THE ECONOMY OF EARLY AMERICA

The Revolutionary Period, 1763–1790

PERSPECTIVES ON THE AMERICAN REVOLUTION

Ronald Hoffman and Peter J. Albert, Editors

The Economy of Early America

The Revolutionary Period,

1763–1790

Edited by RONALD HOFFMAN

JOHN J. MCCUSKER

RUSSELL R. MENARD

and PETER J. ALBERT

Published for the

UNITED STATES CAPITOL HISTORICAL SOCIETY

BY THE UNIVERSITY PRESS OF VIRGINIA

Charlottesville

THE UNIVERSITY PRESS OF VIRGINIA

First Published 1988

Printed in the United States of America

Library of Congress Cataloging-in-Publication Data

The Economy of early America.   330.973

  (Perspectives on the American Revolution)   E19
  Includes index.
    1. United States—Economic conditions—To 1865—Regional
disparities.   2. Great Britain—Colonies—America—Economic conditions—
Regional disparities.
  I. Hoffman, Ronald, 1941–   . II. Series.
  HC104.E26   1987   330.973'02   87-6169
  ISBN 0-8139-1139-7

Contents

CONTENTS

Preface

BY THE SECOND HALF of the eighteenth century an elaborate commercial economy flourished in British North America. Although considerable diversity characterized the various regions that composed this economic system, and levels of prosperity differed within and between these areas, contemporaries viewed Britain's colonies as places that offered opportunities for substantial material advancement. Moreover, despite the primary emphasis on commerce and agriculture, an increasing interest in manufacturing presaged the first steps in the transition from a preindustrial to an early industrial economy.

It has been the aim of this series from the beginning to examine the American Revolutionary era from all relevant perspectives so that the enormous complexity and diversity of this seminal event in American history would be demonstrated. The subject of *The Economy of Early America: The Revolutionary Period, 1763–1790* is absolutely fundamental to carrying out this process. While today there is—or at least there should be—general agreement among historians that historical events cannot be meaningfully understood without reference to the economic context in which they occur, this position has not always commanded respect. And indeed even today the practioners of the art are not unified in their assessment as to how much weight should be given to economic influences in the construction of an overall interpretive scheme.

The most sophisticated early statement demonstrating the reciprocal relationship between politics and the economy was made by Carl L. Becker in his book *The History of Political Parties in the Province of New York, 1760–1776*. One of the most remarkable aspects of Becker's work is its enduring timeliness and the freshness and accuracy of its insights, which make it as modern as any work being produced today. Despite a range of critical assessments that have challenged some of Becker's assertions—and have shown the need for certain modifications—his fundamental approach remains sound and his sense of direction continues to guide, influence, and inform historical scholarship. While Becker's most familiar formulation involved the role of, and motivation behind, factional politics in the struggle for independence—the question as he phrased it of home rule and "who should rule at home"—he also ascribed considerable influence to the impact of economic conditions in shaping the character of the imperial protest that ultimately led to Independence. With respect to the period immediately following the Stamp Act, he wrote:

> The history of these years is far from simple. It can have little meaning for those who regard the Revolution as a spontaneous uprising of the colonies in defense of a political principle, or for those others who can see in it nothing but the achievement of a deliberately planned independence. There was at first a certain reaction from the violence of the stamp act period; purely local issues not infrequently confused party lines altogether; but toward the close of the year 1769, and during the winter of 1770, a combination of various influences, almost wholly economic, contributed to differentiate once more, and more clearly than the stamp act had done, the radical and conservative elements of the population.[1]

From this introductory statement Becker proceeded to explain the effect of the economy on political and social behavior in New York from the enactment of the Townshend duties until the calling of the First Continental Congress. Far from insisting that this enormously complicated period was determined exclusively by economic considerations, Becker acknowledged a host of other influences including a perennial desire for power, popular resentments, and religious prejudices, but these elements, he observed, operated within a context of economic instability. Beginning with a broad delineation of the basic contours of New York's trading patterns

[1] Carl Lotus Becker, *The History of Political Parties in the Province of New York, 1760–1776* (Madison, Wis., 1909), pp. 22, 52.

and then narrowing his focus to portray the colony's particular vulnerability to hard currency shortages, Becker elaborated on the variegated impacts created by this situation in the groups that composed New York City. This is not, I hasten to point out, simple economic determinism since, in the author's words, "the motives of individuals are rarely so simple as that, the motives of classes, never."[2] Nonetheless, for Becker one of the chief defining elements of the society within which people move, act, and interact involves the economic framework within which their most basic decisions about survival are made, and, as his study persuasively argues, their politics, like all the rest of their behaviors, are inextricably related to this reality.

The authors in this volume differ in their emphasis in regard to what Becker and many others have called "political economy," but collectively their essays underscore the extensive regional diversity of eighteenth-century North America in the age of the American Revolution.

In the volume's opening essay, James F. Shepherd provides an overview of the course of American overseas trade between 1763 and 1790, and in particular assesses the impact of the Revolution and its aftermath. Commerce and the production of goods for overseas markets, he points out, were fundamental to the economy of the thirteen colonies, so the changes in these markets and the disruptions in commercial activity brought about by the Revolutionary War and Independence had a significant impact on the economic life of the new nation. In the prewar period the North American colonies supplied Great Britain with staples and the British West Indies with provisions, and traded profitably with the foreign Caribbean islands and southern Europe; in turn, they imported British manufactured goods. The colonies were distinguished by variations in the type (agricultural products, fish, etc.) and value of their exports, and the importance of overseas trade for their respective economies. On the basis of his analysis of the import and export trade between 1763 and 1775, the level of "invisible" earnings from shipping and

[2] Ibid., p. 62.

mercantile activities, the sale of ships, and expenditures by the British government, Shepherd maintains that in the late colonial period the balance of payments was generally favorable to the colonies or was at least roughly balanced. There was considerable indebtedness, of course, consisting of short-term trade credits owing from American debtors to British creditors. This indebtedness was not increasing, however, and because short-term credit was furnished by the British, colonial capital was freed for longer-term investments. Shepherd then addresses the question of the effect of the Revolution on American overseas trade, to the extent that this is feasible given the paucity of statistical evidence. With British markets cut off and the British navy and privateers disrupting shipping, the destinations of exports and the sources of imports changed drastically and the level of commerce declined sharply during the war years. Direct trade with Europe and indirect trade with the West Indies expanded somewhat, but generally the volume of overseas commerce fell considerably and the economy was marked by a greater degree of self-sufficiency as Americans attempted to create substitutes for imports. In the immediate postwar era, the lack of statistics again hampers the economic historian's attempt to generalize, and the picture is further complicated by the degree of local and regional variation. On the whole, however, Shepherd sees the 1780s as a period of change and readjustment, marked by the continuation of self-sufficient or subsistence production. By the 1790s, when reliable statistical evidence for the nation as a whole becomes available, northern continental Europe had emerged as an important market for American exports, southern Europe had regained its prewar position, Great Britain had resumed its importance as a trading partner, and trade with the Caribbean had surpassed its prewar level although it had shifted away from British areas. These statistics from the federal period also indicate changes in the composition of trade following the Revolution, the creation of new trade routes, the continuing growth of mercantile and shipping activities, and alterations in the importance of overseas trade for the various regional economies in the new nation.

James A. Henretta's article parallels Shepherd's by exploring the impact of the American Revolution on the nation's domestic economy. Henretta raises two questions: "Did the War for Independence *accelerate* the process of American economic growth?" and "Did it encourage the transition to a more *capitalistic* society?" He analyzes the late colonial and Revolutionary-era economy of the United States, particularly the manufacture of cloth, using the model of protoindustrialization—a putting-out system of handicraft production organized by merchant capitalists. The American domestic economy was characterized, he argues, by features of the *Kaufsystem,* in which economically viable rural families enjoyed considerable autonomy and owned most of the means of production, and by the avoidance of the *Verlagsystem,* in which merchant-capitalists dominated the manufacturing process and held impoverished rural workers in a condition of economic dependence. He concludes that the American Revolution—especially the ending of British mercantilist restrictions and the exigencies of the war itself—did indeed accelerate American economic growth by expanding the industrial base, increasing agricultural by-employments, fostering the expansion of traditional home manufactures and the generation of new enterprises, creating intraregional zones of production, and encouraging the establishment of entrepreneurs and traders oriented to domestic markets. Nevertheless, he maintains, British competition and the absence of substantial and concentrated markets slowed the process of protoindustrialization. The Revolution delayed the emergence of a more capitalistic society by making western lands available for settlement, thereby draining the surplus agricultural population from more settled regions and discouraging the expansion of rural industries. Moreover, the wars of the French Revolution encouraged the diversion of capital into mercantile ventures rather than investment in domestic manufacturing enterprises.

The next six essays have a regional focus. Three—the articles by Winifred B. Rothenberg, Thomas M. Doerflinger, and John J. McCusker—are primarily economic studies. Spanning the era of the Revolution (indeed, Rothenberg's runs forward to 1838), they describe the salient features of specific regional economies and explicitly or implicitly attempt to evaluate the effect of the Revolution on their development. The other three articles—the pieces by Lewis R. Fischer, Joseph A. Ernst, and Russell R. Menard—also study regional economic development, but with an explicit focus on explaining why the respective colonies that are the subjects of their essays did or did not choose independence. Consequently, these three pieces begin roughly at mid-century and end at 1775.

Lewis R. Fischer's paper studies the mercantile economy of Nova Scotia in the period from mid-century down to the Revolution. Initially, merchants settling in the colony expected that they would be rewarded by quick profits and that Halifax would develop as a major trading port. These expectations were not fulfilled, however: the colony did not attract a sufficiently large number of settlers, there was a shortage of capital investment, and the trade of Halifax was dominated by New England. Fischer then traces the town's mercantile development over the quarter century following its founding and discusses the principal groups that comprised its merchant community. He argues that the disillusionment of the 1750s, the impact of the French and Indian War, and the experience of the postwar depression transformed this community as "dominant merchants and marginal traders" left the town. Over the next decade, however, the commerce of Halifax was marked by stable growth, culminating in 1774–75 with dramatic increases in the volume and significant changes in the pattern of trade. Consequently, the interests of the Halifax merchants increasingly diverged from those of British-American colonists to the south, and, when the southern colonies moved toward independence, these men were convinced that their interests would be better served by Nova Scotia's remaining within the empire.

In the next essay Winifred B. Rothenberg analyzes a selection of Middlesex County probate records, dating from 1730 to 1838, to determine whether they provide evidence of the development of a regional capital market in the county and, by extension, in Massachusetts and throughout the northeast as a whole. Her objective is to verify and date the emergence of a financial market in the rural economy that had the effects of stimulating capital accumulation in the farm sector and encouraging investment in the industrializing sector. She uses the probate records of 512 decedents to test for three indicators of a capital market—that such a market would alter the forms of capital transfer (she finds such evidence beginning after the Revolution in the appearance of securities, the growing proportion of probates charging interest for loans and the higher rates of interest charged, and the increasing negotiability of credit instruments), that individual credit networks would grow in size and geographical extent, and that there would be a growing preference for liquidity of financial instruments. The results of her evidence indicate, she concludes, that "capital market forces emerged in the regional economy in the early 1780s to mobilize savings in agriculture and allocate them to new uses."

Thomas M. Doerflinger then examines the dry goods trade in the hinterland of Philadelphia, analyzing the trade and exploring its impact on the region's economy. Essentially, dry goods exports to this area were handled by ten to fifteen major British houses, which shipped goods to perhaps hundreds of American merchants. These, in turn, each sold to various retailers and artisans. Doerflinger describes the rivalry among these retailers for customers. Price competition was particularly important in the process of building up a clientele, but retailers also vied with one another in advertising, displaying their wares, the terms of payment offered, and in selling merchandise other than dry goods to "build traffic" in their stores. The effect of their efforts was to bring manufactured goods within the reach of a broad segment of the rural population. Doerflinger surveys the great variety of dry goods available for purchase and argues that it indicates the style consciousness of rural consumers, their ability to purchase these commodities (according to Doerflinger, the rural populace definitely did not consist of subsistence farmers with little disposable income), and the impact in the Philadelphia market region of the "consumer revolution" of the eighteenth century.

In the following article, Joseph A. Ernst explores the coming of the Revolution in Virginia and Maryland. Despite

general economic similarities between the two colonies—
he describes the Chesapeake region as largely a tobacco-
producing area, undergoing severe economic difficulties in
the years after the French and Indian War that were exacerbated by British revenue and currency policies—the experience of Virginia differed "radically," he writes, from that of
Maryland. The key to understanding this difference, Ernst
insists, is the concept of political economy, which emphasizes
the intersection of economic conditions, political factors, and
social ideas and ethics. To support his argument, he closely
traces the fluctuations in the tobacco and grain export trades
of Virginia and Maryland between 1760 and 1775 and their
impact on economic conditions within the two colonies. He
goes on to sketch the nature and membership of the principal
factions or coalitions in the colonies, and the personal antagonisms, regional divisions, economic factors, and political
issues that motivated them. Finally, he outlines the "libertarian" political thought and the ideology of virtue and interest
that influenced the perceptions and actions of the Revolutionaries. Ernst shows how the interplay of these forces—
how the political economy as a whole—led Virginia and
Maryland to respond quite differently to the crises of the pre-
Revolutionary era.

In a similar vein, Russell R. Menard analyzes the intercon-
nections between economic growth, slavery, and politics in
the pre-Revolutionary South Carolina lowcountry. He describes the growth of the colony's economy—the increase in
the white and slave populations and the appearance of a
creole majority among the slaves, and the emergence and
development of rice and indigo production. South Carolina's
long-term prosperity in the quarter century preceding the
Revolution, despite periodic short-term disruptions, was
firmly based on these two exports, and Menard illustrates the
extent to which they shaped the plantation society of the Carolina lowcountry and fostered the growth of an indigenous
ruling class. This lowcountry gentry prospered within the
empire, accumulating slaves and land, and building their fortunes on rice and indigo. Why, then, did they choose Revolution? The answer, Menard argues, is that they resented

British interference and perceived British policy as a form of enslavement, a threat to their accomplishments and prosperity, and a restriction of their ability to govern the colony, address local issues, and control their economy.

John J. McCusker's essay assesses the impact of the American Revolution on the economy of the British West Indies. There is, he points out, a scarcity of data that would allow the economic historian to address the question definitively, but the economic importance of the islands makes it a significant one. The long-term decline of the British West Indies, he concludes, began after 1790. The decade after the Treaty of Paris of 1763 saw a major economic expansion in the islands. While the Revolutionary War years were a period of depression, economic difficulties were less severe for the islands than for the continental colonies, and the West Indies recovered more quickly after the war than did the United States. Available evidence demonstrates that the British West Indies continued in the postwar era to experience population growth, steady increases in the quantity of sugar produced and exported as well as in productivity (the value of sugar produced per worker), and a rise in imports as well. In 1790, McCusker argues, their economy was as healthy as it had been before the Revolution.

Jacob M. Price concludes the volume by surveying some of the major topics relating to the economy of Revolutionary America. He discusses the population history of the continental colonies during the seventeenth and eighteenth centuries, probes the reality lying behind such labels as "staple" versus "subsistence" economies and areas of "slave" versus "free" labor, raises the question of what systems of manufacture were employed in the colonies, the nature of the import trade, and the movements of debt, credit, and price levels. He then analyzes the impact of the Revolution on agriculture, domestic production, population, and trading patterns. His essay concludes with a call for further research in many of these areas, employing rigorous quantitative methods.

The editors would like to acknowledge the valuable criticisms of the commentators at the U.S. Capitol Historical Society's symposium on the economy of early America, namely, Stuart Bruchey, Paul G. E. Clemens, Marc Egnal, and Robert E. Gallman. The graphs and map for the volume were prepared by Lisa Blanc and Chris Johnson of the Cartographic Services Laboratory at the University of Maryland, College Park.

THE ECONOMY OF EARLY AMERICA

The Revolutionary Period, 1763–1790

JAMES F. SHEPHERD

British America and
the Atlantic Economy

BY 1763 TRADE AND PRODUCTION FOR MARKETS, especially
those overseas,[1] had become central to the British-American
colonial economy. The slowly improving productivity that
marked this sphere of the economy, together with the stim-
ulus of the ancillary activities associated with the collection,
transportation, and distribution of these goods within overseas markets, brought progress and increased living standards to Americans in the eighteenth century. It importantly
contributed to the level of prosperity that Americans enjoyed
and to the structure of the economy that developed.

It was changes in these markets, and disruptions wrought
by war and political independence for thirteen of the most
populous colonies, that most importantly affected the course
of the American economy after 1775. During the turbulent
years of the Revolution and the years of adjustment and
change in the 1780s, the new nation found itself outside the
comfortable confines of British mercantilism. The major historical question here has always been the state of the economy
as it recovered from the war and adjusted to the new political
realities. Was recovery slow or rapid? Did the economic
health of the United States approach that of the pre-
Revolutionary colonies before the outbreak of war in Europe
in 1793 pulled the young nation into a new period of pros-

[1] "Overseas" and "foreign" areas were obviously not synonymous for
colonial Americans. The mother country, Great Britain, was not a foreign
nation, though it was overseas. Some British colonies in North America
were separated by water (and thus overseas), such as Newfoundland and
the West Indian islands. Because of these semantic difficulties, *overseas* is
used here, and throughout this essay, with reference to those colonies on
the North American continental mainland that were separated by water
from Great Britain, other British colonies, and foreign countries.

perity? It is to these questions that we turn. We will examine, first, the international sector from 1763 to 1775, with emphasis upon the impact of recent evidence on our view of the late colonial economy; second, the impact of the war on commerce and the economy; third, alterations in the new nation's economy resulting from changing overseas economic relations following peace and Independence; and, fourth, the importance of overseas trade to North Americans in relation to American economic development and to overall economic activity.

By 1763 a flourishing Atlantic economy had developed in which Great Britain and her colonies played an important part. England and her satellites, Scotland and Wales, had been transformed over the preceding three centuries from small, underdeveloped countries on the fringes of Europe into the powerful, industrial British nation-state central to this Atlantic economy. The colonies that Britain founded became important suppliers to the mother country of such staples as sugar, tobacco, and indigo. The continental colonies also carried out the important function of provisioning the British West Indian colonies, thereby enabling the latter to concentrate on the more valuable activity of producing sugar. They earned surpluses in trades with foreign Caribbean islands and with southern Europe that enhanced their ability to buy British manufactures and goods reexported by British merchants. By the time of the Revolution, about a third of English exports found customers in the American colonies. They had become a very important market for the British.

Production for these flourishing trades imposed a distinctive pattern of regional specialization upon the British colonies. The abundance of natural resources and relatively scarce labor and capital encouraged production of natural-resource–intensive products. These natural resources consisted of much potentially good agricultural land and a range of climates suitable for growing a wide variety of crops, fisheries that began to be exploited even before permanent settlement was made, and forests from which numerous wood products could be produced. Consequently, agriculture

4

was the main economic activity in the colonies, in all likelihood occupying 80 to 90 percent of the labor force. In addition, many commercial manufacturing activities, for example, flour milling and the manufacture of wooden containers, were dependent upon agricultural production and distribution.

Fishing was also important, particularly in the northern colonies. Newfoundlanders, especially, depended almost exclusively upon the North Atlantic cod fishery. By 1763 the total value of exports of sugar from the West Indies, tobacco from Virginia and Maryland, flour from the middle colonies, and rice from South Carolina and Georgia each surpassed cod exports in total value.[2] Yet the features of Newfoundland's development which made it unique among the colonies—and which have not received sufficient attention from historians—are its high degree of commercialization and the fact that its level of exports relative to its population was far higher than for any of the other British-American colonies, including the British West Indies. The importance of the cod fishery to Newfoundland far surpassed the relative importance of the fur trade to Quebec, a fact that has not been adequately stressed in the literature of Canadian economic history. This nearly exclusive dependence upon the cod fishery also meant that Newfoundland lacked the strong agricultural base that made all the other British continental colonies self-sufficient in food production.[3]

These broad patterns of regional specialization are well known. The only purpose of repeating them at this point is

[2] James F. Shepherd, "Staples and Eighteenth-Century Canadian Development: The Case of Newfoundland," in Roger L. Ransom, Richard Sutch, and Gary M. Walton, eds., *Explorations in the New Economic History: Essays in Honor of Douglass C. North* (New York, 1982), p. 120.

[3] Exceptions were the British West Indies, which could have been self-sufficient in food production (as they later were in the nineteenth century) had they not been so heavily specialized in the production of sugar for export markets, and perhaps New Hampshire and Massachusetts, which imported wheat and flour, exhibiting a net deficit in these products. Because New England exported foodstuffs like fish and Indian corn, it is not clear whether these two colonies would have been self-sufficient in the production of foodstuffs in the overall picture.

5

to establish a frame of reference for examining some of the disputed points about American colonial trade and for assessing the changes and difficulties brought by the Revolution and Independence. Quebec exported furs and skins from the important fur trade, as well as whale oil and some agricultural staples, wheat being the principal one. Nova Scotia's exports were mostly fish, whale oil, and wood products. New Hampshire's were mainly forest products and ships, and Massachusetts', forest products and fish. The other two New England colonies, Rhode Island and Connecticut, exported principally foodstuffs and were more akin to the middle colonies in this respect. The importance of grain and grain products to the middle colonies, as well as the economic role of these colonies more generally, has not been given sufficient attention by historians. Exports from Maryland and Virginia were dominated by tobacco, although wheat and corn were increasing in importance in the later colonial period. Naval stores along with some foodstuffs came out of North Carolina, and rice, indigo, and deerskins from the backcountry were the principal products of South Carolina and Georgia. The British West Indies were, of course, heavily specialized in the production of sugar but exported a wide variety of less valuable tropical and semitropical goods such as molasses (a by-product of sugar refining), rum, coffee, cotton, and a number of dyestuffs.

This picture of regional specialization is well accepted, but it says little about the degree of specialization and the relative importance of overseas trade to the various regions and colonies. The singular importance of the cod fishery to Newfoundland has been mentioned. The heavy reliance of Virginia and Maryland upon the great staple, tobacco, South Carolina and Georgia upon rice and indigo, and the West Indies upon sugar is a well received part of colonial economic history. Even so there were differences in degree. An example is South Carolina, for which per capita exports ranged from £3½–4 sterling.[4] Though considerably less than the

[4] These and the following references to per capita exports came from Shepherd, "Staples and Eighteenth-Century Canadian Development," pp. 98 and 119, and James F. Shepherd and Gary M. Walton, *Shipping, Mari-*

£12–15 sterling per capita for Newfoundland, exports from South Carolina appear to have been in good part produced by the labor of a large slave population (more than 60 percent of the population in 1770 was black). Though South Carolina imported small amounts of wheat and flour, the absence of large imports of foodstuffs indicates a near self-sufficiency in what would have been the principal part of the subsistence income furnished to the slave labor force. If export earnings can therefore be viewed as accruing mostly to the free population, exports per free resident would have been considerably higher—more than £9 sterling. Per capita exports from the British West Indies of £5–6 sterling may be viewed in the same light. Per capita exports from Virginia and Maryland, the tobacco colonies, were less than £2 sterling, and less than £3 sterling per free resident, exhibiting a significantly lower level than South Carolina and the West Indies. The per capita exports of eight colonies (Quebec, Nova Scotia, New Hampshire, Massachusetts, Connecticut, New Jersey, Delaware, and North Carolina) were less than £1 sterling. In some cases, this may have simply indicated that a colony's products were being collected and exported from a larger neighboring port. Surely, this was true for New Jersey, for which the customs records indicated a very low level of exports.[5]

_____

time Trade, and the Economic Development of Colonial North America (Cambridge, 1972), pp. 46–47. They are annual averages for 1768–72. The values of per capita exports from the British West Indies are based upon official values of exports to Great Britain taken from Stanley L. Engerman, "Notes on the Patterns of Economic Growth in the British North American Colonies in the Seventeenth, Eighteenth, and Nineteenth Centuries," in Paul Bairoch and Maurice Lévy-Leboyer, eds., *Disparities in Economic Development since the Industrial Revolution* (London, 1981), p. 48. The West Indian estimates are based upon population data from John J. McCusker, "The Rum Trade and the Balance of Payments of the Thirteen Continental Colonies, 1650–1775," Ph.D. diss., University of Pittsburgh, 1970, p. 712.

[5] See the description of the internal transportation system in which goods were collected and brought to market in Philadelphia by David E. Dauer, "Colonial Philadelphia's Intraregional Transportation System: An Overview," in Glenn Porter and William H. Mulligan, Jr., eds., *Working Papers from the Regional History Research Center* 2 (1979):3–4. Goods were collected up the Delaware River from Trenton, Burlington, and other

7

Subject to this qualification, the customs records indicate a considerable variation in the degree of importance of overseas trade to each colony. Newfoundland was most heavily oriented to producing for overseas markets, followed, as one would suspect, by the British West Indies and the southern continental colonies. Even among these colonies there were substantial variations. Conceptually, one may divide the economic activities of a typical family or plantation in an agrarian society such as that of the British colonies at this time into subsistence production and market production. Subsistence production was comprised of producing economic goods and services for one's own consumption, and included food grown and prepared for home use as well as a wide variety of home manufactures—linen and woolen cloth, clothing made from this cloth, candles, soap, leather and leather products, and furniture and other wooden products. Furthermore, many of the capital goods in American society were produced at home. Examples ranged from houses and farm buildings to tools and fences. Market production, of course, refers to goods and services destined to be sold in markets for cash, credit, or barter. Either the colonies with lower exports relative to their population depended more upon subsistence production and less upon income earned in production for foreign markets, or the production of goods for sale in local and regional markets for domestic consumption was greater. Because the northern colonies were more urbanized, the latter was probably the case. The degree of urbanization, however, even in the northern colonies, was relatively small. Consequently, it seems doubtful that a higher level of production for domestic markets in the northern colonies would have offset the lower relative level of exports. Did lower standards of living coincide with a greater degree of subsistence production? Did those colonies with lower levels of exports experience lower standards of living? Until we know more about the levels of production for domestic markets and subsistence, these questions cannot be answered definitively. Such suppositions seem to be con-

---

towns, and from downstream, reaching to the southern edge of the colony of Delaware.

tradicted by Alice Hanson Jones's findings that the levels of nonhuman wealth in the northern and southern colonies in 1774 were about the same.[6] Any comparison of per capita exports and output between the northern and southern colonies must also take into consideration the differences in organization of production with regard to the use of free, indentured, or slave labor that would likely result in differences in the distribution of incomes. Further speculation about the importance of overseas trade with regard to the overall level of economic activity will be deferred until the final section of the paper, when we may view it in relation to the changes that came during the war and the 1780s.

Estimates of commodity trade indicate that Great Britain was the most important destination of all North American colonial exports during the late colonial period, accounting for 55 percent of the value of all exports in 1768–72, the years for which we have comprehensive trade figures.[7] The estimates reaffirm that the direct trades between the southern colonies and Britain dominated exports to Britain, and that the important southern staples, tobacco, rice, and indigo, were indeed the most valuable commodities in these trades. Southerners used the proceeds of these export earnings to buy British manufactured goods and reexports from Britain such as tea and hemp. For the colonies to the north, which produced fewer commodities suited for British markets, customers were found in the West Indies and southern Europe for surpluses of foodstuffs, livestock, and raw materials. Exports of foodstuffs from the northern colonies allowed the British West Indies to turn heavily toward specialization in the production of sugar that was then exported directly to Britain. Foodstuffs were also exported to the foreign West Indies. Earnings from these exports to the British and the foreign West Indies financed the purchase by continental col-

---

[6] Alice Hanson Jones, *Wealth of a Nation to Be: The American Colonies on the Eve of the Revolution* (New York, 1980), p. 303.

[7] These and following references are to trade estimates in Shepherd and Walton, *Economic Development*. Estimates pertain only to the continental colonies and not to the West Indies although many of the same conclusions might pertain to the West Indies as to the southern continental colonies.

onists of various West Indian goods, such as sugar, molasses, rum, and other produce less valuable in total such as coffee and cotton. Molasses was used as the principal input in colonial rum distilling, an extensive industry particularly in New England in the late colonial period. New Englanders were also in the business of importing West Indian goods and reexporting them in the coastal trade to other colonies. Southern Europe, another food-deficit area, was the other major market for the continental colonies. It was especially important to the middle colonies, and exports of flour to southern Europe and the West Indies made it the second most valuable commodity exported after tobacco. Southern Europe was also the most important market for the products of Newfoundland's fishery. Though some goods were imported from southern Europe, such as wine and salt, it was an area in which the colonies earned a healthy balance-of-payments surplus. Surpluses from here and the West Indies enabled the northern colonies to purchase desired imports from Britain. Though some goods were exported to Africa, they amounted to less than 1 percent of total exports, suggesting that commodity trade with Africa has been overemphasized by historians (the value of slaves brought into the colonies was significant, however).

Though emphasizing the commodity trade, historians have long recognized the importance of the sale of services, particularly shipping and mercantile activities, arising from the distribution of these commodities. By the late colonial period substantial income was generated from "invisible" earnings, particularly for New England and the middle colonies in the West Indian and southern European trades. These earnings for the colonies may well have been larger than for any single commodity exported from the continental colonies including tobacco and eclipsed only by sugar exports from the British West Indies.[8] They were a major source of earnings of sterling that the colonists used to pay for British imports, and they indicated the development of a strong commercial sec-

[8]The value of sugar exported from the British West Indies to Britain was considerably greater than tobacco. See McCusker, "Rum Trade," pp. 232 and 1143.

tor in the colonies by this time. Another source of earnings, not included in the customs records and thus not in the above estimates of commodity exports, was the sale of ships to overseas buyers. Though not nearly of the magnitude of shipping earnings, these were a consistent source of income to the colonies, especially for New England, where most of the shipbuilding took place.

How did these patterns of trade change over the 1760s and the 1770s before the Revolution? Though we do not have comprehensive trade statistics to examine this change, there are two important pieces of evidence. For one, we have the official values of British trade with the colonies (given in the Appendix, table 1).[9] We may also compare the tonnage of ships entering and clearing continental colonial ports for 1760–62 with 1768–72 (averages are given in Appendix, table 2). The official values of imports from Great Britain into the thirteen colonies to 1775 have been adjusted for changes in purchasing power by John J. McCusker. These are shown for 1760–75 in Appendix, table 1, column 1. The unadjusted official values of imports from Great Britain are shown in column 2, these being the sum of imports from England (column 3) and Scotland (column 4). Comparison between the unadjusted official values and McCusker's, adjusted for changes in purchasing power, indicate that the official values can be used for purposes of examining approximate volumes and trends in trade. They show that imports from Britain had increased during the Seven Years' War, but leveled off and fell after 1760. Though highly variable, and perhaps distorted by the aftermath of the war in the early 1760s and by the nonimportation agreements in the

[9]The official values from the English customs records (Customs 3, Public Record Office) originally were based upon current values early in the eighteenth century. Because of a largely horizontal trend in prices for English exports and imports over the century to the beginning of the Napoleonic wars, they may be used as an approximate index of the volume and value of English-American trade in the period under consideration in this paper. The beginning of the Scottish customs records (Customs 14, P.R.O.) in 1755 allows us to view British-American trade rather than English alone. For a more complete discussion of these data, see the sources given in the Appendix, table 1.

late 1760s and early 1770s, they displayed no discernible upward or downward trend for the 1760s. The 1770s up to 1775 appear to have been years of greater trade; they probably included the peak of a business cycle. In 1775 imports were virtually cut off with the colonial trade boycotts. Exports to Britain, on the other hand, fell during the Seven Years' War and rose after 1760. From 1763 through 1770 they displayed a level trend, rose to higher levels during the early 1770s, and fell to negligible levels in 1776.

The tonnage data (Appendix, table 2), too, show little significant change in the volume of shipping entering and clearing colonial ports. Because they end in 1772, these data do not reflect the increase shown in the above trade figures for the 1770s. In New England only the smaller colonies of Rhode Island and Connecticut show significant increases in the volume of shipping. An increase in New York inbound shipping is not as much reflected in outbound shipping from that colony when comparing the two periods. In the overall perspective a decline in New Jersey's volume of shipping, and stagnation of Pennsylvania and Delaware, result in virtually no change in the middle colonies. The same is true for the tobacco colonies. Only the lower South shows much growth as a region. Georgia, especially, shows very rapid growth. The volume of shipping (combined ship entries and clearances) increases by nearly 300 percent, reflecting rapid growth of settlement there. One might tentatively conclude from this evidence that British-American colonial trade had grown to very substantial levels by 1763, and though it continued to increase to 1775, the increase was modest on the average. Only the trade of a few colonies was an exception to this generalization, Georgia being the most spectacular in relative terms, though small in absolute size. During the period from 1763 to 1775, colonial trade had reached its zenith.

One implication of the estimates of trade is for the colonial balance of payments, one of the most serious of concerns for the eighteenth-century mercantilist. We have seen how the American colonists paid for the highly prized manufactured goods and other imports from Britain. The southern colonies and West Indies paid largely with proceeds earned in direct trade with Britain, and the northern colonies with surpluses earned in the West Indian and southern European trades and with "invisible" earnings from shipping and mercantile activities. Other items must be considered, however, such as the sale of ships, payments for slaves and indentured servants imported into the colonies, the collection of taxes and duties, and the expenditures made by the British government in the colonies for the salaries of British civil servants and for military and naval expenditures. With these factors in mind, one can take up the question of whether the colonists were faced with a deficit in the current account of their balance of payments that had to be financed by a growing indebtedness to British creditors. There is a long tradition in American history that the colonists were subjected to both political and economic repression. It is argued that the Navigation Acts and other mercantilist burdens imposed by the British on the colonies, particularly after 1763, led to an ever-growing indebtedness by Americans that consisted of a sort of economic bondage and exploitation.[10] Growing indebtedness would show up as a deficit in the current account of the balance of payments. Estimates of trade and these other balance-of-payments items have been published by this author and Gary M. Walton for 1768–72. The estimates are particularly sensitive to smuggling (which would most critically affect estimates of imports, there being little incentive to engage in the smuggling of exports), the values of imports from Great Britain (which were estimated by revising the official values), the estimates of invisible earnings, the estimates of expenditures by the British government in the colonies, and the sale of colonial-built ships. Recent contributions to the literature would suggest some changes in the Shepherd-Walton estimates. Jacob M. Price, using additional evidence, convincingly places such earnings from ship sales at a higher level, suggesting that these averaged at least £140,000 an-

[10] This traditional view is discussed in John J. McCusker and Russell R. Menard, "The Economy of British America, 1607–1790: Needs and Opportunities for Study" (Paper presented at the Conference on the Economy of British America, Williamsburg, Va., October 1980). McCusker and Menard cite a number of authors who discuss this position.

nually from 1763 to 1775.[11] The Shepherd-Walton estimates had earlier placed sterling exchange earnings from the sale of ships in the approximate range of £50,000 to £100,000. Though not a large absolute difference, it is significant when considering that the remaining estimated deficit on the current account of the colonial balance of payments averaged only £40,000 annually for 1768–72.[12] It is presumably shipbuilding that accounts for the differences between tonnage entering New Hampshire and tonnage clearing that port (see the Appendix, table 2). For both periods, 1760–62 and 1768–72, the volume of shipping leaving is about 50 percent higher than that entering the colony. Though similar differences exist for other colonies, none are consistent with both periods save New Hampshire.

The larger amount of shipping earnings is even more crucial to the balance of payments. John McCusker, in an excellent article on British ship tonnage in the eighteenth century, reminds us that there were different measures of tonnage.[13] Registered tonnage was the figure recorded in official documents and used by governments for levying duties and tonnage fees on ships entering ports. There was, of course, an incentive for shipowners to discount their registered tonnage from measured tonnage, a figure calculated by a standard formula based upon gross dimensions of the hull of the ship and used by shipbuilders in contracting with buyers of ships. Scholars have long been aware of these two different measures of tonnage. Both the United States and Britain changed from the older method of establishing the registered tonnage of vessels to one based upon measured tonnage in the 1780s. Evidence suggests that, on the average, pre-1780 registered tonnage equaled about two-thirds of measured tonnage. But this average varied systematically with the size of the ship, as

---

[11] Jacob M. Price, "A Note on the Value of Colonial Exports of Shipping," *Journal of Economic History* 36 (1976):704–24.

[12] Gary M. Walton and James F. Shepherd, *The Economic Rise of Early America* (Cambridge, 1979), p. 101.

[13] John J. McCusker, "The Tonnage of Ships Engaged in British Colonial Trade during the Eighteenth Century," *Research in Economic History* 6 (1981):73–105.

Year	Hogsheads	Tonnage of shipping cleared
1768	65,946	35,213
1769	77,175	37,894
1770	83,771	37,206
1771	106,693	45,587
1772	99,500	46,919

pointed out by Christopher J. French;[14] it tended to be larger for smaller ships and smaller for larger ones. These differences will be important for comparing pre- and post-Revolutionary tonnage flows. McCusker, however, points out another difference, which is that the cargo tonnage—or the real carrying capacity—of ships may have averaged around twice the amount of pre-Revolutionary registered tonnage. If we are concerned with shipping earnings, it is this latter measure with which we should be concerned.

This may be illustrated by comparing the number of hogsheads shipped to Great Britain from Virginia and Maryland with the registered tonnage that cleared those colonies in the years 1768–72.[15] Peacetime freight rates customarily charged for carrying tobacco in this trade were £7–8 sterling for four hogsheads. Throughout most of the seventeenth century, four hogsheads had occupied roughly one registered ton. However, because of the increase in the size of the hogshead over the eighteenth century, it was said that by the end of the colonial period four hogsheads occupied an average of two registered tons,[16] and this rate was used in the Shepherd-Walton estimates of shipping earnings. Yet the above data suggest that ships were carrying 2.14 hogsheads of tobacco per registered ton plus a number of other commodities upon which freight would have been earned in this British trade with the Chesapeake. McCusker's point, applied to the

[14] Christopher J. French, "Eighteenth-Century Shipping Tonnage Measurements," *Journal of Economic History* 33 (1973):434–43.

[15] The data are from the American customs records, Customs 16/1, P.R.O. See also Shepherd and Walton, *Economic Development*, p. 238n.

[16] Shepherd and Walton, *Economic Development*, pp. 121–25.

Shepherd-Walton estimates of invisible earnings, which were based upon registered tonnage, is that while they are large relative to any single commodity export, they may understate actual pre-Revolutionary shipping earnings. Though the above evidence does not suggest that actual earnings were twice as high as the Shepherd-Walton estimates, it does indicate they were higher. Although the colonists did not have a large stake in the tobacco carrying trade, this same phenomenon may have been true of those trades with the West Indies and southern Europe, where a high proportion of the shipping was owned by colonists. A more precise estimate is not possible at this time because of the lack of specific freight rates for other commodities. Nevertheless, higher shipping earnings would have made a very considerable difference in the balance of payments. It suggests that the Shepherd-Walton estimates, which were intended to be on the conservative side, may be more conservative than the authors had intended.

Other recent research suggests that another large source of sterling, expenditures by the British government in the colonies especially for defense, was probably somewhat larger than earlier estimated.[17] The direction of these revisions concerning the sale of ships, shipping earnings, and British government spending in the colonies would work in the same direction—toward the reduction of any deficit in the colonies' balance of payments with Britain and smaller or negligible capital inflows. Admittedly, the questions are still open about the effect on the colonial balance of payments of smuggling and the actual amount paid by the colonists for imports from Britain. Because both would likely work in the direction of a higher level of imports, modifications would lead in the direction of an unfavorable balance of payments. New evidence is lacking on these elements, however, and the data cited above tend to strengthen the view that by the late colonial period, the balance of payments was usually favor-

[17] Julian Gwyn, "British Government Spending and the North American Colonies, 1740–1775," *Journal of Imperial and Commonwealth History* 8 (1980):74–84, and idem, "The Impact of British Military Spending on the Colonial American Money Markets, 1760–1783," *Historical Papers (Communications Historique)* (1980):77–99.

able to the colonists or was at the least generally balanced. This suggests an economic maturity and self-sufficiency in the sense that the colonies were not being subsidized by Britain to any greater extent (with the important exception of defense). The colonists paid for their purchases overseas. Though there was a high degree of *interdependency* among the participants in this eighteenth-century Atlantic economy that stemmed from the relatively high levels of overseas trade, the colonists were not in a position of *dependency*. It might be noted that this conclusion holds principally for the thirteen colonies that revolted. The British colonies that did not revolt had large deficits relative to their populations. Though economic independence may not be a causal factor on the road to political independence, it may be a likely prerequisite.

One should quickly add at this point that an approximately balanced current account means only that colonial indebtedness abroad was not increasing. A large amount of indebtedness existed, and on balance this ran from American debtors to British creditors. In any economy, the process of getting a good from the producer to the ultimate consumer takes time and involves a cost in real economic resources since the activities comprising the distribution of goods must be financed. An excellent account of how this was done in the eighteenth century has been given recently by Jacob Price.[18] Merchants, factors, warehousemen, storekeepers, and others between the producer and consumer furnished this finance in the trade between Britain and the American colonies. Because the usual time interval needed to market products across the Atlantic was long, it resulted in a duration of credits that might extend for a year or longer. At any given time, then, a large amount of debt would be outstanding. It was the British, by and large, who provided this short-term trade credit to the colonies. It might be furnished by a London export merchant, financing sales of woolens to a Philadelphia importer, or it might be a Scottish factor in the Virginia piedmont furnishing credit to a small tobacco planter. The colo-

---

[18] Jacob M. Price, *Capital and Credit in British Overseas Trade: The View from the Chesapeake, 1700–1776* (Cambridge, Mass., 1980).

nists usually paid for this credit in the prices charged for the goods. This indebtedness did not exist because the colonies were incurring an unfavorable balance of payments, nor was it necessarily a device by which the British merchant could exploit the American consumer. It was the result of the necessity of financing eighteenth-century trade. Furthermore, it was of a short-term nature, suggesting that the colonists were financing longer-term investments by their own savings, which resulted in an increasing stock of physical capital in the colonies. Because short-term trade credit was furnished by the British, colonial savings were freed for these longer-term investments.

There were other ways in which the international sector affected American colonial development. Immigration, both free and forced, provided more workers for a labor-scarce economy. Imports of slaves were especially important to the lower South in the late colonial period. The skills and knowledge of immigrants, as well as their muscle, can make an important contribution to progress. It has been suggested, for example, that the knowledge of black slaves was instrumental in the establishment of rice production in South Carolina in the late seventeenth century.[19] By the late colonial period, the institution of slavery was firmly established, and blacks constituted over a fifth of the population. Though it was to create tragic circumstances later in our national history, slavery was a valuable source of labor to the colonial economy.

It is apparent that overseas trade had become very important to the British colonies before the American Revolution and that an eighteenth-century Atlantic economy flourished. The question concerning the importance of trade in relation to overall economic activity will be deferred until the final section of the paper when we may view it in relation to the changes that came during the war and with Independence in the 1780s. It is clear that each continental colony save Newfoundland had developed a strong agricultural base, and that

[19] Peter H. Wood, *Black Majority: Negroes in Colonial South Carolina from 1670 through the Stono Rebellion* (New York, 1974), pp. 35–36.

each was self-sufficient in the production of foodstuffs.[20] Overseas trade provided the markets for colonial producers to specialize in those activities that they did best and the sources for those commodities for whose production colonial resources were less suited.

The outbreak of the Revolution brought a significant disruption of production for overseas market in the American continental colonies. The British market, the most important, was cut off from the colonies. The British navy and privateers increased the risks to colonial shipping, whether in established routes like the West Indies and southern Europe or in attempting to initiate direct trade with continental northern Europe. This disruption pertained as well to the keeping of records that provide the historian with evidence on this trade. We simply do not have the kind of information furnished by British records kept before 1776, especially any quantitative overview of colonial commerce. We know less about what happened to overseas trade, and our account must be more sketchy and conjectural as a consequence.

Curtis P. Nettels has described four stages of wartime commerce.[21] The first includes the trade restrictions, embargoes, and boycotts of 1774 and 1775, running up to April 1776, which effectively eliminated all direct and legal trade between the thirteen colonies and Britain and other British colonies. This resulted in acute shortages of goods that were usually imported, including arms and ammunition necessary for the war effort. Congress authorized limited trade with the foreign West Indies in late 1775 in order to obtain such goods. The second stage began in April 1776 when Congress authorized a policy of open ports and unrestricted foreign trade; it lasted until mid-1778. France was a major supplier and shipper of imports in this period, shipping goods directly to New England or indirectly to the United States via the West

[20] Parts of New England were net importers of cereals and cereal products. See n. 3.

[21] Curtis P. Nettels, *The Economic History of the United States*, vol. 2, *The Emergence of a National Economy, 1775–1815* (New York, 1962), pp. 13–18.

Indies. Trade may have reached its lowest levels in 1776 and 1777 because of an apparently effective blockade maintained by the British navy in these years. Beginning in mid-1778 Congress began to negotiate formal treaties of commerce, first with France and then with Spain and the Netherlands as they entered the war. From this time until early 1782, wartime commerce was at its peak. During this period the Europeans, particularly the Dutch, became active in carrying tobacco from the Chesapeake, and the Dutch island of St. Eustatius became an entrepôt for that and other American products. This third stage lasted until 1782, when the British began to concentrate upon naval attacks on American vessels trading with the West Indies, causing trade to decrease sharply during this last full year of the war.

Though we know these general outlines of trade, without more comprehensive evidence it is difficult to give a more complete picture of wartime commerce. Though illegal, direct trade with Europe began even before the war. For example, the correspondence of Anthony Bleecker, a New York commission merchant, includes a letter sent on June 10, 1774, to John der Neusville, an Amsterdam merchant, in which Bleecker ordered sixteen boxes of "best Bohea tea" sending 1,125 Spanish dollars in payment.[22] Apparently the goods were to be sent directly to New York. In this letter he mentioned previous contact with Neusville, but it is not clear whether he had earlier ordered goods directly from the Dutch merchant.

Even though this direct trade with Europe grew during the war, together with indirect trade through the West Indies, there are many reasons why it remained significantly below prewar levels. During earlier eighteenth-century conflicts, levels of commerce were sharply reduced. In general, the higher risks and increased problems of obtaining timely information increased the costs of trade during wartime. Freight and insurance rates rose. The supply of shipping was reduced as British ships were precluded from entering the

[22] Letterbook of Anthony Lispenard Bleecker, 1767–87, New-York Historical Society, New York City.

colonies and as American ships were captured or used in privateering. Problems of monetary exchanges were magnified as rapid inflation occurred. The greater difficulties and costs of carrying on trade may be illustrated by a number of specific examples. Clearly, prices of imported goods rose more than those of domestic produce. The French consul for New England writing in 1781 to the minister of marine in France stated: "What I buy here costs me three or four times as much. Import costs are high because of insurance and freight."[23] Many of his other letters complained of the high cost of living or insufficient salary. Anthony Bleecker, the New York merchant, moved to Morristown, N.J., from New York sometime between June 1776 and May 1777, perhaps to avoid the fighting or the British occupation. He lived and conducted his business from there in his "retired situation from a seaport town."[24] After 1775 the volume of his correspondence fell and his problems of obtaining current information multiplied. Communications were slower and less dependable. In some letters Bleecker prodded his overseas correspondents for answers. He wrote Neusville and Hercules Daniel Bize,[25] a merchant in St. Eustatius, about earlier orders and the disposition of his goods, complaining that he had had no word from them. After 1775 orders from Neusville were routed through St. Eustatius. Apparently in a dispute over either charges or security on a note sent by Bleecker (the reason was not clear to Bleecker), Bize ignored Bleecker's requests concerning the disposition of his goods, and Bleecker brought suit against him through a St. Eustatius

[23] Philippe André Joseph de Létombe to the marquis de Castries, Oct. 27, 1781, printed in Abraham P. Nasatir and Gary Elwyn Monell, *French Consuls in the United States: A Calendar of Their Correspondence in the Archives Nationales* (Washington, D.C., 1967), p. 14. I am indebted to John McCusker for knowledge of this source. The French consular reports remain a valuable but unexploited source of information on American Revolutionary commerce.

[24] Anthony Bleecker to John der Neusville, undated, Bleecker Letterbook. The letter is on p. 152 of the letterbook, following that of Dec. 5, 1779, and preceding that of Aug. 2, 1780.

[25] In places the name appears to be Bire.

law firm in 1780.[26] Information in the colonies was sometimes slower and less dependable, too. In a letter to Matthew Irwin of Reading, Pa., in 1778 Bleecker stated: "This is my fourth letter to you since I have had any of your favours. I conclude that some of these may have miscarried, or that you must have been from home, otherwise you would not have been so long silent."[27] Another letter to Irwin in 1779 illustrates the difficulty of purchasing goods. Bleecker asked that the last chest of his tea (which had been purchased from Neusville and sent through St. Eustatius to Baltimore) be sent to him in Morristown for his own use "in order to procure provisions and other necessaries for family use, by way of barter with the farmers."[28]

Though imported goods became more costly and scarcer in the colonies during the war, it was the export trade that was reduced most.[29] Higher freight and insurance and the scarcity of shipping weighed more heavily on bulky American products. American production was disrupted by military operations and as manpower and other resources were channeled into the war effort. The British market, which had been the most important before the war, was lost along with those in the British West Indies and Newfoundland. American tobacco exports, which had reached an all-time high just before the Revolution, began to go directly to France and the Netherlands after the war began, but not at prewar levels.[30] This decline in exports, of course, caused an unfavorable balance of payments during the war years. This deficit was paid in

[26] Bleecker to Messrs. Curson and Goveneur, Aug. 2, 1780, Bleecker Letterbook.

[27] Bleecker to Matthew Irwin, Dec. 21, 1778, ibid.

[28] Bleecker to Irwin, Feb. 5, 1779, ibid.

[29] McCusker and Menard, "Economy of British America," pp. 231–32.

[30] See Jacob M. Price, *France and the Chesapeake: A History of the French Tobacco Monopoly, 1674–1791*, 2 vols. (Ann Arbor, 1973), 2:681–727, Nettels, *Emergence of a National Economy*, p. 19, and Edward C. Papenfuse, *In Pursuit of Profit: The Annapolis Merchants in the Era of the American Revolution, 1763–1805* (Baltimore, 1975), especially chap. 3.

three ways.[31] Subsidies and loans from European allies, especially France, totaled nearly $10 million. British and French military and naval expenditures in the United States also resulted in earnings of foreign exchange. Finally, privateering became a major source of funds during the war: American privateers took 2,000 British vessels, with cargoes valued at an estimated £18 million sterling during the conflict.[32]

As overseas trade declined, Americans were forced into a greater degree of self-sufficiency. Resources were channeled into the production of goods that substituted for imports. Examples of this process of import substitution abound. The production of both household and commercial manufacturing of textiles increased. The output of the colonial iron industry rose. The use of grain in making alcoholic beverages turned tastes from imported rum and wine to beer and whiskey.[33] Americans were remarkably resourceful at these pursuits, and the ability of the economy to be sufficiently flexible to accomplish this indicates a maturity of economic development that would be beneficial and perhaps necessary for political independence. Nevertheless, these activities were less productive and resulted in lower standards of living for Americans during the Revolution.

The difficulties encountered by the new nation in the 1780s have stirred controversy among both contemporary observers and historians over the question of the health of the American economy during this decade. For example, Tench Coxe, a Philadelphia merchant and writer on the American economy, contended that affairs had reached "a very disagreeable condition by the year 1786." Benjamin Franklin, on the other hand, upon returning from France in 1785 after a long residence abroad, said that perhaps the state of the

[31] Nettels, *Emergence of a National Economy*, pp. 20–21.

[32] Ibid., pp. 8–13.

[33] James F. Shepherd and Gary M. Walton, "Economic Change after the American Revolution: Pre- and Post-War Comparisons of Maritime Shipping and Trade," *Explorations in Economic History* 13 (1976):399.

economy was "less gloomy than has been imagined."[34] Historians also have expressed sharp differences of opinion. Merrill Jensen has called the period "one of extraordinary economic growth." He goes on to assert: "By 1790 the export of agricultural produce was double what it had been before the war. American cities grew rapidly."[35] Curtis Nettels, on the other hand, entitled his two chapters pertaining to the 1780s "Postwar Trade and Depression" and "Depression Remedies," painting a picture of serious economic decline for the country.[36]

One reason for such differences of opinion stems from the lack of any overall statistical picture of output and trade for the American economy during the 1780s as for the war years. Another reason is that there were great variations in economic prospects among localities and regions of the country. As during the Revolution, one suspects that subsistence production was less affected by the above difficulties. This important base of economic activity provided Americans with a higher degree of stabililty in their economic welfare than would have been possible if they had been wholly dependent upon market production for their incomes. With regard to the health of the economy, though, production for markets is at issue.

Gordon C. Bjork has suggested an interpretation that strikes a path between the optimism of Jensen and the pessimism of Nettels.[37] During the 1780s recovery was mixed. The Confederation period was one of change and readjustment. The new nation was forced to cope both with peacetime conditions and with being outside the British Empire. The latter fact meant that the United States was subject, like any other foreign country, to British mercantilist restrictions. The im-

[34] The quotations are taken from Gordon C. Bjork, "The Weaning of the American Economy: Independence, Market Changes and Economic Development," *Journal of Economic History* 24 (1964):541.

[35] Merrill Jensen, *The New Nation: A History of the United States during the Confederation, 1781–1789* (New York, 1950), p. 423.

[36] Nettels, *Emergence of a National Economy.*

[37] Bjork, "Weaning of the American Economy."

Table 1. Average annual exports to overseas areas: the thirteen colonies, 1768–72, and the United States, 1790–92 (in thousands of pounds sterling; 1768–72 prices)

Destination	1768–72	Percentage of total	1790–92	Percentage of total
Great Britain and Ireland	1,616	58	1,234	31
Northern Europe	—		643	16
Southern Europe	406	14	557	14
British West Indies ⎱	759	27	⎰402	10
Foreign West Indies ⎰			⎱956	24
Africa	21	1	42	1
Canadian colonies	—		60	2
Other	—		59	1
Total	2,802	100	3,953	100

SOURCE: James F. Shepherd and Gary M. Walton, "Economic Change after the American Revolution: Pre- and Post-War Comparisons of Maritime Shipping and Trade," *Explorations in Economic History* 13 (1976):406.

NOTE: Components may not sum to the total because of rounding.

pact of these changes had different effects upon the several regions and the various overseas trades. This fact, together with the lack of evidence, makes it difficult to generalize about the 1780s. Late in 1789, after the adoption of the Constitution, the federal government began to collect statistics on foreign trade. With this evidence the patterns, magnitudes, and composition of foreign trade for the years 1790–92 can be compared with the statistical picture of trade in 1768–72.

In table 1 annual average exports from America to major overseas areas are compared (in order to make the values comparable, the dollar values of 1790–92 have been converted to pounds sterling and to 1768–72 prices). It is clear that by 1790 the United States had taken advantage of its new freedom to trade directly with northern European countries. The major part of this trade was with France and the Netherlands, and the major commodity exported to these countries was tobacco, although rice, flour, wheat, and maize (Indian corn) were important because these were years of poor crops in Europe. As has been noted, though, the establishment of this trade with northern Europe, which must stand as a most important consequence of Independence, did not preclude the major share of American exports from reverting to Great Britain, though prewar levels of exports were not reached by 1790–92. The official values show the trade with Scotland, dominated by tobacco exports before the Revolution, fell off especially sharply with the reorganization of these markets in the 1780s (Appendix, table 1). The official values of American trade with Britain show a sharp increase for imports into the new United States in 1784 to meet pent-up demand, but then they fell off over the rest of the 1780s to lower levels than had existed in the early 1770s. Imports increased again to higher levels in 1790–91, comparable with high levels that had existed in 1770–72. So, by the early 1790s, imports from Britain had reached about the same absolute levels as before the war, but exports had not, and Americans had to seek new markets for their products.

By 1790 American trade with the Caribbean had surpassed its prewar level, and trade with southern Europe, which had been severely disrupted by the war, had just regained its relative position. In the Caribbean, trade had shifted away from the British areas and more to those controlled by the other European nations (except for the Spanish colonies, from which Americans were excluded). One reason was prohibition of American shipping from the British West Indies after the war, although the trend had existed before the Revolution as the non-British West Indian islands became more important markets for American products. Consequently, this shift was probably only accelerated by Independence and British restrictions upon American shipping. Changes in the composition of trade accompanied the growing importance of the Caribbean as a market for American products. Contrary to what some historians have said, the great colonial staple, tobacco, was no longer the single most valuable export (in terms of current value) by the early 1790s, although tobacco exports came to exceed prewar levels by the mid-1780s. Higher prices for tobacco in the later 1780s, together with higher levels of output, resulted in modest recovery in the tobacco-producing areas of Virginia and Maryland, and stimulated the spread of tobacco growing in the piedmont region of North Carolina.

This appears not to have been the case for the other important southern staples: rice, indigo, and naval stores. Although the statistics may be faulty, exports of rice do not appear to have kept pace with the rise in population. Indigo production recovered, but fell off in the 1790s as the British developed sources of supply in their Caribbean islands. Naval stores about recovered their total prewar value, but this was small relative to tobacco, rice, and indigo. The most dramatic change in the composition of exports was the increased amount of foodstuffs, such as salted beef and pork, flour, and maize—the most important commodities in the West Indian trade. This trend was under way before the Revolution; the shift into grain production in the upper South in the later colonial period was a part of this change. In any event, not all of the increased export of foodstuffs can be attributed to Independence.

Other, less valuable trades came into existence. An Asian trade (included in "Other" in table 1) began in the mid-1780s. About this time Americans began shipping foodstuffs and naval stores to French islands in the Indian Ocean. The China trade began with the return to New York of the *Empress of China* from its first voyage to Canton in 1785. It gradually developed into a trade of manufactured goods for furs on the Pacific Northwest coast, with the furs shipped to China in exchange for tea, silk, and other Oriental goods. Although of relatively minor importance in terms of value, the China trade led, among other things, to the first American claim on the Oregon territory.

Overall, there was an increase of about 37 percent in the real value of exports from the late colonial period to the early 1790s. But since population increased by 80 percent over this period, the rise of exports did not keep pace with population growth. The relative importance of foreign markets to the American economy declined somewhat, as can be seen by the fall in per capita exports shown in table 2.

This view, though, obscures significant regional differences. It is clear that the increase in real exports was due almost entirely to increased exports from the New England and Middle Atlantic regions. Compared with prewar proportions, overseas trade gained slightly in relative importance in the North and more so in the Middle Atlantic states. It did this despite the depressed economy of New Hampshire,

Table 2. Average annual exports from colonies and regions of the thirteen colonies, 1768–92, and states and regions of the United States, 1791–92 (total exports in thousands of pounds sterling; per capita exports in pounds sterling; 1768–72 prices)

Origin	1768–72			1791–92		
	Total exports	Percentage of total	Per capita exports	Total exports	Percentage of total	Per capita exports
New England						
New Hampshire	46	2	0.74	33	1	0.23
Massachusetts	258	9	0.97	542	14	1.14
Rhode Island	81	3	1.39	119	3	1.72
Connecticut	92	3	0.50	148	4	0.62
Total	477	17	0.82	842	22	0.83
Middle Atlantic						
New York	187	7	1.15	512	14	1.51
New Jersey	2	—	0.02	5	—	0.03
Pennsylvania	353	13	1.47	584	16	1.34
Delaware	18	1	0.51	26	1	0.44
Total	559	20	1.01	1,127	30	1.11
Upper South						
Maryland	392	14	1.93	482	13	1.51
Virginia	770	27	1.72	678	18	0.91
Total	1,162	41	1.79	1,160	31	1.09
Lower South						
North Carolina	75	3	0.38	104	3	0.27
South Carolina	455	16	3.66	436	12	1.75
Georgia	74	3	3.17	97	3	1.17
Total	603	22	1.75	637	17	0.88
Grand total	2,802	100	1.31	3,766	100	0.99

SOURCE: James F. Shepherd and Gary M. Walton, "Economic Change after the American Revolution: Pre- and Post-War Comparisons of Maritime Shipping and Trade," *Explorations in Economic History* 13 (1976):413.

NOTE: Components may not sum to the total because of rounding.

which suffered because of a falling off in shipbuilding and the timber trade. The increase in per capita exports in all the New England colonies except New Hampshire indicates a vigorous recovery in trade there by the early 1790s. How rapidly this recovery occurred over the 1780s is impossible to say without more complete evidence, but export data for 1787 compiled by Gordon Bjork indicate that exports for Massachusetts for that year may have been as much as they were before the Revolution.[38] Though population was growing, growth was not so rapid as in the Middle Atlantic region, probably due to the lack of geographic frontiers within their boundaries.[39] The slim evidence we have suggests that the overseas trade of the New England states, with the exception of New Hampshire, had more than recovered by the early 1790s, and that this recovery took place rapidly beginning in the mid-1780s.[40]

The increase in exports relative to population in the Middle Atlantic states was due solely to the large relative increase of New York's exports. In per capita terms Pennsylvania's and Delaware's per capita exports declined moderately. What was the source of this large relative increase in New York's trade with overseas areas?[41] The traditional explana-

[38] Gordon C. Bjork, "Stagnation and Growth in the American Economy, 1784–1792," Ph.D. diss., University of Washington, 1963, p. 85.

[39] Ibid., p. 37.

[40] Ibid., pp. 31–37, also cites qualitative accounts of improving trade in Massachusetts following 1786.

[41] It seems odd that such a large change has been ignored in the literature. This seems to be the case for more than just economic questions, as many scholars of the middle Atlantic colonies/states note. See Milton M. Klein, *The Politics of Diversity: Essays in the History of Colonial New York* (Port Washington, N.Y., 1974), p. 181, where he writes, "This categorization reflects the failure of historians to organize an appropriate frame of reference into which to fit the variegated pattern of the Middle Colonies' economic, social, and political development." Thomas C. Cochran "The Middle Atlantic Area in the Economic History of the United States," *Proceedings of the American Philosophical Society* 108 (1964):156–57, discusses this lack of an integrated regional treatment of the middle Atlantic area by historians. He maintains that it has been due to geographic and cultural differences that make it difficult, if not impossible, to treat these middle

tion of such differences among the states has been that associated with the "critical period" school of history, which says that the 1780s was a period of confusion where the individual states discriminated against one another in all possible ways while the federal government stood by powerless to bring cooperation and coordination.[42] The tariffs and trade restrictions imposed by most states were one of the most important ways by which the states supposedly discriminated against one another. It seems far more likely, however, that New York's explosive increase in exports was due to increased agricultural output based upon rapid population growth and settlement of upstate New York. Before the Revolution, white settlement was confined to Long Island, Manhattan, the Hudson Valley to Albany, scattered settlements north of Albany and west along the Mohawk, and a few outposts on the upper Susquehanna.[43] Robert V. Wells states: "The process that produced record proportions of rural New Yorkers in the early years of the new nation began about the middle of the eighteenth century as population began to move up the Hudson, before exploding westward along the Mohawk toward the Genessee in the years after independence."[44] This growth of New York City's hinterland continued rapidly after 1790, and was the most important factor in New York surpassing Philadelphia and becoming the preeminent American port.[45] The roots of this preeminence lay in the rapid expansion of its hinterland that began in the 1780s.

Atlantic colonies and states as a region. See also Thomas C. Cochran, *New York in the Confederation: An Economic Study* (Port Washington, N.Y., 1932).

[42] See William Frank Zornow, "New Hampshire Tariff Policies, 1775–1789," *Social Studies* 45 (1954):252.

[43] Mary Jo Kline, "The 'New' New York: An Expanding State in the New Nation," in Manfred Jones and Robert V. Wells, eds., *New Opportunities in a New Nation: The Development of New York after the Revolution* (Schenectady, N.Y., 1982), p. 14. A more specific view of this growth of settlement seems sketchy. Kline goes on to say: "We do not, for instance, even know where the New York frontier line lay during the decades of the state's expansion" (p. 30).

[44] Robert V. Wells, "What Then Is New York, This New State? An Introduction," in Jones and Wells, eds., *New Opportunities in a New Nation*, p. 10.

[45] This point seems to have been missed by Gordon C. Bjork and his

Philadelphia's hinterland, on the other hand, was largely settled by the end of the colonial period.[46] As settlement and cultivation moved into the west of the Susquehanna River valley, Baltimore began to siphon Pennsylvania trade away from Philadelphia.[47] Other factors besides the spread of settlement also contributed to Baltimore's growth. A better network of roads together with the natural advantages of water transportation on the Susquehanna and Chesapeake favored the city.[48] Its growth was spurred during the Revolution as the British appeared in the Chesapeake only intermittently and for short periods until 1780.[49] Baltimore also benefited from the well-known shift of agricultural production in Maryland from tobacco to wheat.[50] Baltimore's flour shipments to overseas destinations increased from around 40,000 to 200,000 barrels between 1770 and the early 1790s.[51] Despite Philadelphia's failure to grow as rapidly as New York and Baltimore, its exports did increase following the end of the war and were considerably higher in 1784 than 1773.[52] Part of Philadelphia's relative decline was due to the loss of tobacco exports, which reverted to the upper South after 1784, and part was due to a decrease in exports of foodstuffs, most importantly flour. Recovery occurred by 1789, however, and Pennsylvania's total exports were considerably

---

discussants. See "Foreign Trade," in David T. Gilchrist, ed., *The Growth of the Seaport Cities, 1790–1825* (Charlottesville, Va., 1967), pp. 54–82.

[46] James T. Lemon, *The Best Poor Man's Country: A Geographical Study of Early Southeastern Pennsylvania* (Baltimore, 1972), especially chap. 5.

[47] Ibid., p. 129; Ronald Hoffman, *A Spirit of Dissension: Economics, Politics, and the Revolution in Maryland* (Baltimore, 1973), pp. 74–80; and Gary Lawson Browne, *Baltimore in the Nation, 1789–1861* (Chapel Hill, N.C., 1980), pp. 3–4. Baltimore also benefited from settlement in the northern and western parts of Maryland as well as south-central Pennsylvania.

[48] Hoffman, *A Spirit of Dissension*, p. 77.

[49] Browne, *Baltimore in the Nation*, p. 9.

[50] Paul G. E. Clemens, *The Atlantic Economy and Colonial Maryland's Eastern Shore: From Tobacco to Grain* (Ithaca, N.Y., 1980), pp. 168–205.

[51] Geoffrey Gilbert, "The Role of Breadstuffs in American Trade, 1770–1790," *Explorations in Economic History* 14 (1977):380.

[52] Bjork, "Stagnation and Growth," pp. 53–56.

higher in the early 1790s than they had been before the Revolution, even though the level of exports relative to population was not quite so high.

In the upper South the disruptions caused by the war, especially the loss of field hands, made the restoration of tobacco production to the high prewar levels impossible.[53] Nevertheless, American tobacco exports had recovered their prewar levels by 1786 and remained there until 1792.[54] This, together with the growing grain and flour exports provided moderate recovery for the upper South. Maryland did better than Virginia. Though per capita exports fell, the value of total exports rose by 23 percent from 1768–72 to the early 1790s. For Virginia both total and per capita exports fell. The tonnage figures (Appendix, table 2), too, bear out better performance for Maryland's trade. Even so, as indicated by the fall in per capita exports, the overseas trade of the upper South—which had been so important to the colonies—was not keeping pace with a growing population.

This was even more true in the lower South. British occupation of coastal South Carolina during the last four years of the war, the loss of slaves, and the flight of loyalist elements severely reduced the productive capacity of rice and indigo plantations there during the Confederation period.[55] North Carolina, having a different economic structure, was less oriented toward overseas trade, and consequently suffered less. However, South Carolina and Georgia experienced a large fall in per capital exports. South Carolina's exports dropped in absolute terms from the 1770s to the early 1790s.

To what extent were state and regional variations in recovery due to the tariff and related legislation enacted by the states during the 1780s? This question is difficult to answer because it is impossible to quantify the impact of the various state duties and restrictions. Furthermore, there is no system-

[53] Price, *France and the Chesapeake*, pp. 728–31. See also Papenfuse, *In Pursuit of Profit*, p. 177, for estimates of Maryland exports in the mid-1780s.

[54] If Virginia and Maryland fell somewhat short of complete recovery, the difference was made up by increased production in the Carolinas and Georgia (Price, *France and the Chesapeake*, p. 731).

[55] Bjork, "Stagnation and Growth," pp. 17–18.

atic account of the structure and level of state tariffs, nor any comparative study of the differences among states.[56] Such tariffs ranged from various specific duties on a long (and varied) list of enumerated goods, to general ad valorem rates ranging from 1 percent in Maryland in 1782 (raised to 2 percent later that year) to 5 percent in New Hampshire, Massachusetts, New York, Pennsylvania, and North Carolina. Changes in specific duties often occurred, together with occasional changes in ad valorem rates. Exemptions were frequently made, especially for raw materials or tools used in domestic manufacturing that were not available locally. Usually, too, goods produced in other states were exempt. Discriminatory duties were often levied on both goods imported in foreign ships and on the tonnage of those ships. The purpose of the state tariffs initially was to provide revenue, and some states such as New York secured a large proportion of state revenues from them.[57] By the mid-1780s, however, tariff acts passed by Pennsylvania and all the New England states began specifically to mention protection of domestic manufacturing as a goal. In addition, a number of retaliatory measures were passed by states aimed directly at the British after that government adopted an Order in Council in 1783 that closed British West Indian ports to American shipping.

But did this system of state tariffs and trade regulation

[56] There are, however, the following older works about colonial and early American tariffs and trade legislation: W. C. Fisher, "American Trade Regulation before 1789," American Historical Association *Papers* 3 (1889):467–93; Albert A. Giesecke, *American Commercial Legislation before 1789* (Philadelphia, 1910); and William Hill, "Colonial Tariffs," *Quarterly Journal of Economics* 7 (1892):78–100. Also, William Frank Zornow has written about the tariff laws of seven of the states: "Georgia Tariff Policies, 1775 to 1789," *Georgia Historical Quarterly* 38 (1954):1–10; "Massachusetts Tariff Policies, 1775 to 1789," *Essex Institute Historical Collections* 90 (1954):194–215; "New Hampshire Tariff Policies, 1775–1789," *Social Studies* 45 (1954):252–56; "The Tariff Policies of Virginia, 1775–1789," *Virginia Magazine of History and Biography* 62 (1954):306–19; "North Carolina Tariff Policies, 1775–1789," *North Carolina Historical Review* 32 (1955):151–64; "Tariff Policies in South Carolina, 1775–1789," *South Carolina Historical Magazine* 56 (1955):31–44; and "New York Tariff Policies, 1775–1789," *New York History* 37 (1956):40–63.

[57] Forrest McDonald, *E Pluribus Unum: The Formation of the American Republic, 1776–1790*, 2d ed. (Indianapolis, 1979), pp. 109–10.

cause discrimination among states and stifle interstate and foreign trade, as the "critical period" view suggests? Erroneous statements by contemporary observers supported this view. Tench Coxe maintained that duties upon goods from other states were greater than those imposed upon foreign goods of a similar kind by the enacting state. He added that there was discrimination in tonnage duties by some American states against other states. A specific example often cited is that a New York act of 1787 provided that foreign goods brought into New York from Connecticut and New Jersey were to pay entrance and clearance fees four times higher than American goods. This had arisen from New Jersey's refusal to discriminate against British goods and ships with higher duties as most of the other states were doing, and from Connecticut's attempt to build up its own direct foreign trade by taxing foreign goods coming into Connecticut from other states. Some historians more recently have expressed this same view. Robert G. Albion states: "Interstate rivalry and the jumbled condition of the state currencies . . . seriously hampered the merchants—a depressed and at times desperate tone runs through their letter-books of those years."[58]

Such discrimination among states was not typical, however. Albert A. Giesecke, in an older study of early American commercial legislation, noted that it was exceptional, "for it was usual during the period to exempt goods of the growth or produce of any of the United States from import duties by the legislating state."[59] Merrill Jensen would agree, saying that "trade 'barriers,' contrary to the ["critical period"] tradition, were the exception rather than the rule."[60] This supports his view that the young United States was growing rapidly during the 1780s, and that the national political system provided by the Articles of Confederation did not hamper this vigorous growth. Curtis Nettels emphasized that some of the state tariffs were ones that "gave substantial pro-

[58] Robert G. Albion, *The Rise of the Port of New York* (Hamden, Conn., 1961), p. 7.

[59] Giesecke, *American Commercial Legislation*, p. 135.

[60] Jensen, *The New Nation*, p. 340.

tection to local industries, which were then being injured by the competition of low-priced foreign products."[61] Nettels also emphasized the *potential* for discrimination under the Articles of Confederation, and their failure to give Congress "the power to enact navigation laws or otherwise to put pressure on foreign states that adhered to policies injurious to American shipping and trade."[62] Despite these effects of the state tariffs and trade legislation, the evidence does not suggest that either interstate or foreign trade was greatly hampered, or that the regional differences in recovery and adjustment to being outside the British Empire had much to do with this tariff system. Most importantly, the states usually erected no barriers to interstate trade, and it was relatively free to American merchants and shipowners during the 1780s. Lower tariffs generally were established in the southern states, where trade was more depressed.

These regional variations have not been sufficiently emphasized by historians. Exports from the northern states increased relatively more than their population (with the exceptions of New Hampshire, Pennsylvania, and Delaware). In particular, exports from New York boomed, reflecting the increased agricultural output of that state. In contrast, the fall in per capita export values for the southern states was in part the result of a slowing in the growth of demand for southern staples and partly the consequence of market alterations stemming from Independence and new economic and political alliances rather than discrimination and restrictions imposed by the states upon one another's trade.

It should be emphasized that it was the export trade in the traditional southern staples that was stagnating—not the aggregate size of the southern economy. The following percentage changes in population during the 1770s and 1780s indicate that population growth and settlement were rapidly taking place.[63] The most rapid growth, however, was in more recently and less densely settled areas. New York's growth in the 1780s stands out as high. So, too, does that in the western

[61] Nettels, *Emergence of a National Economy*, p. 69.

[62] Ibid., p. 75.

[63] The percentage changes are computed from the 1770 and 1780

State	1770–80	1780–90
Maine	57	97
New Hampshire	41	62
Vermont	376	78
Massachusetts	14	41
Rhode Island	(9)	30
Connecticut	12	15
New York	29	61
New Jersey	19	32
Pennsylvania	36	33
Delaware	28	30
Maryland	21	30
Virginia	20	29
North Carolina	37	46
South Carolina	45	38
Georgia	140	48
Kentucky	187	64
Tennessee	900	260

parts of the original southern states and in the future states of Kentucky and Tennessee, rather than in the older, staple-producing areas. Soon there would be a great new staple, but in the early 1790s the older staples were beginning to fall into eclipse.

Paralleling the growth of commodity trade in the northern states was the growth of mercantile and shipping activities, which had been so important to New England and the middle colonies before the Revolution. It is difficult to know these changes with any degree of precision because of the lack of evidence and a change in the prewar and postwar definitions of tonnage. Nevertheless, an examination of the evidence on tonnage (see the Appendix, table 2) indicates that there probably was at least a 45 percent increase—and perhaps more— in the volume of shipping entering American ports between the late colonial period and the early 1790s. Furthermore, the proportion of that shipping owned by Americans increased in all but that connected with the important West Indian trade, the latter fall reflecting the British prohibition

---

Greene-Harrington-Sutherland total population data in the U.S. Bureau of the Census, *Historical Statistics of the United States: Colonial Times to 1970*, 2 vols. (Washington, D.C., 1975), 2:1168. The 1790 data are from the census of that year, 1:24–37.

on American ships trading directly with the British islands.[64]

This evidence suggests that shipping earnings and mercantile profits, too, probably recovered from the disruption of trade caused by the war and the readjustments that took place in the 1780s. This recovery, both of commodity trade and of shipping and mercantile activities in the New England and Middle Atlantic states, was of great importance to the new nation. The maintenance of a strong commercial base in these regions allowed the United States to take advantage of the new economic possibilities that were to come with the outbreak of war in Europe in 1793.

What, then, were the effects of these developments in the international sector of the late colonial, Revolutionary, and early national periods on the American economy?[65] Most importantly, what were the consequences for the economic welfare of Americans living during these times? For an answer to these questions, scholars have often turned to the "staple theory" of economic development. This theory has suggested that growth and progress in a newly-settled region have come from concentration on the production of a few primary products (products in which the natural-resource content of the product is relatively large) for export. The exploitation of these resources allows the newer region to increase its average productivity and trade for goods in whose production it does not have a comparative advantage (which are usually manufactured goods from the older, mature region). This specialization results in increasing levels of trade, migration of mobile economic resources—labor and capital—and

[64] Shepherd and Walton, "Economic Change," pp. 415 and 419.

[65] Many sources address this question. The reader may wish to see Richard E. Caves, "Export-Led Growth and the New Economic History," in Jagdish N. Bhagwati et al., eds., *Trade, Balance of Payments, and Growth* (Amsterdam, 1971), pp. 403–42; Marc Egnal, "The Economic Development of the Thirteen Continental Colonies, 1720 to 1775," *William and Mary Quarterly*, 3d ser. 32 (1975):191–222; Stanley L. Engerman and Robert E. Gallman, "U.S. Economic Growth, 1783–1860," *Research in Economic History* 8 (1983):1–46; Robert E. Gallman, "The Pace and Pattern of American Economic Growth," in Lance E. Davis et al., eds., *American Economic Growth: An Economist's History of the United States* (New York, 1972), pp. 15–60; McCusker and Menard, "Economy of British America," pp. 1–56; and Shepherd and Walton, *Economic Development*, pp. 6–26.

higher living standards than would be achieved by following a course of complete self-sufficiency for the newly settled region.

Not all would agree that this scenario comprises the staple theory, but it does conform to the American colonial experience. The important questions that arise are what proportion these activities for production for overseas markets comprised of overall economic activity, and what other sources of economic progress existed. Was improving agricultural productivity, for example, a more important source of growth?[66] Current speculation about the relative importance of overseas trade to the American colonies would put it in the range of 15 to 20 percent of total output around 1770 and 10 to 15 percent during the last decade of the eighteenth century.[67] Unless production for domestic markets was substantial, this suggests that subsistence production was a major part of economic activity. However crude this calculated guess regarding the relative importance of production for overseas markets may be, the inescapable conclusion is that subsistence production dominated early American economic activity. Through this period subsistence production provided an important base to American economic welfare (though it, too, may have been affected by the war). Still, 15 to 20 percent is enough to matter at the margin. It would not have been all-important, yet it would have made a difference. A more definite answer to this question will continue to elude us until we have a more complete picture of early American economic life. Certainly we need to give more emphasis to studying subsistence activities and those associated with production for domestic markets in order to examine the process of early American growth. We should look at consumption and investment patterns for various types of households and producing units. Undoubtedly probate records will continue to be exploited heavily in the future as our most abundant records of colonial life. We need to study the credit and financial structure of the economy. Needless to say, the big questions

[66] Agricultural productivity was not an independent component of colonial growth because most exports were agricultural products.

[67] Robert E. Lipsey, "Foreign Trade," in Davis et al., eds., *American Economic Growth*, p. 554.

must be explored. However, they will be more easily addressed once we have better answers to these and other questions about the colonial economy. The staple theory can serve as an organizing framework (it is not a comprehensive theory of growth), but proper attention must be paid to domestic production.

Regional differences have been stressed in this paper. The differences in the degree of dependence upon overseas markets of various regions and colonies in the late colonial period are striking. Changes that came after the Revolution are marked and have not been sufficiently emphasized in our histories of this period. Fuller explorations of the causes of these changes are required. They cannot be simply chalked up to the effects of the war and Independence in a hostile, mercantilistic Atlantic economy. The Revolution and Independence should not be taken to be the great watershed in our economic history that it usually is assumed to have been.

Clearly, Americans had developed a strong commercial base in the form of a resident mercantile sector by the end of the colonial period, especially in the northern regions. It allowed the new nation to take advantage of its neutral position in the European wars following 1792 and attain new levels of trade and prosperity. It undoubtedly contributed to the accumulation of capital and know-how necessary for the growth of manufacturing and industry. It sharply differentiated the British-American colonies from others in Latin America and elsewhere, playing an important role in American economic prosperity. This development of a strong commercial base rivals the important institutions and strong central government established by the Constitution as a factor in successful American economic growth.

Not all was rosy. Recent research has shown a growing inequality in the distribution of income and wealth in the colonies. This surely carried into the early national period. The existence of the plantation system had firmly grounded the institution of slavery in American society, and it soon was to be perpetuated by the beginning of cotton production in the South. None of this should detract, however, from the fact that most white Americans had achieved a relatively high material standard of living, perhaps the highest in the world for their time.

Appendix table 1. Official value of imports from, and exports to, Great Britain to and from the American continental colonies,* 1760–91; and the current value of imports from Great Britain to the American continental colonies, 1760–75 (rounded to the nearest thousand pounds sterling)

	(1) Current value of imports from Great Britain	(2) Official value of imports from		(3)	(4)	(5) Official value of exports to		(6)	(7)
		Great Britain	England	Scotland		Great Britain	England	Scotland	
1760	2,786	2,798	2,612	186		1,150	761	389	
1761	1,782	1,797	1,652	145		1,161	848	313	
1762	1,474	1,547	1,377	170		1,069	743	326	
1763	1,859	1,893	1,632	261		1,460	1,106	354	
1764	2,442	2,475	2,250	225		1,449	1,111	338	
1765	2,114	2,120	1,944	176		1,574	1,152	422	
1766	1,984	1,982	1,804	178		1,428	1,044	384	
1767	2,192	2,168	1,901	267		1,473	1,096	377	
1768	2,393	2,390	2,157	233		1,657†	1,251	405	
1769	1,491	1,605	1,336	269		1,532†	1,060	471	
1770	2,133	2,262	1,926	336		1,498	1,016	482	
1771	4,462	4,577†	4,202	374		1,946	1,340	606	
1772	3,460	3,311	3,013	298		1,800†	1,259	542	
1773	2,451	2,312	2,079	233		1,887	1,369	518	
1774	2,953	2,843	2,590	253		1,847	1,374	473	
1775	226	220	196	24		2,457	1,921	536	
1776		56	55	1		186	104	82	

Year						
1777	93	57	36	17	13	4
1778	69	34	35	43	18	25
1779	412†	350	63	54†	21	34
1780	997†	825	171	98†	19	80
1781	995†	848	148	144	100	44
1782	301†	256	44	136	29	107
1783	1,544	1,435	109	349	314	35
1784	3,738	3,418	320	749	701	48
1785	2,308	2,079	229	894	776	118
1786	1,603	1,431	172	843	744	99
1787	2,014	1,794	220	894†	780	113
1788	1,886	1,710	176	1,024	884	140
1789	2,495†	2,307	189	1,050	893	157
1790	3,432	3,258	174	1,191	1,043	148
1791	4,223	4,014	209	1,194	1,011	183

SOURCES: Column 1, John J. McCusker, "The Rum Trade and the Balance of Payments of the Thirteen Continental Colonies, 1650–1775," Ph.D. diss., University of Pittsburgh, 1970, p. 1210; columns 2 through 7, U.S. Bureau of the Census, *Historical Statistics of the United States: Colonial Times to 1970*, 2 vols. (Washington, D.C., 1975), 2:1176–77.

*These were given in the English and Scottish customs records (Customs 3 and 14, respectively, Public Record Office), for New England, New York, Pennsylvania, Virginia and Maryland, the Carolinas, and Georgia.

†The components for England and Scotland do not sum to the total for Great Britain because of rounding.

Appendix table 2. Tonnage of shipping entering and clearing the British North American continental colonies from and to overseas areas, averages for 1760–62 and 1768–72, and the United States, average for 1790–92

	Average 1760–62		Average 1768–72		Average 1790–92 (unadjusted)*	Average 1790–92 (adjusted)†
	Tons entered	Tons cleared	Tons entered	Tons cleared	Tons entered	Tons entered
Canadian colonies						
Newfoundland	——	——	11,049	11,864	—	
Nova Scotia	9,772‡	10,564‡	2,542	2,488	—	
Quebec	5,471§	6,175§	4,346	4,466	—	
Total	15,243	16,739	17,937	18,818		
New England						
New Hampshire	9,946	16,132	10,857	15,172	12,216	6,700
Massachusetts	34,517	41,231	39,333	38,324	115,732	63,700
Rhode Island	3,806‖	5,991	7,559	8,365	16,394	9,000
Connecticut	4,528‖	4,595	8,707	10,212	22,583	12,400
Total	52,797	67,949	66,456	72,073	166,925	91,800
Middle colonies/states						
New York	9,980	14,762	16,928	16,734	81,790	45,000
New Jersey	2,194	2,166	560	671	595	300
Pennsylvania	30,241	31,896	30,055	29,428	85,512	47,000
Delaware	3,276	3,399	2,811	935	5,862	3,200
Total	45,691	52,223	50,354	47,768	173,759	95,500
Upper South						
Maryland	24,722	24,730	22,468	25,925	59,496	32,700
Virginia	43,064	40,565	38,702	42,120	83,510	45,900
Total	67,786	65,295	61,170	68,045	143,006	78,600

Lower South						
North Carolina	11,538	11,616	12,618	15,478	36,531	20,100
South Carolina	18,894	19,268	25,783	26,973	43,320	23,800
Georgia	1,972	1,961	7,021	8,535	23,923	13,200
Total	32,404	32,845	45,422	50,986	103,774	57,100
Grand total	213,921	235,051	241,339	257,690	587,464	323,000

SOURCES: Add. Ms. 38335, British Library, for 1760–62; Customs 16/1, Public Record Office, for 1768–72; United States, *American State Papers*, Class IV, *Commerce and Navigation* (Washington, D.C., 1832), vol. 7, for 1790–92:

NOTE: No statistics are available for ships clearing U.S. ports in the 1700s. The figures for 1760–62 and 1768–72 are registered tonnage and were used as the official measure of the size of ships. Due to a change in the definition of tonnage in the 1780s, the 1790–92 data are not comparable with those from the prewar years. The postwar figures are based upon measured tonnage, the figure calculated by a standard formula based upon the gross dimensions of the hull of the ship and used by shipbuilders in contracting with buyers. The relationship between the prewar registered tonnage and the postwar measured tonnage has been investigated by McCusker, Walton, and French (John J. McCusker, "Colonial Tonnage Measurement: Five Philadelphia Merchant Ships as a Sample," *Journal of Economic History* 27 [1967]:82–91; idem, "The Tonnage of Ships Engaged in British Colonial Trade during the Eighteenth Century," *Research in Economic History* 6 [1981]:73–105; Gary M. Walton, "Colonial Tonnage Measurements; A Comment," *Journal of Economic History* 27 [1967]:392–97; and Christopher J. French, "Eighteenth-Century Shipping Tonnage Measurements," *Journal of Economic History* 33 [1973]:434–43). Evidence suggests that, on the average, prewar registered tonnage was equal to about two-thirds of measured tonnage. However, this average varied systematically with the size of the ship. The difference tended to be larger for smaller ships, and smaller for larger ships. Registered tonnage was approximately 43 to 45 percent less than measured tonnage for ships ranging from 51 to 150 registered tons, and 30 to 32 percent less for ships in the range of 151 to 250 registered tons (French, "Eighteenth-Century Shipping Tonnage Measurements," p. 440). In order to present the most conservative (smallest) measure of 1790–92 tonnage, a correction factor of 0.55 was used to obtain the adjusted tonnage figures.

*Only tonnage entering the states was given in the source.

†The adjusted figures were computed by multiplying the unadjusted tonnage figures by a factor of 0.55 and rounding to the nearest hundred.

‡No figures were given for the port district of Annapolis Royal (Canso) for 1760 and 1761. During 1762, the tonnage entering this port district was 2,530 tons and the tonnage clearing was 2,495 tons. The above averages include no amounts for this port district for 1760 and 1761.

(*continued*)

§The figures for Quebec are for 1762 only.

‖No tonnage was given for New Haven for 1760. Tonnage entering New Haven was 982 tons in 1761 and 1,560 tons in 1762, and tonnage clearing was 1,298 tons in 1761 and 2,188 tons in 1762. The above averages include no amounts for New Haven for 1760.

JAMES A. HENRETTA

The War for Independence and American Economic Development

In 1960 Thomas C. Cochran advanced the provocative thesis that the Civil War retarded the industrialization of the United States. Cochran based his argument on statistical indices of total commodity output—the production of coal, pig iron, textiles, farm machinery, as well as the rate of construction of new railroad lines. His analysis of these key economic indicators demonstrated that the pace of economic growth slowed during the 1860s. Cochran's short paper forced a revaluation of the traditional thesis that the war, as Harold U. Faulkner had phrased it, "speeded the Industrial Revolution and the development of capitalism."

Ultimately most scholars agreed with Cochran that wartime economic growth fell below that of the preceding period. At the same time they argued that the war shifted the pattern of economic development in significant ways and, equally important, that it bolstered the financial resources and the political power of industrial capitalists. Seen from

An earlier version of this paper was presented at the Shelby Cullom Davis Center at Princeton University. Lawrence Stone, John Murrin, and Paul Clemens offered useful criticisms and suggestions, as did participants in the 1984 United States Capitol Historical Society Symposium—notably James Walsh, Jacob Price, and Franklin Mendels. I am especially grateful to Lois Carr for providing me with unpublished materials, to Stanley Engerman for a perceptive critique of my manuscript, and to Michael Merrill for showing me the inner logic of my interpretation.

the widest perspective, therefore, the Civil War had a much greater total economic impact than Cochran had allowed.

Cochran's argument also turned the attention of historians to the initial decades of American economic growth. For two decades various scholars—Douglass North, Paul David, Robert E. Gallman, George Rogers Taylor, and, most recently, Diane Lindstrom—have advanced stimulating hypotheses to explain the expansion of the per capita gross national product between 1790 and 1840.[1]

Historians of the Revolutionary era have largely ignored this debate over the timing of the American economic "take-off." With a few exceptions, they have not directly addressed the economic impact of the War for Independence. Our understanding of the wartime economy rests largely on four books written a generation ago. Robert A. East published his study of entrepreneurial activity, *Business Enterprise in the American Revolutionary Era,* in 1938. Richard B. Morris added a detailed examination of workers' occupations and lives in *Government and Labor in Early America* in 1946. Then, in 1947, Oscar and Mary Handlin provided an institutional synthesis in *Commonwealth; A Study of the Role of Government in the American Economy: Massachusetts, 1774–1861.* These studies fleshed out the valuable statistical analyses offered by Anne Bezanson beginning in 1935 and culminating in *Prices and Inflation during the American Revolution: Pennsylvania, 1770–1790,* published in 1951.

Subsequent biographies of individual merchants, such as the Beekmans of New York and the Browns of Providence, did not attempt an overview of the wartime economy. Nor did they ground their narratives in a set of theoretical statements. Rather, they described how merchants and other social groups suffered, gained, or simply coped during the war and the economically difficult decade of the 1780s.[2]

---

[1] Thomas C. Cochran, "Did the Civil War Retard Industrialization?" *Mississippi Valley Historical Review* 48 (1961):197–210. The Faulkner quotation is on p. 197. For a review of this debate see Ralph Andreano, *The Economic Impact of the American Civil War* (Cambridge, Mass., 1962).

[2] Robert A. East, *Business Enterprise in the American Revolutionary Era* (1938; reprint ed., Gloucester, Mass., 1964); Richard B. Morris, *Government and Labor in Early America* (1946; reprint ed., Boston, 1981); Oscar

Even as this picture of the war economy remained fragmentary, important scholarly works revised our understanding of colonial society. First, quantitatively-based commercial studies outlined the long-term movement of tobacco prices, the transatlantic flow of African slaves and white indentured servants, the amazing growth of exports in wheat and rice, and the complete American balance of trade for the years 1768–72.[3] Second, historians used local tax and probate records to describe the structure of property ownership in the colonies, and Jackson T. Main attempted to link the extent of wealth inequalities to participation in commercial activity.[4] Finally, demographic studies raised the specter of a Malthusian subsistence crisis in the dominant rural sector. As Kenneth A. Lockridge suggested in his brief but influential survey "Land, Population, and the Evolution of New England Society, 1630–1780," "this part of America was becoming more and more an old world society; old world in the sense of the size of farms, . . . an increasingly wide and articulated hierarchy [with] . . . the poor ever permanent and in increasing numbers."[5]

---

and Mary Handlin, *Commonwealth; A Study of the Role of Government in the American Economy: Massachusetts, 1774–1861* (Cambridge: Mass., 1947); Anne Bezanson, *Prices and Inflation during the American Revolution: Pennsylvania, 1770–1790* (Philadelphia, 1951); Philip L. White, *The Beekmans of New York in Politics and Commerce, 1647–1877* (New York, 1956); James B. Hedges, *The Browns of Providence Plantation: Colonial Years* (Cambridge, Mass., 1952).

[3] Jacob M. Price, "The Economic Growth of the Chesapeake and the European Market, 1697–1775," *Journal of Economic History* 24 (1964):496–511; U.S. Bureau of the Census, *Historical Statistics of the United States: Colonial Times to 1970*, 2 vols. (Washington, D.C., 1975), ser. Z441-72; Philip D. Curtin, *The Atlantic Slave Trade: A Census* (Madison, Wis., 1969); David W. Galenson, *White Servitude in Colonial America: An Economic Analysis* (Cambridge, 1981); Paul G. E. Clemens, *The Atlantic Economy and Colonial Maryland's Eastern Shore: From Tobacco to Grain* (Ithaca, N.Y., 1980); James F. Shepherd and Gary M. Walton, *Shipping, Maritime Trade, and the Economic Development of Colonial North America* (Cambridge, 1972).

[4] Jackson T. Main, *The Social Structure of Revolutionary America* (Princeton, 1965); Alice Hanson Jones, *Wealth of a Nation to Be: The American Colonies on the Eve of the Revolution* (New York, 1980).

[5] Kenneth A. Lockridge, "Land, Population, and the Evolution of New England Society, 1630–1780," in Stanley N. Katz, ed., *Colonial America:*

This new scholarship holds immense significance for the Revolutionary era. To bring it to bear on the interpretation of the wartime economy requires the creation of an analytical hypothesis similar to that constructed by Cochran. Let us ask, therefore, "Did the War for Independence *accelerate* the process of American economic growth?" and "Did it encourage the transition to a more *capitalistic* society?" To answer these questions, we must first examine the character of the prewar economy both in terms of traditional mercantilist theory and with reference to the new literature on European "protoindustrialization." With this conceptual framework in place, we can then proceed to an analysis of wartime events. Finally, a short discussion of economic change and political policies after 1790 will suggest the similarities and the differences between the economic impact of the Civil and the Revolutionary wars.

In many respects, the British mainland colonies constituted a classic case of a mercantilist economy. In the southern plantation colonies, freemen and slaves produced tobacco, rice, and wheat for export to Europe, and they consumed manufactured goods imported from the mother country. By the 1740s the middle colonies likewise boasted a strong export sector. Increased production of wheat for European markets and corn for the West Indies permitted the importation of consumer goods—textiles, ironware, and ceramics. In New England, merchants sold meat, timber, and fish to the West Indies to pay for British manufactures.

The *absolute* size of the mercantilist economy grew rapidly during the eighteenth century. The American mainland population doubled each generation, stimulating export and import markets. Between 1750 and 1810, the number of people per square mile in most seaboard counties tripled.

Greater population density also prompted the *relative* growth of the domestic economy. Unlike the staple-

---

Essays in Politics and Social Development (Boston, 1971), p. 484. Also see Philip J. Greven, Jr., *Four Generations: Population, Land and Family in Colonial Andover, Massachusetts* (Ithaca, N.Y., 1970), and James A. Henretta, "The Morphology of New England Society in the Colonial Period," *Journal of Interdisciplinary History* 2 (1971):379–98.

producing export sector, American domestic production has received little scholarly attention. Yet the proportion of the mainland's gross output that was produced by American farmers, artisans, and merchants was undoubtedly higher in 1775 than ever before. Despite their astounding growth, imports composed an ever-smaller component of the American economy.

Just as mercantilism provides a framework for the study of the export economy, so the theory of "protoindustrialization" offers a conceptual perspective on the domestic sector. As a set of interpretative propositions, protoindustrialization focuses on the putting-out system of handicraft production organized by merchant capitalists. The logic of the system, Sidney Pollard has recently written, consisted "on the one hand, of capital and entrepreneurship able and willing to grasp the opportunities of distant markets . . . and supply them on a large scale; and, on the other, dispersed manufacture in the countryside enjoying low costs of production . . . by the widespread use of 'inferior labour,' i.e., women and children, by the depression of real wages made possible by the agricultural part-incomes of the workers, and by an advanced division of labour."[6]

The initial studies of the outwork system in preindustrial Europe focused on the activities of merchants. These skilled entrepreneurs managed the distribution of raw materials and finished products. Then, in the 1950s, Joan Thirsk and H. J. Habakkuk linked the emergence of the rural textile industry with the rapid population growth encouraged by the custom of partible inheritance. In his study of economic development in Flanders, Franklin F. Mendels gave these demographic propositions a theoretical cast. He carefully delineated the process whereby "areas which turned to cottage industry tended to attract immigration, had earlier and more marriages, and had higher fertility than other rural areas." "An impressive growth of this type of manufacturing" was hardly salutary, Mendels concluded, for it "was accompanied by an equally impressive poverty," by the loss of peas-

---

[6]Sidney Pollard, *Peaceful Conquest: The Industrialization of Europe, 1760–1970* (Oxford, 1981), p. 65.

ants' control over land and other means of production, and, ultimately, by the appearance of a substantial rural proletariat.[7]

The existence of cottage industry is one precondition for protoindustrialization. The presence of an impoverished rural labor force is usually (but not necessarily) another aspect of a protoindustrialized society. The final ingredient is intraregional specialization. As Mendels and a trio of German historians—Hans Medick, Peter Kriedte, and Jurgen Schlumbohm—have described it, protoindustrialization involves the simultaneous appearance, in adjacent areas, of rural industries and a symbiotic commercial agriculture. This specialization of function increases the level of intraregional exchange as well as extraregional trade, resulting in a significant expansion of production for market.

Other scholars have suggested even broader theoretical perspectives. Charles Tilly has pointed to the complementary nature of rural and urban manufacturing and underlined the importance of local or regional (rather than distant) markets for manufactured goods. For Frank Perlin, protoindustrialization was part of the massive expansion of capitalist relations of production in the early modern world. In his study of the subcontinent of India in the late eighteenth century, Perlin found that "local economic life was becoming more dense and vigorous even in essentially agricultural hinterlands." There was an increased use of money, he explained, with "a knowledge of quantity, calculation, attribution of value, widely dispersed among ordinary people." What were the structural preconditions, Perlin asked, "that made it possible for manufactures to exist as an aspect of a greater organization of production and marketing relationships embracing towns, production of foodstuffs, and financial institutions" at this particular historical moment?[8]

[7] Joan Thirsk, "Industries in the Countryside," in F. J. Fisher, ed., *Essays in the Economic and Social History of Tudor and Stuart England* (Cambridge, 1961); H. J. Habakkuk, "Family Structure and Economic Change in Nineteenth-Century Europe," *Journal of Economic History* 15 (1955): 1–12; Franklin F. Mendels, "Proto-Industrialization: The First Phase of the Industrialization Process," *Journal of Economic History* 32 (1972):203.

[8] Peter Kriedte, Hans Medick, and Jurgen Schlumbohm, *Industrialization*

Perlin's question, raised with respect to one region affected by British commercial activity in the late eighteenth century, applies to North America as well. As on the Indian subcontinent, a combination of increased foreign trade and home manufacturing created a more dense, vigorous, and prosperous economic system in the American colonies.

Protoindustrial theory must be applied to British North America with careful attention to its distinctive social character. The colonies lacked "the poverty of the peasantry [that] was a major precondition for the expansion of cottage industry" in many parts of Europe. Living standards for the 500,000 enslaved blacks on the American mainland were as low as those of poor peasants, but slaves mainly produced agricultural crops for export to Europe and not manufactured goods. While increasing numbers of the "strolling poor" wandered through the countryside on the eve of American Independence, these whites amounted to less than 5 percent of the rural population. In times of economic downturn, the poor in the towns numbered between 15 and 20 percent of the residents. However, these urban centers were small and few in number. And the mainland colonies completely escaped the subsistence crises that devastated parts of Europe. In protoindustrial Saxony, for example, 60,000 people (6 percent of the population) starved to death or succumbed to disease in the 1770s.[9]

---

before Industrialization: Rural Industry in the Genesis of Capitalism, trans. by Beate Schempp (Cambridge, 1981); Charles Tilly, "Flows of Capital and Forms of Industry in Europe, 1500–1900," *Theory and Society* 12 (1983); Hans Medick, "The Proto-Industrial Family Economy: The Structural Function of Household and Family during the Transition from Peasant Society to Industrial Capitalism," *Social History* 3 (1976):291–315; Frank Perlin, "Proto-Industrialization and Pre-Colonial South Asia," *Past and Present* 98 (1983):84, 70, 51.

[9]Catherina Lis and Hugo Soly, *Poverty and Capitalism in Pre-Industrial Europe* (Atlantic Highlands, N.J., 1979), pp. 149, 171–93; Karl Tilman Winkler, "Social Mobility in Eighteenth-Century North America" (Paper presented at the Krefeld Conference, Krefeld, Germany, June 1983); James A. Henretta, "Wealth and Social Structure," in Jack P. Greene and J. R. Pole, eds., *Colonial British America: Essays in the New History of the Early Modern Era* (Baltimore, 1983), pp. 262–89; and Paul G. E. Clemens,

These differences between Europe and the American mainland colonies can be stated more precisely in terms of the traditional theoretical distinctions applied to the putting-out system. Virtually none of the inhabitants of colonial America worked within the rigid confines of the *Verlagsystem*. In this highly developed form of cottage industry, capitalist merchants dominated the manufacturing process. They owned all the raw materials and held rural workers in a position of nearly complete economic dependence. However, some American farmers and rural artisans participated in a *Kaufsystem*. These rural families owned most of the means of production and enjoyed considerable economic autonomy. Yet they had to sell their domestic manufactures (and crops) at the prices set by local storekeepers and seaport merchants. These commercial middlemen charged commissions for their services and often extracted excess profits through their knowledge of the market system. Many areas of the European cottage industry, such as Flanders, participated in a *Kaufsystem* and a set of market relationships similar to those in British North America.[10]

Recent scholarship has revealed both the causes of the emergence of the colonial *Kaufsystem* and its specific features. Especially in long-settled towns in New England, but in Pennsylvania and the Chesapeake as well, the rapidly increasing population pressed heavily on existing agricultural resources. Prime arable land grew scarce. As a consequence, tenant farming and western migration were everywhere on the increase.

However, the Malthusian crisis postulated by Lockridge did not materialize. Creative adaption averted inexorable decline. In Guilford, Conn., for example, families adopted (or strengthened) a "stem family" pattern of residence and inheritance. A single son and his spouse inherited the subdivided farm bequeathed by the third generation of Guilford

---

"Commerce and Community: Reflections on the Social History of Early American Agriculture" (unpublished paper, 1984).

[10] See Robert E. Mutch, "Yeoman and Merchant in Pre-industrial America: Eighteenth-Century Massachusetts as a Case Study," *Societas—A Review of Social History* 7 (1977):279–302.

parents. Other siblings received money, apprenticeship contracts, or title to lands in newly opened communities. In Wenham, in coastal Essex County, Mass., traditional forms of family limitation remained strong until 1750. Nonmigrant males delayed marriage until they gained access to land (at age twenty-six or twenty-seven), while out-migrants married earlier (age twenty-three) and then departed. The male age at marriage dropped to twenty-two between 1750 and 1820, but the rate of out-migration increased. The safety valve of the frontier inhibited the appearance of a substantial agricultural proletariat.[11]

Migration conflicted with a cultural preference in America, as in most Western European peasant communities, for partible inheritance. In Chebacco (near Ipswich), Mass., 90 percent of all decedents with more than one son chose to divide their small farms. Similar practices throughout Massachusetts produced an abundance of marginal farms. As Bettye Pruitt's analysis of the 1771 tax list demonstrates, only 53 percent of Massachusetts' farms contained enough acres of pasture, tons of hay, and bushels of grain to feed their inhabitants and livestock. Yet most of the colony's towns remained viable economic units. "Many farmers kept more cattle than their land could hold, and many kept fewer," Pruitt concluded, "and only in the town as a whole did it all balance out."[12]

The creation of an interdependent economic community increased productivity through a more complete utilization of resources. Diaries and account books reveal an elaborate

[11] John J. Waters, "Patrimony, Succession, and Social Structure: Guilford, Connecticut, in the Eighteenth Century," *Perspectives in American History* 10 (1976):131–60; Douglas Lamar Jones, *Village and Seaport: Migration and Society in Eighteenth-Century Massachusetts* (Hanover, N.H., 1981), chap. 5; Robert A. Gross, *The Minutemen and Their World* (New York, 1976), chap. 4; John J. Waters, "Family, Inheritance, and Migration," *William and Mary Quarterly*, 3d ser. 39 (1982):64–86.

[12] Christopher Jedrey, *The World of John Cleaveland: Family and Community in Eighteenth-Century New England* (New York, 1979), pp. 63–84; Bettye Hobbs Pruitt, "Agriculture and Society in the Towns of Massachusetts, 1771: A Statistical Analysis," Ph.D. diss., Boston University, 1971, table 27 and pp.172–79.

exchange of female labor, especially for the production of textiles. They also document the diversification of male economic activity and the increase of year-round labor. Jonathan Burnham, the owner of a relatively large farm of seventy acres in Ipswich, Mass., sold his surplus grain and livestock. To make ends meet, he also fished and dug clams for sale, plowed his neighbors' fields, and made leather clothes and shoes during the winter. In the western Massachusetts town of Northampton, Ebenezer Hunt presided over a store and hatmaking enterprise that had 550 open accounts in 1773. In return for store goods and felt and worsted hats, local men and women provided Hunt with dressed deerskins and beaver pelts, meat, hoops, and barrels. They also spun and wove and lined hats for this small-scale merchant entrepreneur. The returns from domestic manufacturing thus bolstered local farm income and raised living standards. In 1776, over one-third of Northampton families had some nonfarm income.[13]

Occupational diversity appeared in more densely settled areas. In Ipswich only half the male population engaged in farming as a primary occupation, 20 percent were artisans, and another 18 percent engaged in various maritime enterprises. In the neighboring agricultural town of Andover, nearly 30 percent of the third-generation descendants of the original proprietors followed a trade or craft at some point in their lives. In Connecticut, craftsmen's estates comprised 25 percent of the inventories probated in the late colonial period. The booming export trade in grain brought prosperity and occupational complexity to Pennsylvania as well. Twenty percent of the taxpayers in rural Lancaster County were craftsmen in 1758. In the small towns of Lancaster, Reading, and York, artisans numbered 30 to 40 percent of the population.[14]

---

[13] Arlen I. Ginsburg, "The Political and Economic Impact of the American Revolution on Ipswich, Massachusetts" (unpublished paper, 1976); Anne Baxter Webb, "On the Eve of the Revolution: Northampton, Massachusetts, 1750–1775," Ph.D. diss., University of Minnesota, 1976, pp. 223–29.

[14] Jackson T. Main, "The Distribution of Property in Colonial Connect-

While older men turned to agricultural by-employments and artisanry to cope with a shifting rural economy, younger propertyless men opted for military service whenever it was available. Both in Maryland and New Jersey, the majority of recruits into the Continental army during the Revolutionary War came from families with little or no property. This enlistment pattern likewise appeared among 2,300 militiamen raised in Massachusetts in 1756 for service in the Seven Years' War. A detailed analysis by Fred Anderson demonstrates that most of these recruits were young—aged seventeen to twenty-six—and "temporarily poor." They lived at or near their families' homes, working either "for themselves" or to build up the family patrimony. Military service, Anderson argues, was simply a new means to achieve the traditional goal of landed independence. With the £15 in Massachusetts currency earned in the 1756 campaign, a young man could buy 15 to 30 acres of unbroken land in an old community like Andover or as many as 150 acres of unimproved upland in Northampton.[15]

These adaptive strategies had sharp limitations. Among Essex County fishermen, the population "grew faster than the capacity of the industry to absorb it." As a result, the character of the industry changed profoundly during the mid-eighteenth century. Merchants no longer extended credit to trustworthy fishermen to finance their ownership of boats and their fishing voyages. Taking advantage of the labor surplus, merchant capitalists outfitted their own boats and employed wage laborers who were young, strong, and expendable. "The industry was no longer an effective agent for social mobility," its historian Daniel Vickers concludes.

---

icut," in James Kirby Martin, ed., *The Human Dimensions of Nation Making: Essays on Colonial and Revolutionary America* (Madison, Wis., 1976), pp. 70, 89, and table 4; James T. Lemon, *The Best Poor Man's Country: A Geographical Study of Early Southeastern Pennsylvania* (Baltimore, 1972), table 23 and pp. 7–8, 96, 128, 139, 147.

[15] James Kirby Martin and Mark Edward Lender, *A Respectable Army: The Military Origins of the Republic, 1763–1789* (Arlington Heights, Ill., 1982), pp. 90–91; Fred Anderson, "A People's Army: Provincial Military Service in Massachusetts during the Seven Years' War," *William and Mary Quarterly*, 3d ser. 40 (1983):500–527.

"Poor immigrants stayed poor; well-born craftsmen's sons returned to their fathers' trades; and fishermen trained up to support their parents in old age, bred sons of their own to follow them. . . . Young men . . . emerged from their stints at sea on the same level at which they had entered."[16]

The story was only slightly better in the predominant agricultural society. In the quarter century before the War for Independence, the white inhabitants of British North America maintained, and perhaps even improved, their standard of living. But the cost was high. To provide for their numerous children, many parents worked harder and in more diverse occupations. Geographical mobility left emotional scars. Winter by-employments required additional labor. The fluctuating demand for craft goods meant psychological uncertainty and physical hardship.

More significantly, this economic evolution threatened a fundamental transformation in social relationships. In the more complex environment of the late colonial period, a growing proportion of rural families found themselves in positions of partial financial dependence. Some were tenants. Others owned land but fell into continuing debt to village storekeepers, landlords, or millowners. And nearly all the inhabitants of established communities increasingly depended on their neighbors for special craft skills, land-use rights, or labor. As Robert A. Gross has demonstrated, only affluent farmers were truly self-sufficient.[17]

Nonetheless, the new bonds of economic interdependence were mostly reciprocal and symmetrical. They tied families of roughly equal financial status to one another, often in mutually supportive relationships. "He wove for grain," a weaver testified in a court case heard in Schenectady, N.Y., in 1779, "and did not weave much for money." Or these financial ties

[16] Daniel Vickers, "From Clientage to Free Labor: The Cod Fishery of Colonial Essex County, Massachusetts, Reconsidered as a Labor System" (Paper presented at the Sixth Annual Meeting of the Social Science History Association, Washington, D.C., October 1983), pp. 11–12.

[17] Robert A. Gross, "Culture and Cultivation: Agriculture and Society in Thoreau's Concord," *Journal of American History* 64 (1982):51.

linked merchant entrepreneurs to "petty producers" who had some economic autonomy.[18]

American distinctiveness stemmed, therefore, not from the absence of the *Kaufsystem,* but rather from a successful effort to avoid the oppressive *Verlagsystem.* In various parts of Europe, the spread of cottage industry increased the existing high rate of population growth stemming from partible inheritance. Deprived of their farms, landless cottagers could no longer use inheritance incentives to delay the age of marriage and thereby reduce fertility. Their children married earlier and, as a result, had even greater numbers of offspring. Even severe fluctuations in market prices for domestic manufactures did not cut fertility. Rather, high prices allowed young men and women to marry and to create new economic units. Low prices also failed to reduce fertility, for declining incomes prompted parents to work young children harder and to urge older siblings to marry. Once they had lost control of the means of production, European cottagers were caught in a process of "self-exploitation" that increased the rate of demographic growth and the extent of impoverishment.[19]

In America, by contrast, the availability of land guaranteed the primacy of agriculture and traditional family patterns. Moreover, colonial parents reduced their fertility (from an average of six to seven births per completed family in 1700 to five to six births in 1800) in order to provide their sons and daughters with land, either nearby or in a newly settled community. As Toby Ditz has demonstrated, farm families both in lowland and in upland communities in the Connecticut River valley provided some land for 70–75 percent of *all* their children on the eve of the American Revolution. Confronted by land shortages, some of these parents excluded daughters from landed inheritances or wrote wills that re-

[18] Quoted in Richard B. Morris, "Labor and Mercantilism in the Revolutionary Era," in Richard B. Morris, ed., *The Era of the American Revolution* (1939; reprint ed., New York, 1965), p. 129.

[19] Kriedte, Medick, and Schlumbohm, *Industrialization before Industrialization,* p. 99.

quired favored heirs to provide financial assistance to their siblings.[20]

Thus the circumstances of American life and the cultural values of its inhabitants militated constantly against the preconditions of the *Verlagsystem:* widespread landlessness, grinding poverty, and overdependence on cottage industry. As a result, the American revolt against Great Britain stemmed more from mercantilist pressures, such as imperial administrative reform and trade imbalances, than from an oppressive protoindustrial rural economy.

Yet British mercantilism intersected with the nascent American *Kaufsystem* in important ways, notably in the textile industry. Historically, cloth production was the major activity in European protoindustrial regions. The industry spanned the Continent and encompassed a wide range of fabrics and markets. Some French weavers specialized in high-quality silks. German, Flemish, and Irish peasants fabricated durable linens. And English cottagers wove wool into cloth of many varieties and prices. Merchants marketed these rurally produced textiles in cities, in other European regions, and throughout the world. On the eve of the American Revolution, the mainland colonies imported ten to thirteen million yards of linen and woolen cloth from Great Britain each year, at a cost of £800,000 sterling. In addition, the colonists consumed a significant quantity of German linens.[21]

At this point it is impossible to estimate the proportion of American cloth consumption met by imports. There are no reliable data (from probate inventories or other sources) indicating requirements for clothing or the amount of heavy linen used for other purposes, such as sacking and bagging. Nor have the records of storekeepers been carefully analyzed to determine the extent of cloth purchases by ordinary arti-

[20]Toby Ditz, "Proto-industrialization and the Household Economy in the American North: Inheritance Patterns in Five Connecticut Towns, 1750–1820" (Paper presented at the Eighth International Congress of Economic History, Budapest, 1982), p. 15.

[21]Shepherd and Walton, *Economic Development*, pp. 110–13, 182, and appendix 2.

sans or farm families. Literary sources, such as letters and diaries, indicate extensive use of imported cloth in urban and commercial agricultural areas. They also suggest heavy reliance on domestically manufactured homespun by the rest of the rural population.

The statistical evidence is equally contradictory. The per capita volume of British imports increased between 1740 and 1775, but probate records also suggest a rising number of female spinners and weavers and of rising domestic production. Apparently, increased imports and higher American output went hand-in-hand—resulting in a better-clothed population over the course of the eighteenth century. It seems probable that in 1775 Americans manufactured more textiles per capita than ever before. Even stronger evidence indicates that per capita domestic production increased significantly between 1775 and 1825.[22]

Three excellent studies, published between 1916 and 1926, provide a wealth of information about the American textile industry both before and after the War of Independence. In *Household Manufactures in the United States, 1640–1860,* Rolla Milton Tryon focused primarily on goods made in the household from farm-produced goods and intended for home use. His account offers a comprehensive survey of family production and consumption, including an extensive discussion of the manufacture of woolen cloth. Because Tryon assumed that only agricultural products—and not home manufactures—were sold or bartered, he minimized the extent to which these handicrafts were exchanged.

Percy Wells Bidwell likewise de-emphasized the importance of home manufactures in the exchange systems of early America. "The real meaning of the term 'manufactures,'" Bidwell wrote in "The Rural Economy in New England," and "the only sense in which it is significant for the purposes of this essay, and indeed, for any economic history . . . includes only articles produced for a wide market, by persons who

[22]Clemens, "Commerce and Community," p. 11, argues that involvement in international trade and population increase brought "a growth in rural demand that allowed the establishment of more rural retailing, manufacturing, and food processing operations."

depend entirely upon the income derived from such activity for their support." "Of manufactures in this sense," he concluded, "there were practically none in New England in 1810." These studies thus systematically underestimated the production of textiles for exchange or sale. Nevertheless, along with Arthur Harrison Cole's exemplary analysis, *The American Wool Manufacture*, they offer a fairly complete description of textile production in the late colonial period.[23]

"The custom of making Coarse Cloths in private families prevails throughout the entire province," Sir Henry Moore, the governor of New York, reported to the Board of Trade in 1767, "and almost in every House a sufficient quantity is manufactured for the use of the family." "Every house swarms with children," he continued, "who are set to work as soon as they are able to Spin and Card; and as every family is furnished with a loom, the itinerant weavers who travel about the country, put the finishing hand to the work." However, Moore added, there was not "the least design of sending any of it to market." Gov. William Tryon of North Carolina also stressed the widespread production of textiles and their consumption within the family. "I have not heard of a piece of woolen or linnen cloth being ever sold that was the manufacture of this province," he told the Board of Trade.[24]

Given the mercantilist character of the southern economy, the local production of textiles even for household consumption is surprising. In times of high export prices, well-to-do planters preferred imported cloth for themselves and for their slaves. In the 1740s Lieutenant Governor Bull of South Carolina reported the annual importation of 500,000 yards of "Welsh plains" for use by the black population. When export income fell, however, local output increased. In 1710

[23] Rolla Milton Tryon, *Household Manufactures in the United States, 1640–1860: A Study in Industrial History* (Chicago, 1917), pp. 1–12; Percy Wells Bidwell, "Rural Economy in New England at the Beginning of the Nineteenth Century," Connecticut Academy of Arts and Sciences *Transactions* 20 (1916):275; Arthur Harrison Cole, *The American Wool Manufacture*, 2 vols. (Cambridge, Mass., 1926).

[24] Moore quoted in Victor S. Clark, *History of Manufactures in the United States*, 2 vols. (New York, 1929), 1:16; Tryon quoted in Cole, *Wool Manufacture*, p. 32.

Governor Spotswood of Virginia indicated the domestic manufacture of "above 40,000 yards of diverse sorts of Woolen, Cotton, and Linnen Cloth." A poor market for tobacco, Spotswood explained, placed the people "under the necessity of attempting to Cloath themselves with their own Manufactures . . . planting Cotton and Sowing flax . . . mixing the first with wool to supply the wants of coarse Cloathing and Linnen, not only for their Negroes, but for many of the poorer sort of housekeepers."[25]

The testimony of later observers suggests that this experience generated a strong tradition of household cloth production among poor and middling white farm families in the southern colonies. There was "no grand manufactory" in Virginia (where he had lived for twenty-five years), a London merchant told Parliament in 1776, "but all the people do manufacture." "The planters' wives spin the cotton of this country," Lt. Gov. Francis Fauquier reported from Virginia the following year, and "make a coarse strong cloth with which they make gowns for themselves and their children. And sometimes they come to this town and offer some for sale."[26]

The existence of a local market for domestic cloth in the Chesapeake is even more surprising. Yet a variety of evidence clearly indicates its presence. John Pemberton lived on the Eastern Shore of Maryland. His account book for 1722 records the purchase of five yards of "country cloth" and a pair of "country-made stockings" for a slave. Fifty years later, William Sharp, who lived in the same region, left an estate that included £10 of wearing apparel and seventeen yards of country-made cloth.[27]

These cases are not unique. Probate records clearly reveal the growth in domestic textile-making capacity. In Prince George's County, Md., 32 percent of estate inventories in the 1730s and 1740s indicated cloth-making capacity—sheep

[25] Clark, *History of Manufactures*, 1:210; Spotswood quoted in Tryon, *Household Manufactures*, pp. 49–50.

[26] Merchant and Fauquier quoted in Clark, *History of Manufactures*, 1:209 and 211.

[27] Clemens, *Atlantic Economy*, pp. 92, 142, and table 15.

and a combination of spinning wheels, looms, or cards for combing cotton or wool.[28] And, as table 1 demonstrates, the proportion of estates in six Chesapeake counties with these craft tools (but not necessarily sheep) increased steadily in the succeeding decades.

Spinning and weaving had become agricultural by-employments for many women in the Chesapeake. Many households produced yarn from wool or flax and sold or exchanged it with weavers, receiving cloth in return. Some merchants and planters had significant investments in home industry. When the merchant Isaac Hardy died in 1762, he owned sheep and raised flax and cotton. In addition, his inventory listed "a wheel for spinning wool and two wheels for spinning linen; hackles for preparing flax; 43 pounds of washed wool ready for carding, 30 pounds of hackled flax ready for spinning, 30 pounds of tow, and ten pounds of cotton" as well as a loom and a tackle for weaving.[29]

The families of small-scale freeholders and tenant farmers provided the labor for textile production. Most white planters in the Chesapeake operated on a very narrow economic margin. A family of four might produce an annual crop of 2,000 pounds of tobacco and pay taxes of 140 pounds. To purchase clothing would take an additional 840 pounds of tobacco, leaving about 1,000 pounds (worth about £4.5) for needed food, supplies, and farm equipment. Among tenant farmers rent averaged 500–600 pounds of tobacco, cutting disposable income even further. In these circumstances many white women spun yarn, wove or bartered it for country-made cloth, and sewed it into clothes for their families. By the 1760s the estates of poor planters (worth less than £50) usually contained spinning wheels, and their wives and daughters wove cloth on the looms owned by richer planters. "Among the poor," Thomas Jefferson noted during the War for Independence, "the wife weaves generally and the rich

[28] Allan Kulikoff, "Economic Growth and Opportunity in Eighteenth-Century Prince George's County, Maryland" (Paper presented at the Cliometrics Conference, Madison, Wis., April 1976), table 1.

[29] Lois Green Carr, "The Economy of Colonial Somerset County, Maryland, in Comparative Perspective" (unpublished paper, 1984), p. 17.

Table *1*. Percentage of Maryland and Virginia estates with yarn- or cloth-making tools

	County					
Date	Somerset	Anne Arundel	Prince George's	St. Mary's	Talbot	York
1665–77	11	3	0	3		3
1678–87	14	0	0	5		0
1688–99	53	8	9	15		8
1700–1709	53	17	9	16		17
1710–22	66	20	11	32	46	20
1723–32	74	33	29	43	58	33
1733–44	72	57	55	50	73	57
1745–54	89	61	81	71	80	61
1755–67	82	56	75	75	76	56
1768–77	80	59	94	78	78	59

SOURCE: Adapted from Lois Green Carr, "The Economy of Colonial Somerset County, Maryland, in Comparative Perspective" (unpublished paper, 1984), table 2.

either have a weaver among their servants or employ their poor neighbors." For his part, George Washington expected the wives of white overseers, carpenters, and other workers to make clothes for his slaves.[30]

Cloth manufacture was even more widespread in the middle and New England colonies. Many farm families in rural New England produced few export crops. They accumulated specie or credits to pay for imported goods only with great difficulty and had no option but to make their own yarn. Forty percent of the household inventories in York County, Maine, listed spinning wheels in the 1730s, as did 38 percent of those in more highly commercialized Essex County, Mass.[31]

The middle colonies exported substantial quantities of wheat, corn, and flour, especially after 1740, and imported large amounts of British dry goods. They also received thousands of Scotch-Irish, German, and Swiss settlers from proto-industrial regions of Europe. Weavers from Krefeld in Germany were among the original settlers of Germantown, Pa. (Many of their relatives must have been among the 6,000 cloth outworkers employed by the firm of Johann Heinrich Scheibler in the Krefeld region in 1762.) These migrants carried their craft skills to America. Working in their own handicraft shops—probably with small networks of female outwork spinners—Germantown weavers produced high quality worsted fabrics and stockings. They sold these goods both locally and in the Chesapeake colonies. Other German migrants pursued similar economic strategies. Palatinate Germans settled in Frederick, Md., in the 1740s and carried on a commerce in domestic linen, woolen, and leather goods. To clothe their slaves, some tidewater planters purchased Osnaburg-type fabrics woven by Germans in the western county of Augusta, Va. Part of this production took place outside

[30] Clemens, *Atlantic Economy*, pp. 159–60; Jefferson quoted in Tryon, *Household Manufactures*, p. 121; Julia Cherry Spruill, *Women's Life and Work in the Southern Colonies* (1938; reprint ed., New York, 1972), pp. 75, 78, and 83.

[31] Laurel Thatcher Ulrich, "Martha Ballard and Her 'Girls': Women's Work in Eighteenth-Century Maine" (unpublished paper, 1984), p. 29.

artisans' shops. In 1772 weavers in Somerset County, N.J., asked the assembly "to prohibit Farmers and others keeping Looms in their Houses and following the Weaving Business."[32]

Linen production had a particularly strong base in the agricultural countryside. Middle colony farmers formed part of a transatlantic system of textile production. To make soft, high-quality linens, Irish manufacturers harvested their flax before it was fully mature. To plant the next year's crop, they imported thousands of bushels of flaxseed from America. This mercantilist-inspired export system unwittingly encouraged colonial production of rough linens for local use. By seeding an acre with one bushel of flaxseed, a middle colony farmer harvested four to ten bushels of seed (worth 12s. a bushel). Each acre also yielded 80 to 200 pounds of hackled fiber for the production of coarse cloth.[33]

New England farmers grew flax as well. They exported some to Ireland but used even more for domestic textile production. Scotch-Irish communities in New Hampshire fabricated high-quality linens. Farmers of English ancestry in Massachusetts and Connecticut mixed flax with wool from their abundant flocks of sheep to make durable linsey-woolsey. In addition, the New England colonies imported 300,000 pounds of West Indian cotton annually between 1768 and 1772, presumably for use by home manufacturers.[34] Throughout the mainland settlements, textile production was an integral part of the yearly activities of most of the white population.

Suddenly, rough homespun garments became fashionable, as the colonists protested against restrictions imposed by the British mercantile system. Following the Stamp Act crisis of 1765 and the Nonimportation agreements, political leaders

[32] Lis and Soly, *Poverty and Capitalism*, p. 151; Jeffrey M. Diefendorf, "Social Mobility in the Rhineland in the Eighteenth Century" (Paper presented at the Krefeld Conference); Clark, *History of Manufactures*, 1:206–7 and 223; weavers quoted in Morris, "Labor and Mercantilism," p. 81.

[33] Lemon, *Best Poor Man's Country*, p. 158, n. 33; Shepherd and Walton, *Economic Development*, appendix 4, table 2.

[34] Shepherd and Walton, *Economic Development*, appendix 4, table 8.

advocated the wearing of American-made cloth. Previously, affluent colonials had shunned the coarse fabrics made and worn by rural folk. Now they laid away their smooth imported cloth and elevated the humble fabricators of homespun to the status of patriotic heroines. Newspapers celebrated the spinning and weaving exploits of worthy "Daughters of Liberty" and reported their productive achievements. One Massachusetts town claimed an annual output of 30,000 yards of cloth, East Hartford, Conn., reported 17,000, and the borough of Elizabeth, N.J., declared an output of "upwards of 100,000 yards of linnen and woolen cloth." For individual families, an annual output of 500 yards of cloth became a newsworthy event. From Woodbridge, N.J., the Freeman, Smith, and Heard families proudly announced they had attained this goal.[35]

In the past some domestic cloth produced in households or in ethnic communities had entered regional markets. Boston merchants sold "white and striped homespun" in the 1740s, and shipped 200 homespun jackets to Albany a few years later. By the late 1760s, however, documentary evidence of production for sale becomes much more abundant. Governor Wentworth of New Hampshire estimated the annual sale of 25,000 yards of high-priced but durable linen in his province. Merchant Enoch Brown advertised that he took "all Sorts of Country-made Clothes at his Store on Boston Neck, either on Commission, or in Exchange for any kind of West India Goods at a reasonable Rate." In Philadelphia, middling traders and artisans (and not transatlantic mercantile houses) formed the "United Company for Promoting American Manufactures." By employing three hundred women and children in their homes, the company avoided the capital expenditures and worker unrest that had doomed earlier urban manufactory ventures. Two years after its first meeting, the company declared a dividend.[36]

[35] Tryon, *Household Manufactures*, pp. 108–9; Cole, *Wool Manufacture*, 1:191.

[36] Clark, *History of Manufactures*, 1:207; Cole, *Wool Manufacture*, 1:31n and 62n; Gary B. Nash, *The Urban Crucible: Social Change, Political Con-*

The United Company was nearly unique. Even after the Nonimportation agreements American merchants and entrepreneurs did not develop an extensive putting-out system. Their hesitancy did not reflect the absence of skilled and willing workers. As early as 1762 the merchant William Pollard reported that many older people in Lancaster, Pa., had turned to linen making. By 1776 the *Pennsylvania Gazette* argued that "many poor people (old and young) would spin a little if they knew where to turn it into ready money at the end of the week or month."[37] The availability of cheaper and better textiles from protoindustrial regions of England and Germany represented a more significant barrier. Ocean transport was inexpensive, and the skilled but impoverished cottagers of Europe had no choice but to accept low prices for their fabrics.

In fact, colonial merchants generally avoided the mobilization of rural households for market production. They relied primarily on consumer demand for West Indian or British goods to secure a supply of goods for market. Merchant houses invested significantly in production only in the New England fishing industry, backcountry Chesapeake tobacco-growing regions, and lowcountry South Carolina rice plantations. Mostly they used their surplus income in other ways. As Virginia D. Harrington has demonstrated, New York merchants bought provincial bonds, extended loans to individuals, and purchased real estate—both urban rental properties and speculative frontier tracts. Some merchants invested in urban industries directly related to commerce, such as distilling, shipbuilding, and sugar refining. A few devoted capital resources to the production of iron for export, thus providing rural by-employment in woodcutting and hauling. And, during the Seven Years' War, merchants with military contracts systematically tapped the agricultural market for grain and meat. Even then, however, most mer-

---

sciousness, and the Origins of the American Revolution (Cambridge, Mass., 1979), p. 336.

[37] Lemon, *Best Poor Man's Country,* p. 96; Clark, *History of Manufactures,* 1:217.

cantile capital flowed into the more speculative (and the potentially more lucrative) enterpries of marine insurance and privateering.[38]

Thus, on the eve of the War for Independence, textile manufacture in the American mainland colonies was extensive, but its marketing was limited. Most rural folk made some or all of their own cloth, thus restricting the demand for fabrics. The availability of imported textiles, both cheap cloth for slaves and fine fabrics for the well-to-do, similarly discouraged entrepreneurs from mobilizing rural producers in a putting-out system. Finally, the traditional merchant preference for investment in financial instruments, real estate, and speculative maritime ventures deprived the textile industry of commercial leadership. Even so, a *Kaufsystem* of textile production existed among Germans in the middle and southern colonies and Scotch-Irish settlers in northern New England, and many English households exchanged or sold some textile products. The *Verlagsystem,* however, was conspicuously absent because of mercantilist policies and an abundance of fertile land.

The Revolutionary War severely disrupted established commercial patterns. The Royal Navy and British privateers destroyed the New England fishing industry and seized hundreds of American ships bound for Europe and the West Indies. British troops occupied major American ports and raided towns and supply depots along the coast. The court system functioned erratically, making it difficult to collect debts. Patriot armies requisitioned goods and offered increasingly worthless notes and currency in return. Merchants of a conservative temperament, such as James Beekman of New York, retired to the countryside to await the return of financial stability. They lived off the proceeds of prewar profits and returned to trade only as inflation sapped their incomes.

More adventurous merchants exploited the speculative op-

---

[38] Virginia D. Harrington, *The New York Merchant on the Eve of the Revolution* (1935; reprint ed., Gloucester, Mass., 1964), chap. 4.

portunities provided by the wartime economy. They braved capture to trade with Europe, charging high fees and selling scarce goods at exorbitant prices. Many merchants profited handsomely from privateering early in the war. Then, after 1777, they lost many of their ships to the Royal Navy. Agile entrepreneurs began speculating in the financial paper spewed forth by the printing presses of the state governments and the Continental Congress. By 1781 in Maryland, merchants offered soldiers immediate credit for store goods, taking currency and western land patents at one-seventh their face value. "Speculation, peculation and an insatiable thirst for riches," Washington complained, had infected "every order of Men."[39]

Speculation in depreciated currency indicated the growing financial importance of the state governments. The government of Maryland spent £500,000 between 1776 and 1779, twelve times its prewar expenditures. The drain on Maryland's treasury doubled during the following three years. Supplying military needs became a major enterprise. Before 1779, clothing, munitions, and other military supplies consumed 60 percent of the state's budget.

These imported manufactures came primarily from new European sources. The location of Nantes on the Loire River "makes it the only port for the American trade," noted one French trader, "as we draw the linen and woolen manufactures of the North by water carriage and even those of Flanders and Switzerland." Maryland army contractors promptly dispatched orders for "oznaburgs, coarse linens and woolens, Russian drabbs and sheeting, some shoes if they can be had good and reasonable." Most European manufactures cost more than English goods and were of lower quality. Nevertheless, they commanded high prices in wartime America. French and German fabrics sold quickly in Baltimore at three times their invoice value, which already included charges for

[39] White, *Beekmans of New York*, pp. 480–515; Edward C. Papenfuse, *In Pursuit of Profit: The Annapolis Merchants in the Era of the American Revolution, 1763–1805* (Baltimore, 1975), p. 94; Washington quoted in East, *Business Enterprise*, p. 30.

freight and insurance. This markup was double or triple that on prewar English imports.[40]

Neither this trade nor the fortuitous capture of British supply ships met civilian or military demand. To insure adequate supplies for its military forces, the Revolutionary government of Connecticut placed an embargo in 1776 on the export of cloth, shoes, and tanned leather. In New Haven the committee of inspection urged merchants to purchase wool and flax and to promote the manufacture of cloth. "Clothing is what we are deficient in," the *Connecticut Journal* complained, while from Maryland Charles Carroll lamented that "arms are still wanting and cloathing still more so."[41]

Household producers increased their output in a brave but futile attempt to compensate for the annual loss of ten to thirteen million yards of imported fabrics. As early as 1776 patriot forces in New York City wore country linens from Pennsylvania. The steady parade of British victories and American retreats accentuated existing shortages. In the Battle of Long Island, Capt. Edward Rogers of Cornwall, Conn., lost "all the shirts except the one on my back & all the stocking except thos on my legs" as well as two coats and a blanket. "The making of cloath . . . must go on," he wrote plaintively to his wife. "I must have shirts and stockings & a jacket sent me as son as possable & a blankit."[42]

Throughout the rebellious provinces, the production of domestic cloth increased, both for private and military purposes. When the marquis de Chastellux visited a farmstead in Farmington, Conn., he found its residents "making a sort of camblet, as well as another woolen stuff with blue and white stripes for women's dress. . . . The sons and grandsons of the family were at work; one workman can make five yards a day." Encouraged by the state government, a Maryland

---

[40] Papenfuse, *In Pursuit of Profit*, pp. 92–93, 118, 100, 128; Cole, *Wool Manufacture*, 1:50.

[41] Linda Susan Luchowski, "Sunshine Soldiers: New Haven and the American Revolution," Ph.D. diss., State University of New York, Buffalo, 1976, pp. 82–85; Papenfuse, *In Pursuit of Profit*, p. 97.

[42] Quoted in James P. Walsh, *Connecticut Industry and the Revolution* (Hartford, Conn., 1978), p. 22.

clothing contractor set up a small factory with sixteen looms. Soon he had engaged enough outwork spinners to produce 100 yards of linen per day. Yet production remained both limited and expensive. Weavers in "great numbers in our parts have enlisted," he complained; "those that remain have advanced their prices." To cope with soaring prices (the result, in this case, both of currency inflation and the scarcity of cloth), town authorities in New England regulated the cost of homemade fabrics and the rates charged by spinners and weavers.[43]

State governments likewise attempted to obtain adequate supplies of military clothing at reasonable prices. The requisition system employed in Connecticut was the most elaborate and successful. In July 1776 the governor and council of safety imposed a clothing levy. They called upon the citizens of Hartford to provide 1,000 coats, 1,000 vests, and 1,600 shirts, and assessed smaller towns on a proportionate basis. The council assumed that these items would be mostly "homemade" and authorized additional purchases of shoes, hats, and blankets. In October state officials requisitioned tents, iron pots, wooden bowls, and canteens. A year later the state government asked the towns to provide shirts, woolen "overhalls," stockings, and shoes for each of their men serving in the Connecticut Continental Line.[44]

While the authorities promised to pay a "fair price," they gathered these military supplies through the political process rather than the market system. Town meetings delegated responsibility for these levies to special committees of fifteen to thirty men. The committees sent the clothing to the state's purchasing clothier; he immediately dispatched it to the state clothier, who traveled with Connecticut's Continental troops. The state clothier distributed the goods and received payment from Congress, which deducted the cost from the

---

[43] Clark, *History of Manufactures*, 1:225; Morris, *Government and Labor*, pp. 300–303; Papenfuse, *In Pursuit of Profit*, pp. 89–90; Cole, *Wool Manufacture*, 1:20n.

[44] Walsh, *Connecticut Industry*, pp. 19–20; Albert E. Van Dusen, "The Trade of Revolutionary Connecticut," Ph.D. diss., University of Pennsylvania, 1948, pp. 187–88, 266, and 299.

soldiers' pay.[45] Initially, this requisition process worked smoothly. Local committees encouraged domestic manufacturing and paid for clothing at prices determined by the wages of Continental troops. Waterbury provided shirts, frocks, shoes, and tow cloth worth £700. The town charged the state government only 28s. in constables' fees for impressing various items. As wartime demands increased and inflation spiraled, the supply of clothing steadily diminished. By October 1779 Norwich had to pay interest on clothing "loaned" to the town and the town meeting issued a mandatory order requiring citizens to contribute goods.[46]

Direct requisition of clothing worked as well as it did for a number of reasons. Many Americans made their own fabrics and shoes or obtained them by barter with friends or neighbors. They were therefore accustomed to a nonmarket exchange system. Moreover, the inhabitants of many towns had traditionally paid local taxes in labor or in kind. Finally, the existing market for clothes was even smaller than that for cloth fabrics. Families either sewed their own garments or employed the services of a tailor. This absence of a commercial market for shirts, trousers, and other items of clothing encouraged families to comply with political requisitions.

More important yet, these levies provided patriot women with the opportunity to contribute directly to the war effort. Women and daughters traditionally handled many aspects of cloth manufacture. Men usually sheared sheep and hackled flax, but women washed and combed these fibers, spun them into thread and yarn, and sewed the finished fabrics into garments for each family member. The Nonimportation agreements of the 1760s momentarily wrapped these mundane female activities in patriotic glory. The real contribution of women to American independence came during the Revolutionary War, however, when it attracted less public attention (and, subsequently, much less study by scholars). As patriot and loyalist soldiers and militiamen marched back and forth across the countryside, fighting occasional battles, their wives and children worked constantly on farms and in

[45] Walsh, *Connecticut Industry*, pp. 20–21.

[46] Ibid., pp. 23–25.

workshops. In general, they maintained a sufficient level of production to supply the state governments with the grain, meat, and clothing requisitioned for military purposes.

Documentary records from the 1780s and early 1790s suggest that the wartime experience broadened the scope of women's work. Many women now added weaving to their repertoire of domestic skills. In 1785 the daughters of Martha Ballard of Hallowell, Maine, were spinning flax and carrying it to three women to weave. Two years later the Ballards acquired their own loom. During the next five years their teen-aged daughters (and young female servants) wove a wide variety of fabrics, often assisted by the skilled women of the neighborhood. By the 1790s 50 percent of the probate inventories in Hallowell listed looms, a clear indication that weaving had become a normal female household responsibility.[47]

A similar evolution took place in the Hudson River valley, despite easy access to imported goods. Alexander Coventry, a relatively well-to-do Scottish immigrant, lived on a river-front property in Columbia County, N.Y. Yet he employed a series of spinners and weavers in the early 1790s and had a "short coat and trousers . . . made from wool off my own sheep." Twenty-three of the forty-four itemized probate inventories in nearby Ulster County between 1788 and 1792 contained one or more spinning wheels. In addition, the inventories listed twenty-one woolen wheels and sixteen looms. The production of cloth in Ulster County increased steadily in subsequent decades, reaching 6.1 yards per capita in 1820 and peaking at 8.6 yards in 1825. By that time, the county's cloth industry supported thirty fulling mills and thirty-eight carding machines. Even as early as the end of the War of Independence, clothmaking had become part of the production and exchange systems of a majority of rural families.[48]

---

[47] Ulrich, "Martha Ballard," pp. 29–31, provides some interesting data, but there is no systematic and detailed study of women's productive activities during the Revolution. See, in general, Mary Beth Norton, *Liberty's Daughters: The Revolutionary Experience of American Women, 1750–1800* (Boston, 1980) and Nancy F. Cott, *The Bonds of Womanhood: "Women's Sphere" in New England, 1780–1835* (New Haven, 1977), chap. 1.

[48] Alexander Coventry, *Memoirs of an Emigrant: The Journal of Alexander*

The political requisition of foodstuffs was a less successful aspect of the war effort. Established markets for food existed both in the West Indies and in Europe. British occupation of American ports and the depredations of privateers partially closed these export markets, but military demands provided new outlets for farmers. Originally the British ministry planned to supply its army completely from American sources, but patriot domination of the countryside made this impossible. The ministry therefore shipped flour and salted meat from Britain, as well as tents, clothing, and munitions. Even so, the British army depended on local farmers for fresh food, fodder, horses, and fuel. Each day the main army of 35,000 men and 4,000 horses consumed 37 tons of food, 38 tons of hay and oats, and (during the winter) huge supplies of wood. To attract these supplies, British officials paid in specie—not the depreciating currency offered by patriot merchants and the commissariat of the American army. Merchants and farmers with access to British encampments in New York, Newport, Philadelphia, Savannah, and elsewhere frequently traded with the enemy.[49]

This lucrative commerce provoked accusations of treason and, on many occasions, armed confrontations with patriot militiamen. Yet the flow of British specie aided the rebel cause. Eventually this hard currency found its way into the hands of patriot merchants. They used it to purchase desperately needed arms, clothing, and other supplies in Europe. Connecticut authorities frequently bowed to this economic reality. In 1781, for example, they allowed the town of Windsor to export 1,000 bushels of corn and used the specie to purchase linen cloth.[50]

To supply its own forces, the Continental Congress created an army commissariat. This new bureaucracy was not large.

Coventry, M.D., 2 vols. (Albany, 1978), 1:450, 536, 620, 629, 645; David M. Ellis, *Landlords and Farmers in the Hudson and Mohawk Region, 1790–1850* (Ithaca, N.Y., 1946), p. 110; Michael Merrill, "The Transformation of Ulster County, 1750–1850" (unpublished paper, 1985).

[49] R. Arthur Bowler, *Logistics and the Failure of the British Army in America, 1775–1783* (Princeton, 1975), pp. 30, 57, and 156.

[50] Van Dusen, "Trade of Revolutionary Connecticut," p. 349.

The office of the clothier general employed only a few sub- and purchasing-clothiers in each state. Yet locally based merchant-agents extended the reach of this administrative system into hundreds of counties and townships. Farmers in the Hudson Valley would only sell a part of their wheat in the winter of 1776–77, a local correspondent told Gen. Philip Schuyler: "The remainder they are determined to Grind themselves and sell the Flour to the Army in the Spring when they expect the price will be much higher."[51]

Beginning in late 1777 there were consistent and, at times, severe shortages of grain throughout the Middle Atlantic and New England states. After Saratoga, General Burgoyne's army of 5,000 men and their 1,500 patriot guards depleted supplies of food and fuel near Boston. The return of the main British army to New York in 1778, trailed by a sizable force of Continentals, likewise created shortages. In conjunction with the arrival of a French expeditionary force in Rhode Island, these troop movements set off a mad scramble for scarce resources. Military contractors estimated the French demand for flour for the five months beginning in May 1779 at 45,000 barrels. This total was more than triple the amount of bread and flour shipped annually from New England to the West Indies between 1768 and 1772. It comprised one-fourth of annual exports of bread and flour exported from the grain-rich middle colonies during the same years.[52] Commissariat agents, merchants with French military contracts, and traders engaged in illicit commerce with the British army competed for food, wood, and fodder across a four-state region.

This extraordinary military demand may have increased the commercial orientation of many farming communities in the northern states. Before the Revolutionary War farmers in some regions were closely tied to the market, but others participated in the commercial world in a very limited fash-

[51] Schuyler quoted in East, *Business Enterprise*, pp. 101–2.

[52] Richard Buel, Jr., *Dear Liberty: Connecticut's Mobilization for the Revolutionary War* (Middletown, Conn., 1980), pp. 150 and 159; Shepherd and Walton, *Economic Development*, appendix 4, table 5; East; *Business Enterprise*, pp. 153–63.

ion. Their families consumed most of the output of their farms or bartered it within the local community. Only the surplus, a relatively small proportion of total production, entered into the wider market. During the war, state officials requisitioned food, clothing, and other supplies from every village and hamlet. Army contractors roamed the countryside, offering high prices for food, horses, and wagon transport. By the end of the war more farm households undoubtedly understood the potential opportunities (and dangers) offered by the market exchange system.

This economic change involved shifts in the realms of production, distribution, and credit. In the first place, the upward movement of prices prompted some farm families to increase their output. In Massachusetts, for example, Winifred B. Rothenberg's weighted index of on-the-farm prices demonstrates that producers received from 30 percent to 50 percent more between 1776 and 1783. Farmers had to pay higher prices for supplies and equipment as well, cutting their profits from increased sales. Yet many families raised more crops for sale and expanded their winter by-industries. Farmers in Windham, Conn., increased their production of saltpeter for gunpowder, while the manufacture of shoes became a major enterprise in New Jersey and Massachusetts.[53]

The specialization of work and intensification of labor continued after the war. In Concord, Mass., the proportion of the population engaged in crafts and trade increased from 15 percent to 33 percent between 1771 and 1801. And the farmers of the town, Robert Gross has argued, now "labored more intensively than ever . . . chopping wood, reclaiming land for English hay, digging potatoes, making butter."[54]

Significant changes in the distribution system occurred as well. Stimulated by wartime opportunities, country traders and local entrepreneurs became more avid and aggressive in the pursuit of business. These small-scale traders now had

[53] Winifred B. Rothenberg, "A Price Index for Rural Massachusetts, 1750–1855," *Journal of Economic History* 39 (1979):table 2; Alan Dawley, *Class and Community: The Industrial Revolution in Lynn* (Cambridge, Mass., 1976), pp. 14–15 and appendix A.

[54] Gross, "Culture and Cultivation," p. 57.

greater freedom, for the war broke the hold of established merchants and their backcountry trading networks. In 1766 major New York City merchants had secured legislation that prohibited peddlers from plying their trade. In 1770 the colonial assembly removed this absolute ban (probably because it was unenforceable), but continued to discourage itinerant trading through licensing fees.[55] These legal restraints evaporated during the Revolutionary War, and many small-scale traders and storekeepers became prominent military contractors.

The career of Oliver Phelps of Granville, Conn., indicates the new opportunities created by the wartime demand. In 1777 Phelps won appointment as state superintendent of army purchases. Once a mere shopkeeper, Phelps now prospered by supplying the state through his own firm and through newly formed partnerships with other entrepreneurs. In 1780 Phelps emerged as a leading supplier of beef to the French army, working as a subcontractor for the resourceful Jeremiah Wadsworth.[56]

Wadsworth himself rose through the ranks of the wartime bureaucracy. His ascent to a position of great wealth and prominence began in 1775. As a young man of thirty-two (with an inherited estate of £2,000 from his minister-father), Wadsworth became commissary of supplies for Connecticut. By 1776 he had advanced to the post of deputy commissary general, responsible for the requisition of Continental army supplies throughout New England. Recognizing his superb administrative talents, the Continental Congress elevated Wadsworth to the rank of commissary general. Wadsworth held this position from April 1778 to December 1779, and it made him a wealthy man. As commissary general, he received a commission of one-half of 1 percent on all purchases. Equally important, this post provided Wadsworth with the political leverage to win the lucrative supply contract for the French army in America.[57]

---

[55] White, *Beekmans of New York*, p. 467.

[56] East, *Business Enterprise*, p. 56.

[57] Ibid., chap. 4, especially pp. 80–92.

Scores of country traders pursued similar, if less glorious, administrative and mercantile careers during the Revolutionary War. Their entrepreneurship expanded the *Kaufsystem* of protoindustrial production during and after the war. In the Connecticut Valley, for example, merchants, peddlers, and itinerant traders appeared in growing numbers during the 1780s. They bought cheese, potatoes, and salted meat from farmers, as well as substantial quantities of household manufactures. While traveling through Berlin, N.H., in 1797, Timothy Dwight learned that, before Independence, locally produced tinware had been sold by peddlers with a "horse and two baskets." "After the war," he reported, "carts and wagons were used for this purpose. . . . A young man is furnished by the proprietor with a horse, and a cart covered with a box. . . . This vehicle within a few years has, indeed, been frequently exchanged for a wagon; and then . . . these young men direct themselves to the Southern States."[58]

As a result of the system of wartime finance, these traders operated in a world filled with new and diverse monetary instruments. In 1784 merchants in New Haven advertised goods for sale in return for specie or for "banknotes, Morris' notes, Mr. Hillegas' notes, Pickering's certificates, soldiers' notes, state money." Major merchants, such as the Burrells of Boston, speculated heavily in these paper certificates. In December 1784 the Burrells purchased £2,445 in Pierce's Continental notes, paying three to five shillings on the pound. Redemption at face value would yield a 400 percent profit. Panicked by Shays's Rebellion, the Burrells settled for a smaller return, selling their notes at seven shillings on the pound in 1786.[59]

The uncertainties of the Revolutionary era prompted many men and women to adopt this calculating form of economic behavior. While relatively few Americans were speculators, everyone had to contend with the flood of paper

[58] Christopher S. Clark, "Household Economy, Market Exchange, and the Rise of Capitalism in the Connecticut Valley, 1800–1860," *Journal of Social History* 13 (1979):170; Bidwell, "Rural Economy," p. 259; Dwight quoted in Tryon, *Household Manufactures*, pp. 265–66.

[59] East, *Business Enterprise*, pp. 271–73.

currency. Most rural folk tried to avoid cash transactions; instead they expanded their reliance on traditional non-market systems of exchange among families and neighbors. If farmers did sell their grain, meat, and household manu-factures, they demanded specie—or a premium for currency transactions. Local traders would accept printed notes in re-turn for store goods, but only at a substantial discount. The greatest inflationary spiral in American history forced nearly every family to look out more carefully and more persistently for its economic self-interest.

The War for Independence, the Pennsylvania *Centinel* sug-gested in 1785, had suppressed that "great reluctance to innovation, so remarkable in old communities." David Ram-say, the contemporary historian of the Revolution, argued that the demands of war had encouraged—at times, even forced—Americans to act "in a line far beyond that to which they had been accustomed."[60]

While the most dramatic transformations came in the po-litical sphere, economic change was not insignificant. House-hold manufacturing and artisan production increased substantially throughout the Middle Atlantic and New En-gland states during the war. And greater quantities of rural manufactures now entered the commercial exchange system. The experience of the Rev. Medad Rogers, minister of the small town of New Fairfield, Conn. (population 742 in 1790), offers a humble but instructive example. As his salary, Rogers received the use of a 100-acre farm and an annual stipend of $100, payable in cash or in kind. During one eighteen-month period in the early 1790s, the minister traded for store goods with no less than 450 pounds of cheese—made by his parish-ioners, paid as salary, and distributed through his barter into the wider world of commerce.[61]

The sum of thousands of similar local transactions had a significant impact on the American economy. The British consul at Philadelphia reported in 1789 that "among the

[60] Quotations from East, *Business Enterprise*, p. 323; Duane Ball and Gary M. Walton, "Productivity Change in Pennsylvania Agriculture," *Journal of Economic History* 36 (1976):113.

[61] Bidwell, "Rural Economy," pp. 366–67.

country people in Mass. Bay coarse linens of their own making are in such general use as to lessen the importation of
checks and even of coarse Irish linens nearly 2/3rds." "In the
4 Eastern States viz. New Hampshire, Mass. Bay, Rhode I.
and Connect.," Phineas Bond continued, "the people manufacture much larger quantities of woolens for their own use
than they did before the war. . . . 40,000 yards of coarse New
England linen have been sold in Philada within the last year."
"Here then is *a surplus* of household manufactures sold *out of
the state*," Tench Coxe noted with evident satisfaction a few
years later; "it is an acknowledged fact that New England
linens have affected the price and importation of that article
from New York to Georgia."[62]
Nonetheless, demand far outstripped domestic supplies.
"America must always look to other countries for a supply of
woolen manufactures," Bond concluded in his detailed state-
by-state survey. At the same time he warned that "many useful domestic manufactures . . . have lately been resumed in
the Eastern and Middle States from motives of economy."[63]
In the winter season," one traveler to Massachusetts noted,
"the inhabitants of Middleborough are principally employed
in making nails, of which they send large quantities to market. This business is a profitable addition to their husbandry;
and fills up a part of the year, in which, otherwise, many of
them would find little employment." By expanding their by-
industries during the wartime crisis, northern farm families
had found yet another way to cope with the traditional problem of population growth. Moreover, their efforts partially
offset the decline in foreign trade during the Revolutionary
War and nearly maintained traditional living standards.[64]
This process of "internal" economic development resembled that described by Diane Lindstrom for the Philadelphia region in the early nineteenth century. The rural, small
town, and urban settlements in this area "reaped the highest

[62] Report enclosed in Phineas Bond to the duke of Leeds, Nov. 10, 1789,
in American Historical Association, *Annual Report . . . 1896*, 2 vols. (Washington, D.C., 1897), 1:651; Coxe in Tryon, *Household Manufactures*, p. 134.

[63] Bond, *Report*, 1:632 and 631.

[64] Quotation from Bidwell, "Rural Economy," p. 272n.

per capita incomes of any section," she explains, "by producing an abundance of agricultural, extractive, and in some cases manufactured commodities" and by increasing "the quantity of trade" among themselves. A similar, if more limited, diversification of economic activity and exchange had taken place during the Revolutionary War. When Brissot de Warville visited Worcester County, Mass., in 1795, he found "almost all these houses . . . inhabited by men who are both cultivators and artisans; one is a tanner, another a shoemaker, another sells goods; but all are farmers."[65]

Thus, Americans emerged from the Revolutionary era with an expanded domestic industrial base. They participated as well in more active systems of local exchange and commercial markets. In fact, they were now full members in a system of protoindustrial production that spanned the North Atlantic Ocean. Like their European counterparts, American households processed a greater variety of farm products for market sale: salted beef and pork, hides for shoes, wool and flax for cloth, and milk for cheese. Rural manufacturers also processed increasing quantities of nonagricultural goods, such as tinware, nails, and furniture.

However, as of 1790 or even 1815, the United States had only experienced one mode of protoindustrialization. Unlike parts of Britain and Europe, the American countryside still did not contain a large population of impoverished cottagers. Most domestic manufacturers remained members of economically viable farm families. The *Kaufsystem* of protoindustrialization remained the norm. As various historians of the European experience have demonstrated, this type of cottage system often maintained or even raised rural incomes. As yet, merchant capitalists did not dominate rural production through an oppressive *Verlagssystem*. The appearance of dependent outworkers and a capitalist-run system of production in New England and parts of the Middle Atlantic states occurred mainly after 1815, with the massive expansion of

[65] Diane Lindstrom, *Economic Development in the Philadelphia Region, 1810–1850* (New York, 1978), pp. 8–12; quotation from Bidwell, "Rural Economy," p. 263.

the shoe, palm-leaf hat, and button industries. By that time as well, the growing production of yarn and thread in factories had generated additional rural outworkers, especially weavers.[66]

A few studies, based on careful research in local records, describe the *Kaufsystem* of protoindustrialization that predominated during the first half century of American independence. They demonstrate increased agricultural by-employments and cottage industry in many seaboard areas and hint at the existence of intraregional zones of production. This defining characteristic of protoindustrialization appears in the evolution of "local economies" based on "soil resources, new crops, and . . . crafts and home industries" in late colonial Maryland.[67] It is suggested as well by the emergence of new inheritance patterns in the commercial agricultural town of Wethersfield, Conn., in the early nineteenth century and the continuation of traditional practices in "subsistence plus" agriculture and craft towns in the nearby uplands.[68]

The best documented case of intraregional specialization also comes from Connecticut. The research of Edward S. Cooke indicates the evolution of distinct types of social-economic structures and furniture-making traditions in the adjoining Connecticut towns of Newtown and Woodbury.[69] As table 2 suggests, Newtown residents developed a strong craft orientation within a diversified agricultural economy in the early nineteenth century. The value of the artisanal equipment in Newtown rose, while production of wheat declined sharply and the output of dairy and meat remained

[66] Clark, "Household Economy," pp. 169–80; Thomas Dublin, "Women and the Dimensions of Outwork in Nineteenth-Century New England" (Paper presented at Berkshire Conference, Smith College, Northampton, Mass., June 1981).

[67] Carr, "Economy of Somerset County," pp. 1–2.

[68] Ditz, "Proto-industrialization" and *Property and Kinship: Inheritance in Early Connecticut, 1750–1820* (Princeton, 1986).

[69] Edward S. Cooke, Jr., "Rural Artisanal Culture: The Preindustrial Joiners of Newton and Woodbury, Connecticut, 1760–1820," Ph.D. diss., Boston University, 1984.

Table 2. Production in Newtown and Woodbury, 1770–1824

Date	Mean value of artisanal equipment		Estates with wheat in the inventory		Inventory value of meat and dairy products	
	Newtown	Woodbury	Newtown	Woodbury	Newtown	Woodbury
1770–74	£1.0s	£3.3s	53%	46%	£19.12s	£4.11s
1780–84	2.9	1.0	50	55	9.2	12.5
1790–94	5.7	1.1	47	35	4.19	8.4
1800–1804	2.10	3.6	17	35	9.2	14.14
1810–14	7.6	1.19	15	25	8.12	11.12
1820–24	10.6	3.13	6	28	5.0	8.17

SOURCE: Adapted from Edward S. Cooke, Jr., "Rural Artisanal Culture: The Preindustrial Joiners of Newtown and Woodbury, Connecticut, 1760–1820," Ph.D. diss., Boston University, 1984, tables 6, 8, and 11.

steady. In contrast, Woodbury farmers maintained, and perhaps expanded, their agricultural output.

If economic upheavals during the Revolutionary era initiated these structural changes, they nevertheless took more than a generation to come to fruition. Various factors account for the slow maturation of protoindustrial regions in the United States. First, the absence of a substantial and concentrated market for finished goods discouraged merchant investment in rural industry. Fewer than four million people lived in the United States in 1790, and they were dispersed over a large geographic area. Significantly, the first market for American manufactures emerged in the plantation regions of the Chesapeake and South Carolina, with the demand for cheaply made shoes for the large population of enslaved blacks. Second, rigorous British competition inhibited domestic production of textiles. An advanced *Verlagsystem* of protoindustrialization and a highly skilled work force in various regions of England enabled merchants to flood the American market with low-priced, high-quality fabrics.

However substantial, these obstacles were not insurmountable. In the aftermath of Independence, purposeful action by American merchants and governments could have fostered domestic manufacturing and a much more diverse and substantial putting-out system. The experience of two textile enterprises suggests both the potential for the development of a *Verlagsystem* and the reasons for its failure. Both the Hartford Manufactory and the Massachusetts Woolen Manufactory owed their genesis to the investment capital generated by the Revolutionary War. Jeremiah Wadsworth was the driving force behind the Hartford enterprise. In 1788 Wadsworth organized production on a putting-out basis, using a central workshop (staffed by English army deserters and former prisoners of war) for wool sorting and cloth finishing. When President Washington visited the manufactory in 1792, he reported that most of the spinning and weaving was done "by the country people, who are paid by the cut."[70]

Dr. John Manning organized a similar enterprise in Ips-

[70] Cole, *Wool Manufacture*, pp. 65–69.

wich, Mass., in 1794. "The Town's Poor . . . are daily increasing," Manning informed the state legislature: "Almost all the farms have been divided and subdivided so as to yield little more than a supply of provisions for the owners, and being so full of inhabitants, is well calculated for a manufacturing town." Manning's almost classic description of the preconditions for a substantial cottage industry neglected to mention that Ipswich was already a manufacturing center. In 1790 six hundred women and children employed by local entrepreneurs had fabricated 28,000 yards of lace and 13,000 yards of edging.[71]

Taking advantage of this ample labor supply, Manning invested the returns from his Massachusetts state securities in looms. He housed them in both private homes and a central factory and began the production of coarse woolens, blankets, and flannels. By 1800, however, Manning and Wadsworth were out of the textile business. Both fledgling enterprises were the victims of competition from British goods, as were earlier American textile ventures. On July 4, 1788, calico printers joined other artisans in a Philaldelphia parade celebrating the ratification of the new United States Constitution. Their intricately designed flag carried the motto "May the union government protect the manufacturers of America."[72]

In fact, as John R. Nelson, Jr., has argued, the Hamiltonian Federalists largely ignored the pleas of these textile workers and of other domestic manufacturers. Indeed, Hamilton's financial policies deprived the handicraft and putting-out industries of funds and of tariff protection. The Treasury secretary's ingenious schemes for debt redemption and assumption ignited a fierce speculation in Continental and state securities. Merchants and urban investors used their capital to buy war certificates and bonds rather than to invest in rural manufacturing. Moreover, Hamilton's funding program depended upon tariff revenues to pay interest on the

[71] Ginsburg, "Political and Economic Impact," p. 16.

[72] Motto quoted in David J. Jeremy, *Transatlantic Industrial Revolution: The Diffusion of Textile Technologies between Britain and America, 1790–1830s* (Cambridge, Mass., 1981), p. 20.

national debt. The Treasury secretary therefore opposed high duties for they would cut revenues as well as imports.[73]

Even Hamilton's "Society for Establishing Useful Manufactures" did not assist protoindustrial entrepreneurs like Wadsworth and Manning. Rather, the society encouraged mercantile capitalists to invest in factory production using the latest English technology. Most Federalist merchants had no financial incentive to invest in manufacturing until the embargo of 1807, and every reason not to do so. For these American traders were still tied, by their past experience and present shipping investments, to the old British mercantile system. As in England itself at an earlier point in time, "commercial capitalism inhibited the growth of domestic manufacturing capacity because its greatest profits came from trade in imported goods."[74]

Like the Civil War, the War of Independence disrupted the existing systems of production and exchange. The Revolutionary War likewise altered the character of the American economy. The end of British mercantilist restrictions and wartime exigencies brought the expansion of traditional home manufactures, the creation of new rural enterprises, and appearance of domestically oriented traders and entrepreneurs. Other developments, however, delayed the emergence of a strong manufacturing sector. By opening western lands for settlement, the treaty of 1783 drained off the surplus agricultural population, inhibiting the expansion of rural industries. By providing American merchants with the status of neutral carriers, Independence also diverted capital into maritime investments during the wars of the French Revolution. Unlike the Civil War, the War of Independence did not vest political and financial power in the hands of an elite committed to domestic industrial development.

This comparison provides an answer to the two questions posed at the beginning of this essay. The net effect of these

[73] John R. Nelson, Jr., "Alexander Hamilton and American Manufacturing: A Re-Examination," *Journal of American History* 65 (1979):971–95.

[74] John R. Gillis, *The Development of European Society* (Boston, 1977), pp. 13 and 15.

contradictory events was to *accelerate* American economic development and to *delay* the emergence of a more capitalistic society. The War of Independence expanded the *Kaufsystem,* thereby increasing the number of independent household producers and the overall level of market activity. Yet merchants continued to invest primarily in foreign trade, inhibiting the emergence of the more capitalistic *Verlagsystem* of manufacturing until after 1815. Unlike Europe, the United States would experience capitalist protoindustrialization simultaneously with the Industrial Revolution.

LEWIS R. FISCHER

Revolution without Independence: The Canadian Colonies, 1749–1775

THE REVOLUTIONARY ERA, however defined, was an epoch of sweeping political and economic change throughout much of North America. While the political and military aspects of the age have long attracted scholarly attention, students of the thirteen Revolutionary colonies have in recent years produced a number of important macro- and micro-economic analyses that have finally allowed us to comprehend the functioning of their economies.[1] Unfortunately, it is not possible to make a similar claim for scholarly activity concerned with the northern colonies that eventually coalesced between 1867 and 1949 to form the Dominion of Canada.[2] The economic

The author would like to thank the Social Sciences and Humanities Research Council of Canada for various grants-in-aid in support of this research. In addition, the departments of history at York University, the University of Western Ontario, and Memorial University of Newfoundland have been generous in the provision of computer time for the study. Joseph A. Ernst made invaluable suggestions on various problems relating to this study.

[1] The most satisfactory broad survey of the colonial economy is Gary M. Walton and James F. Shepherd, *The Economic Rise of Early America* (Cambridge, 1979). This has been superseded in many important respects by John J. McCusker and Russell R. Menard, *The Economy of British America, 1607–1789* (Chapel Hill, N.C., 1985).

[2] In this paper the term *Canada* is used to refer to all the colonies that eventually joined the dominion. In most cases current place-names have been used to avoid confusion; thus, I refer to Quebec rather than to the province of Canada.

history of these colonies in the Revolutionary period remains to be written.

There are a number of factors that may explain this neglect. In part the lack of attention devoted to this period may be related to the national belief that for Canada this was not an era of cataclysmic, or even interesting, change. Indeed, one Canadian historian has characterized the period before 1812 as a time in which society seemed in "slow motion."[3] While many Quebecois have lamented the fall of New France and the descendants of loyalists have glorified the "great exodus to the north," for the mass of the Canadian populace it was continuity rather than change that was the norm. Viewed in the broader perspective of Canadian national history, such a conception is at least understandable: after all, rather than forging a new nation, as "British North America" these colonies, along with the West Indies and India, formed the nucleus of the second British Empire.

The lack of sharp political change suggests a related explanation for the relative neglect of the Revolutionary period in Canadian historiography. Thirty-five years ago Carl Bridenbaugh, then the director of the Institute of Early American History and Culture, deplored the lack of interest within the American historical profession in prenational United States history.[4] But the euphoria associated with the celebration of the bicentennial combined with the population explosion in American graduate schools in the 1960s and 1970s has provided impetus to the creation of a lively and controversial field in Revolutionary studies. Canada, by contrast, has enjoyed a much more modest growth of graduate education, and the enthusiasm generated by the Canadian centenary in 1967 directed both popular and scholarly attention to a later century.

But perhaps the most compelling rationale for the disregard accorded this period by Canadian historians has to do with the effects of regionalism. To a degree unparalleled in

[3] J. K. Johnson, "Introduction," in J. K. Johnson, ed., *Historical Essays on Upper Canada* (Toronto, 1975), p. viii.

[4] Carl Bridenbaugh, "The Neglected First Half of American History," *American Historical Review* 53 (1948):506–17.

the United States, Canada has always been a "nation of re-gions," and regional shibboleths have always done a great deal to shape the perspectives of Canadian historians. Forty percent of Canada's population, along with its largest and most prestigious universities, are located in Ontario, an area which was barely populated during the Revolution and which did not achieve colonial status until the Canada Act of 1791. Two of the four Atlantic provinces (Prince Edward Island and New Brunswick) did not exist at the time of Lexington and Concord, and a third (Newfoundland) would not achieve colonial status until the 1820s. The other Atlantic colony, Nova Scotia, clung to a perilous existence and owed its growth chiefly to the influx of loyalists after 1783; not sur-prisingly, the descendants of these migrants have tended to treat the pre-Revolutionary period as singularly unimpor-tant. It is in Quebec, however, that studies of the Revolution-ary era have been arguably the most important. Quebec historiography has burgeoned in recent years, yet the interval between the fall of New France and the partition of the Can-adas in 1791 has continued to be the "forgotten decades" in the writing of that province's history. The emphasis on re-gions may be one of the constructs that differentiate Canada from the United States, but it has not conferred upon the historical profession wholly unmixed blessings.

In particular, the effects of regionalism have added to the isolation of Quebec in scholarly circles. Despite veneers of bilingualism in scholarly journals and academic conferences, the historical profession in Canada reflects vividly the "two solitudes" of national life. English and French historians sel-dom communicate, and this has allowed historians of "la belle province" to develop a particularly inbred agenda for histor-ical research. While some important and innovative research is being undertaken, a distressing amount of scholarship in French Canada has been concerned myopically only with An-glo-French relations. Two contending schools of historical in-terpretation have arisen, both at least as much concerned with providing prescriptions for Quebec's future as with in-terpreting its past. More important to our purposes here, neither has yet produced a major economic history of the

Revolutionary period.[5] Instead they have debated, often with little regard for the historical record, about the nature of relations between the country's two founding races following the defeat of Montcalm on the Plains of Abraham. One group of historians, noting the outflow of population following the conquest, alleges that this represented a "decapitation" in which a sizable portion of the bourgeoisie chose emigration to domination by English "imperialists." The other side counters that no such selective migration occurred, and that the new rulers moved gradually to allow greater Francophone participation in colonial life while simultaneously "modernizing" Quebec society.[6] Neither camp has yet produced much convincing evidence.

The sterility of this debate means that what we know for certain about Quebec in the Revolutionary era can be summarized briefly. Clearly these years witnessed striking demographic change. At the time of the conquest, the colony contained perhaps 80,000 souls. The transformation to English rule did indeed witness an out-migration (although just who left remains uncertain), so that by 1765 the population base had declined by about a seventh. With the infusion of some English settlers, particularly in the urban areas, and a continuance of high rates of natural increase, the population recovered to about 90,000 on the eve of the Revolution. By 1790 the population of Quebec may have been as high as 160,000.[7]

[5] The two conflicting schools are generally referred to as the Montreal and Laval interpretations. The best general economic history of Quebec in this period is Fernand Ouellet, *Histoire Economique du Québec, 1760–1850: Structures et Conjunctures* (Montreal, 1966), although it concentrates on the period after 1791. But see also his "Dualité économique et changement technologique au Québec (1760–1790)," *Histoire Sociale/Social History* 18 (1976):256–96.

[6] Perhaps the most striking example of the way in which ideology can blind rather than inform scholarship is Maurice Seguin, *"Nation Canadienne" et l'Agriculture, 1760–1850: Essai d'Histoire Economique* (Trois-Rivieres, 1970).

[7] Canada, Dominion Bureau of the Census, "Chronological Summary of Population Growth in Canada, with Sources of Information, 1605–1731,"

The chief economic activities of the society remained subsistence farming and the ubiquitous fur trade. The latter continued to provide the principal export commodity, although British markets replaced La Rochelle as the European terminus of the trade. The trade was also undergoing structural shifts in this period. In 1754–55, for example, the volume of beaver skins exported averaged just over 140,000 pounds annually; by 1769–72 this had declined to 134,000 pounds, and increasingly fur traders were having to venture further afield for their supplies.[8] But despite the fascination that the fur trade has held for Canadian historians, the extent to which this decline was either caused or exacerbated by factors of political economy as opposed to depletion of the resource base is still unclear.

The dominant economic activity in the province remained subsistence farming, based largely upon the seigneurial system. The English initially left the seigneuries alone, but the removal of the political and cultural legitimization for the system may have had some impact upon production. Regardless, Quebec was an insignificant exporter of agricultural produce both before and after the conquest. In the first decade of the nineteenth century the colony suffered an "agricultural crisis," but it remains unclear as to what extent the roots for this failure lay in the pre-Revolutionary period.[9] In short,

---

Seventh Census of Canada, 1931 (Ottawa, 1936), 1:133–53. The extremely high crude birth rate in Quebec is documented and analyzed in J. Henripin and Y. Peron, "The Demographic Transition of the Province of Quebec," in D. V. Glass and R. Revelle, eds., *Population and Social Change* (New York, 1972), pp. 213–31.

[8] The statistics on the fur trade are taken from William L. Marr and Donald G. Patterson, *Canada: An Economic History* (Toronto, 1980), p. 59. See also Murray G. Lawson, *Fur: A Study in English Mercantilism, 1700–1775* (Toronto, 1943). The most important study of the fur trade remains Harold A. Innis, *The Fur Trade in Canada*, rev. ed. (Toronto, 1956).

[9] On the seigneurial system, the standard work is R. Cole Harris, *The Seigneurial System in Early Canada: A Geographical Study* (Madison, Wis., 1968). See also Guy Fregault, *Canadian Society in the French Regime* (Ottawa, 1962); Marcel Trudel, *The Seigneurial Regime* (Ottawa, 1971). On the agricultural crisis, see Fernand Ouellet, "L'Agriculture Bas-Canadienne Vue a Travers les Dimes et la Rente en Nature," *Histoire Sociale/Social History* 8

our knowledge of either the state or operation of the Quebec economy before 1791 remains less than satisfactory.[10]

The gaps in our understanding of the Quebec economy also are characteristic of the other areas of settlement. Newfoundland, on the extreme eastern slope of the North American littoral, was officially only a "fishing station" until the 1820s. Despite a resident population which had reached 11,500 by 1770 and which by recent estimates was producing fully a third of the volume of cod exports, functionaries in Whitehall persisted in subordinating the interests of the local populace to the concerns of West Countrymen who operated the migratory fishery.[11] By and large historians of Newfoundland in this period have followed the proclivities of the Board of Trade in this regard by treating the economy as merely an extension of the metropolitan economy rather than as a quasi-separate entity.[12] While some recent works have begun

---

(1971):5–44; Gilles Paquet and Jean-Paul Wallot, "Aperçu sur le Commerce Internationale et la Prix Domestiques dans le Bas-Canada, 1793–1812," *Revue d'Histoire de l'Amérique Française* 21 (1967):447–73; Paquet and Wallot, "Crise Agricole et Tensions Socio-Ethniques dans le Bas-Canada, 1802–1812: Elements pour un Re-interprétation," *Revue d'Histoire de l'Amérique Française* 26 (1972):185–237; Jean Hamelin and Fernand Ouellet, "La Mouvement des Prix Agricoles dans le Province de Québec, 1760–1851," in C. Galarmeau and E. Lavoie, eds., *La France et le Canada Français du XVIe au XXe Siècle* (Quebec, 1966), pp. 35–48; T. J. A. LeGoff, "The Agricultural Crisis in Lower Canada, 1801–12: A Review of a Controversy," *Canadian Historical Review* 55 (1974):1–31; Paquet and Wallot, "The Agricultural Crisis in Lower Canada, 1802–12: Mise au Point, A Reply to T. J. A. LeGoff," and LeGoff, "A Reply," *Canadian Historical Review* 56 (1975):133–61 and 162–68.

[10] The Canada Act of 1791 has often been taken as a watershed by historians of early Canada. It divided the province of Canada into Lower (Quebec) and Upper (Ontario) units.

[11] C. Grant Head, *Eighteenth-Century Newfoundland: A Geographer's Perspective* (Toronto, 1976), pp. 61–81, contains the most thorough statistics on the Newfoundland fishery to mid-century. See also James F. Shepherd, "Staples and Eighteenth-Century Canadian Development: The Case of Newfoundland," in Roger L. Ransom, Richard Sutch, and Gary M. Walton, eds., *Explorations in the New Economic History: Essays in Honor of Douglass C. North* (New York, 1982), pp. 97–124.

[12] A good example of this, although an admirable work, is Keith Mat-

to rectify this problem, the gaps in our knowledge of the Newfoundland economy in this era are as serious as those for Quebec.[13]

These were of course not the only areas of settlement on the northern fringe of the continent. The island of St. John (Prince Edward Island) was the home to several thousand Acadian fishermen and small-scale husbandmen; not until the nineteenth century would any significant English settlement occur on this outpost in the Gulf of St. Lawrence. No scholarly study of the economy has yet been undertaken, but we do know that it developed little more than a subsistence economy before 1800.[14] Cape Breton, wrested from France after the fall of Louisbourg in 1758, was largely unpopulated. Both islands were administratively and economically linked to their larger neighbor to the south, Nova Scotia, for most of the period.

This brings us to Nova Scotia, which before 1784 included all of present-day New Brunswick as well. It would be a gross misreading of the available literature to suggest that the economy of Revolutionary Nova Scotia has been the subject of a great deal of serious concern. Yet the ingredients for at least a tentative economic history of the colony are in place. Further, the way in which the economy of this colony functioned may well shed some important light on the Re-

thews, "The West of England–Newfoundland Fisheries," Ph.D. diss., Oxford, 1968. See also D. W. Prowse, *A History of Newfoundland from the English, Colonial and Foreign Records* (London, 1895); St. John Chadwick, *Newfoundland: Island into Province* (London, 1967); Frederick W. Rowe, *A History of Newfoundland and Labrador* (St. John's, 1982).

[13] The standard work on the Newfoundland fisheries is Shannon Ryan, *Fish Out of Water: The Newfoundland Saltfish Trade, 1814–1914* (St. John's, 1986), which unfortunately does not examine the eighteenth century. But see n. 11, above, and the essays in John J. Mannion, ed., *The Peopling of Newfoundland: Essays in Historical Geography* (St. John's, 1977).

[14] On Prince Edward Island, see Andrew H. Clark, *Three Centuries and the Island: A Historical Geography of Settlement and Agriculture in Prince Edward Island Canada* (Toronto, 1959); Francis W. P. Bolger, ed., *Canada's Smallest Province: A History of Prince Edward Island* (Charlottetown, 1973); Lewis R. Fischer, *Enterprise in a Maritime Setting: The Shipping Industry of Prince Edward Island, 1787–1914* (St. John's, forthcoming), chap. 1.

volutionary colonies to the south. Alone among the predominantly English-speaking mainland colonies, Nova Scotia failed to join the Revolutionary movement. Despite geographic, political, religious, and demographic links with New England, Nova Scotians proved relatively immune to Revolutionary rhetoric and blandishments. If the "new" economic interpretations of the Revolution are correct, we would expect to find an economy in this province that operated very differently than elsewhere on the Atlantic seaboard.[15]

Indeed the economic experience of Nova Scotia, and particularly of its capital, Halifax, was very different. In order to provide colonialists with this important comparative dimension, I will focus my attention on the Halifax-based economy, outlining its principal features and advancing a new interpretation of why this colony rejected revolution.

By the middle of the eighteenth century, Englishmen had been resident in Nova Scotia for almost 150 years. The colony was frequently a pawn in international diplomacy, switching rulers at the close of virtually every colonial war. But peninsular Nova Scotia was ceded to Britain for the final time by the Treaty of Aix-la-Chapelle, which formally concluded King George's War. Since France was permitted to retain the great garrison at Louisbourg, it seemed prudent to imperial officials to establish a competing armed town to protect its more southerly colonies from possible future incursions. This decision marked the genesis of Halifax. While the military origins of the proposed town are undeniable, historians have too often been remiss in recognizing that planners in Whitehall also entertained high hopes for the economic future of both Halifax and its hinterland. Nova Scotia was to be peopled with "industrious Protestants" who would rapidly produce exportable surpluses; Halifax would be the entrepôt

[15] See especially Marc Egnal and Joseph A. Ernst, "An Economic Interpretation of the American Revolution," *William and Mary Quarterly*, 3d ser. 29 (1972):3–32; Egnal, "The Changing Structure of Philadelphia's Trade with the British West Indies, 1750–1775," *Pennsylvania Magazine of History and Biography* 99 (1975):156–79; Ronald Hoffman, *A Spirit of Dissension: Economics, Politics and the Revolution in Maryland* (Baltimore, 1973).

through which would flow a growing and economically important trade.[16]

Even disregarding clearly stated but unrealistic hopes that Nova Scotia would develop into the perfect mercantilist colony, there were sound reasons for believing that it was possible to establish a solid economic base. One cornerstone of prosperity was to be based upon a flourishing fishery. Early observers confidently predicted that the "fishery will draw great numbers to it, and it is hop'd by this means [that] the Principal [will be] paid to Great Britain in a few years by an Increase of Trade."[17] The instructions delivered to Gov. Edward Cornwallis as he prepared to embark for the colony enjoined him to be "protective" of this "primary activity."[18] Based upon previous British experiences with the northern fisheries at both Canso and Newfoundland, officials had every reason to be sanguine about the prospects. In good years, it was reported, the fishery at Canso attracted "two hundred vessels or more from New England, Some from New York also, and from Annapolis Royal, the Metropolis of Nova Scotia, with some few from the West of England."[19] Even more impressive were the returns from Newfoundland, where landings exceeded 500,000 quintals of dry fish per annum by the late 1740s.[20]

The other economic pillar was expected to be agriculture. Prospects for that sector looked no less bright than for the fishery. Royal officials were well aware of the success enjoyed by Acadian farmers in the Annapolis valley and along the

[16] See T. B. Akins, *History of Halifax City* (Halifax, 1895), pp. 15–20.

[17] William Shirley to the earl of Bedford, Mar. 3, 1748, Record Group 1/29, Public Archives of Nova Scotia.

[18] "Instructions to Governor Cornwallis," Mar. 29, 1749, C.O. 218/3/391, Public Record Office.

[19] C.O. 217/7/107, P.R.O. See also Andrew H. Clark, *Acadia: The Geography of Early Nova Scotia to 1760* (Madison, Wis., 1968), especially pp. 224–29. Clark's book, the first of a projected two-volume study that was to have carried the analysis up to 1867, remains unquestionably the finest work yet produced on any phase of Nova Scotian history. Unfortunately, he died before he could complete the second volume.

[20] Head, *Eighteenth-Century Newfoundland*, pp. 61–81.

shores of the Bay of Fundy. By mid-century between seven and ten thousand Acadians resided in that portion of the colony, and they had succeeded in reclaiming approximately twenty thousand acres of extremely fertile marshland, most of which was planted in wheat and oats.[21] Grain production in this region of Nova Scotia had been yielding exportable surpluses for more than forty years. Before 1740 it appears that most of the exports had gone to the French garrison on Cape Breton, but increasing amounts were shipped south by enterprising New England traders who sailed into the Bay of Fundy each fall to barter imported goods and other luxuries for agricultural produce.[22] While most British officials were far too xenophobic to place much trust in "papist plowmen," their long-range plans called for the replacement of the Acadians by "practical English husbandmen."[23] At least part of this proposal came to fruition in 1755 with the expulsion of the majority of the French settlers.

The glue that was to cement this system was the development of Halifax as a major trading port. To help ensure its development, Cornwallis was instructed to locate the town on the best harbor he could find on the Atlantic coast. He certainly did well in this regard: Chebucto, where he planted his town, was situated on arguably the largest and most sheltered harbor in North America. And he certainly brought with him a sufficient number of men interested in trade: perhaps a tenth of the 2,576 settlers who sailed with Cornwallis were merchants, and a number of others were members of that class of men who while primarily concerned with other mat-

[21] Clark, *Acadia*, pp. 230–44; Graeme Wynn, "Late Eighteenth-Century Agriculture on the Bay of Fundy Marshlands," *Acadiensis* 8 (1979):80–89; R. Cole Harris and John Warkentin, *Canada before Confederation* (Toronto, 1974), pp. 25–32.

[22] This trade is discussed more fully in Lewis R. Fischer, "The Fruits of Stability: Merchant Shipping and Societal Growth in Pre-Revolutionary Halifax," in W. A. B. Douglas, ed., *Canada's Atlantic Connection* (Ottawa, 1985), pp. 1–34.

[23] An exception to this stereotype was the colonial surveyor-general Charles Morris, who has provided us with the best contemporary accounts of Acadian farming. See especially his "Brief Survey of Nova Scotia," MG 18/F10 (1748), Public Archives of Canada.

ters were not averse to turning their hands to commerce from time to time.[24] Trade was to be the lifeblood of the town, and most of the nonmilitary settlers had their eyes focused clearly on commerce. As one observer reported in 1762, "Not one family in the town or the parts adjacent subsist by Husbandry. They all are in some branch of Trade."[25]

On the surface, the expectations of both the Board of Trade and the new settlers appeared rational. Yet the economy did not develop in the manner that they hoped. For most of the quarter century preceding the outbreak of the Revolution, the colonial economy failed to function as predicted. As one historian has so correctly put it, this was a "marginal colony" on the fringe of the larger North American economy.[26] What went wrong?

Part of the problem was demographic: the colony was never able to attract large numbers of settlers. On the eve of the Revolution perhaps 20,000 souls resided in Nova Scotia, a net increase of about 25 percent in a quarter century.[27] The population shortage was of course exacerbated by the expulsion of the Acadians, and only partially rectified by the campaign to recruit New Englanders to take up Acadian farms in the 1760s.[28] Halifax suffered similar difficulties, peaking

[24] This figure is estimated from C.O. 217/38/116–19, P.R.O.

[25] "Report of Charles Morris," Jan. 11, 1762, Record Group 1/37, Publ. Arch. of N.S.

[26] John Bartlett Brebner, *The Neutral Yankees of Nova Scotia: A Marginal Colony during the Revolutionary Years* (New York, 1937).

[27] Population figures for pre-Revolutionary Nova Scotia are of dubious accuracy. Here I have followed in general the estimates in Dominion Bureau of the Census, "Chronological Summary."

[28] Governor Lawrence's descriptions and proclamations inviting settlement are conveniently reprinted in W. O. Raymond, "Colonel Alexander McNutt and the Pre-Loyalist Settlements of Nova Scotia," Royal Society of Canada *Proceedings and Transactions*, 3d ser. 4 (1911):80. On the pace of New England settlement in the vacated Acadian lands, see Brebner, *Neutral Yankees*, pp. 19–40; A. W. H. Eaton, "Rhode Island Settlers on the French Lands of Nova Scotia in 1760 and 1761," *Americana* 10 (1915):1–43; R. G. Huling, "The Rhode Island Emigration to Nova Scotia," *Nar-*

at about 3,000 in the late 1750s, declining to about 1,800 in the early 1760s, and recovering to perhaps 2,500 by 1775.[29]

An additional factor was a shortage of capital investment. It took capital to develop the fishery, particularly investment in small boats to prosecute the inshore fishery and larger vessels to reach the fertile grounds on the offshore banks. While quantitative evidence on ownership of smaller vessels is scarce, certainly a series of governors and other officials suggested that investment in this area lagged.[30] The data collected thus far on larger vessels (see below) indicate that for the most part this sector of the fishery was also undercapitalized. A similar problem existed in the agricultural sector, although a recent study suggests that the lack of settlers rather than a paucity of capital may have been more important in explaining stagnation in the farm sector.[31]

But the crux of the problem was an inadequate comprehension of the system of trade that predated the establishment of Halifax. Imperial officials, and all too many of the settlers, simply seemed to assume that the fish caught off the Nova Scotian coast and the harvests from colonial fields would find their way to the new port. Such an assumption, however, showed an abysmal ignorance of the trading interests of New Englanders, many of whom had grown accustomed to treating Nova Scotia as an economic hinterland.[32]

---

ragansett *Historical Register* 7 (1889):89–135; J. S. Martell, "Pre-Loyalist Settlements around the Basin of Minas," M.A. thesis, Dalhousie University, 1933; W. F. Ganong, "Origins of Settlements in the Province of New Brunswick," Royal Society of Canada, *Proceedings and Transactions,* 2d ser. 10 (1904):3–185; S. Hollingsworth, *The Present State of Nova Scotia* (Edinburgh, 1787); Wynn, "Late Eighteenth-Century Agriculture," pp. 81–89.

[29] See Akins, *History of Halifax City,* for estimates of the urban population.

[30] See for example, Charles Lawrence to the Board of Trade, Aug. 1, 1754, Nov. 3, 1756, Record Group 1/36, Publ. Arch. of N.S.

[31] Wynn, "Late Eighteenth-Century Agriculture," pp. 80–89.

[32] See Andrew H. Clark, "New England's Role in the Underdevelopment of Cape Breton Island during the French Regime, 1713–1785," *Canadian Geographer* 9 (1965):1–12; John Bartlett Brebner, *New England's Outpost:*

For men of commerce in ports such as Boston, Salem, Marblehead, Portsmouth, Newport, and a score of smaller places in the Puritan commonwealths, trade with Nova Scotia was an integral part of their operations. Further, they enjoyed a host of comparative advantages. Established merchants possessed the vessels to prosecute trade and the contacts in far-flung markets to export profitably the grain and fish collected. These men could also offer a wider range of less expensive trade goods than could the newly arrived Haligonians, and if necessary they could afford to pay higher prices for local produce. All of these advantages mitigated against the penetration of the hinterland by Halifax interests. Needless to say, without some type of economic integration between the port and its hinterland, it was virtually impossible to develop the type of economic system envisaged by the Board of Trade and the town's boosters.[33]

To understand the mercantile economy more clearly, we can divide the pre-Revolutionary era into more-or-less distinct periods. The first, lasting from 1749 to roughly 1756, was an era during which the town became established. Drawn by visions of expanding opportunities and the promises of lucrative profits, merchants flocked there in large numbers. When confronted with the hard rocks of economic reality, many foundered and departed as swiftly as they had come. The second period coincided with the Seven Years' War; it was transitional. Until 1760 the merchant community in general benefited from the conflict, but after that date the town entered a period of intense depression similar to the economic downturns experienced elsewhere in America after the cessation of hostilities. By 1764 this severe contraction had abated, and in the third period the merchants were able to establish a more stable, if somewhat marginal, mercantile system that continued virtually unaltered through 1773. Fi-

---

Acadia before the Conquest of Canada (New York, 1927); George A. Rawlyk, *Nova Scotia's Massachusetts: A Study of Massachusetts–Nova Scotia Relations, 1630 to 1784* (Montreal, 1973).

[33] See, for example, the comments in Board of Trade to Lawrence, May 7, 1755, C.O. 218/5/118–29, P.R.O., for the naiveté of the Board about entrenched New England interests.

nally, the years 1774 and 1775 were marked by dramatic increases in trade and shifts in its pattern. These years were indeed revolutionary. But rather than culminating in independence, the sudden change in conditions convinced a majority of merchants that their interests would be better served within the framework of the British Empire.

The generalized picture of the Halifax-centered economy can be discerned more readily if we examine some hard economic data. A logical place to begin is with an examination of the merchant community itself. In Halifax these men were leaders in both politics and society. But, more important, they were the central figures in the emerging economy through their control of trade.

A study of the Halifax merchants, however, is fraught with difficulties. Unlike similar men in the colonies to the south, Nova Scotia merchants have left us no great collections of records. Nor did they write long letters to the newspapers or produce pamphlets or broadsides about commerce or the great issues of the day. Students of the mercantile community are also frustrated by the fragmentary nature of some other standard primary sources, such as newspapers, court records, and tax lists. Nevertheless, by using the sources we do possess it is possible to sketch at least a broad picture of merchant behavior.[34]

Between 1749 and 1775 at least 420 merchants were active in Halifax.[35] For ease in analysis we may divide these men into three broad groups. The first comprised those who had been interested in Nova Scotian trade before the establish-

[34] Most of the material on individual merchants was drawn from the advertisements in local newspapers. No papers have survived for the period 1757–61, and the *Halifax Gazette* suspended publication during 1767. For these years data have been drawn from court records and official correspondence.

[35] Given the gaps in sources, there may well have been more. In addition, an individual was not counted unless fairly definitive evidence existed to indicate that he actually engaged in trade. With so many people "dabbling" in trade, this figure almost certainly underestimates the total number involved in commerce, although it should be a relatively accurate total of those who considered themselves merchants.

ment of Halifax, generally through contacts with Annapolis, Canso, or one of the French settlements. Membership in this group was not large, and the origins of its members were divided about equally between New England and elsewhere. Almost all were active before 1760. A second group consisted of those who might be termed "camp followers," men whose primary interest was to profit by supplying the needs of the civil and military establishments. Competing for contracts funded by large Parliamentary grants, and engaging in other trade only part-time, these men formed a slightly larger group than the first category in the first decade. Primarily of English origin, most departed after 1760 when the Parliamentary grants were sharply reduced. By far the greatest number of merchants in all periods belonged to a third group. We may label these individuals the "entrepreneurs." Mostly from New England, they flocked to the town in the early years to tap the expected opportunities. Many left quickly when the boom failed to materialize, but others proved more enduring. Not surprisingly, this last group was both enterprising and unstable.

Men of the first group exhibited many of the characteristics of the Jersey-born sea captain turned trader Joshua Mauger. Mauger had long been involved in trade with the French on Cape Breton, but following Cornwallis's arrival he shifted his headquarters to Halifax. While he was successful in winning supply contracts and even became agent-victualler to the naval station for a time, Mauger's chief interests centered on trade. He entered the import-export business at Halifax and established stores both there and elsewhere in the colony. He also founded distilleries, producing a commodity which proved vital to the local economy and in which he achieved a dominant position by the mid-1750s. Evidence of his success was his ability to "retire" to England after 1760, leaving his Nova Scotia interests in the hands of a capable assistant, John Butler. Mauger went on to become the member of Parliament for Poole, but he never forgot Nova Scotia: for most of the remainder of his life he was the principal expert on Nova Scotian affairs for the Board of Trade.[36]

[36] See Donald F. Chard, "Joshua Mauger: The Creation and Defense of

An important member of the second group was Thomas Saul. Saul seems never to have engaged in general trade on a regular basis, preferring instead to enrich himself by acting as the commissary agent for Sir William Martin and others in Britain who held lucrative contracts for the supply of the town and its garrison. Saul's prosperous activities naturally excited the jealousies of competitors, at least some of whom managed to initiate an official inquiry in 1751 into charges that Saul was swindling the public by setting the price of flour at twice the "usual rate."[37] Exonerated by Gov. Peregrine Hopson, Saul proceeded to a career as a member of the Council; he also was the recipient of numerous other official appointments during the 1750s.[38] Like most other members of the "camp followers," Saul returned to England in the early 1760s.[39]

Characteristics of merchants in the third category were exemplified by Malachi Salter. Although Salter, like so many successful merchants, managed to gain his shares of place-holdings, his principal interests were always in trade and commerce. His connections, both mercantile and familial, were chiefly with New England, but his network of commercial correspondents stretched at least as far down the coast as Philadelphia. To serve his expanding trading interests, Salter invested heavily in shipping, becoming the most important shipowner in Halifax following Mauger's departure. His will-

---

a Colonial Fortune and Its Implication for Nova Scotia's Relationship to New England, 1749–1784" (Paper presented at the Fifty-fifth Annual Meeting of the Canadian Historical Association, June 1976), for a convenient summary of Mauger's career.

[37] This charge was repeated in two petitions. The first, signed by Samuel Shipton, William Bourn, and Jacob Hurd, is in C.O. 217/13/H46, P.R.O. The second, from Daniel Shatford and Thomas Thomas, is in C.O. 217/13/H45, P.R.O. See also Benjamin Gerrish to Cornwallis, Nov. 26, 1751, C.O. 217/13/H49, P.R.O.; Ronald Rompkey, ed., *Expeditions of Honour: The Journal of John Salusbury in Halifax, Nova Scotia, 1749–53* (Newark, Del., 1982), especially pp. 123–26.

[38] Peregrine Hopson to the Board of Trade, Oct. 20, 1752, Record Group 1/35, Publ. Arch. of N.S.

[39] See Brebner, *Neutral Yankees*, p. 15, for a thumbnail sketch of Saul's career.

Table 1. Parliamentary grants to Nova Scotia, 1749–75

Period	Value	% of total	Average annual grant
1749–56	£529,861	75.7%	£66,233
1757–62	112,375	16.1	18,729
1763–75	57,700	8.2	4,438
1749–75	699,936	100.0	25,923

SOURCE: Derived from C.O. 218, Public Record Office; Record Groups 29–32, Public Archives of Nova Scotia.

NOTE: Before 1758 the value of the grants includes the amount appropriated for civil accounts plus capital funds for military projects. From 1759 onward it includes only civil accounts. Since military capital projects were almost nonexistent after 1758, this does not distort the time series in any significant way. The grants for 1763–75 include approximately £3,000 appropriated for expenses related to the island of St. John. Military salaries are excluded throughout.

For estimates that reflect the level of noncapital military spending, see Julian Gwyn, "British Government Spending and the North American Colonies, 1740–1775," *Journal of Imperial and Commonwealth History* 8 (1980):74–84; idem, "The Impact of British Military Spending on the Colonial American Money Markets, 1760–1783," Canadian Historical Association *Historical Papers* (Montreal, 1980), pp. 77–99.

ingness to innovate was demonstrated by, among other things, the establishment of a sugar house, which was producing twenty-five tons of loaf sugar annually by the late 1760s.[40]

Only the second group of merchants, those most interested in profits from supply contracts, enjoyed continuous prosperity in the period before 1756. The source of their success is easily detectable: it lay in the ability to win contracts funded by the generous Parliamentary grants. While no measure of economic output is available for pre-Revolutionary Halifax, it is clear that these grants formed the most important single source of funds to stimulate trade. The funds voted for the support of the civil and military establishments were large and heavily concentrated in the early years (see table 1). Over

[40] The material on Salter is drawn from scattered sources, but see especially the review of his holdings in "The State of Manufactures in Nova Scotia," July 11, 1768, C.O. 217/45/184–226, P.R.O.

three-quarters of the money appropriated by Parliament in the period before the Revolution was approved in the first eight years of settlement. Those, like Saul, who had suitable connections found the situation highly profitable. The grants continued at a reasonably high rate for the next four years as well, averaging just under £25,000 per annum. After 1760 a drastic reduction in Parliamentary largesse, coupled with a shift in military objectives, provides ample explanation for the departure of most merchants of this stripe.

Neither of the other two mercantile groups fared so well in the early years. Economic growth lagged, and there were simply too many merchants for a town the size of Halifax. The result was a highly unstable mercantile climate. It is possible to provide a rough measure of this instability by examining an index of business failures and dissolutions (see figure 1).[41] Merchants failed or departed the town in relatively large numbers before 1756. The number of unsuccessful merchants remained above average from 1752, the first year in which it is possible to construct this measure, through 1755. Not until 1756, when rumors of impending war were transformed into reality, did business dissolutions even ap-

[41] Business failures are calculated primarily from extant newspapers and court records held at the Publ. Arch. of N.S. The newspapers were used as the primary source. Ads noting that a merchant was "going out of business" or "removing from the province" were tallied for each year. Only unique instances were counted. These lists were then checked, where possible, against other sources. When information indicated that the merchant had been successful but was leaving by choice, the case was excluded. For years in which the newspapers were incomplete, the number of failures was indexed by the simple method of calculating a mean number of failures per surviving issue and multiplying by 52. Since there was no seasonality to merchant failures (although in many years there were insignificant concentrations in the late spring and late fall), such a procedure should not introduce distortions, regardless of which issues were missing. The figures for 1757–61 and 1767 were calculated from court records, official reports, and biographical information collected from a variety of sources. I would like to thank Marc Egnal for suggesting this methodology to me.

Because of the methodology used, it should be apparent that figure 1 does not necessarily indicate the actual number of failures but rather the magnitude. If anything, the conservative criteria for identifying failures have probably lead to a slight underestimation of the phenomenon.

Figure 1

Business failures and dissolutions at Halifax, 1752-75

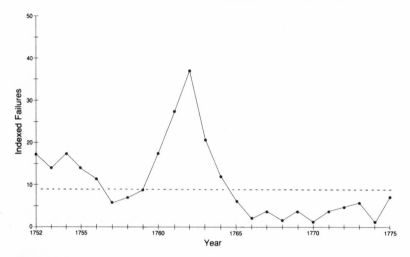

SOURCE: See note 41.

NOTE: Period mean equals 8.9.

proach the mean for the pre-Revolutionary period (8.9 per
year). Not surprisingly, almost all the failures were accounted
for by merchants in groups one and three; only one failure
unearthed in the sources involved a merchant in group two.[42]

Wartime spending was the basis for a new stability that
characterized the late 1750s. Parliamentary grants remained
at acceptable levels, and increased military spending added
to the mercantile opportunities. The annual number of business failures dropped below the mean for the first time since
the founding of Halifax and remained low through 1759 in
spite of an influx of new arrivals to the mercantile community. But the boom collapsed in 1760 and merchant dissolutions rose sharply, peaking in 1761 and remaining above
average through 1764. At the same time both Parliamentary
grants and military spending were curtailed. This led to an
exodus of the merchants in group two; only three such men

[42] The one failure in group two was Thomas Shatford, a Guernsey-born
merchant who held supply contracts to provide building materials for the
town. He advertised that he was "quitting the province" in the *Halifax
Gazette*, Dec. 6, 1754.

remained in Halifax after 1763. Many of the members of group one also departed. Some, like Mauger, had accumulated high profits during the war, but others simply judged future prospects to be limited. Most of those who departed were Englishmen.[43]

The mercantile exodus of the early 1760s changed the face of the Halifax business community in important ways. First, it greatly reduced the size of the mercantile sector. At least 204 merchants were active in the town in 1758; by 1764 the number had been reduced by about two-thirds. With the departure of many of the dominant English merchants in groups one and two, there was a new ascendancy for the component of the community born in New England. While such men had always enjoyed a numerical majority, their dominance was now overwhelming: after 1764 New Englanders never comprised less than 85 percent of all merchants. Finally, by the mid-1760s the Halifax mercantile sector bore little resemblance to the unstructured scene of the previous decade. Many of the marginal traders, and most who hoped for windfall profits, had gone; those who remained were more committed to making their careers in the town. While there were still some "men on the make," such as Salter and Richard Wenman, who established a ropewalk in 1767, the Halifax merchants had become more homogeneous, and in a sense less competitive, than before.[44]

The commercial sector had also become more stable. In comparison to conditions elsewhere, this mercantile stability of the 1760s and early 1770s stands out sharply. As William S. Sachs has shown, business conditions in the northern colonies fluctuated wildly in the decade preceding the Revolution.[45] In Halifax, by contrast, business failures dropped below the mean in 1765 and remained low for the remainder of the pre-Revolutionary period. The Halifax mercantile sec-

[43] See notes 36, 39, and 40, above.

[44] Brebner, *Neutral Yankees*, p. 83; "The State of Manufactures in Nova Scotia," July 11, 1768, C.O. 217/45/184–226, P.R.O.

[45] William S. Sachs, "The Business Outlook in the Northern Colonies, 1750–1775," Ph.D. diss., Columbia University, 1957, especially pp. 97–126.

tor had achieved a balance that was uncharacteristic of its counterparts to the south.

In a town as concerned with trade as Halifax, mercantile fortunes were obviously connected intimately with trade. Commerce began even before Cornwallis and his party had landed, as "a number of boats from New England, who come to this place to fish and trade with the Indians," opened commercial contacts with the settlers.[46] The governor promptly appointed a Naval Officer, Benjamin Green, and the new official began reporting information about trade in the new port.

The Naval Officer's records form the backbone of the analysis to follow. They are complete from 1749 through 1766, one of the longest runs of this kind of document in the eighteenth century.[47] The years 1768–72 can be reconstructed with equal accuracy through an analysis of Customs 16/1, a marvelous document that provides data on shipping and trade for all British possessions.[48] For the years 1767 and 1773–75, however, the historian must resort to a more painstaking procedure, estimating the patterns of commerce through government records, newspapers, and shipping lists of the most likely trading partners.[49] The results of this ex-

[46] Cornwallis to the Board of Trade, June 23, 1749, C.O. 217/18/106–7, P.R.O.

[47] The Naval Officer's lists contain the following items: date of entrance or clearance, name of vessel, rig, tonnage, port of registry, number of men, number of guns, place bound (or from), master, principal owner(s), and cargo. They are contained in C.O. 217 and 218, P.R.O. All have been computerized and are currently in the machine-readable data archive at Memorial University of Newfoundland.

[48] For a full description of Customs 16/1, see James F. Shepherd and Gary M. Walton, *Shipping, Maritime Trade, and the Economic Development of Colonial North America* (Cambridge, 1972). The Customs 16/1 data for Nova Scotia have been incorporated in a slightly modified form into the data file described in n. 47.

[49] As a control, a series of weighted regression equations was used to predict expected frequencies of voyages and trade flows. In general, it yielded good fits, thus increasing the confidence in this technique for capturing the vast majority of data. For a full description of this technique,

Table 2. Shipping entrances and clearances: Halifax, 1749–75

Year	Entrances	Tonnage	Clearances	Tonnage
1749	112	5,410	116	6,505
1750	265	13,546	279	14,787
1751	196	9,180	200	9,147
1752	174	8,073	176	8,050
1753	172	7,670	190	8,243
1754	143	6,187	138	5,879
1755	186	7,794	195	8,665
1756	176	7,819	183	8,134
1757	255	10,775	256	11,963
1758	242	9,993	251	11,382
1759	270	12,223	226	10,263
1760	185	8,026	175	8,340
1761	203	9,540	171	7,935
1762	124	6,308	121	6,596
1763	96	4,916	80	3,806
1764	114	5,436	106	5,501
1765	117	5,661	122	5,866
1766	90	4,428	98	5,506
1767	93	4,609	103	5,883
1768	95	4,955	104	5,944
1769	145	7,006	162	7,324
1770	158	8,363	192	9,399
1771	130	6,928	159	7,378
1772	126	6,319	164	7,577
1773	179	8,326	186	8,601
1774	204	9,672	201	9,438
1775	249	10,786	251	10,819

SOURCES: Naval Officer's Lists, C.O. 217 and 218, and Customs 16/1, Public Record Office, and newspaper reports of entrances and clearances, all hereinafter referred to as Halifax Shipping File.

NOTE: Entrances and clearances for 1749 are for the period July–December only.

ercise allow us to examine the patterns of shipping and trade in a detail that far surpasses what has previously been possible.

In general the fortunes of trade paralleled the success of the merchants discussed in the last section (see table 2). Trade was highly variable before 1756; after peaking in 1750, tonnage clearing the port declined at a rate of 17.7 percent per

see Lewis R. Fischer, "Estimating Trade Patterns," unpublished technical paper 79-11, Maritime History Group, Memorial University of Newfoundland.

annum through 1754. With the resumption of imperial conflicts, the volume of shipping leaving the port grew by 9.7 percent per year between 1755 and 1759. The good times were short, though, and the termination of hostilities plunged port traffic into its second and steepest trough of the pre-Revolutionary period, clearances falling by 19.9 percent per annum between 1759 and 1763. In the decade after 1764, Halifax clearances enjoyed a period of sustained growth, growing on average by 8.4 percent annually. After 1774 port traffic soared, as a combination of events boosted the local economy.[50]

Given the state of the records, it is not currently possible to make a direct comparison between Halifax and other northern ports in the 1750s. William Sachs's account of the business climate in the northern colonies, however, suggests that conditions there were for the most part more stable than in Halifax.[51] But the reverse held true in the 1760s. Table 3 reconstructs total port movements (entrances plus clearances) for four other northern ports after 1763. It demonstrates that the stability of growth found in Halifax was indeed unusual. Only Salem comes close to matching the sustained growth of Halifax, in large measure due to the success of the New England port in the West Indian cod trade.[52] Boston, New York, and Philadelphia were all characterized by wide fluctuations in the volume of shipping. Part of this instability may be explained by the effectiveness of protest movements such as nonimportation, but the timing of the fluctuations suggests that even without such trade boycotts

[50] All growth rates were calculated by a regression equation of the form $LogY = a + bt$. The results for Halifax clearances were as follows:

1750–54: $LnY = 9.082 - .194t$
1755–59: $LnY = 9.117 + .092t$
1760–63: $LnY = 8.856 - .221t$
1764–73: $LnY = 8.747 + .081t$

[51] Sachs, "The Business Outlook."

[52] Jacob M. Price, "Economic Function and the Growth of American Port Towns in the Eighteenth Century," *Perspectives in American History* 8 (1974):142–49.

Table 3. Entrances and clearances, selected ports, 1763–73

Year	Halifax	Salem	Boston	New York	Philadelphia
1763	8.7	31.1	52.3	31.7	67.4
1764	10.9	31.8	52.8	41.9	76.9
1765	11.5	34.8	64.2	33.9	67.4
1766	9.9	29.4	54.6	39.2	83.7
1767	10.5	34.5	60.9	42.9	69.0
1768	10.9	33.5	45.7	35.2	71.9
1769	14.3	30.3	59.3	52.5	83.1
1770	17.8	35.4	75.0	52.1	94.6
1771	14.3	37.1	68.6	50.3	84.7
1772	13.9	34.0	86.3	57.3	73.1
1773	16.9	39.7	65.1	48.6	87.7

SOURCES: Halifax Shipping File; William S. Sachs, "The Business Outlook in the Northern Colonies, 1750–1775," Ph.D. diss., Columbia University, 1957, pp. 295–300; "Early Coastwise and Foreign Shipping of Salem: A Record of Entrances and Clearances, 1750–1769," Essex Institute Historical Collections 67 (1931):49–64, 241–56, 337–52; Jacob M. Price, "Economic Function and the Growth of American Port Towns in the Eighteenth Century," Perspectives in American History 8 (1974):123–86; Murray G. Lawson, "The Routes of Boston's Trades, 1752–1765," Publications of the Colonial Society of Massachusetts 38 (1959):514–21; William I. Davisson and Lawrence J. Bradley, "New York Maritime Trade: Ship Voyage Patterns, 1715–1765," New-York Historical Society Quarterly 55 (1971):309–17; Arthur L. Jensen, The Maritime Commerce of Colonial Philadelphia (Madison, 1963).

NOTES: Tonnage figures derived by adding entrances and clearances.

the three largest colonial ports were wildly unstable after 1763.[53]

The trading patterns emanating from Halifax also appear to be unique among the major northern ports. Nowhere else was the coasting trade of such importance, particularly commerce to and from New England. On the other hand, no other port for which we have data conducted such a small percentage of its trade with offshore areas.[54] A detailed schema of Halifax trade is presented in Appendix tables 1 and 2. These show clearly the overwhelming importance of the coastal trade. Trade with the mainland colonies and Newfoundland over the period accounted for over 80 percent of entrances and clearances by number and almost 75 percent by tonnage. New England was consistently the most important trading partner: between 1749 and 1775 about 54 percent of all clearances were bound for a New England port, while just over 56 percent of all entrances originated in that region. Boston alone accounted for half the New England total, and the other ports in Massachusetts (including Maine) added another third of both entrances and clearances. The ports in the middle colonies contributed 15 percent of clearances and 12 percent of entrances. Britain, including Ireland, was not so well represented as the literature suggests,[55] but since vessels that engaged in transatlantic trade were consistently larger than coastal craft, trade with the mother

[53] On the economic effects of nonimportation, see Robert J. Chaffin, "The Townshend Acts of 1767," *William and Mary Quarterly* 3d ser. 27 (1970):90–121. Introducing statistical controls for the boycotts, in the form of dummy variables, removed almost none of the variance, which suggests that the instability of the three largest ports was independent of such economic sanctions.

[54] See, for example, Sachs, "The Business Outlook," pp. 295–300; Murray G. Lawson, "The Routes of Boston's Trades, 1752–1765," *Publications of the Colonial Society of Massachusetts* 38 (1959):514–21; William I. Davisson and Lawrence J. Bradley, "New York Maritime Trade: Ship Voyage Patterns, 1715–1765," *New-York Historical Society Quarterly* 55 (1971):309–17.

[55] Brebner, *Neutral Yankees*, pp. 8–9, makes the oft-repeated claim that 50 percent of shipping entering Halifax sailed from Great Britain. As the data show, whether the criterion used is number of entrances or tonnage, in no year was the British share nearly this high.

country contributed a disproportionate share of tonnage, particularly to entrances.

Trading patterns were far from stable, however. Trade with New England was characterized by several cyclical patterns, and entrances in particular declined linearly after 1759. Trade with the middle colonies was more important in the decade after 1754 than either before or after. New York was the primary trading partner in this region before 1760, but Philadelphia became more significant later. British trade remained fairly stable, by contrast, except during the war period. Of particular concern, especially given the plan for Halifax to become a major exporter of fish, was trade with the West Indies and southern Europe. Both trades exhibited distinctly rising trends toward the end of the period, particularly after 1773. The volume of shipping clearing for the West Indies more than doubled between 1773 and 1775, and tonnage clearing for southern Europe rose by 75 percent. Similarly, trade with other Nova Scotian ports requires some mention. If Halifax was to become the export entrepôt for Nova Scotian agricultural products, regular contact with the farming areas on the Bay of Fundy was essential. Although the nature of the records from which these data were derived makes the results somewhat suspect,[56] trade with other areas of Nova Scotia was generally disappointing. There were no entrances at all between 1756 and 1760 from the hinterland, and clearances also languished for much of the period. But the volume of tonnage engaged in this trade increased about fivefold between 1773 and 1775, years that were crucial to Halifax's development.

The nature of trade in the port was obviously affected by the availability of cargoes. Halifax unfortunately offered few outward freights through much of the period. One way of

---

[56] Neither the Naval Officer's lists, Customs 16/1, nor the newspapers ever showed any sustained interest in intraprovincial trade. Thus, it is possible that the figures presented here distort the strength of the links between Halifax and its hinterland. If there is distortion, there is certainly no evidence of any bias in individual years. However, when placed in the context of the ongoing laments by Halifax merchants concerning their exclusion from this trade, it seems unlikely that the data seriously underestimate the number of voyages.

measuring this is by calculating the number of vessels listed as clearing in ballast (see table 4). Between 1749 and 1754 almost 70 percent of tonnage cleared the port in ballast. While this proportion improved somewhat during the war years, the postwar slump was characterized by a rising percentage of vessels leaving with no profitable cargo. The situation improved markedly after 1763, however, and in the next decade less than a third of all tonnage was unproductively utilized on outbound voyages. The two years immediately preceding the war saw an even greater improvement, with only about a sixth of tonnage being unable to procure a paying freight out of the port.

What trade existed was carried principally in vessels owned elsewhere. Vessels owned or registered in Halifax played a distinctly secondary role in the port's maritime commerce throughout the pre-Revolutionary period (see table 5).[57] New England vessels predominated in roughly the same proportions in which they were represented among voyage origins and destinations. Before 1760, about three-quarters of all vessels and approximately five-eighths of all tonnage entering or clearing with cargoes was registered in New England ports. While this proportion decreased over time, craft from New England ports were numerically the most important throughout the period, although they were surpassed in carrying capacity by British vessels after 1773. Ships registered in the mid-Atlantic ports generally increased their share of the trade, while vessels registered in the mother country enjoyed a fairly stable share of the commerce. Sailing vessels with some connection to the local Halifax mercantile community were almost nonexistent before 1754, accounting for less than 2 percent of either numbers or tonnage. The situation improved somewhat during the war years, due largely

[57] When identifying Halifax vessels, I have employed two criteria. First, whether the vessel was listed as being registered in Halifax; if the source indicated that it was, it was counted. But if one or more listed owners were known to be resident in the town at the time the vessel entered or cleared, it was also counted. While this happened infrequently, it was necessary to do this since registry laws were so loose that many vessels were never reregistered even after their owner or owners shifted residence. No registry book has survived for Halifax in these years.

Table 4. Percentage of tonnage clearing Halifax in ballast, 1749–75

Period	Nfld.	Canada	N.S.	N.Eng.	Mid-Atl.	S.Atl.	G.B.	W.I.	Other	Total
					Trade Route					
1749–54	86.3	N/A	100.0	73.2	89.1	100.0	57.2	0.0	20.0	69.2
1755–59	58.2	N/A	83.7	54.8	62.6	100.0	33.3	0.0	33.3	58.6
1760–63	100.0	N/A	100.0	69.2	78.3	90.9	62.0	0.0	51.5	71.1
1764–73	26.0	7.3	25.0	30.9	42.6	49.2	23.0	0.0	15.2	32.2
1774–75	16.7	12.5	7.7	16.8	26.1	33.3	11.1	0.0	0.0	17.0

SOURCE: Halifax Shipping File.

NOTES: Vessels are counted as being in ballast if they are so designated in the records. Craft that are partially in ballast are considered laden. Canada includes the island of St. John; Great Britain includes Ireland.

Table 5. Percentage of Halifax shipping movements accounted for by vessels registered in selected locales, 1749–75

Period	Halifax		New England		Mid-Atlantic		South Atlantic		Great Britain		Other	
	N	Tons	N	Tons	N	Tons	N	Tons	N	Tons	N	Tons
					Port of Registry							
1749–54	1.8	1.3	72.4	66.1	6.3	3.8	1.1	1.4	17.5	26.3	0.9	1.1
1755–59	3.4	2.6	76.7	66.9	3.9	2.9	1.4	1.6	13.2	22.4	1.4	3.6
1760–63	2.2	2.0	68.2	63.7	7.8	7.3	1.3	1.8	15.8	23.0	4.7	2.2
1764–73	3.9	3.1	57.8	50.6	16.1	14.3	1.1	2.2	13.9	21.4	7.2	8.4
1774–75	16.8	17.6	38.5	29.8	13.0	12.2	0.9	1.6	23.0	32.4	7.8	6.4

SOURCES: Halifax Shipping File.

NOTES: Shipping movements are comprised of entrances plus clearances. Vessels in ballast excluded. Great Britain includes Ireland.

Table 6. New investments in shipping, Halifax, 1749–75

Period	Tons registered	Average tons per year	Peak year
1749–54	2,077	346	1753
1755–59	4,651	930	1758
1760–63	1,097	274	1761
1764–73	6,159	616	1770
1774–75	2,352	1,176	1774

SOURCE: Halifax Shipping File.

NOTE: De novo registrations excluded.

to the multitude of prizes captured off the coast and brought to Halifax to be condemned and sold by the Vice-Admiralty Court.[58] The economic slump of the early 1760s was accompanied by a diminution of Halifax's share of the trade, while the growth period after 1763 witnessed renewed participation by locally owned craft. Only in the period 1774–75 did Halifax vessels make a substantial contribution to the port's carrying trade, but even in those years they accounted for considerably less tonnage than either New England or British-owned ships.

The lack of participation by local owners was a direct reflection of the pattern of investment in shipping by local entrepreneurs. As table 6 indicates, local investors registered little tonnage before 1754. Of the limited total, 1,819 tons (87.5 percent) were accounted for by the two largest shipowners in the first decade, Joshua Mauger and Ephraim Cooke.[59] The war-induced boom convinced more merchants

[58] The role of privateering in Halifax is discussed in Lewis R. Fischer, "Privateering in Halifax during the Seven Years War" (Paper presented at the Atlantic Eighteenth-Century Studies Conference, Wolfville, N.S., October 1983). I have estimated there that profits on Halifax privateers averaged about 60 percent. This accords well with the estimate of 70 percent in Carl E. Swanson, "Predators and Prizes: Privateering in the British Colonies during the War of 1739–1748," Ph.D. diss., University of Western Ontario, 1979, chap. 7. A much higher estimate (about 140 percent) based upon scanty evidence is found in James G. Lydon, Prizes, Privateers and Profits (Upper Saddle River, N.J., 1970).

[59] John J. McCusker, "The Shipowners of British America before 1775" (Paper presented at the Shipowner in History Conference, Greenwich,

to invest, but about two-thirds of the tonnage added to the local fleet between 1755 and 1759 consisted of prizes. Many of these vessels never participated in a mercantile voyage; instead, owners had them refitted and dispatched in search of more lucrative returns as privateers.[60] Diminishing opportunities for trade during the depression of 1760–63 were reflected in the collective decision to retrench during that period: the average annual investment was the lowest for the entire pre-Revolutionary era. This caution continued after 1763, despite the renewed strength of trade. Almost two-thirds of all investments in shipping between 1764 and 1773 occurred after 1769, and there is some tantalizing evidence to suggest that merchants were attempting to profit from trade disruptions elsewhere on the seaboard.[61] Of particular importance is the unprecedented spurt of investment in 1774 and 1775, which parallels the rise in participation in the carrying trades by Haligonians in those years.

The yearly variance in shipping investments was high. A number of variables were examined, but only two exhibited strong relationships with investment: the volume of cod exported and the number of clearances to the Bay of Fundy. These were related to the two great staples that the founders of the town hoped to exploit, so it is hardly surprising that in calculating the potential return on their investments, merchants gave great weight to these trades.

The first of these staples was cod. Exports were disappointing before 1764 (see table 7). The great improvement in cod exports commenced about 1768, and the rise in shipping in-

September 1984), argues correctly that in most colonial ports it was not the practice to list all shipowners in Naval Officer's returns. But in Halifax the various officers seem always to have listed each owner resident in the town separately. This makes it possible to compile lists of all vessels in which an individual held shares, although it remains impossible from this source to determine precisely what proportion of tonnage each individual owned.

[60] See n. 58, above.

[61] Some of the commodities imported and exported during nonimportation look suspiciously like goods destined for smuggling. See also the note on Halifax smuggling in Benjamin W. Labaree, *The Boston Tea Party* (New York, 1964), p. 35.

Table 7. Cod exports from Halifax, 1749–75

Period	Total quintals	Yearly average	Percent exported on Halifax vessels
1749–54	53,789	8,965	15.7%
1755–59	14,115	2,823	3.9
1760–63	8,701	2,900	8.3
1764–73	216,125	21,613	18.2
1774–75	64,215	32,108	76.4
Total	356,945	13,220	21.8

SOURCE: Halifax Shipping File.

NOTE. Dry fish only; pickled fish excluded.

vestment began the following year. If the volume of fish exports is correlated with new investments in shipping, lagged by one year to simulate a reasonable pattern of demand, the results (+.62 between 1749/50 and 1767/68 and +.93 between 1768/69 and 1774/75) clearly show the relationship between the two variables. As much as 38 percent of the variance in shipping investment may be explained by the previous year's cod exports before 1768 and perhaps 86 percent of the variance thereafter.[62] Local investors clearly considered the prospects for the export of cod when placing orders for new sailing vessels.

The data in table 7 suggest something else: the inability of the Halifax merchants to wrest control of the trade from their competitors. Before 1764 they carried only a small proportion of fish exports; the overwhelming majority cleared in New England vessels. And even that tiny fraction of exports shipped in locally owned vessels was predominantly channeled through New England. Of the 9,718 quintals of dried cod exported in Halifax vessels between 1749 and 1763, only 1,845 (19 percent) cleared directly for the West Indies; the remainder went to New England, principally to Salem and Boston. Presumably it was transshipped in those ports for its eventual destination. The situation improved somewhat after 1764, primarily due to the influence of Mal-

[62] The amount of variance explained by this variable cannot be determined accurately because of the effects of multicollinearity. Clearances to Fundy also correlated well with the level of investment, but the nature of the data makes it difficult to separate the effects of this other variable.

achi Salter. Almost 40 percent of the cod exported in Halifax vessels in these years was consigned directly to the West Indies or southern Europe, and 92 percent was carried in vessels in which Salter had a share. He was also the most prominent merchant involved in the dramatic rise of local participation in the cod trades in 1774–75.

Shipping investment also correlated strongly with clearances to the Bay of Fundy, although less strongly than with cod exports. This is to be expected, since trade was nonexistent in some years, and the expulsion of the Acadians in 1755 and the slow resettlement of the region by New Englanders caused stagnation in the agricultural sector before the mid-1760s. But between 1765 and 1775, investment in shipping correlated with clearances to Fundy at a moderate +.48, which suggests that the Halifax merchants had not forgotten their dream of engrossing this trade.

The patterns of trade illustrated in Appendix tables 1 and 2 make it clear that Haligonians were unable to break the New England monopoly in the early years. But by the mid-1760s they had managed to obtain a small but stable share of the trade. Once again, as in the cod trade, it was the 1774–75 period that witnessed a dramatic shift. It is not possible to determine with any precision what proportion of this trade was gained by Halifax interests, but the sizable rise in the number of both entrances and clearances suggests that the long-awaited breakthrough had finally arrived, just at that critical juncture when North Americans were to be forced to choose between independence and loyalty.

The material discussed thus far provides the basis for advancing a new interpretation of the failure of Nova Scotia to join the Revolution. This is one of the few subjects in Canadian history during the Revolutionary era that has received its full share of scholarly attention, but few historians have considered the economic dimension.[63] While space will not

---

[63] E. D. Poole, *Annals of Yarmouth and Barrington in the Revolutionary War* (Yarmouth, 1899); Beamish Murdoch, *A History of Nova Scotia*, 3 vols. (Halifax, 1865–67); Emily P. Weaver, "Nova Scotia and New England during the Revolution," *American Historical Review* 10 (1904):52–56; D. C.

permit a detailed treatment of the subject, it is possible to sketch out at least the broad outlines of an interpretation that accords with the economic realities of the Halifax experience.

The merchants who first settled in the town brought with them dreams of riches. To reach this goal, they believed that they needed to control both the fishery and the exports from the farms along the Bay of Fundy. Instead of achieving immediate success, however, they encountered an entrenched and well-developed trading system based in New England. Regardless of whether they were New Englanders or Englishmen, the Halifax merchants came to agree on one thing very quickly: New England traders were a barrier to their success. In the first decade, though, they merely complained about this state of affairs, as the numerous petitions and letters to imperial authorities attest. The community was far too divided on other matters to take concerted action. The men who would have been natural leaders of any effort to wrest control from the New Englanders were for the most part too involved with the scramble for largesse generated by the Parliamentary grants, and the bulk of the mercantile sector was too unstable to undertake any long-range activities.

But the Seven Years' War and the subsequent trade depression transformed the community. As many of the dominant merchants and marginal traders exited, a new homogeneity

Harvey, "The Struggle for the New England Form of Township Government in Nova Scotia," Canadian Historical Association *Report* (1933):15–22; idem, "Machias and the Invasion of Nova Scotia," Canadian Historical Association *Report* (1932):21–28; Viola F. Barnes, "Francis Legge, Governor of Loyalist Nova Scotia, 1773–1776," *New England Quarterly* 4 (1931):424–46; Maurice W. Armstrong, "Neutrality and Religion in Revolutionary Nova Scotia," *New England Quarterly* 19 (1946):50–62; idem, *The Great Awakening in Nova Scotia, 1776–1809* (Hartford, 1948); George A. Rawlyk, "The American Revolution and Nova Scotia Reconsidered," *Dalhousie Review* 43 (1963):379–94; idem, *Nova Scotia's Massachusetts;* idem, ed., *Revolution Rejected, 1775–1776* (Scarborough, Ont., 1968); Gordon Stewart and George A. Rawlyk, *A People Highly Favoured of God: The Nova Scotia Yankees and the American Revolution* (Toronto, 1972); Jack M. Bumsted, *Henry Alline, 1748–1784* (Toronto, 1971). Exceptions to this rule include Brebner, *Neutral Yankees;* Wilfred B. Kerr, "The Merchants of Nova Scotia and the American Revolution," *Canadian Historical Review* 13 (1932):20–36; idem, *The Maritime Provinces of British North America and the American Revolution* (Sackville, N.B., 1941).

became evident among the merchants. Led by men such as Malachi Salter, the merchants were able to stabilize their marginal trading system and to eke out at least satisfactory rewards. Complaints about the New England merchants continued to abound, but to many in Halifax it must have appeared that they had carved out a satisfactory economic niche.

Indeed, this new stability was reflected in the willingness of the Halifax merchants to accept conditions that elicited widespread protest elsewhere in colonial America. Conditions and experiences separated the Halifax merchants from their colleagues to the south, and their behavior showed it. While other merchants complained about inflated inventories, vendue sales, dumping by British merchants, and restrictive legislation, there is no evidence of any widespread grievance in Halifax. None of the "panic advertising" so common in many colonial towns appeared in the local newspapers.[64] Response to British legislation was generally restrained. Only the Stamp Act excited any protest, but popular disturbances were extremely limited.[65] The Currency Act, which alarmed merchants up and down the seaboard, did not seem to trouble Haligonians at all.[66] And when merchants in the northern colonies invited their counterparts in Nova Scotia to join the nonimportation movement in response to the Townshend duties, the Halifax merchants did not even bother to reply.[67]

As the men of commerce in Halifax increasingly diverged ideologically from other colonial traders, they also discovered that there was money to be earned by acting independently. That they did so is unquestionable. Haligonians were often

[64] Compare the description of the northern cities in Egnal and Ernst, "An Economic Interpretation."

[65] Wilfred B. Kerr, "The Stamp Act in Nova Scotia," *New England Quarterly* 6 (1933):552–66.

[66] Joseph A. Ernst, *Money and Politics in America, 1755–1775: A Study in the Currency Act of 1764 and the Political Economy of Revolution* (Chapel Hill, N.C., 1973).

[67] The fate of the petition is summarized in Brebner, *Neutral Yankees*, p. 141.

able to reap short-term profits by this stance, as they did during nonimportation. As a Philadelphia merchant observed bitterly in 1770, while businesses in other ports suffered, the level of goods imported into Halifax from Britain actually rose during nonimportation.[68] Imports of tea, for example, which had averaged only about 500 pounds per year in 1768 and 1769, soared to over 13,000 pounds in 1770, doubtless to be smuggled at a high markup to eager consumers in New England.[69]

These experiences also help to explain the new willingness on the part of Halifax merchants to invest in shipping in the late 1760s and early 1770s. And the ownership of vessels enabled them to take decisive advantage of the next disruption in trade and virtually to seal their destiny as "neutral Yankees." In 1774 an angry majority in Parliament responded to what it considered to be open defiance by closing the port of Boston. This did not halt Boston's trading activities, but it did hinder them; one of the principal results was a shortage of shipping tonnage in a number of colonial trades. The merchants of Salem, who had come to rival the Bostonians in the cod trades, shifted their assets out of Nova Scotia trade and into the more lucrative Newfoundland fishery.[70] At the same time, Boston merchants shifted their vessels out of the marginal Fundy trades into more profitable employment. The result, as all the data on the Halifax trading system indicate, was a "revolution in trade." Clearances by Halifax vessels to the West Indies rose dramatically in late 1774 and continued their ascent through 1775. Local merchants were also able to fill the vacuum in the Bay of Fundy, capturing a significant portion of the Nova Scotian grain trade for the first time.

[68] *Halifax Chronicle*, June 12, 1770.

[69] Customs 16/1, P.R.O.

[70] This point is discussed at length in Keith Matthews, "Newfoundland Trade in the Revolutionary Era" (Paper presented at the Atlantic Eighteenth-Century Studies Conference, Wolfville, N.S., October 1983). Professor Matthews died before this splendid essay could be revised for publication, but plans are being made to publish it as part of a forthcoming testimonial volume.

While merchants in other colonies embraced revolution to gain control of their economic destiny, Haligonians had no need to follow.[71] Their divergent behavior, combined with a good measure of luck, had fulfilled the dream of the founders. In a very real sense their peculiar economic development had enabled them to achieve economic sovereignty without forcing Haligonians to sever their ties with Great Britain.

[71] Compare the argument in Egnal and Ernst, "An Economic Interpretation."

Appendix table 1. Halifax clearances, 1749–75

Year	Nfld.		Canada		Nova Scotia		New England		Mid-Atlantic		South Atlantic		U.K.		West Indies		Other		Totals	
	N	Tons	N	Tons	N	Tons	N	Tons	N	Tons	N	Tons	N	Tons	N	Tons	N	Tons	N	Tons
1749	4.3	4.0	0.0	0.0	16.4	13.1	64.7	54.7	6.9	3.7	3.5	7.8	2.6	15.1	0.9	1.2	0.9	0.6	116	6505
1750	10.0	9.8	0.0	0.0	4.7	4.1	67.2	60.8	9.4	8.6	2.2	5.6	1.8	4.1	1.1	1.0	4.0	6.3	279	14787
1751	8.5	8.3	0.0	0.0	6.0	4.6	53.0	51.0	16.0	10.3	9.0	15.7	2.0	2.9	2.0	2.1	3.5	5.2	200	9147
1752	6.8	8.7	0.0	0.0	4.0	2.5	60.2	56.0	13.6	13.3	6.8	9.3	0.6	0.7	3.4	3.9	4.6	5.8	176	8050
1753	14.2	13.6	0.0	0.0	4.2	2.4	50.0	51.9	16.8	13.2	2.1	2.4	1.1	1.5	6.3	7.0	5.3	8.1	190	8243
1754	17.4	15.9	0.0	0.0	5.1	2.2	42.8	41.2	18.2	17.5	3.0	4.0	4.4	7.4	3.6	4.3	5.9	7.8	138	5879
1755	2.6	3.3	0.0	0.0	9.2	13.7	64.7	59.5	15.9	12.4	1.0	1.4	2.5	3.6	1.0	0.8	3.1	5.6	195	8665
1756	1.6	1.4	0.0	0.0	1.1	1.1	67.8	67.6	19.7	17.1	3.3	2.8	2.8	4.0	2.7	5.5	1.1	0.5	183	8134
1757	1.2	1.4	0.0	0.0	0.0	0.0	74.4	68.9	18.0	18.5	2.0	4.2	0.8	1.5	2.4	2.7	1.6	2.1	256	11963
1758	2.4	2.1	0.0	0.0	0.8	0.8	67.8	63.4	20.0	18.2	4.4	9.1	1.6	2.1	1.2	1.0	2.0	3.3	251	11382
1759	0.5	1.4	0.0	0.0	0.0	0.0	78.9	71.4	13.7	14.4	4.4	9.0	0.5	1.1	0.9	0.8	1.3	2.2	226	10263
1760	0.6	1.0	0.0	0.0	0.6	0.2	69.2	64.5	14.9	17.4	6.3	6.6	2.3	3.4	3.4	4.7	2.9	2.4	175	8340
1761	0.0	0.0	0.0	0.0	1.2	1.0	67.3	60.4	18.7	18.3	4.8	10.6	3.5	4.6	2.3	2.7	2.3	2.5	171	7935
1762	0.0	0.0	0.0	0.0	0.0	0.0	67.8	63.2	17.4	16.7	3.4	7.6	3.4	3.7	4.1	4.2	3.3	4.0	121	6596
1763	0.0	0.0	0.0	0.0	0.0	0.0	53.8	49.7	23.9	18.8	3.9	8.0	6.3	12.0	8.8	7.1	3.8	4.6	80	3866
1764	0.0	0.0	0.0	0.0	2.8	1.8	50.1	42.5	23.6	19.0	5.7	15.6	1.0	0.9	9.4	10.6	7.6	9.6	106	5501
1765	1.6	2.0	3.3	3.1	8.2	8.0	46.7	41.1	14.7	11.8	3.2	7.6	4.1	5.0	11.5	10.7	6.5	11.0	122	5866
1766	3.1	3.3	2.0	7.3	12.3	8.2	42.9	38.5	22.4	17.5	0.0	0.0	9.2	15.5	4.1	3.9	4.1	6.0	98	5506
1767	3.2	3.3	0.0	0.0	6.9	4.2	50.2	47.5	20.0	16.1	2.4	3.7	7.1	13.6	6.2	5.8	4.1	6.0	103	5883
1768	2.9	3.4	0.0	0.0	0.0	0.0	56.8	39.6	18.3	16.0	0.0	0.0	6.7	23.9	8.7	6.6	6.7	10.6	104	5944
1769	1.2	1.6	0.6	0.6	0.0	0.0	65.4	50.5	16.0	19.2	1.8	3.2	4.3	10.9	4.3	4.4	6.2	9.8	162	7324
1770	0.5	0.3	0.5	0.4	0.5	0.3	66.2	48.7	12.5	11.2	2.1	2.3	8.3	24.7	4.2	3.7	5.2	8.3	192	9399
1771	1.3	0.6	3.8	5.1	0.0	0.0	71.1	61.4	12.0	10.8	0.6	0.7	5.7	13.8	2.5	2.7	3.2	5.2	159	7378
1772	1.2	0.7	0.6	1.7	0.0	0.0	69.5	52.8	9.7	6.5	0.6	0.5	9.8	26.5	1.2	1.6	7.3	9.8	164	7577
1773	1.1	0.5	2.2	2.0	2.7	2.4	61.8	41.3	10.1	9.0	1.1	2.8	10.1	28.7	3.5	6.1	7.3	7.2	186	8601
1774	1.0	0.3	2.5	2.1	7.0	5.8	46.2	34.9	10.8	9.0	2.5	2.9	11.3	30.3	8.9	4.9	9.8	9.8	201	9438
1775	0.8	0.2	2.4	2.0	11.6	8.4	32.9	26.1	9.7	8.4	3.1	3.0	14.8	29.5	17.4	14.8	7.3	7.6	251	10819

SOURCE: Halifax Shipping File.

NOTE: Figures are expressed as a percentage of total clearances; row totals equal 100 percent.

Appendix table 2. Halifax entrances, 1749–75

Year	Nfld. N	Nfld. Tons	Canada N	Canada Tons	Nova Scotia N	Nova Scotia Tons	New England N	New England Tons	Mid-Atlantic N	Mid-Atlantic Tons	South Atlantic N	South Atlantic Tons	U.K. N	U.K. Tons	West Indies N	West Indies Tons	Other N	Other Tons	Totals N	Totals Tons
1749	0.0	0.0	0.0	0.0	27.7	27.5	62.4	61.7	8.1	5.6	0.0	0.0	1.8	5.2	0.0	0.0	0.0	0.0	112	5410
1750	3.8	4.0	0.0	0.0	1.9	0.9	76.7	67.0	8.0	5.4	0.4	0.2	7.6	17.5	0.4	0.2	3.4	5.0	265	13546
1751	2.6	2.2	0.0	0.0	2.0	1.3	58.7	55.3	15.8	9.3	0.5	0.2	12.2	19.7	2.6	2.6	5.6	9.6	196	9180
1752	2.3	1.2	0.0	0.0	1.2	0.6	63.8	59.5	14.4	10.6	1.7	1.5	8.1	13.9	3.5	3.2	5.0	9.6	174	8073
1753	4.1	5.7	0.0	0.0	4.7	2.9	56.0	53.0	16.3	12.1	2.4	2.1	14.5	21.3	3.5	4.2	1.8	2.2	172	7670
1754	5.6	4.5	0.0	0.0	6.3	4.5	46.9	39.6	15.4	13.4	5.6	4.0	11.9	23.3	2.8	3.4	5.6	7.4	186	6187
1755	1.1	0.7	0.0	0.0	0.5	0.8	65.1	59.4	16.1	12.1	2.0	1.9	9.7	17.4	2.2	3.0	3.2	4.9	143	7794
1756	0.6	0.5	0.0	0.0	0.0	0.0	72.2	71.0	17.0	14.7	2.8	1.8	5.2	10.3	1.1	1.9	1.1	0.8	176	7819
1757	1.2	0.8	0.0	0.0	0.0	0.0	70.7	66.0	19.7	16.5	1.2	0.8	5.2	11.3	2.4	2.9	1.2	1.4	255	10775
1758	0.4	0.3	0.0	0.0	0.0	0.0	67.0	62.8	21.5	19.1	1.6	1.4	4.1	11.0	0.4	0.2	2.5	2.8	242	9993
1759	0.0	0.0	0.0	0.0	0.0	0.0	78.2	68.9	10.1	9.0	1.9	1.2	7.5	17.2	0.7	0.7	1.9	3.2	270	12223
1760	0.0	0.0	0.0	0.0	0.0	0.0	69.8	63.9	14.1	14.2	4.9	2.7	7.6	15.1	3.3	3.0	0.5	1.3	185	8026
1761	1.0	1.9	4.4	4.4	4.4	5.9	63.5	55.3	13.4	11.9	2.0	1.7	6.9	15.0	2.0	1.8	2.5	2.3	203	9540
1762	0.8	1.0	0.0	0.0	0.0	0.0	64.6	51.4	16.9	16.0	2.4	1.4	10.5	24.7	3.2	3.3	1.6	1.6	124	6308
1763	0.0	0.0	1.1	0.8	0.0	0.0	55.2	45.2	19.8	15.3	4.2	3.4	12.5	24.0	3.1	4.2	4.2	7.2	96	4916
1764	0.9	0.3	0.0	0.0	0.9	1.5	49.1	45.0	30.8	27.9	3.6	2.0	9.6	16.7	5.3	5.9	0.9	0.9	114	5436
1765	2.6	3.5	6.0	6.6	6.0	5.0	48.0	42.2	20.6	14.6	1.8	1.5	9.4	17.6	2.6	3.4	3.4	5.5	117	5661
1766	0.0	0.0	5.6	5.4	6.7	4.2	46.8	41.4	23.3	18.3	1.1	0.8	11.1	24.1	3.3	3.2	2.2	2.7	90	4428
1767	0.0	0.0	1.1	5.1	6.2	3.1	56.0	47.7	17.9	13.0	2.2	4.0	9.5	20.7	6.3	5.7	1.1	0.9	93	4609
1768	0.7	0.4	1.4	2.7	4.1	4.9	57.2	40.5	18.6	14.7	1.4	1.0	12.4	29.6	2.8	2.9	1.4	3.3	95	4955
1769	0.7	0.5	1.3	2.6	4.2	4.9	54.2	46.5	21.6	15.7	0.0	0.0	13.8	32.6	2.8	5.8	1.4	3.4	145	7006
1770	0.0	0.0	0.6	0.8	6.6	6.2	55.4	39.9	15.8	12.8	1.9	0.8	12.7	29.5	5.1	4.0	1.9	6.2	158	8363
1771	0.8	3.2	3.1	2.7	6.6	6.1	59.6	40.5	13.8	12.2	0.8	1.0	10.0	27.2	3.1	2.9	2.3	4.4	130	6928
1772	0.8	1.1	0.8	1.3	6.4	5.9	52.4	35.9	17.5	13.7	0.0	0.0	15.1	34.4	5.6	5.2	1.6	2.5	126	6319
1773	1.1	1.3	2.2	2.2	6.1	6.0	50.3	32.8	13.6	12.0	0.0	0.0	15.5	35.6	6.1	5.1	5.1	5.0	179	8326
1774	1.0	0.6	2.9	2.7	7.3	6.5	46.2	30.3	12.8	10.2	0.0	0.0	18.3	38.1	7.0	7.0	4.5	4.6	204	9672
1775	1.2	1.0	2.4	2.5	9.1	8.0	31.8	25.6	9.4	7.7	0.0	0.0	32.9	41.4	10.1	10.6	3.1	3.4	249	10786

SOURCE: Halifax Shipping File.

NOTE: Figures are expressed as a percentage of total entrances; row totals equal 100 percent

WINIFRED B. ROTHENBERG

The Emergence of a
Capital Market in
Rural Massachusetts,
1730–1838

It is a divine thing to lend; to owe an heroic virtue.

François Rabelais

I. INTRODUCTION

ON THE EVE of the Revolution, New England had the lowest per capita wealth and "the most dismal outlook" of any colonial region.[1] For over a century the colonial South, embed-

An earlier version of this article appeared in the *Journal of Economic History* 45 (1985). The author takes this opportunity publicly to express her deep gratitude to Webster David Brown and Don Hickey at the Middlesex County Probate Court, who bent every effort to facilitate her data gathering; and to the community of scholars who sustained her: Jerome Rothenberg, Kenneth Sokoloff, Barry Eichengreen, Peter Temin, Robert Margo, Jeremy Atack, Marc Egnal, Robert Gallman, and Lance Davis. Much has been gained by presentation of successive versions of this paper at the U.S. Capitol Historical Society's symposium on the economy of early America, the Social Science History Association, at the Harvard, Berkeley, Stanford, University of Pennsylvania, Washington, D.C.-Area, and All-University of California Economic History Workshops, and at the Brandeis Economics Department Seminar. She is indebted to Frank Flynn at the University of British Columbia for skillful programming, to Claudia Goldin and Carol Petraitis for careful and caring editing, and to an anonymous referee for unusually helpful and warmly appreciated guidance. This article is dedicated to the beloved memory of Alice Hanson Jones.

[1] Alice Hanson Jones, *Wealth of a Nation to Be: The American Colonies on the Eve of the Revolution* (New York, 1980), p. 141.

ded as it was in world commodity markets, had grown far more rapidly and was, on a per capita basis, far wealthier. Yet so rapid was the rate of growth in the North in the decades following Independence that by 1840 per capita northern income was over 30 percent higher than southern. This remarkable reversal happened not because southern growth had slowed—apparently it had not—but was due "entirely" to what had become, in barely two generations, "the extraordinarily high income of the Northeast."[2]

That impressive growth story was centered in Massachusetts with the industrialization of cotton-textile and machine-tool manufacture, but had had its beginnings in the farm economy long before, with the unheralded emergence, proliferation, and articulation of local markets, a thickening network in place by the mid-1780s.[3] Less spectacular than the export-led growth of the South, New England's development pattern was ultimately a more fruitful one, nourishing "ramifying nests of symbiotic enterprises" to cushion against the devastating consequences of change.[4]

The challenges came from Vermont grain and dairy farms, from Pennsylvania and Genesee valley wheat farms, from Cincinnati hog markets. It came by coastal schooner, overland wagon, canal barge, railroad, and live on the hoof. Local markets relayed the shocks as changing relative prices and resilient farmers responded by shifting from grains to hay, from hay to dairying, and finally from agriculture to commerce and industry.

Central to such a transformation must have been the development of an effective mechanism for increasing the liquidity of the regional economy, for motivating the accumulation of capital in the farm sector, and for channeling savings through credit networks that became increasingly

[2] Robert W. Fogel and Stanley L. Engerman, *Time on the Cross: The Economics of American Negro Slavery,* 2 vols. (Boston, 1974), 1:249.

[3] Winifred B. Rothenberg, "The Market and Massachusetts Farmers, 1750–1855," *Journal of Economic History* 41 (1981): 283–314.

[4] This apt phrase, taken out of its original context, appeared in Jane Jacobs, "Why the TVA Failed," *New York Review of Books* 31 (May 10, 1984), p. 45.

multilateral and impersonal, out of declining sectors on the fringes of the development process and toward higher returns generated in infrastructure and manufacturing sectors. The mechanism to effect that transformation is a regional capital market.[5]

The problem I confront here, then, is to confirm and date the emergence of that market, relying on probate data for the evidentiary base. Because the test of capital market function most often used, the convergence of risk-standardized rates of return, cannot be documented from probate data, the study tests for the appearance of three other attributes of market penetration. (1) A developing capital market alters the "structural elements" of the capital-transfer process. Interest rates are freed to behave like market-clearing prices, credit instruments become more fully negotiable, and new investment opportunities appear, accompanied by new financial intermediaries to service them. (2) A developing capital market both thickens in density and expands in space, as evidenced by the increasing size and widening geographical spread of individual credit networks. (3) A developing capital market enhances the liquidity of financial instruments and therefore the propensity of rural wealthholders to substitute them for physical assets. This may be the most important role the capital market played in the transformation of the agricultural economy, and it is tested here in two ways. The first is a wealth-quartile analysis of shifts in portfolio composition over time. The second is regression analysis identifying the determinants of that shift.

The Data Base

The data through which farmers will be observed as demanders and suppliers of loanable funds come from the debts and

---

[5] That the southern economy was unable in the antebellum period to generate a comparable growth spurt may have been due to its failure to evolve a comparable capital market, a failure due, perhaps, to the anomaly of increasing risk aversion in the South over time, even into the 1870s. So suggest Jeremy Atack, Fred Bateman, and Thomas Weiss in their "Risk, the Rate of Return, and the Pattern of Investment in Nineteenth-Century American Manufacturing," Bureau of Economics and Business Research of the University of Illinois, reprint no. 464 (Champaign-Urbana, n.d.).

credits of 512 probated decedents in Middlesex County, Mass., between 1730 and 1838. (Nationally aggregated data on private capital formation become available in 1839.) Middlesex County—the agricultural hinterland of Boston, 800 square miles stretching from the New Hampshire border to the sea—has a probate archive that is probably unsurpassed for historical coverage, for the quality of the inventories, and most particularly for the completeness of the executors' and administrators' accounts that accompany the inventories. A study of this kind depends on those accounts, for the inventories alone contain nothing of the debts owed by the estate, and only little of the debts owed to it. For a study of a sample of New England counties that excluded Middlesex, Alice Hanson Jones found those accounts missing for 55 percent of her decedents. It was possible in Middlesex County to locate 86 percent of the documentation for the sample. The probate process and the data are discussed in the Appendix.[6] The complete data base, with colonial currencies converted to dollars, is available upon request from the author.

Probates are problematical in a variety of ways, some of which present special difficulties for a study of indebtedness. One suspects that probate inventories may understate wealth, both real and portable, for the dying have always had the same incentives to conceal property from debt collectors as the living have to conceal it from tax collectors. To the extent that the intergenerational transfer of property was arranged by the deceased before his death, such properties will not appear in inventories of the deceased's wealth. Eleven of the 512 in the sample had disposed of their real estate in this way so that it had escaped appraisal, and the underreporting of personal property must have been much more widespread.

More serious is the problem of representativeness. All attempts to make a probate sample representative of its contemporary universe have had to confront two sources of bias: the probated are wealthier than the nonprobated, and the

---

[6] For any serious student of probates, the discussion of the probate process in the appendix will be inadequate, and they are referred to Alice Hanson Jones, *American Colonial Wealth: Documents and Methods,* 3 vols. (New York, 1977), vol. 1.

dead are older (and therefore wealthier) than the living. To offset these biases, the best probate studies have either stratified the sample or twice weighted the relevant magnitudes.[7] In the present study the sample was more impressionistically selected to constitute an "interesting mix"—principally, but not entirely, from rural towns; principally, but not entirely, farmers from the ranks of the poor, the middling, the prosperous, and the very wealthy. Table 1 summarizes some of the sample characteristics.

In defense of an "interesting mix," I would distinguish between two ways of arguing from sample data. The first argument would confirm that a capital market was functioning from evidence that the sample behaved as though it were. The second argument would confirm the hypothesis by inferring from the behavior of the sample to that of a whole population. In this article I am making the first kind of argument. It is the second, it seems to me, that requires that the sample be made in the image of its living universe. One relates to the presence of a capital market; the other to its pervasiveness. These are distinct and separable issues.

However, acknowledging that a sample was drawn impressionistically must act to constrain generalizations one might be tempted to make along the way. For example, one characteristic of the sample is a more than 200 percent increase in the wealth (in constant dollars) of all quartiles in the second period. There is no intent to generalize that finding to the population as a whole. Nevertheless, the fact is that the wealth distribution of the sample does closely approximate that for the universe from which it came. A Gini coefficient calculated for the sample ranked by total wealth, which is the sum of the values of real estate, portable physical wealth (henceforth *PPW*), and financial assets, is .675. The top 10 percent of the sample population held 54 percent of the wealth. This compares well with Alice Hanson Jones's estimate of a Gini of .64 for free wealthholders in the New England colonies in 1774,

---

[7] This is an issue definitively explored by Jones in *American Colonial Wealth*, pp. 1878–1901. For Jones's purposes it was imperative that her probate sample be made as nearly as possible a mirror image of the living universe: America on the eve of the Revolution.

and with Jeremy Atack and Fred Bateman's Gini of .63 for the whole rural North in 1860.[8] The sample, then, does not oversample the rich, but where their presence distorts the findings, the upper tail is removed and separate results produced. The absence of the top 5 percent, the wealthiest 23 decedents, lowers the Gini of the remaining 95 percent to .53.

Also relevant is the distribution of sample occupations. Just over 80 percent of decedents in the sample were farmers. According to the Fourth U.S. Population Census, this mirrors the proportion of the Massachusetts population "engaged in agriculture" in 1820. But of those farmers in the sample, more than 40 percent had by-employments in which they engaged, along with nonfarmers, in as many as twenty-two artisan crafts and five professions. The ubiquity of by-employments among these decedents may accurately reflect the versatility and ingenuity of the Yankee farmer, but it has, for the purpose at hand, the disadvantage of so blurring the distinction between agriculture and commerce, between farmer and nonfarmer, that it will frustrate the specification of an occupational dummy in the regression analysis below.

Drawing a data base from probates may bias a study of indebtedness in still another, more subtle way, and in a direction difficult even to identify, let alone measure. Compared, say, to debts litigated in the Court of Common Pleas, it would appear that the relations between debtors and their creditors at probate may have been softened by "some degree of familiarity and trust."[9] If so, that would explain my finding that

[8] Jones, *Wealth of a Nation to Be,* p. 164, table 6.2. Jones ranked her sample by total physical wealth, which is real estate + *PPW.* Also Jeremy Atack and Fred Bateman, "The 'Egalitarian Ideal' and the Distribution of Wealth in the Northern Agricultural Community: A Backward Look," *Review of Economics and Statistics* 43 (1981): 125. Massachusetts was not included in their sample of the rural North, but their Ginis for Connecticut and Vermont are .66 and .67 respectively.

[9] David Thomas Konig, in his study of seventeenth-century Essex County, was able to locate on a contemporary map of Lynn the homesteads of a few parties to probated loans and found that they lived within two miles of each other and could therefore be presumed to have had face-to-face contact; whereas parties to litigated loans were unlikely, given the

Table 1. Characteristics of the sample

	1730–80		1781–1838		1730–1838	
	Number of decedents	Percent of known	Number of decedents	Percent of known	Number of decedents	Percent of known
Total	292		220		512	
Occupation						
Known	277	100%	217	100%	494	100%
Farmer	242	87	167	77	409	83
Farmer only	145	52	87	40	232	47
Artisan	78	28	69	32	147	30
Artisan only	10	4	13	6	23	5
Merchant	42	14	44	20	86	17
Professional	18	6	40	18	58	12
Acreage owned						
Known	229	100	187	100	416	100
0	38	17	19	10	57	14
1–10	15	7	12	6	27	6
11–50	58	25	47	25	105	25
51–99	67	29	34	18	101	24
100–199	33	14	43	23	76	18
200–5224+	17	7	33	18	50	12

Table 1. Characteristics of the sample (cont.)

	1730–80		1781–1838		1730–1838	
	Number of decedents	Percent of known	Number of decedents	Percent of known	Number of decedents	Percent of known
Number of creditors per decedent						
Known	239	100	193	100	432	100
1–19	122	51	86	44	208	48
20–50	91	38	81	42	172	40
Over 50	14	6	19	10	33	8
Number of debtors per decedent						
Known	225	100	186	100	411	100
1–19	132	59	121	65	253	62
20–50	7	3	20	11	27	7
Over 50	3	1	14	7	17	4
Number with credits	205	70	182	83	387	75
Number with debts						
Known	245	100	198	100	443	100
Number	231	94	182	92	413	93

SOURCE: Probate documents, Middlesex County Probate Court

15 percent of the notes—excluding mortgages—held by the richest quartile of probated decedents after 1781 had been outstanding for more than ten years; 2 percent for over twenty years; and some for over thirty. Yet in the courts "a creditor could proceed against his debtor's person or property, which he could either seize or sell, in any Massachusetts county for an indefinite period after the rendition of judgment."[10] And once in litigation, creditors appear to have initiated collection proceedings immediately, the outcome of which was (more often than not) "to attach the goods or Estate of the debtor to twice the debt," and for want thereof (more often than not) "to take the Body of the said debtor and him safely to keep."

Granted that there is a difference in ambiance between litigated debts and debts outstanding at probate, it is still not clear what bias that difference may have imparted to this study. On the one hand, one of the responses of Massachusetts courts to the commercial transformation of the economy after Independence was to soften the legal remedies creditors could seek against debtors. Judge-made law, thus instrumentally conceived, was moving in the direction of making market relations between debtors and creditors look more and more like the forgiving links between kith and kin at probate. On the other hand, if probate indebtedness does indeed overrepresent "personalized transactions," then the evidence for this study has been biased against its hypothesis, which only strengthens its findings.

Periodization

Part 2 catalogues a number of alterations in what I am calling the structural elements of the capital-transfer process. In these respects, at least, the world of the rural wealthholder

---

distances that separated them, to encounter each other in the course of their daily interchanges. See his *Law and Society in Puritan Massachusetts: Essex County, 1629–1692* (Chapel Hill, N.C., 1979), p. 82. I would add that a large majority of the plaintiffs and defendants in prosecutions for debt at the Middlesex County Court of Common Pleas lived in different towns.

[10] William E. Nelson, *Americanization of the Common Law: The Impact of Legal Change on Massachusetts Society, 1760–1830* (Cambridge, Mass., 1975), p. 42.

will be seen to have changed dramatically and in some cases abruptly in the first quinquennium of independence. The balance of the study explores the depth and breadth of that transformation. It hypothesizes a breakpoint at 1781, and makes cross-sectional comparisons between the first period (1730 to 1780) and the second (1781 to 1838). The validity of the periodization is supported not only from the kinds of evidence adduced in Part 2 but by significance and chi-square tests of the evidence presented in Part 3, by sizable shifts in the quartile analysis of portfolio composition in Part 4, and by Chow tests of the period regressions in Part 5. But by Donald N. McCloskey's "Jewish mother test" the periodization is best confirmed by asking, "So what else is new?"[11] On that test the decade of the American Revolution was an extraordinary breakpoint, ushering in "a new era of shared ideation" affecting (according to the new social history) a stunning number and variety of social indicators.[12]

II. CHANGES IN THE STRUCTURAL ELEMENTS OF CAPITAL TRANSFER

A Widened Menu of Investment Opportunities

There is a sudden alteration at the close of the Revolutionary War in the portfolio holdings of sample decedents. Beginning in 1778, securities appear for the first time: shares in bridges (the Charles River, Malden, Chelsea, Andover, Merrimac, Piscataqua, West Boston, Cayuga), in turnpikes (the Medford & Andover, the Worcester, the Providence), the Middlesex Canal, and the Boston Aquaduct Co. There are shares in the U.S. Bank, Union Bank, Boston Bank, Salem Bank, Lowell Bank, Neptune Bank, Bunker Hill Bank, Farmers' Exchange Bank, and something called the Railroad

---

[11] Donald N. McCloskey, "The Loss Function Has Been Mislaid: The Rhetoric of Significance Tests," *American Economics Association Papers and Proceedings*, 75 (May 1985), p. 201.

[12] William E. Nelson, for example, has explored the vast consequences for the common law alone of "the gradual breakdown of ethical unity in Massachusetts over a thirty-year period beginning in the 1780s," in *Americanization of the Common Law;* the quotation is from p. 117.

Bank; in the New England Marine Life Insurance Co., the Massachusetts Marine & Fire Insurance Co., Union Insurance Co., the Charlestown Fire & Marine Insurance Co., and in the Massachusetts Hospital Life Insurance Co. Holdings of Massachusetts State 5 percent notes appear as early as 1778, followed by New Hampshire, New York, and Rhode Island State Notes, U.S. Loan Office Certificates, Continental Loan Office Notes, 3 percent and 6 percent deferred stocks, something called U.S. Stocks, and Treasurers' Notes. Sample decedents died "seized of" shares in the Boston Manufacturing Co., the Boston Hat Manufactory, the Glass Manufactory, Newton Iron Works, Hamilton Manufacturing Co., Merrimac Manufacturing Co., Boott Cotton Mills, Lawrence Manufacturing Co., Tremont Mills, Otcheco Manufacturing Co., Nashua Manufacturing Co., several railroads, and the Boston Type and Stenotype Foundry. If "large holdings of securities were common in eastern cities by the late 1840s," it is clear that they had begun to be important in the Massachusetts countryside sixty years earlier.[13]

Securities, then as now, were not widely held. They appear in the accounts of only 13 percent of the second-period decedents (the financial assets of the majority continued to be loans), and of the 13 percent half lived in Cambridge and Charlestown, the urban places in the county.[14] It is therefore all the more interesting that the other half of securities holders lived in the rural communities of Framingham, Dunstable, Stoneham, Wilmington, Stow, Chelmsford, Malden, Weston, Woburn, Concord, Groton, Newton, and Tewksbury.

Why this sudden appearance of securities in the composition of financial assets in the early 1780s? Funding the prosecution of the war in the absence of banks of any kind had placed U.S. and state government bonds in the hands of a wide cross-section of the population who had accepted them

[13] James L. Sturm, "Investing in the United States, 1798–1893: Upper Wealth-Holders in a Market Economy," Ph.D. diss., University of Wisconsin, 1969, p. 72.

[14] Charlestown was then part of Middlesex County. It was annexed to Boston (Suffolk County) in 1873.

in payment for army requisitions, in payment for military service, or as an act of patriotism. Independence unleashed a demand for internal improvements and, in turn, for innovative and reliable sources of borrowed capital to finance them—a demand that found expression in the clamor of the free chartering of limited-liability corporations generally and of banks in particular. Those internal improvements may very well have played the same role in mobilizing capital that the turnpike and canal trusts were playing in contemporary England. They tapped into idle savings "which may not have been made available for more risky direct investment in industry or commerce, and applied them towards the development of a form of social overhead capital essential for industrial and commercial expansion. In this sense they acted as 'conduits' connecting the 'reservoirs of savings' with the 'wheels of industry.'"[15]

It was not until 1830 that limited liability was fully established in Massachusetts corporation law, and it is in the 1830s that the bulk of manufacturing shares show up in decedents' estates. But the securities of insurance companies are evident as early as 1778 and of banks in 1784, which speaks to the role played by financial intermediaries in channeling rural savings to industrializing firms. Much of the start-up capital of the Boston Manufacturing Co., for example, came from the Massachusetts Hospital Life Insurance Co., whose securities were held by rural investors.

Interest

It was during the Revolution that administrators suddenly began to speak of interest as the "improvement" of money, a metaphor carried over from land management to portfolio management. With the prospect of improvement, the lending of money lost the character of "mutual aid among men exposed to the common risks . . .[where] the charitable man comes to the help of distress out of goodwill," and became investment, that is, the productive use of a resource the re-

[15] William Albert, *The Turnpike Road System in England, 1663–1840* (Cambridge, 1972), p. 119.

turn to which is interest.[16] Also in 1783, and again for the first time, appears evidence of interest as the money value of time. Interest begins to be charged by the courts on delayed administration of estates, on delayed payment of court costs, on delays in disbursements of legacies, and even on late payments of rents.

But arguably the most important changes between the colonial and early national periods occurred in the notion of interest as the price of money, and that involves two separable issues: the increased incidence of interest charges and market determination of the level of rates.

From 1781 to 1800, interest was charged on 20 percent of sample administration accounts, increasing to 33 percent from 1800 to 1810, and to 37 percent from 1810 to 1838. This stands in sharp contrast to the years before the Revolution, when interest appeared in only about 5 percent of sample probates. Is it plausible that something like 95 percent of loans in the colonial period were interest-free? Or is this only a reporting bias? Was the taking of interest in fact widespread throughout the eighteenth century but sufficiently under the cloud of usury laws in the Bible Commonwealth that it was disguised or discounted in advance?[17]

Because the notion of a price for money is intimately related to the emergence of a market for money, a choice must be made between these two interpretations. At litigation "lawful interest" was exacted at least as early as 1718, but only when the debt arose from the borrowing of money. Debt that stemmed from unpaid account-book balances remained customarily interest-free throughout the period. Thus, the marked increase in the frequency with which interest was charged in second-period probates might be explained in one of two ways: either there was in fact an increase in the incidence of charging interest, or there was a shift in the struc-

[16] R. H. Tawney, Introduction to Thomas Wilson's *Discourse upon Usury* (1925; reprint ed., New York, 1963), p. 23.

[17] "I would as much abhorre to lend money for gaine hereafter as I doe abhorre to steale by the high waye, or to murdr any man violentlye for his goods, which god forbyd that ever I shoulde thinke or minde to doe" (Thomas Wilson, *Discourse upon Usury*, p. 379).

ture of debt away from accounts receivable (which did not carry interest even in litigation) and toward the "traffic in money" (which did).

The format of administration accounts does permit a test of this distinction (insofar as it is a real distinction) because they frequently identify obligations as notes, bonds, mortgages, or book accounts.[18] "Due on book" continued to bulk large enough in the debts of second-period decedents as to reject the hypothesis of a shift in the composition of debt and to argue instead for an increase in the incidence of interest taking after 1781. But even if the apparent increase in incidence of interest is really a shift to money lending, that too would have enhanced the liquidity of the economy.

In litigation during the colonial period neither promissory notes between the parties nor the documents issued by the Court of Common Pleas against the debtor specified a rate of interest. It was written simply as "Lawful Interest," which was 6 percent. Similarly, in probate documents before 1781, the rate—when it was given, or when it could be calculated from information that was given—was also 6 percent; sometimes less, but never more. Then, beginning in 1785, interest rates began to climb to 7, 8, and 9 percent, floating free of their ancient and customary restraints, free enough, presumably, to rise to the level of the returns on physical capital, a phenomenon critical to the historical development of capital markets.[19]

---

[18]Apparently bonds, unlike notes, were protected from the operation of usury laws. "That the issue of negotiability first arose in connection with bonds seems to confirm the suspicion that until the nineteenth century bonds were widely used to prevent judicial interference with commercial transcations . . . (and) . . . almost surely could successfully immunize usurious contracts from legal attack" (Morton J. Horwitz, *The Transformation of American Law, 1780–1860* [Cambridge, Mass., 1977], p. 217). That may account for the preponderance of bonds among the credits of the wealthiest decedents.

[19]"The capital market in a 'developed' economy successfully monitors the efficiency with which the existing capital stock is deployed by pushing returns on physical and financial assets toward equality, thereby significantly increasing the average return. Economic development so defined is necessary and sufficient to generate high rates of saving and investment

To find rates as high as 9 percent as early as 1785 is worthy of attention because the prohibition of usury, legislated in Massachusetts in 1693 but enforced by the Puritan churches from the very beginning, was still on the books at the outbreak of the Civil War. Of course, rising rates are not in themselves usurious. It is only exceeding statutory limits that makes them so. And while with one hand Massachusetts continued until the Civil War to legislate limits on interest rates, with the other hand it began to dismantle, bit by bit, the complex structure of legal remedies that penalized usurious contracts. In doing so the courts were acknowledging mounting pressure from commercial interests to free money from the notion of "just price" from which the "will theory of contract" had already freed other commodity prices.[20]

Negotiability

That credit instruments be empowered to "pass like currency from debtor to creditor almost indefinitely" took on a special urgency after the Revolution, when the chronic currency shortage that had plagued Massachusetts since its founding was exacerbated by the withdrawal of British bills of exchange.[21] Negotiability is an attribute not so much of the creditworthiness of the instrument as of the evolved state of the capital market within which it moves and of the body of commercial law that guarantees, all the way to the last holder, a right of recovery "against the world." I quote here at some length from Morton J. Horwitz:

> No development had a more shattering effect on American conceptions of the nature of contract than the necessity of forging a body of commercial law during the last decade of the 18th century. At the heart of all commercial problems lay the question of negotiable instruments and of whether the American le-

---

(accurately reflecting social and private time preference), the adoption of best-practice technologies, and learning-by-doing" (Ronald McKinnon, *Money and Capital in Economic Development* [Washington, D.C., 1973], p. 9).

[20] Horwitz, *Transformation of American Law*, pp. 237–45.

[21] Tony A. Freyer, "Negotiable Instruments and the Federal Courts in Antebellum American Business," *Business History Review* 50 (1976): 441, and Horwitz, *Transformation of American Law*, p. 215.

gal system could assimilate the principle of negotiability into a conception of contract that challenged a whole range of accepted legal notions. . . . How could A, who had given a promissory note to B, be sued by C, to whom B had transferred the note, when nothing passed between A and C? . . . Where C endorsed a note over to D, could D sue B, a prior endorser, if the original promisor defaulted? Could C, a subsequent endorsee, receive a better title to [a defective] instrument than B had . . . so that subsequent innocent purchasers of an instrument might depend on payment regardless of any known defects in the obligation arising out of the original transaction between distant parties?[22]

And, most important of all, can C or D, "innocent purchasers," recover against A even if A has already paid B the value of the note? For it is this, "to allow an endorsee to recover against a promisor who had paid the value of the note to his original promisee," that constitutes full negotiability. On this "crucial" point Massachusetts courts balked until some time after 1809.[23]

In other respects, the passing of endorsed paper was legitimate even in the colonial period. Evidence in the probate records that notes have left the world of face-to-face contacts is the presence in administration accounts of notes addressed to the payee "Or Order," notes made out "To Bearer," acceptances, and endorsements. It is not always clear what was meant by "indorsements." There are third-party signatures as early as 1754, but at that early date they may have been merely sureties, extending face-to-face contact to include "the friend of my friend," and would not constitute evidence of "personal divorcement in the capital transfer" necessary for a market in these instruments.[24]

But when the word *indorsement* appears juxtaposed to scheduled payments of principal and interest, the instrument

[22] Horwitz, *Transformation of American Law*, pp. 212–13.

[23] Ibid., p. 338, n. 6.

[24] Lance E. Davis, "Capital Immobilities and Finance Capitalism: A Study of Economic Evolution in the United States, 1820–1920," *Explorations in Entrepreneurial History* 2 (1963/64): 89.

in question may be truly negotiable (even if falling short of being "fully" negotiable). Each time such an instrument was transferred it was necessary not only to endorse it but also to compute interest at the time of transfer.[25] And evidence of this sort appears in the probate documents of eleven first-period decedents beginning as early as 1764, but there are thirty-eight decedents with notes so endorsed in the second period. Again, we cannot know from probates whether these instruments achieved full negotiability in Horwitz's sense, for that required nothing less than the transformation of the privity notion of contract. What is certain is that the financial intermediaries to effect their passage were in place by 1785.

III. THE MOBILITY OF CAPITAL: WIDENED AND THICKENED CREDIT NETWORKS

The emergence and proper functioning of a regional capital market will be retarded or much impaired by the combination of risk aversion and the high transactions costs traditional in a rural economy. Evidence that can date the weakening of those inhibitions will go a long way toward dating the presence and penetration of the market.[26]

The evidence economists typically look for is the convergence of rates of return on risk-standardized investments across a spectrum of enterprises. Another approach, one that

[25] Stuart W. Bruchey, *Robert Oliver, Merchant of Baltimore, 1783–1819* (Baltimore, 1956), p. 112.

[26] I say weakening, not disappearance. These inhibitions remain to this day. A major factor affecting household portfolio behavior of even the very wealthy as recently as 1978 "may be the costs of acquiring and processing the information required to make decisions about how best to allocate resources across different assets. We would expect such costs to vary among households and, in particular, with observable variables such as the level of educational attainment and occupation" (Mervyn A. King and Jonathan I. Leape, "Wealth and Portfolio Composition: Theory and Evidence," *NBER Working Paper no. 1468* [Sept. 1984], p. 34). If this is true of a sample whose mean net worth was a quarter of a million dollars (in 1978), how much truer it must have been of my sample, whose mean net worth, in 1800 dollars, was $3,600.

lies within the limitations of probate data, is to find evidence that over time individual credit networks both thickened (each decedent in the second period networked to more credit partners than decedents in the first) and widened (each decedent in the second period networked to more distant credit partners than were decedents in the first). Evidence is presented on both the thickening and widening of markets as an operational restatement of Lance E. Davis's notion of "personal divorcement" to serve as a measure of increasing capital mobility.

From administration accounts the names were taken of every borrower and lender involved in the credit networks of the sample decedents, and with those names three approximations are attempted. The simplest is to count. For the period as a whole, each decedent left on average 17 creditors and/or debtors. But there was enormous variance in the size of these networks, ranging from those who died holding or beholden to no one, to Newell Bent of Cambridge (1831) who left 490 debtors, Abel Bancroft of Groton (1786) who left a young widow to settle with 166 debtors, Tilley Merrick, the Concord storekeeper (1768) with 135 debtors, and Benjamin Blaney of Malden, who in 1750 left his estate to 140 creditors.

Here attention centers on changes over time in the size of these networks. Table 2 compares the average size, standard deviation, and maximum size of networks for five time intervals between 1730 and 1838.

The number of creditors of the average decedent increased from under nineteen in the first period to over twenty-six in the last, and the number of debtors from under four to over twenty-six. Even omitting the aforementioned individuals with exceptionally large networks, the number of credit links decedents had forged increased steadily. When it is recalled that administration accounts at probate contain only those credits and debts outstanding at death—only the unpaid balances left over after a lifetime of borrowing, lending, and litigation—the size of the networks in table 2 may safely be characterized as vastly understating the credit networks of the living.

It is much more difficult to test the hypothesis that credit networks widened in space. To observe changes over time in

Table 2. The average size of credit networks across 5 periods, 1730–1838

	Creditors				Debtors			
Period dates	N	Mean	S.D.	Max.	N	Mean	S.D.	Max.
1730–50	110 (109)	18.7 (17.5)	18.2 (13.9)	140 (81)	107	3.8	9.8	74
1751–70	93	22.2	17.4	75	110 (109)	6.5 (5.1)	15.8 (8.4)	135
1771–90	56	26.0	19.7	106	57 (56)	9.0 (6.2)	24.3 (11.6)	166
1791–1810	116	22.4	17.5	67	124	12.7	17.1	75
1811–38	34	26.1	19.8	73	36 (35)	26.2 (12.9)	81.0 (15.5)	490

SOURCE: Probate documents, Middlesex County Probate Court

NOTE: The numbers in parentheses are calculated omiting the exceptionally large networks. The mean number of creditors (omiting outliers) is significantly different at the 5 percent level in the 5 time periods. Mean number of debtors (omiting outliers) is significantly different at the 1 percent level in the 5 time periods.

the distance between credit partners, one must know the towns both of the decedent and of his partners, but the latter are seldom given in administration accounts. One cannot, in other words, complete the exercise by locating the partners to whom decedents were linked, but some success rewarded the attempt to locate the decedents to whom partners were linked. Just over one-fifth, 22 percent, of the borrowers and lenders were found to be partners of more than one sample decedent.[27] Because the towns of decedents are known, the test consisted in determining whether the decedents to whom these borrowers and lenders were linked were more widely spaced in the second period than in the first. There was dramatic confirmation of some very wide networks in which the same individuals appeared as partners of fifteen, sixteen, even twenty-one different sample decedents in as many as nine different towns across the county. But the hypothesis that there was a significant difference between the first and second periods in the spread of networks could not be confirmed.

There were, however, over 700 instances—468 in the first period, as it happens, and 236 in the second—in which the towns of both parties to each credit transaction were given. For them two grids were drawn with the town of credit partner across the top and the town of decedent down the side; the number of instances of each pairing appears in each cell. In the first-period grid the cells with the largest numbers ran along the diagonal; that is, for the subset of cases for which both towns are known, more loans took place between parties in the same town than between parties in different towns.[28]

---

[27] Because of the ubiquity of parent-naming and Bible-naming in Massachusetts, the pool of names was not large, and it would have been a mistake to have assumed that all appearances of the same name referred to the same individual. John Adamses, for example, abounded. To avoid this problem, various algorithms were employed, but in the end the distinction was made by time: it was assumed that the same name denoted the same individual only if the time interval between appearances of that name was less than 20 years. By holding to this perhaps too stringent rule, the 11,956 names reduced to 8,515 presumably different debtors and creditors, of whom 1,873 or 22 percent appear as partners of two or more sample decedents, and 627 as partners of three or more.

[28] It appears that Concord occupied the center of gravity of the grid in

After the Revolution this pattern changed. In the second-period grid the diagonal lost its dominance. No special bond linked townspeople to one another in what had once been the intimate business of extending credit. Rather one senses a widening search for more far-flung credit partners.

To say "far-flung" suggests a measure of distance, a proxy for which appears in table 3. Here the distance between credit partners in the subset of 700 networks is measured as the number of "towns apart" they are on a county map held constant at its 1838 conformation. The vanishing diagonal appears in the table as a 42 percent decrease in the proportion of networks within the same town. Most of the decrease spills over into a 60 percent increase in links to contiguous towns, and a near doubling of the proportion of networks reaching out of Middlesex County. Indeed, ties to Worcester County alone nearly tripled (as a percent of the whole) after 1781. In the first period, partners living more than two towns away from each other accounted for one-third of these networks; in the second period for 42 percent. This small subsample—700 out of 11,956 borrowers and lenders—modestly confirms the process of market penetration in space (see map).

IV. QUARTILE ANALYSIS OF SHIFTS IN PORTFOLIO COMPOSITION

Table 4 presents a two-period cross-sectional comparison by total wealth quartile of decedents' total wealth, financial assets, debts, and various physical assets. The wealth quartiles,

---

the first period. Not only were there more instances of Concord residents transacting with each other than of any other pairing, but more decedents from all over the county were linked to Concord borrowers and lenders than to any other. While it is true that Concord is both centrally located in the county and was a shire town in the colonial period, the centrality of Concord in the county's credit networks may be an artifact of a local tradition of painstaking estate administration. If such were the case, Concord ties would dominate a subset like this one which, in naming the towns of both credit partners, is unusually painstaking. Incidentally, credit flows between Cambridge and Worcester County ran second to Concord/Concord networks. Thirty decedents owned outlying property in at least one town in Worcester County.

Table 3. The geographical spread of credit networks

	1730–80		1781–1838	
	Number of observations	Percentage of sample	Number of observations	Percentage of sample
Total	468	100.0%	236	100.0%
Same town	155	33.1	45	19.1
Contiguous towns	83	17.7	67	28.4
Two towns apart	74	15.8	26	11.0
Three towns apart	40	8.5	20	8.5
Four towns apart	31	6.6	15	6.4
Five towns apart	20	4.3	11	4.7
Six towns apart	20	4.3	13	5.5
Seven towns apart	3	0.6	3	1.3
Out of Middlesex County	34	7.3	32	13.6
Out of Massachusetts	8	1.7	4	1.7

SOURCE: See text.

NOTES: Based upon the configuration of towns in Middlesex County as of 1838. Significance level of the chi-square statistic = .0005.

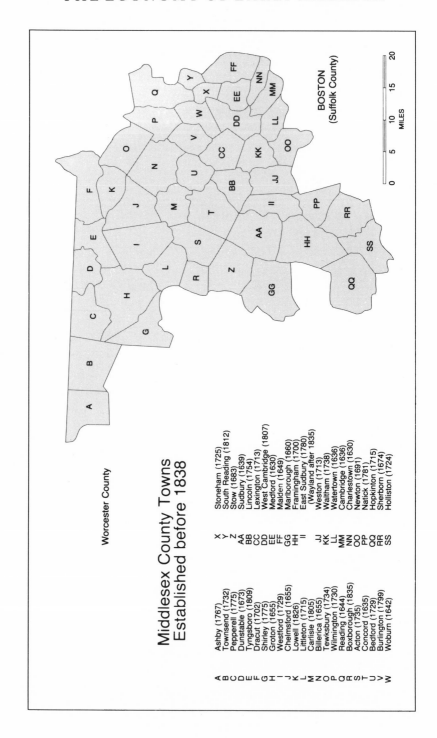

Middlesex County Towns
Established before 1838

A	Ashby (1767)
B	Townsend (1732)
C	Pepperell (1775)
D	Dunstable (1673)
E	Tyngsboro (1809)
F	Dracut (1702)
G	Shirley (1775)
H	Groton (1655)
I	Westford (1729)
J	Chelmsford (1655)
K	Lowell (1826)
L	Littleton (1715)
M	Carlisle (1805)
N	Billerica (1655)
O	Tewksbury (1734)
P	Wilmington (1730)
Q	Reading (1644)
R	Boxborough (1835)
S	Acton (1735)
T	Concord (1635)
U	Bedford (1729)
V	Burlington (1799)
W	Woburn (1642)

X	Stoneham (1725)
Y	South Reading (1812)
Z	Stow (1683)
AA	Sudbury (1639)
BB	Lincoln (1754)
CC	Lexington (1713)
DD	West Cambridge (1807)
EE	Medford (1630)
FF	Malden (1649)
GG	Marlborough (1660)
HH	Framingham (1700)
II	East Sudbury (1780) (Wayland after 1835)
JJ	Weston (1713)
KK	Waltham (1738)
LL	Watertown (1636)
MM	Cambridge (1636)
NN	Charlestown (1630)
OO	Newton (1691)
PP	Natick (1781)
QQ	Hopkinton (1715)
RR	Sherborn (1674)
SS	Holliston (1724)

Worcester County

BOSTON
(Suffolk County)

MILES

0   5   10   15   20

Table 4. Credit activity by wealth: quartile behavior, 1730–1838

	A: Wealth defined as undeflated total wealth							
	First Quartile		Second Quartile		Third Quartile		Fourth Quartile	
	(1) 1730–80	(2) 1781–1838	(1) 1730–80	(2) 1781–1838	(1) 1730–80	(2) 1781–1838	(1) 1730–80	(2) 1781–1838
Total wealth								
Quartile maximum	318.70	1694.90	736.90	3554.60	1583.20	7583.10	23425.10	210199.10
Number observations	71	54	71	54	71	54	70	53
Mean	173.57	1049.13	525.77	2613.61	1096.62	5372.30	3484.79	26457.55
S.D.	77.33	413.19	123.98	560.43	245.02	1139.71	3517.90	36009.69
Real estate								
Maximum	283.30	1500.00	629.40	3152.00	1381.70	6260.00	18099.10	76620.00
Mean	51.45	470.34	302.88	1688.73	749.62	3629.75	2484.56	10818.28
S.D.	70.11	424.61	177.57	783.98	292.55	1289.53	2884.97	11719.95
Real estate/Wealth								
Maximum	.99	.95	.99	.99	.94	.97	.96	.96
Mean	.27	.41	.56	.63	.68	.68	.69	.54
Distance (mean)	4.68	5.00	4.75	4.70	4.40	4.30	3.70	3.30
PPW								
Maximum	318.70	1080.20	522.20	1100.30	625.20	2936.60	2473.10	41094.00
Mean	80.35	285.35	158.96	471.50	243.56	915.52	536.62	2731.82
S.D.	64.27	186.33	104.11	219.39	102.72	593.78	474.27	5794.87
PPW/Wealth								
Maximum	1.00	1.00	.89	.40	.84	.53	.50	.60
Mean	.48	.33	.31	.18	.23	.17	.17	.12
Financial assets								
Maximum	264.60	1455.60	458.30	2454.50	1162.00	4926.10	4088.30	130886.60
Mean	41.76	293.44	63.93	453.38	103.44	827.02	463.61	12907.45

Table 4. Credit activity by wealth: quartile behavior, 1730–1838 *(continued)*

A: Wealth defined as undeflated total wealth

	First Quartile		Second Quartile		Third Quartile		Fourth Quartile	
	(1) 1730–80	(2) 1781–1838	(1) 1730–80	(2) 1781–1838	(1) 1730–80	(2) 1781–1838	(1) 1730–80	(2) 1781–1838
Financial assets/Wealth								
Maximum	1.00	.90	.89	.98	.80	.69	1.00	.96
Mean	.25	.26	.13	.18	.09	.15	.14	.34
Acres								
Maximum	100.00	399.00	171.00	230.00	505.00	379.00	5224.50	10000.00
Mean	16.00	30.00	45.00	80.00	83.50	134.00	267.00	429.00
Debts								
Maximum	469.60	7698.50	1318.90	5226.20	938.70	7391.00	4770.20	188975.50
Mean	71.92	576.68	135.23	857.35	203.43	1794.00	650.18	6268.95
Debts/Wealth								
Maximum	1.99	7.13	3.16	2.89	.75	1.37	1.48	1.18
Mean	.41	.60	.27	.38	.19	.34	.20	.18
Net assets (financial assets − debts)								
Maximum	165.50	1455.60	448.20	2189.20	1122.30	3112.90	2804.10	124904.60
Mean	−31.94	−321.91	−74.26	−423.90	−94.59	−903.64	−168.60	6960.45
S.D.	108.19	1336.54	223.97	1187.72	326.65	1990.39	1058.61	25026.45
Net worth (wealth − debts)								
Maximum	296.20	1674.60	687.90	3467.90	1519.80	7530.80	19894.10	136785.10
Mean	107.53	441.49	385.63	1802.36	881.48	3442.16	2628.46	20966.84
S.D.	104.89	1266.71	222.67	1378.94	286.63	1830.23	2902.30	25873.34
FPC/Wealth								
Maximum	.69	.49	.52	.18	.31	.14	.19	.07
Mean	.19	.08	.14	.06	.10	.05	.07	.02
NFPC/Wealth								
Maximum	.33	.15	.14	.09	.11	.21	.24	.52
Mean	.01	.01	.01	.01	.01	.01	.01	.02

B: Wealth defined as deflated total wealth

	First Quartile		Second Quartile		Third Quartile		Fourth Quartile	
	(1) 1730–80	(2) 1781–1838	(1) 1730–80	(2) 1781–1838	(1) 1730–80	(2) 1781–1838	(1) 1730–80	(2) 1781–1838
Total wealth								
Quartile maximum	597.70	1679.43	1372.71	3649.58	2713.51	7067.19	47095.72	195898.50
Number observations	71	54	71	54	70	53	71	54
Mean	341.15	1058.67	998.27	2663.56	1978.49	5229.91	6188.73	24407.64
S.D.	153.42	433.61	245.97	607.97	413.98	1046.53	7091.58	32691.77
Real estate								
Maximum	481.51	1382.98	1182.24	3062.88	2290.94	5864.84	39099.60	71407.25
Mean	91.84	497.43	600.55	1710.61	1389.62	3538.23	4397.89	10121.96
S.D.	129.10	434.92	339.58	810.71	526.10	1395.33	5881.83	10805.52
Real estate/Wealth								
Maximum	0.94	0.95	0.99	0.99	0.94	0.97	0.96	0.96
Mean	0.24	0.42	0.59	0.63	0.70	0.68	0.68	0.55
Distance (mean)	4.90	4.90	4.60	4.50	4.40	4.60	3.60	3.20
PPW								
Maximum	524.18	976.67	790.27	1115.92	1346.29	2848.31	6868.77	37155.52
Mean	159.91	297.13	296.72	468.19	432.20	876.59	943.99	2540.25
S.D.	121.83	197.60	168.34	231.94	200.71	546.02	1039.86	5237.25
PPW/Wealth								
Maximum	1.00	1.00	0.89	0.40	0.84	0.53	0.50	0.60
Mean	0.49	0.33	0.31	0.18	0.22	0.17	0.17	0.13
Financial assets								
Maximum	455.18	1651.06	1048.17	2229.34	1833.01	6351.31	6901.12	121981.30
Mean	89.40	264.11	101.00	484.75	156.67	815.10	846.85	11745.43
Financial assets/Wealth								
Maximum	1.00	0.98	0.82	0.90	0.70	0.96	1.00	0.95
Mean	0.27	0.25	0.11	0.20	0.08	0.16	0.15	0.33

Table 4. Credit activity by wealth: quartile behavior, 1730–1838 (*continued*)

B: Wealth defined as deflated total wealth

	First Quartile		Second Quartile		Third Quartile		Fourth Quartile	
	(1) 1730–80	(2) 1781–1838	(1) 1730–80	(2) 1781–1838	(1) 1730–80	(2) 1781–1838	(1) 1730–80	(2) 1781–1838
Acres								
Maximum	100.00	399.00	102.00	243.00	505.00	379.00	5224.00	10000.00
Mean	14.00	30.50	44.00	79.00	83.00	140.00	265.00	411.00
Debts								
Maximum	984.54	6960.67	3663.11	6350.18	1895.44	6415.80	8240.98	176118.80
Mean	140.50	598.19	257.66	928.33	402.35	1574.42	1088.17	5809.85
Debts/Wealth								
Maximum	2.00	7.13	3.16	2.89	0.75	1.37	1.48	1.18
Mean	0.42	0.63	0.25	0.37	0.21	0.31	0.18	0.19
Net assets (financial assets − debts)								
Maximum	448.33	1324.60	1048.17	1988.37	1797.37	2784.35	6036.26	110731.10
Mean	−49.76	−359.86	−154.50	−468.28	−250.45	−817.97	−212.22	6110.98
S.D.	216.76	1231.79	457.37	1341.98	499.12	1809.93	2016.34	21827.21
Net worth (wealth − debts)								
Maximum	586.45	1562.34	1340.59	3517.14	2588.40	6883.88	32087.26	121263.46
Mean	211.56	441.79	755.18	1792.05	1563.52	3487.10	4576.03	18948.84
S.D.	207.22	1171.25	504.15	1447.19	530.98	1713.40	4602.26	22778.92
FPC/Wealth								
Maximum	0.69	0.49	0.52	0.18	0.31	0.14	0.19	0.09
Mean	0.19	0.08	0.14	0.06	0.09	0.05	0.07	0.02
NFPC/Wealth								
Maximum	0.33	0.15	0.14	0.08	0.11	0.21	0.24	0.52
Mean	0.01	0.01	0.01	0.01	0.01	0.01	0.01	0.02

SOURCES: See text.

NOTES: Definitions of variables: *PPW* = portable physical wealth; *FPC* = farm physical capital; *NFPC* = nonfarm physical capital; Wealth = Total wealth. See text for definitions of other variables and for deflator. All magnitudes in part A are in current dollars; all magnitudes in part B are in constant dollars deflated by my Massachusetts farm-product price index (1795–1805 = 100) constructed for the period 1750 to 1855 and extrapolated backwards to 1730 using a nonlinear trend fitted by an OLS regression:

Index/1000 = 0.221 + 0.145 × 10⁻¹ Time − 0.51 × 10⁻⁴ Time squared

This procedure yields values for observations before 1750 as follows: 1730 = 23.5, 1739 = 36.0, 1742 = 40.0, 1743 = 41.3, 1744 = 42.6, 1745 = 43.9, 1746 = 45.2, 1747 = 46.4, 1748 = 47.7, 1749 = 48.9. See Winifred B. Rothenberg, "A Price Index for Rural Massachusetts, 1750–1855," *Journal of Economic History* 39 (1979): 975–1001; index is on pp. 983–85.

columns 1 in the first period and columns 2 in the second, reveal the striking increase over time in borrowing, lending, and the shift of wealth shares from physical to financial assets across the wealth spectrum.

The sample decedents in each period are here ranked and sorted by total wealth, that is, by the value of real estate + *PPW* + financial assets. Financial assets are defined as loans and mortgages + securities + cash.

Attention should be drawn at the outset to the finding that the quartile results are sensitive to the wealth measure employed to rank and sort the cases. Using total wealth results in all but the wealthiest second-period decedents emerging as net debtors. But if the sample had been ranked and sorted by *PPW,* all second-period quartiles except one (the second) would have appeared as net creditors, a spurious outcome, as it happens, but one that would have had momentous implications. This sensitivity lies in the fact that the share of wealth invested in *PPW* across quartiles diminishes with increasing wealth and over time (see figure 1) so that sorting by *PPW* acts perversely to deposit in the *bottom* quartiles just those wealthy decedents who had invested most heavily in financial assets. But far from handicapping the exercise, this very lack of robustness itself confirms the shift in the composition of wealth away from physical capital and toward financial instruments.

But there is more direct evidence of that shift in table 4. Farm physical capital (*FPC*) as a share of total wealth decreased sharply between the first and second periods in every quartile, and nonfarm physical capital (*NFPC*) maintained, with curious constancy, its 1 percent share of wealth, while mean holdings of financial assets tripled for the poorest, quadrupled for the second, increased fivefold for the third and nearly thirteenfold for the richest quartile. Financial assets/wealth, that is financial assets as a share of wealth, doubled for all but the poorest. Debts, in the meantime, increased in each quartile in a pattern that suggests that debt is a logistically shaped function of wealth.

Although all quartiles, save the last one in the second period, remain on average net debtors, there are decedents in each who appear to be specialized lenders, whose holdings of

Figure 1
Shift in the debt share and asset shares of wealth by quartile and period

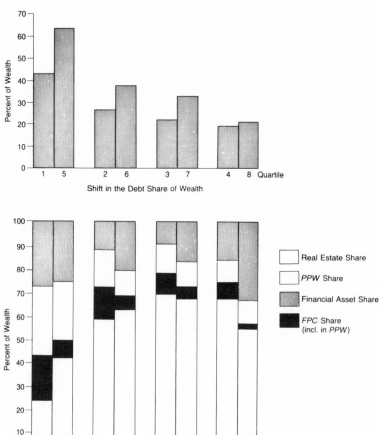

NOTES: Quartiles 1-4 = first period; quartiles 5-8 = second period.

financial assets far exceed their debts. That this is true in each quartile and that the variance (standard deviation) of net financial position, net assets = (financial assets − debts), rises sharply with wealth, suggests that wealth is not determining, or is not acting alone to determine, those net outcomes. The regression analysis in the next section tests the hypothetical determinants of the marked increases in financial activities across wealth quartiles and over time.

V. THE DETERMINANTS OF PORTFOLIO COMPOSITION: REGRESSION ANALYSIS

Farmers have always extended credit to one another. Farming, with its long production periods, seasonal discontinuities, and periodic disasters is unimaginable without credit. It is not, then, the presence of promissory notes in rural portfolios that makes a capital market. Rather it is the displacement by financial assets of embodied physical capital, the shift in the composition of rural assets away from cattle and implements and toward evanescent forms of wealth whose liquidity is énhanced by the collective willingness to make that shift. In the previous quartile analysis the shift was placed between the first and second periods and confirmed at all wealth levels. What remains to be explored is the causal path: Upon what variables did market forces work to explain the observed changes?

The specification of the regressions hypothesizes that decedents' financial behavior is explained by the following variables: total wealth, distance (from Boston), owned acres, and time, which picks up the development of the regional economy generally.[29] The strength of the overall specification is confirmed by the high R^2 values on the pooled sample. The strength of the periodization—indeed the strength of the hypothesis of this article—is abundantly confirmed by the gains in R^2 in all second-period equations using the entire sample, and by the Chow-test results, which reveal that the

[29] The variable acres in these regressions is carrying added freight as a proxy for that elusive thing, a noncommercial mentalité. A simple farmer/nonfarmer occupational dummy would have been preferable, but it is compromised by the ubiquity of by-employments; and investment in farm versus nonfarm physical capital raises simultaneity problems with total wealth of which they are components. I am grateful to Robert Margo and an anonymous referee for bringing the simultaneity problem to my attention.

structure of explanation of portfolio behavior in the two periods is very different.

Financial Asset Holdings

(1) The total wealth variable: Column 1 of table 5 gives the
regression results with an $R^2 = .91$ for the pooled sample.
Decedents' wealth is the principal determinant of financial
holdings. Additional equations, not presented here, confirm
that those holdings increased more than proportionally with
increasing wealth, and that wealth is the dominant determinant also of the share of wealth held in the form of financial
instruments.

Following the procedure used throughout the study, regressions are run on the pooled sample and on the two subperiods, and these in turn are compared both with and without the wealthiest 5 percent of decedents. The comparisons
reveal three subfindings. First, the strength of the relationship between total wealth and financial assets is a postwar
phenomenon, shown by the very large increase between the
first and second periods in both the size and significance of
the coefficient on total wealth. Second, the high wealth elasticity of these holdings, 2.5 at the mean for the pooled
sample, is also a second-period phenomenon; wealth elasticity shifts from 0.4 before the war to 2.0 after. Third, when
the wealthiest 5 percent of the sample is removed and the
behavior of the poorest 95 percent is observed separately, the
sharp discontinuity between the two periods is muted. The
coefficient on total wealth increases, is always positive and
confidently significant, and the elasticity at the mean (always
above unity) increases slightly, but these are not dramatic
shifts. They are rather a strengthening of relationships that
were as true in the earlier years as in the later.

I see this finding as revealing the behavioral consequences
of the observations, made previously, about changes in the
structural elements of capital transfer. New types of credit
instruments emerged in the postwar period and were taken
up by the very rich whose portfolio behavior was transformed
by their appearance, while poorer decedents were making
incremental adjustments to patterns of lending traditional to
farmers. In other words, this reading of the results would

Table 5. The determinants of liquidity

<table>
<tr><td rowspan="3"></td><td colspan="6">A. Financial assets[a]</td></tr>
<tr><td colspan="2">Pooled
1730–1838</td><td colspan="2">First period
1730–80</td><td colspan="2">Second period
1781–1838</td></tr>
<tr><td>Entire
sample</td><td>Lowest 95
percent[b]</td><td>Entire
sample</td><td>Lowest 95
percent</td><td>Entire
sample</td><td>Lowest 95
percent</td></tr>
<tr><td>Constant</td><td>−2000.6
(−4.84)</td><td>−192.25
(−1.25)</td><td>182.33
(1.05)</td><td>57.88
(.38)</td><td>−3219.8
(−2.10)</td><td>−520.66
(−.80)</td></tr>
<tr><td>Total wealth[c]</td><td>.83
(48.49)</td><td>.30
(13.40)</td><td>.05
(2.75)</td><td>.19
(7.55)</td><td>.85
(38.01)</td><td>.34
(9.66)</td></tr>
<tr><td>Acres</td><td>−4.71
(−12.70)</td><td>−3.53
(−5.21)</td><td>.61
(3.11)</td><td>−1.09
(−1.63)</td><td>−4.60
(−8.54)</td><td>−4.60
(−3.92)</td></tr>
<tr><td>Distance (from Boston)[d]</td><td>269.44
(3.61)</td><td>20.20
(.71)</td><td>−55.05
(−2.04)</td><td>−9.13
(−.36)</td><td>256.83
(2.11)</td><td>27.98
(.53)</td></tr>
<tr><td>Time</td><td>−19.31
(−3.70)</td><td>.54
(.27)</td><td>7.29
(1.57)</td><td>−2.34
(−.54)</td><td>−6.86
(−.36)</td><td>3.36
(.42)</td></tr>
<tr><td>Number of observations</td><td>415</td><td>397</td><td>228</td><td>225</td><td>187</td><td>172</td></tr>
<tr><td>R^2</td><td>.91</td><td>.38</td><td>.32</td><td>.29</td><td>.94</td><td>.38</td></tr>
</table>

<table>
<tr><td rowspan="3"></td><td colspan="6">B. Debts</td></tr>
<tr><td colspan="2">Pooled
1730–1838</td><td colspan="2">First period
1730–80</td><td colspan="2">Second period
1781–1838</td></tr>
<tr><td>Entire
sample</td><td>Lowest 95
percent</td><td>Entire
sample</td><td>Lowest 95
percent</td><td>Entire
sample</td><td>Lowest 95
percent</td></tr>
<tr><td>Constant</td><td>−1234.7
(−1.84)</td><td>−42.48
(−.21)</td><td>−76.86
(−.32)</td><td>−16.55
(−.77)</td><td>−1061.9
(−.73)</td><td>−198.22
(−.25)</td></tr>
<tr><td>Total wealth</td><td>.17
(6.56)</td><td>.11
(3.96)</td><td>.25
(8.87)</td><td>.08
(2.18)</td><td>.0011
(.053)</td><td>.13
(2.94)</td></tr>
<tr><td>Acres</td><td>10.87
(19.21)</td><td>1.77
(2.06)</td><td>−.64
(−2.46)</td><td>4.20
(4.71)</td><td>17.04
(34.57)</td><td>.045
(.03)</td></tr>
<tr><td>Distance (from Boston)</td><td>121.46
(1.00)</td><td>−40.54
(−1.1)</td><td>−12.34
(−.33)</td><td>−74.86
(−2.13)</td><td>−183.77
(−1.57)</td><td>−9.46
(−0.14)</td></tr>
<tr><td>Time</td><td>−2.28
(−.27)</td><td>11.37
(4.30)</td><td>4.32
(.68)</td><td>12.63
(2.15)</td><td>19.46
(1.07)</td><td>12.65
(1.28)</td></tr>
<tr><td>Number of observations</td><td>358</td><td>342</td><td>190</td><td>188</td><td>168</td><td>154</td></tr>
<tr><td>R^2</td><td>.91</td><td>.21</td><td>.44</td><td>.31</td><td>.95</td><td>.09</td></tr>
</table>

SOURCES: See text.

NOTES: t-statistics are in parentheses. A Chow test of the difference between the first and second period regressions is significant at the 0.1 percent level.

[a] Financial assets = (loans + mortgages) + securities + cash.

[b] Refers to the lowest 95% of the sample, that is, it excludes the top 5%, the wealthiest 23 estates as measured by total wealth.

[c] Total wealth = value of (real estate + PPW + financial assets).

[d] Distance is measured as the number of towns on a straight line between decedent's town and Boston. See text.

suggest that the capital market was rather thin throughout the period.

Speaking more generally, however, the increasingly close association over time between financial asset holdings and total wealth must have had important macroeconomic consequences, for it suggests that the rise in wealth, both nominal and real, observed across all wealth quartiles in table 4, itself contributed, through the increasing wealth elasticity of demand for credit instruments, to the enhanced liquidity of these instruments and hence to the emergence and integration of a capital market.

(2) The acres variable: The strongly negative coefficients on farm size in the pooled regressions support the hypothesis of competition between investment in land, on the one hand, and investment in financial assets on the other. And this is true whether the very rich are present or not. But the period breakdowns reveal that the coefficients on acres are not all negative. That the sign on acres is positive for the full sample in the first period suggests that in the early years the income effect of the wealth of the very rich on landholdings overwhelmed the substitution effect between landholdings and financial holdings, until a market emerged in financial holdings. The decision of the wealthy in the second period to substitute ephemeral forms of property for land itself is of enormous consequence for the economic development of Massachusetts, and it appears in the regressions as a shift in sign, an increase in significance, and an increase in the size of the coefficient on acres.

(3) The distance variable: Distance (from Boston) measures the decedents' access to the center of the financial market. Its use as an independent variable in these regressions, like the analysis of the mobility of capital particularly in table 3, treats the capital market as an economic phenomenon with spatial extension. The implicit hypothesis is that the "magnetic field" of an underdeveloped market will extend (geographically) little if at all beyond its center, while the magnetic field of a more developed and integrated market will penetrate (geographically) farther from its center, and that penetration can then be used to testify to the development of that market.

Distance is construed in the regressions as an integer variable that measures, not miles, but the number of towns (on a straight line) between the decedent's town and Boston. Distance values run from one, for towns contiguous to Boston, to nine, for Ashby, the westernmost town in the county. Because the unit in which distance is measured is the number of "towns between," that unit is standardized across time by holding the county map constant at its configuration as of 1838. Thus, the seventeen new towns carved out of the corners of old ones and incorporated between 1730 and 1838 are assumed for this purpose to have been there throughout the period. Distance was measured the same way in table 3. In 1838 the size and configuration of towns were nearly equal, making "towns between" in 1838 not a bad unit for measuring distance.

Because the cardinal ordering of the distance variable increases as distance increases, a negative sign on its coefficient would imply a narrow capital market restricted to the immediate hinterland of its center, while a positive sign would imply a wider and thicker capital market penetrating the more distant reaches of the county. The signs in the regression results confirm the hypothesis of market extension. The impact of distance from Boston upon the holding of financial assets shifts from negative in the first period to positive in the second.

But there is an interesting lack of transitivity in the relations between the three variables: total wealth decreases with distance from Boston and financial assets move with total wealth. That nevertheless a positive relation emerges in the second period between distance and financial assets becomes a phenomenon of considerable interest. The decision of more distant decedents to increase their financial holdings was being made in the face of first-order pressures acting to decrease their wealth.

Debts

Using the same specification to explain the level of debt as was used to explain the level of financial assets gives a very strong $R^2 = .91$, but only in the pooled sample when the very rich are included. The hypothesis of a discontinuity between

Figure 2

Shift in the composition of financial assets by quartile and period

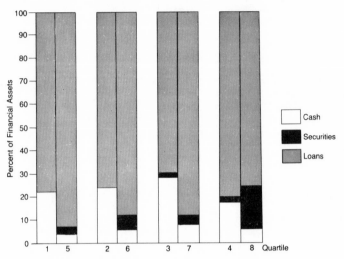

NOTES: Financial assets = (loans and mortgages) + securities + cash. Quartiles 1-4 = first period; quartiles 5-8 = second period.

the first and second periods is amply confirmed with both the full and the truncated samples, but they seem to have experienced the discontinuity differently. For poorer decedents, wealth is a significant (and, notice, positive) determinant of the level of debts. For the very rich, wealth, which had been important in the first period, fades into insignificance in the second, and acres alone explains their second-period debts. In other words, there appears to have been what may be called an "implicit mortgage market," where acreage set limits on the level of borrowing, but stopped short of being collateral.

What were the rich borrowing for? Not for private physical capital formation—that was retreating as a share of assets (see figure 2). The very rich were borrowing in order to lend, using their acreage in some as yet undefined way to underwrite their borrowing while at the same time shifting the composition of their assets out of farming and into commercial paper. The very rich were coming into the capital market on both sides. And they alone were emerging as net creditors.

VI. CONCLUSION

Why did industrialization happen first in Massachusetts? Why, once begun, did it take root so successfully? What had prepared the rural economy for such a transformation? In an earlier study I confirmed that a network of integrated product markets had emerged in the farm economy of Massachusetts considerably in advance of industrialization. The present study confirms that, at about the same time, a regional capital market emerged in Boston's agricultural hinterland; it mobilized the supply of agricultural savings and channeled them toward new investments on the cutting edge of growth.

Using a data base built on the indebtedness of a probate sample of 512 decedents in rural Middlesex County between 1730 and 1838, this article has tested three propositions about a capital market: the appearance of developmental financial institutions, the increased mobility of capital, and the enhanced liquidity of asset holdings. It has also explored the determinants of that critical metamorphosis.

How is the enhanced liquidity of rural portfolios related to the transformation of the rural economy? The answer emerges from the network, quartile, and regression analyses. The enhanced liquidity of rural portfolios *is* the transformation of the rural economy. This phenomenon, it seems to me, must henceforth loom large in whatever is meant by the coming of capitalism to the New England village economy. Capitalism is necessarily, even if not sufficiently, the creature of a developed capital market. And that market, in eastern Massachusetts, can be dated to the early years of national independence.

APPENDIX

After death, then as now, an inventory was usually filed in the county probate court, and the debts and bequests of the deceased were then paid out of the value of the estate by an executor (if there was a will), or by an administrator (if there was none) who lodged one or several accounts with the court as debts were paid and outstanding credits collected. The usual form of the administration account was, first, for the administrator to acknowledge his responsibility for ("he charges himself with") the value of total personal estate left by the deceased as per the inventory. To that was added whatever may have been received since the inventory was taken (revenues from the sale of personal property, payments of debts owed to the estate), or additional property that may have been overlooked.

The administrator then "craves allowance" for expenditures he made out of the estate to pay its debts, and those payments were usually listed in the accounts by name and amount. It is these, together with the credits, that constitute the data in my analysis. I omit other charges the administrator claimed such as probate fees, journeys to settle debts, the cost of legal advice, of surveying, of advertising for creditors, or medical care for the deceased's last illness, of mourning clothes for the family, of the funeral, and of digging the grave.

If there was no will, the first claim upon the estate, before debts were paid and before legacies were distributed, was the widow's portion—her "dower" was one-third of the personal estate, her "thirds" was one-third of the real estate. Claims to widows' portions are also omitted from this analysis.

Obligations to creditors were paid, first, out of cash in the hands of the administrator; if that was not sufficient, out of court-ordered sales of two-thirds of the personal estate. What remained was distributed according to the will, if there was one; or if there was none, according to Massachusetts law which prescribed equal shares to the children. (A double share went to the eldest son by law until 1784).

If, however, debts still remained, the court ordered the sale of as much real estate as was needed to pay them, again saving out of the sale the widow's thirds. There were a very few cases where the widow relinquished her claim to satisfy all creditors of her late husband, but she need not. If claims still remained after two-thirds of the real estate and two-thirds of the personal estate had been sold to pay them, then the estate was declared insolvent, and creditors paid off proportionately, so many pence on the pound or cents on the dollar which, in the judge's words, "is all they can receive until the widow's death," at which time creditors were able once again to attach liens to the property.

Inventories, administrators' accounts, wills, reports of the real estate commissioners, reports of the insolvency commissioners, reports of the sale of personal estate—these are the documents that yielded the data base for this study. The 512 individuals came from 47 towns (a uniquely New England way of referring to what are in fact not towns) in Middlesex County, only one of which (Charlestown, now and since 1873 a part of Boston) was urban throughout the period 1730 to 1838. Confirming the rural nature of this sample is the fact that of the 479 males, 419 were farmers; that is, their inventories contained a full complement of husbandry tools and of livestock.

For each individual the following data were obtained: (1) Year of inventory, which, because inventories were supposed to be taken within one month of death, is usually the year of death. (2) Town in which the homestead is located; other towns in which the deceased owned property. (3) Number of acres owned in that town, and in outlying towns. (4) The value of all real estate (taken from the inventory unless superseded by a more careful reappraisal by the court-appointed real estate commissioners). (5) Occupation(s), ascertained from how he or she was described in the records, or from the kind of tools dominating the inventory, or from the ownership of a shop, store, mill or wharf. Of the occupations coded, twenty-two were artisan crafts, five were professions, four were what one might call "condition": widow, soldier, tenant, Indian. The most frequent occupation was yeoman or husbandman; the terms seem to have been used interchangeably in American parlance. (6) The value of all husbandry tools. Carriages and chaises were excluded. (7)

The value of all nonfarm tools, raw material inventories, stock-in-trade, in other words, nonfarm physical capital. (8) The value of all livestock, including bees and barnyard fowl. (9) The value of all provisions and animal feeds, that is, the output of the farm. The sum of items 6 through 9, plus the value of wearing apparel and all household goods, constitute the portable physical wealth (*PPW*) of the deceased.

Financial assets, if any, are defined as loans and mortgages plus securities plus cash, and included: (10) Cash on hand, usually paper, but occasionally silver or gold coins, and, rarely, bank deposits. The posthumous payments of soldiers' wages for the several campaigns of this period were also placed here. (11) The value of securities. I used the realized market value which appears in administration accounts, not the par value that appeared in inventories. (12) The value of outstanding notes and book accounts owed to the estate and not on interest. (13) The value of notes and bonds on interest, the interest, and (where it can be calculated) the interest rate. (14) The value of mortgages held by the deceased. When these were interest-bearing (and even these were not always so), the interest was placed in the previous column. (15) The value of notes deemed uncollectable. I included these "bad" notes among the financial assets of the creditor—the loan had in fact been made, after all—but deducted them from financial assets in the calculation of net worth on the assumption that if not collected, those funds were not available to the estate for the payment of its debts. But estate administrators often erred; some debts called bad were in fact paid, some considered good were not.

The payments of accrued rents due to the estate were viewed as a flow variable, and hence were excluded from financial assets, viewed here as stocks. Debts were: (16) Notes and book accounts owed to others and not on interest. (17) Notes and bonds owed to others which were demonstrably on interest. (18) Mortgages held against the deceased, and rents owed to others.

In addition, three characteristics were flagged: (19) Insolvency. (20) Whether the interest rate, if it can be calculated, was equal to, greater than, or less than the 6 percent customary rate. (21) The presence of endorsements on notes.

Currency Conversions

While comparative studies—of two or more colonial economies, or of a colony and England—typically convert provincial currencies into pound-sterling equivalents, here it was preferable to render all money values into their U.S. dollar equivalents. Over the study period, in addition to specie, five paper currencies circulated at one time or another in Massachusetts: New Tenor, Old Tenor, Lawful Money, Continentals, and U.S. dollars. Excepting the Continental, these currencies bore a statutory relationship to one another at the time that each redeemed the "sunken" one that went before it. Old Tenor equalled four (sometimes 4.5) times the New Tenor which had preceded it—New Tenor appears occasionally on inventories from the 1730s—and 7.5 times the Lawful Money which followed it; one pound Lawful Money = 3.334 U.S. dollars. Therefore, entries in Old Tenor were divided by 7.5 to convert to Lawful Money and multiplied by 3.334 to convert to dollars. Entries in New Tenor were multiplied by 0.533 or by 0.6 (that is, multiplied by 4 or 4.5 and divided by 7.5) to convert to Lawful Money and then multiplied by 3.334 to convert to dollars. The Continental was almost never used as a medium of account. On the two occasions when it was, conversion rates could be ascertained from other values in the document or from other documents in the packet, or from the monthly conversion ratios that were discovered in the Executor's Account of Hannah Cordis (Curtis), Middlesex County Probate, 1st ser., no. 330.

THOMAS M. DOERFLINGER

Farmers and Dry Goods in the Philadelphia Market Area, 1750–1800

UPON PERUSING HIS COPY of the *Pennsylvania Gazette* for April 14, 1773, a subscriber would immediately notice a long advertisement that took up more than a third of the front page. "Lately imported from London, Bristol, and Holland," the announcement began, "and to be Sold on the cheapest terms by DANIEL BENEZET at his STORE in Arch-Street, four doors below the corner of Second Street." There followed a monotonous list of the goods that Benezet was offering for sale, a catalogue that ran to 199 classes of merchandise. Some of these goods are familiar enough to the modern consumer— "horn combs," "common hand-saws," and "common pewter table spoons," for example—but much of Benezet's inventory bore bizarre labels that are meaningless today. "Double-pressed superfine durrants," "blue, green and brown calimancoes," "common plain camblets," and "broad Scotch cambletees" were to be found on Benezet's shelves, along with superfine ratinets, common grazets, black padusoys, and single tandem silesias. Benezet was particularly proud of his selection of "fine ell wide pompadour, purple and light grounds true Indian chintz morees." Obscure enough to us, these terms for various styles and grades of cloth were full of meaning to the advertisement's intended readers, the retail shopkeepers of Philadelphia and its far-flung agricultural hinterland. From Reading, Pa., to Newcastle, Del., from Trenton, N.J., to Winchester, Va., retailers intently inspected Benezet's list to learn whether the rich old Quaker merchant

was selling anything that might appeal to the farmers, craftsmen, and housewives of their neighborhoods.

For precisely this reason, Benezet's advertisement should
be of interest to historians as well. Benezet and his customers
were the central figures in a major branch of commerce in
the Middle Atlantic region during much of the eighteenth
century, the dry goods trade.[1] Because it moved a great variety of goods from the factories of Great Britain to the cup-
boards and chests in thousands of rural homesteads, this
well-documented commercial circuit is, in effect, a window
overlooking economic life in the early American countryside.
Yet few historians have peered through this window to view
the world of the Middle Atlantic rural consumer. Such is the
purpose of the present paper. After describing the dry goods
trade in the Philadelphia market area in the latter half of the
eighteenth century, the essay will explore the relevance of
that trade to the region's rural economy as a whole.

By the late colonial period, Philadelphia's dry goods trade
had assumed a well-defined structure.[2] The key figures on

---

[1] The dry goods trade was extremely important and fairly standardized
by the 1770s. Certain merchants were known as "dry goods merchants,"
although they might also deal in other goods, and these wholesalers, in
advertisements to the public, used standard phrases such as "Merchandise" and "European and East India Goods" to refer to dry goods. When
the items for sale were enumerated, as in the advertisement by Daniel
Benezet discussed above, cloth was almost always featured.

From the perspective of the Pennsylvania farmer, the dry goods trade
did not change importantly during the Revolutionary era, but of course it
was far from static. After the Revolution a larger number of British firms,
as well as many Continental ones, became involved in the dry goods trade,
and as the Industrial Revolution progressed in England it moved north-
ward toward Liverpool. Control tended to shift from a handful of Lon-
don-based merchant-bankers to wealthy manufacturing houses based in
the Midlands. Many European merchants, including junior partners of
major firms, moved to Philadelphia during the 1780s to sell goods. Consequently, the trade was less clearly organized, and more fluid and volatile,
than it had been before the war.

[2] See Arthur L. Jensen, *The Maritime Commerce of Colonial Philadelphia*
(Madison, Wis., 1963); Philip L. White, *The Beekmans of New York in Politics
and Commerce, 1647–1877* (New York, 1956), pp. 335–485. Marc Egnal,

the European side of the Atlantic were a small group of ten to fifteen English export merchants located in London, Bristol, and Liverpool. These great commercial houses, which were among the most powerful in the empire, received orders for merchandise from hundreds of merchants in Philadelphia and other American ports. They purchased the goods from English middlemen and shipped them across the Atlantic, extending twelve months' credit to their American customers, who took title to the goods. For these commercial and financial services, the English firms charged a 2½ percent commission on the invoice value of the goods. In the period 1749–75, and again during the 1780s and 1790s, these aggressive English firms freely granted credit to American traders, who ranged in stature from ambitious shopkeepers to "merchant princes" like Daniel Benezet. By the 1770s well over half of Philadelphia's 320 merchants were importing dry goods, though the larger importers were frequently involved in other commercial activities as well.

Although he typically maintained open accounts with scores of customers, the Philadelphia importer sold the majority of his goods to a core group of retailers and artisans, usually numbering between ten and forty. To these accounts he would send several large shipments of dry goods, ranging in value from £50 to £600, each year.[3] Some of the rural shopkeepers operated small neighborhood establishments on an informal basis; others were locally prominent businessmen who sold thousands of pounds of dry goods annually and carried on a variety of related business activities. Not a few retailers were successful businesswomen. Whether large or small, rural retailers were usually careful not to become

---

"The Pennsylvania Economy, 1748–1762: An Analysis of Short-Run Fluctuations in the Context of Long-Run Changes in the Atlantic Trading Community," Ph.D. diss., University of Wisconsin, 1974, pp. 13–272, places the dry goods trade within its larger economic context. Among the dozens of relevant manuscript collections, see particularly the William Pollard Letterbook, 1772–74, and Joseph Turner Letterbook, 1753–74, both in the Historical Society of Pennsylvania (HSPA), Philadelphia, and the Stephen Collins Papers, Library of Congress.

[3] All monetary values are stated in pounds Pennsylvania currency unless otherwise stated; £167 currency equals £100 sterling.

dependent on just one dry goods supplier, and they also did business with a provision merchant or wholesale grocer in Philadelphia who sold them rum, sugar, molasses, coffee, spices, and other "groceries."[4]

In the country towns, as in Philadelphia, purveyors of dry goods were numerous. Thirty-eight shopkeepers lived in Lancaster, Pa., in 1759 (although competition later reduced the number dramatically), and 10 of Reading's 267 taxpayers were retailers in 1767.[5] These traders battled aggressively for customers, using a wide range of tactics to best their ubiquitous rivals. Though still underdeveloped in America, the art of advertising was not altogether neglected. Advertisements for dry goods abounded in inland newspapers, and one retailer ran off 500 handbills announcing the opening of his store.[6] Knowing how fussy and demanding their customers could be, shopkeepers were careful to stock merchandise of the most popular styles. More than one Philadelphia importer went broke by ignoring the whims of the rural consumer; itinerant wholesalers from Europe were particularly prone to this fate.[7] In a typical comment, a Philadelphia merchant remarked to his English supplier, "Should they be such

[4] See Thomas Armat to John Lorain, Aug. 28, 1789, Thomas Armat Letterbook, 1782–92, Loudoun Papers, Thomas Armat Section, HSPA, for an informative, if in some respects atypical, example of a shopkeeper's business strategy. Armat figured that Lorain should have an inventory of £800—£600 in dry goods and £200 in groceries—which could be turned over three times annually, producing sales of £2,400 and a projected gross profit of 25 percent.

[5] Jerome H. Wood, Jr., *Conestoga Crossroads: Lancaster, Pennsylvania, 1730–1790* (Harrisburg, Pa., 1979), p. 97; Laura Leff Becker, "The American Revolution as a Community Experience: A Case Study of Reading, Pennsylvania," Ph.D. diss., University of Pennsylvania, 1978, pp. 110–12. See Grace Hutchinson Larsen, "Profile of a Colonial Merchant: Thomas Clifford of Pre-Revolutionary Philadelphia," Ph.D. diss., Columbia University, 1955, pp. 282–83, on the rivalry between two shopkeepers.

[6] Kuhn and Risberg to William French and Co., June 8, 1785, Kuhn and Risberg Letterbook, 1785–88, Kuhn and Risberg Papers, Bucks County Historical Society, Doylestown, Pa.

[7] John Chaloner to Wadsworth and Carter, Nov. 1, 1773, John Chaloner Letterbook, 1782–84, p. 197, Chaloner and White Papers, HSPA.

colours or qualities as does not suit this place I know it wont be in my power to give satisfaction, of which I have had too much experience."[8] Once a suitable inventory had been purchased, it was important to display it effectively. One trader suggested to a rural partner that "the different Articles of Groceries could be mentioned in large characters on the doors, etc. with labels on the Casks."[9] As for the dry goods in this particular store, the merchant remarked that "we observe there being a very Considerable quantity of muslins and fine white handkerchiefs on hand. As the sale of all white goods much depend on their not being exposed to the air by which they lose their clear Whiteness, we find it best to keep all of that description in small hand trunks and band boxes."[10] The other dry goods, however, were to be clearly displayed, "which is a matter very *essential to promote the Sales,* as every Article is expected to be *in view.*"[11]

Terms of payment were yet another area of competition. A storekeeper could expand sales volume by accepting as payment not only cash (specie and paper money) but also a variety of "country produce," such as wheat, hemp, corn, beeswax, deerskins, furs, ginseng, butter, flour, and homespun. Most of these goods would be shipped to Philadelphia or Baltimore for export, but such perishable items as butter were sold locally. In either case, country produce had to be stored in a warehouse, a costly and cumbersome undertaking.[12] A less troublesome but more financially risky way to

[8]William Pollard to John Woolmer, Dec. 13, 1764, William Pollard Letterbook, 1764–68, p. 36, Montgomery Collection, Columbia University, New York City.

[9]Kuhn and Risberg to French and Co., Aug. 17, 1786, Kuhn and Risberg Letterbook.

[10]Ibid., Oct. 17, 1785.

[11]Ibid., Aug. 17, 1786.

[12]See ibid. This was a common practice in the West, although country produce did not take the place of cash completely. See the *Kentucky Gazette* (Lexington) for 1789 or the *Pittsburgh Gazette* for 1788 and 1789. See also Unidentified Account Book, 1793–96 (Muddy Creek, Pa.), microfilm, and John Patterson Daybook E, 1797–1800, microfilm, both in Pennsylvania Historical and Museum Commission (PHMC), Harrisburg.

attract customers was to extend credit generously. This was standard practice in the sale of dry goods where credit sales of several months, often stretching on to several years, were common. But farmers sometimes demanded the opportunity to purchase groceries "on account" as well. As one retailer explained to a Philadelphia merchant, "Note What you say in Regard of Trusting & shall take all the Care possible, but if I dont Trust some Farmers for Rum & other Articles till After Harvest dont think it will Be to the Advantage of the store as there is Many Able Farmers here has not cash at this time of the Year that may be good Customers hereafter & there has been Many here that is safe hand asking for Credit some short time, & says they Can have Cr. of Jinkins With Whome they have formerly dealt."[13]

Groceries held an important place in the business strategy of retailers because they served, in modern parlance, to "build traffic" in the store. Sales of dry goods were highly seasonal, reaching peak volume during the few weeks after the spring planting and the autumn harvest. There was no better way to maintain the loyalty of a clientele from one busy season to the next, while also drawing new customers into the store, than by offering choice groceries at a good price. "Sugar Tea coffee & Som other Trifling thing is only the one thing that Brings a store Customers," wrote one shopkeeper, "Especially if we have good Sugar Tea & Coffee then we soon will have the Towns Custom & then whenever their Friends Comes to Town and Wants to Buy Anything than they Always will recommend to that Store where they get their things."[14] Alcoholic beverages could also attract customers. One merchant wrote approvingly to a retailer, "You concluded to keep a Quarter cask of each kind of your liquors in the upper store for retail, the great Convenience of which you no doubt experience."[15] The effect of this strategem was to turn successful stores into neighborhood centers resembling taverns. The

[13] John Taylor to John Mitchell, May 31, 1773, John Mitchell Papers, Box 2, PHMC.

[14] Peter Anspach to Mitchell, Feb. 14, 1773, ibid.

[15] Kuhn and Risberg to French and Co., Aug. 17, 1786, Kuhn and Risberg Letterbook.

account books of two different retailers show that they served between seven and seventeen customers daily, many of whom regularly purchased small amounts of groceries.[16] Elizabeth Nutt of Burlington, N.J., complained that her store was always so full of people that she could hardly think.[17]

Important though they were, all of these diverse merchandising strategems—credit sales, flexible payment terms, advertising, effective display of merchandise, and the sale of groceries—were overshadowed by price competition as a determinant of success. At every level of the dry goods trade, from the countinghouses of London to the cabins of Pittsburgh, cutthroat price competition was the rule. Because British suppliers were so aggressive in extending credit to American importers, the Philadelphia market was almost chronically glutted with European manufactures. The constant cry in the Delaware valley was that dry goods were cheaper in Philadelphia than in Manchester, that a multitude of importers tottered on the brink of bankruptcy. This was an exaggeration, no doubt, but an exaggeration of reality. Failures were indeed common among Philadelphia importers, particularly during the commercial depressions that followed every war. The inventories of failed firms were often dumped on an already glutted market via the vendues or auction houses where the consumer who paid cash could indeed buy European manufactures for less than their "first cost."[18]

Naturally the keen price competition in Philadelphia extended into the port's hinterland. Retailers took careful note of their neighbors' prices and attempted to match or beat them. Remarked one Lancaster merchant to his Philadelphia supplier, "I do not know how it comes, But Sansinger Always seems to Undersell me in these Articles. I request your Care in sending them good in quality and as low as you can."[19] A

[16] Thomas Scully Daybook, 1773–75 (Christianna Bridge, Del.), HSPA; Greensburg, Pa., Ledger, 1798–1802, PHMC.

[17] Larsen, "Thomas Clifford," p. 282.

[18] In addition to the sources cited in n. 2, above, see Marc Egnal and Joseph A. Ernst, "An Economic Interpretation of the American Revolution" *William and Mary Quarterly*, 3d ser. 29 (1972):3–32.

[19] Wood, *Conestoga Crossroads*, p. 106.

trader in Reading remarked, "Our neighbors take all Opportunities of reducing the price of many things. endeavoring to carry trade. As soon as we know we endeavor to be lower than any one and shall do the best we can to gain on the triffling Credit that Mr. Patton left the store in."[20] The power of low prices to devastate the competition was graphically demonstrated by John Cameron, a rich Lancaster shopkeeper who was supplied on remarkably low terms by Daniel Wister of Philadelphia. Cameron "gave it out publickly that he was resolved to undersell everyone both in Town and Country in order to draw all the Custom to himself, and he was as good as his Word." Cameron traded on a massive scale and "knoct up the Shopkeepers small and great (and ruined most of them)"—before going bankrupt himself.[21]

The effect of the multifaceted competition in the dry goods trade was to bring manufactured goods into the reach of a very broad segment of the rural population. As one Philadelphian observed, "People of this country have got into a bad practice of importing the lowest priced Goods of every kind and the lower sort of people seem not to have found their mistake in purchasing these kinds yet."[22] Newspapers of the Revolutionary period were filled with lamentations about the spread of luxuries throughout American society. In 1770 one newspaper contributor observed that the colonies were in a state of "Misery and Ruin, as a Consequence of the unnecessary Imports of European Goods." Trading so much upon Credit, and aping the Extravagances and Luxuries of the rich and opulent," American merchants had "already done the Colonies irreparable Damage, sunk their Character, and sapped their Virtue."[23] While the abundance of consumer goods did tend to be greater as one approached Philadelphia, their availability was by no means limited to affluent

[20] Murray and Connelly to Mitchell, Feb. 15, 1773, Mitchell Papers, Box 2.

[21] Wood, *Conestoga Crossroads*, p. 100.

[22] Pollard to William Crosby, Jr., and Co., May 6, 1773, Pollard Letterbook, p. 210, HSPA.

[23] Quoted in J. E. Crowley, *This Sheba, Self: The Conceptualization of Economic Life in Eighteenth-Century America* (Baltimore, 1974), p. 127.

coastal areas. In 1789 the *Pittsburgh Gazette* carried an advertisement enumerating 143 items, including "an elegant assortment of Queen's ware," "elegant shawls," and "Sattia and common ribband of the most fashionable colors."[24] Further down the Ohio, in the infant settlement of Kentucky, a Lexington newspaper during the first six months of 1789 carried the advertisements of nine different retailers, six of whom were just opening their stores.[25] And when the Quaker merchant and land speculator Henry Drinker fitted out a store for his settlement on Pennsylvania's extreme northern frontier, he included in the inventory twenty-seven different types of cloth and nine varieties of buckles.[26] The records of western shopkeepers show that they also sold a wide variety of dry goods to their customers.[27] Since the frontier settlements of Kentucky and western Pennsylvania were relatively unstratified societies, lacking large and wealthy elites, there is no doubt that farmers and craftsmen purchased a large share of the European dry goods available in these regions.

Probate inventories provide strong evidence of the widespread distribution of imported manufactures in rural households. Table 1 reveals the possessions to be found in the households of farmers in five counties in the Philadelphia market area, which were randomly selected by Alice Hanson Jones as part of her study of American wealth levels in 1774.[28] The ninety-six farmers in Jones's sample owned an impressive variety of goods. Sixty-two (65 percent) owned pewter and forty-one (43 percent) owned earthenware; between twenty-five and thirty farmers were owners of clocks, table-

24 *Pittsburgh Gazette*, May 9, 1789.

25 See the *Kentucky Gazette*.

26 See Henry Drinker Journal, 1780–98, Dec. 14, 1791, p. 68, Henry Drinker Papers, HSPA.

27 See Anonymous Ledger, 1750–54 (Shippensburg area, Pa.) (PHMC), John Patterson Daybook E, 1797–1800, and Unidentified Account Book, 1793–96 (Muddy Creek, Pa.). See also the Daniel Wister Ledger, 1762–70, Wister Family Papers, HSPA, showing extensive shipments of dry goods to western settlements.

28 Alice Hanson Jones, *American Colonial Wealth: Documents and Methods*, 3 vols. (New York, 1977), 1:69–401.

Table 1. Incidence of selected items in the inventories of 96 middle colony farmers, 1774*

	Number owning item	%
Earthenware	41	43
Pewter	62	65
Silver	10	10
Clock or watch	25	26
Looking glass	30	31
Handkerchief	9	9
Tablecloth	25	26
Hosiery	9	9
Feather beds	29	30
Servants or slaves	10	10
1 or 2	6	6
3 or more	4	4

SOURCE: Alice Hanson Jones, *American Colonial Wealth: Documents and Methods,* 3 vols. (New York, 1977), 1:67–401.

*In Westmoreland, Northampton, and Philadelphia counties, Pa.; Kent County, Del.; Burlington County, N.J.

cloths, and looking glasses. Fifty-five of the ninety-six farmers (57 percent) owned at least one looking glass, clock, tablecloth, handkerchief, or pair of stockings. As for the all-important category of textiles, feather beds were common in the eastern counties, and the median value of bedding in the seventy-one households reporting the amount was £7.4. For the seventy-five inventories indicating the value of the decedent's apparel, the median figure was £5.6. If we assume that the farmer's wife with children owned apparel equal in value to his own (a conservative assumption, given the large amount of cloth needed to make a full-length dress or skirt), then the median value of a household's apparel and bedding was £18.6. Since the cash income of the typical farm family has been variously estimated at between £8 and £40,[29] it is apparent that the investment in textiles was considerable.

A macroeconomic view likewise attests to the abundance of imported manufactures in the Philadelphia market area. In the period 1758–62, average imports from England and Wales amounted to £365,400 sterling per year. After adjusting this figure for both the exchange rate between sterling

[29] For a discussion of this question, see below.

and Pennsylvania currency and the markups of the Philadelphia merchants and the retailers, we can calculate that the average rural family spent about £12 per year on European goods.[30] This figure excludes not only purchases of most imported groceries, which entered from the West Indies, Iberian, and coastal trades, but of such domestic manufactures as pottery, ironware, paper, glass, and hosiery. Naturally this specific figure of £12 Pennsylvania currency in imports per year is a crude estimate that could be adjusted upward or

[30] The figures and assumptions used for this calculation are as follows.

Retail value of imports: (1) Mean annual value of imports from England and Wales to Pennsylvania, 1758–62 = £365,400 sterling (John J. McCusker, "The Current Value of English Exports, 1697 to 1800," *William and Mary Quarterly*, 3d ser. 28 [1971]:624). (2) Price at which these goods were sold by Philadelphia importers to retailers: 2.30 × £365,400 sterling = £840,420 Pa. currency. This premium of 130 percent, which follows the method of conversion used by Philadelphia merchants, accounts for both the exchange from sterling to currency and the importer's markup. Naturally the premium varied with business conditions, within a range of about 100 to 150 (see Jensen, *Maritime Commerce*, pp. 105–6). (3) The retailer's markup of goods purchased from wholesalers = 10 percent; 1.1 × £840,420 = £924,462. This figure of 10 percent for the retailer's markup is a very conservative guess.

Number of families in Philadelphia market but outside the city in 1760: (1) population in Philadelphia market, 1760 = 375,000 (John Flexner Walzer, "Transportation in the Philadelphia Trading Area, 1740–1775," Ph.D. diss., University of Wisconsin, 1968, p. 4). (2) Of these 375,000 people, about 17,000 lived in Philadelphia, leaving a rural population of 358,000 (Gary B. Nash, *The Urban Crucible: Social Change, Political Consciousness, and the Origins of the American Revolution* [Cambridge, Mass., 1979], p. 408). (3) Number of families in market at 5 people/family: 358,000/5 = 71,600 families. (The factor of 5 is used in James T. Lemon, *The Best Poor Man's Country: A Geographical Study of Early Southeastern Pennsylvania* [Baltimore, 1972], p. 180).

Consumption per rural family: (1) If urban and rural families have equal per capita consumption of British imports: 71,600 rural families = 95.5 percent of total population. Rural consumption = .955 × £924,462 (total imports at retail prices) = £882,861 currency. £882,861/71,600 = £12.33/family. (2) If urban families consume 50 percent more than rural families, then urban families, accounting for 4.55 percent of total population, consume 6.83 percent of goods and rural families consume 93.17 percent of goods. Rural consumption = .9317 × £924,462 = £861,321.24. £861,321.24/71,600 families = £12.03/family.

downward for a variety of plausible reasons. But there is no doubt that rural consumers spent a significant proportion of their income on the dry goods that poured into the Delaware valley.

By all accounts, the farmers of the mid-Atlantic region, particularly the Germans and Quakers, were thrifty and conservative agriculturists whose modest dwellings were overshadowed by magnificent barns. Nevertheless, they spent large sums on imported dry goods when they could have made do with homespun. To understand their motivation for doing so, we need to know exactly what they purchased at their neighborhood shops. The journals of Philadelphia merchants provide part of the answer to this question, for they enumerate the specific items that were shipped to rural shopkeepers. Table 2 breaks down fifty-five shipments of dry goods sent by nine different importers to retailers throughout the Philadelphia hinterland. The vital fact that emerges from this tabulation is that fully three-quarters of the goods shipped consisted of cloth and sewing materials. Another 10 percent was comprised of handkerchiefs, hosiery, and hats. Hardware, writing implements, combs, and books were all to be found in these general stores (probably in greater quantity than this table suggests) but the heart of the inventory consisted of textiles and the materials needed to turn fabric into clothing, bedding, and curtains. A typical purchase might include eighteen vest buttons, three large buttons, three-and-a-half yards of blue woolen cloth, four yards of blue ribbon, and a length of silk.[31] In making such a purchase, few shop-

[31] Table 1 strongly documents the fact that, in their trade with the hinterland, "dry goods merchants" handled cloth primarily. Nevertheless, rural shopkeepers also dealt with specialized Philadelphia importers, ironmongers, apothecaries, booksellers, and others who specialized in noncloth items. Consequently the inventories of rural shopkeepers were probably less heavily weighted toward cloth than Table 1 suggests. For examples of purchases see Unidentified Account Book, 1793–96 (Muddy Creek, Pa.), p. 449, Thomas Scully Account Book, 1773–75, Nov. 23, 25, and 29, 1773, HSPA. Also revealing is the purchase by Aaron Leaming, a wealthy South Jersey farmer, of 7 yards of shalloons, 14 buttons, 12 jacket buttons, and 2 sticks of hair at a fair (Aaron Leaming Diaries, 1750–77, vol. 1, Apr. 28, 1750, HSPA). See also entries for Aug. 16–21, 1750, con-

Table 2. Product composition of 52 shipments of "dry goods" from Philadelphia merchants to rural customers, 1750–90

			Value*	%
Cloth			£2,587.35	70.1
Handkerchiefs			184.95	5.0
Hosiery			62.70	1.7
Hats			117.30	3.2
Sewing materials			186.10	5.0
Buttons	77.35	41.6%		
Buckles†	32.00	17.2		
Thread	27.35	14.7		
Other	49.40	26.5		
Writing materials			22.15	0.6
Books			4.1	0.1
Snuff equipment			12.35	0.3
Hardware			77.80	2.1
Toiletries			10.60	0.3
Combs			26.65	0.7
Groceries			130.95	3.6
Eating utensils			50.80	1.4
Gunpowder, shot			37.91	1.0
Other			176.95	4.8
Total			£3,688.66	99.9

SOURCES: Richard Waln Journal B, 1769–75, pp. 40, 73, 87, 117, 124, 136, Richard Waln Papers, Historical Society of Pennsylvania (HSPA), Philadelphia; Henry Drinker Journals, 1776–79, pp. 308, 357, and 1790–98, p. 68, Henry Drinker Papers, HSPA; Wister and Aston Daybook, 1788–89, pp. 91, 105, 151, 233, 360, 544, Wister Family Papers, HSPA; Reed and Forde Daybook, 1785–91, pp. 79, 92, 137, 159, 208, 273, Reed and Forde Papers, HSPA; Thomas Wharton Daybook, 1758–62, pp. 9–10, 13, 44, 59, 62, 160, 173, 186, Leonard T. Beale Collection, HSPA; Thomas Riche Journal, 1757–61, Sept. 27, Dec. 28, 1757, Apr. 15, May 20, June 21, 1758, May 7, Apr. 25, 1759, Thomas Riche Papers, HSPA; Jones and Wister Daybook, 1759–62, Apr. 2, Apr. 4, 1760, Wister Family Papers, HSPA; Thomas Armat Journal, 1784–89, pp. 96, 100 (2 shipments), 104, 111, 113, 115, Loudoun Papers, Thomas Armat Section, HSPA; Stephen Collins Papers, vol. 119, pp. 73, 131, 150, vol. 129, pp. 95, 438, Library of Congress.

*Pounds Pennsylvania currency.

†Also used for shoes.

pers were content to settle for whatever buttons and fabrics the storekeeper happened to have on hand. They were far more definite in their tastes—intent on producing a garment or bedspread that achieved a certain look, a particular style. They were, in short, fashion conscious.

It is this fact that explains one of the most striking features of the dry goods trade: the numbing variety of goods sold. To attract customers, retailers carried a huge selection of fabrics, ribbons, buttons, buckles, and threads. The possible variety of goods was truly vast. Fabric, for example, was available in a variety of colors, patterns, weights, weaves, textures, widths, and prices. It could be warm or cool; scratchy or soft; red, blue, green, or black; woolen, linen, cotton, or silk; spotted, solid, or striped. The customer was sovereign and the merchant aimed to please by selling a generous selection among the thousands of possible offerings. We have already encountered the array of merchandise offered by Daniel Benezet, as described in the *Pennsylvania Gazette:* his advertisement mentioned nearly 200 categories of goods, many of which covered a multiplicity of different items. So extensive was the line of dry goods carried by Benezet's fellow merchant, Samuel Neave, that when Neave's executors recorded the items found in his warehouse, the list ran to no less than twenty-five pages.[32] One Lancaster trader received eight different grades of "clear lawns" in a single shipment, and the shopkeeper Miriam Potts offered 65 items for sale in her New Jersey shop and 361 items in her Philadelphia store.[33]

This bewildering diversity attests to the affluence and taste for luxury of the rural consumer. To a considerable extent, it resulted from the presence in stores of relatively exotic goods made of silk, velvet, satin, and other costly materials. Even items fabricated from inexpensive materials were rendered more costly when produced in a multiplicity of pat-

---

cerning a trip to Philadelphia at which Leaming purchased socks, a jacket, breeches, a scythe, nails, rum and other items.

[32] Jones, *American Colonial Wealth,* 1:190 (inventory 13048).

[33] Jones and Wister Daybook, 1759–62, shipment to John Cameron, July 21, 1768, Wister Family Papers; Jones, *American Colonial Wealth,* 1:169–79 (inventory 13040).

terns, colors, and sizes. And a significant hidden cost was connected with the wide range of goods sold: it tended to increase the total size of inventories, thereby raising the cost of financing them. For example, a retailer who carried a line of 300 types of fabric inevitably stocked a significant number of "specialty items" that did not sell as rapidly as the more popular grades of cloth. To justify an investment in this slow-moving inventory (which was particularly liable to damage from moths, rats, mildew, and changing fashions), he had to charge a higher price. Not content to settle for the most common and inexpensive types of goods, the rural consumer willingly paid this additional cost. Thus the Westmoreland County farmer Isaac Cahill had in his possession in 1774 four different types of cloth, ranging from expensive green fabric worth 30 shillings a yard to shaloons costing only 3.25 shillings a yard.[34]

Naturally the farmer's taste for comfort and style extended beyond his wardrobe to other aspects of the domestic environment. As farmers became more wealthy, their horizons broadened and they filled their houses with an expanding array of possessions. We can view this process by comparing the probate inventories of farmers in recently settled Northampton County, Pa., with the inventories of farmers in three wealthier and longer-settled eastern counties.[35] The furnishings in the Northampton farm house were remarkably spare, seldom amounting to more than a table, a stool, a chest, and a couple of chaff beds. Tableware was likewise simple, consisting of pewter plates or wooden trenchards and pewter spoons. By contrast, the houses of many eastern farmers were filled with substantial pieces of furniture. One or two feather beds and chests of drawers, a dinner table, a dressing table, and six or more chairs were a fairly standard complement.[36] Looking glasses, clocks, and armchairs were not uncommon.

[34] Jones, *American Colonial Wealth*, 1:111–12 (inventory 12004).

[35] Ibid., pp. 69–105, 117–352. Needless to say, the affluent eastern areas were far more populous than the spartan West.

[36] In the eastern counties, 28 of 67 farmers owned feather beds. Most feather beds cost £5–£7; all beds in this price range have been counted as feather beds.

In many homes, the finest pieces of furniture were made of walnut, and silver teaspoons or china might lend an air of gentility to the dinner table. Farmers who could afford to do so spent heavily on beds, coverlets, sheets, pillowcases, and bedcurtains—welcome accoutrements in drafty dwellings where illness was common.[37] Yet there seem to have been limits to the material aspirations of these farmers that were not simply a function of wealth. Few farmhouses contained such signs of sophistication as rugs, mahogany furniture, or pictures on the walls—all of which were common in the homes of affluent Philadelphia artisans.[38]

The proliferation of possessions in Delaware valley farmhouses was part of an international phenomenon, centered in England, that has been dubbed the "Consumer Revolution." Clearly emergent by the late seventeenth century and gaining momentum in England during the fine harvests of the 1740s, the revolution finally moved into high gear during the third quarter of the eighteenth century. According to one of its leading chroniclers, Neil McKendrick, the ramifications of this transformation could hardly have been more profound.

> More men and women than ever before in human history enjoyed the experience of acquiring material possessions. . . . What men and women had once hoped to inherit from their parents, they now expected to buy for themselves. What were once bought at the dictates of need, were now bought at the dictate of fashion. What were once bought for life, might now be bought several times over. What were once available only on high days and holidays through the agency of markets, fairs and itinerant pedlars were increasingly made available every day but Sunday through the additional agency of an ever-advancing network of shops and shopkeepers. As a result "luxuries" came

[37] Although the median value of bedding was £7.4, 11 of the 71 farmers (15 percent) owned bedding worth £20 or more.

[38] Based on an inspection of inventories in Jones, *American Colonial Wealth*, 1:117–329. See, for example, inventories 13008 (a baker), 13011 (tallow chandler), 13012 (tailor), 13029 (carpenter), 13051 (brewer), 13084 (house carpenter), 13088 (brickmaker), 13105 (crier).

to be seen as mere "decencies," and "decencies" came to be seen as "necessities." Even "necessities" underwent a dramatic metamorphosis in style, variety, and availability.[39]

The historians who have identified and labeled this new species of revolution are understandably defensive about introducing yet another variety into an already crowded genus. Yet its claims to legitimacy are impressive, for they are firmly rooted in the most fundamental axiom of economics: the equation of supply and demand. What is produced, the logic runs, must be consumed. What was produced in the Industrial Revolution, therefore, must have been consumed in a Consumer Revolution.[40]

And not a little of this consumption occurred in New England and the middle colonies, where per capita imports from Great Britain were generally on the rise between 1744 and 1775 while the population was doubling every twenty-five years.[41] Indeed, the dry goods trade of Philadelphia and other northern ports is best understood as a commercial extension of the Industrial Revolution, for the entrepreneurial ties between the two were very close indeed—especially after the American Revolution, when the dry goods trade was increasingly oriented toward Manchester and Liverpool, whose leading firms sent agents and junior partners to America to drum up orders.[42] Observers were astounded in 1784, as they had been in 1749, 1760, and 1771, at the tidal wave of English manufactures that flooded the Delaware valley. In 1784 one Philadelphia trader remarked, "The arrival of Vessels &

[39] Neil McKendrick et al., *The Birth of a Consumer Society: The Commercialization of Eighteenth-Century England*, (Bloomington, Ind., 1982), p. 1.

[40] Ibid., pp. 9–33.

[41] Egnal, "Pennsylvania Economy," fig. 5, p. 30, shows the per capita value of exports from Britain to the northern colonies rising rapidly from 1745 to 1760, and then declining gradually until 1775.

[42] See, for example, the Clifford Papers, vols. 6 and 7, the Andrew Clow Papers in the Franklin and Marshall Collection and the Gratz Collection, and the Crammond and Philips Papers in the Gratz Collection, all in HSPA.

Goods here for two months past is beyond Credibility."[43] English capitalists were no less astonished; one noted in March 1784, "You will scarce Credit the Circumstance but it is Strictly Fact—that there are orders still in hand at Manchester that will not be ready until Midsummer next tho' actually given out in Octr. & Novr. last—such has been the great demand for goods to that Manufacture particularly."[44]

Although the same sorts of shops and factories sated the expanding appetites of consumers in eighteenth-century England and America, the tenor of commercial life in the two countries was not identical. The merchandising methods used in America to stimulate consumption were not ineffective, as we have seen, but they were far more primitive than those employed in England. There, by the end of the eighteenth century, "the competitive, socially emulative aspect of fashion was being consciously manipulated by commerce in pursuit of increased consumption."[45] Such industrialists as the potter Josiah Wedgwood and the buttonmaker Matthew Boulton owed much of their success to marketing acumen: high quality and low prices were not enough. As Wedgwood candidly recognized, "*Fashion* is infinitely superior to *merit* in many respects, and it is plain from a thousand instances that if you have a favourite child you wish the public to fondle & take notice of, you have only to make choice of proper sponcers." In his search for "proper sponcers" Wedgwood went straight to the top—the queen of England—and came away with a style of china, known as Queensware, that swept the market. "It is really amazing how rapidly the use of it has spread over the whole Globe," Wedgwood marveled, "& how universally it is liked." As McKendrick has shown, fashion plates, fashion dolls, fashion magazines, and fashion newspapers all played a similar role in altering social perceptions so as to make "men buy 'luxuries' where they had previously

[43] Stephen Collins to Harrisons and Ansley, June 17, 1783, Collins Papers, LX-A.

[44] Champion and Dickason to Armat, Mar. 28, 1784, Box 1, Thomas Armat Papers in Loudoun Papers.

[45] McKendrick et al., *Consumer Society*, p. 43.

bought 'decensies' and 'decensies' where they had previously bought only 'necessities.'"[46]

Farmers in the Philadelphia region, as noted above, were hardly oblivious of fashion: they were by no means content to meet their clothing and bedding needs by purchasing a few standard grades of cloth—let alone subsisting on homespun. Yet there is remarkably little evidence that American businessmen employed sophisticated methods to shape the tastes of the rural consumer. Newspaper advertising tended to be straightforward and factual, containing only a few references to "fashionable" wares. The voluminous transatlantic correspondence of importers says little about specific fashion trends and reveals few efforts to steer customers toward particular styles or brands. It is far from clear why this was so. The most obvious explanation is that American merchants were middlemen who, unlike British manufacturers, did not much care what the consumer bought, so long as he bought it in large quantities. Undoubtedly the absence in America of anything resembling the vast London market drastically reduced the potential payoff from a marketing campaign. Then, too, it was not easy to find cultural symbols that would appeal to a mixed population of Anglican, Quaker, German, and Scotch-Irish consumers. And this very heterogeneity may have expanded consumption through a kind of intergroup demonstration effect: as impoverished German and Scotch-Irish peasants crossed the Atlantic, their taste for consumer goods may have been piqued by the panoply of "decensies" and "luxuries" that prosperous American farmers already possessed.

But the differences in consumer spending in England and America were far outweighed by the essential fact that consumers in both areas were purchasing, in ever-increasing quantities, the vast array of cloth, buttons, buckles, pottery, books, clocks, mirrors, and hardware that spewed forth from English factories. Curiously enough, many influential historians have failed to recognize this fact. The Middle Atlantic farmer, like his New England counterpart, is said to have been a "subsistence farmer" who lived primarily from the

[46] Ibid., pp. 108, 98.

resources of his own farm and local community. This hardy soul produced not only his own food and shelter but also his own cloth; he descended into the commercial marketplace only to buy a handful of "necessities" that could not be produced locally. Thus Jackson Turner Main wrote:

> Even after the frontier stage was over, many farmers produced little beyond their own requirements, and comprised "that class of husbandmen, whose farms are small, but barely sufficient to support their families." . . . Fortunately, the small farmer needed very little cash. He "could do anything, as indeed the countryman in America generally can, himself supplying his own wants in great part or wholly," so that his small holdings furnished "all the necessities, most of the conveniences, and but few of the luxuries of life." There was some exaggeration here. The farmers did indeed furnish most of their own food, but they had to buy salt, molasses, or sugar, and rum. . . . Most of the clothing was made at home. It might consist only of "cotton rags" among the poor southern families or "strong decent homespun" but it was usually adequate for protection from the weather even though it did not satisfy an aesthetic sense of taste for luxury. Shoes, however, had to be purchased, as did hats.[47]

Other historians have accepted this position as well. In *The Best Poor Man's Country* James T. Lemon observed, rather obliquely, that the farmer in southeastern Pennsylvania "produced enough for his family and was able to sell a surplus in the market to buy what he deemed necessities."[48] More recently still, James A. Henretta has endorsed these statements by Main and Lemon and has concluded that the only rural consumers who regularly entered the market to purchase "luxuries" were a small group of "entrepreneurial" farmers who owned slaves and therefore had the labor needed to operate on a large scale. The typical farm household, Henretta suggests, was a "preindustrial" domestic unit characterized by "a household mode of production, limited economic

---

[47] Jackson T. Main, *The Social Structure of Revolutionary America* (Princeton, 1965), pp. 148–49.

[48] Lemon, *Best Poor Man's Country*, p. 180.

possibilities and aspirations, and a safety-first subsistence agriculture within a commercial capitalist market structure."[49]

A cornerstone of this assessment is the idea that the farmer had neither the inclination nor the opportunity to earn substantial cash incomes with which to purchase luxuries in the commercial market. Henretta emphasizes that poor transportation and the absence of slave labor inhibited the development of the market. The typical farmer "planted only 8 or 10 acres of wheat each year, a crop that could conveniently be harvested by the farmer, one or two growing sons, and (in some cases) his wife. Of the normal yield of 80 to 100 bushels, 60 would be consumed by the family or saved for seed; the surplus of 20 to 40 bushels would be sold on the Philadelphia market, bringing a cash income in the early 1770s of £5 to £10 sterling."[50] Henretta implies that this scanty income permitted farmers to buy only necessities in the commercial market.

If this analysis were correct, if in fact the farmer's limited labor supply and poor access to the market held his cash income to £5 to £10 sterling (£8.3 to £17.6 Pennsylvania currency), then the notion that the Consumer Revolution had, by 1775, penetrated deep into Philadelphia's rural hinterland would be called into question. For the £12.5 cash income of Henretta's representative farmer would not go very far. Once he had purchased, for example, a saddle (£1.25), a medium-sized wagon (£6.5), a plow (£1), a good Bible (£2), a gun (£1) and a copper kettle (£1), he would have been in debt—even before paying his taxes, making a contribution to his church, buying other farm equipment, or purchasing *any* groceries or textiles. It is impossible to see how he could have hoped to purchase any of the luxuries that regularly show up in inventories, such as feather beds (£5–£7), a good clock (£11), a fine coat (£2), or a walnut table (£1.125).[51]

---

[49] James A. Henretta, "Families and Farms: *Mentalité* in Pre-Industrial America," *William and Mary Quarterly*, 3d ser. 35 (1978):16–20.

[50] Ibid., pp. 17–18.

[51] These figures are taken from Jones, *American Colonial Wealth*, inven-

But I would argue that the typical farmer earned considerably more cash income than Henretta implies, and he did this by selling many other commodities besides wheat. The great strength of the mid-Atlantic economy in the eighteenth century was its diversity. It supplied several large foreign markets with a variety of commodities, yet was developing a solid manufacturing base centered on shipbuilding, iron-making, weaving, and milling.[52] These developments presented the farmer with a variety of market opportunities that afforded considerable leeway in deploying his limited resources. Instead of committing himself to a single cash crop, he could produce a number of commodities that, together, would employ his family labor supply efficiently throughout the year. Much of what he produced was consumed in the household, but the surplus production of *many* crops and livestock—and not just wheat—was sold in the increasingly sophisticated commodity markets of the Philadelphia area. Lumber could be sold not only for export as staves, heading, and planks, but to supply Philadelphia's prosperous shipbuilding and housing industries or to provide the city with fuel. Pork and beef likewise were sold both for export and for consumption by nonfarm households. Though most of it was fed to livestock, corn, oats, hay, and barley were also sold on the market. Hemp was purchased by Philadelphia ropemakers, and flaxseed was shipped to Ireland in large quantities. Very good prices—£10 to £20 in many cases—could be obtained for riding horses, and farmers in Philadelphia's suburbs supplied the city with vegetables, fruits, beeswax, and dairy products.[53]

It was difficult to become extremely wealthy by engaging in such activities, but according to Lemon farm families in

---

tories 11002, 11007, 11010, 11016, 12001. The wagon listed here was cheap; generally they "sold for from £14 to £19." See Walzer, "Transportation," p. 265.

[52] Lemon, *Best Poor Man's Country*, p. 181, concludes that a third of the population was composed of laborers and craftsmen by the late eighteenth century.

[53] Walzer, "Transportation."

the Lancaster area earned an average cash income of about £40 in 1790.[54] It appears that the most ambitious and successful farmers could achieve incomes considerably above this average figure. Of the sixty-seven probate inventories of farmers who died in three Delaware valley counties in 1774, twenty-seven (40 percent) owned livestock and agricultural commodities worth over £100, and for the top thirteen farms the average figure was £251.[55] The fields, cribs, and barns of these prosperous farmers held a variety of grains, and they typically owned about twenty hogs, ten cows, five horses, and twenty-five sheep, as well as a pair of oxen and miscellaneous items. Part of these holdings was consumed by the family, part was sold in the market, and part was simply held to operate the farm. Without knowing much more about the farm economy, it would be hazardous to estimate the relative importance of these three uses. But it seems highly probable that a farmer owning crops and livestock worth more than £200 could generate an annual cash income of £70 or more. It is not difficult to understand how an enterprising farmer could accumulate a significant estate and assume the title of "a Thousand pound man."[56]

These impressive surpluses would not have been produced if transportation charges had eaten up most of the potential gain from market sales. A careful study of transportation in the Philadelphia area has shown, however, that the cost of getting crops to market "was not exceedingly high."[57] Within the densely settled Delaware valley and upper Chesapeake regions, the great majority of farmers lived "within a half-day's wagon haul of a convenient shallop-landing," and shallop lines provided regular service between Philadelphia and

[54] Lemon, *Best Poor Man's Country*, p. 180.

[55] Based on Jones, *American Colonial Wealth*, 1:107–401.

[56] Nathaniel Blencone to John Steinmetz, May 18, 1767, in Keppelle and Steinmetz Papers, Jaspar Yates Brinton Collection, HSPA. I am most grateful to Marianne Wokeck for bringing to my attention the correspondence with rural shopkeepers in this collection.

[57] Walzer, "Transportation," p. 306. See also Larsen, "Thomas Clifford," p. 298.

such towns as Trenton, Christianna, and Newcastle.[58] Farmers who used water transport paid freight rates "comparable with rail freight charges one hundred years later."[59] Conditions were not so favorable for farmers who had to send their crops to Philadelphia by wagon; the Lancaster-to-Philadelphia run was six times as costly as the trip from Newcastle or Trenton to the great port.[60] Nevertheless, the hundreds of "dutch Wagons" that made the two-day trip from Lancaster to Philadelphia every spring and fall are compelling evidence that a large volume of goods produced on the Lancaster Plain did make its way to the Philadelphia market. It was even worthwhile for farmers living west of the Susquehanna to send their wheat to Philadelphia. Whether by shallop or by wagon, access to transportation routes was clearly important to farmers, for farm advertisements frequently mentioned the property's propinquity to roads and rivers. One farm in Sussex County was said to be "near Delaware River (4 miles distant) and about 9 or 10 miles from a forge."[61] Another notice informed readers that "the main road leading from Gloucester both to Coopers Ferry and Haddonfield passes through the tract, and is very convenient for any person inclining to attend the Philadelphia market."[62]

By the late colonial period, however, it was unnecessary for farmers to deal directly with Philadelphia in order to vend their surplus. The heavy flow of agricultural commodities toward the city and of groceries and dry goods out of it was expedited by the presence of sophisticated milling and marketing centers in the countryside. The volume of business in these towns was heavy enough to justify very substantial investments in mills and stores. By the 1770s travelers frequently remarked upon the series of large stone mills on Delaware's Brandywine River—"8 of them in a quarter of a mile, so convenient that they can take the grain out of the

[58] Walzer, "Transportation," p. 69; see also p. 67.

[59] Ibid., p. 310.

[60] Ibid., p. 309.

[61] "Newspaper Extracts," *New Jersey Archives,* 1st ser. 24 (1902):72.

[62] Ibid., p. 131.

Vessels into the Mills."[63] Flour milling was sometimes carried on in conjunction with other activities, such as lumber milling and retailing. And in the prosperous "pork country" of West Jersey, many storekeepers built warehouses and smokehouses to process the hogs purchased from farmers. One such installation boasted a gristmill, a fulling mill, a sawmill, a brick farmhouse, a smokehouse, a pork house, a store, and several craft shops.[64] Another advertisement for a West Jersey store claimed that 900 barrels of port had been collected in a single year.[65]

Not unlike Chesapeake tobacco merchants, the entrepreneurs who ran these complexes operated two complementary businesses: vending groceries and dry goods, on the one hand, and dealing in certain agricultural commodities, on the other. Wheat, lumber, and pork were the most prominent items of trade, but others could be important. One shopkeeper outside of Trenton, for example, handled large amounts of flaxseed; another retailer in Lancaster sent many wagonloads of hemp to Philadelphia.[66] Such activity was probably distinct from the trading in many types of "country produce" that retailers in the cash-starved western counties needed to engage in if they wanted to make dry goods sales.[67] Further research will probably show that the specialized com-

[63] Peter C. Welsh, "The Brandywine Mills: A Chronicle of an Industry, 1762–1816," *Delaware History* 18 (1956–57):21.

[64] "Newspaper Extracts," *New Jersey Archives*, 1st ser. 28 (1902):90. See the fine discussion of retailers in Max George Schumacher, *The Northern Farmer and His Markets during the Late Colonial Period* (New York, 1975), pp. 73–87.

[65] "Newspaper Extracts," *New Jersey Archives*, 1st ser. 27 (1902):351.

[66] See the correspondence of John Steinmetz with Nathaniel Blencone of Kingwood, N.J., and with William Bell of Lancaster, Keppelle and Steinmetz Papers, Brinton Collection. Bell to Steinmetz, Apr. 27, 1770, mentions the shipment of about ten wagonloads of hemp in the space of a few weeks.

[67] Steinmetz's correspondence shows that cash was used by most shopkeepers to settle balances; other sources confirm this impression. Cash was also common on the frontier, but there "country produce" was more frequently taken in payment by shopkeepers and, one suspects, sent eastward. See the account books cited above, n. 27.

modity trading by retailers was part of a general process of commercialization that was going forth in the Philadelphia region as the volume of trade expanded. Within the port itself, this trend was characterized by the emergence of specialized dry goods importers, shipping merchants, flour merchants, and lumber merchants.

The weight of empirical evidence suggests that neither an inadequate supply of farm labor nor high transportation costs prevented farmers in the Philadelphia region from earning enough cash income to purchase substantial amounts of imported manufactures. Far from being "subsistence farmers" who crept into the market to purchase a few items that could not be produced locally, farmers seem to have been rather closely tied to the market as both producers and consumers. A sudden suspension of commercial relations with the Philadelphia market would have drastically reduced their living standards, depriving them of groceries, bedding, books, and the attractive, comfortable clothing that they had grown accustomed to. The farmers' reaction to such a prospect is shown by the insistent demand of Kentucky's early settlers that the New Orleans market be opened up as an outlet for their produce. Deprived of such a vent for their agricultural surpluses, Kentucky's settlers would have been unable to purchase the dry goods and groceries that filled the pioneer settlement's stores.

Closer to Philadelphia, probate inventories show that, partly in order to introduce "decensies" and "luxuries" into their lives, farmers became enmeshed in financial obligations. Of ninety-six middle colony farmers studied by Jones, the financial assets—cash, bonds, notes, and book debts—are reported for sixty-five, although they probably are not complete in all cases.[68] For such farmers, £50 was a large sum of money, exceeding Lemon's estimate of their annual cash income and equaling about an eighth of the value of their farms.[69] Yet thirty-six of these sixty-five farmers (55 percent)

[68] Jones, *American Colonial Wealth*, 1:69–401.

[69] Ibid. The values of 21 farms are mentioned; the median value was £361.

had financial assets in excess of £50, often far in excess: nine had £500 or more and five had £1,000 or more. Unfortunately we know less about the debts of these farmers because they were not so regularly reported and because complete information on them has not been published. We can determine, however, that thirty-two of the forty-seven farmers reporting had more than ten creditors, and seventeen had more than twenty. The largest single debt was often substantial, exceeding £50 in fourteen of the forty-seven cases. Given the large sums involved, it is not surprising that these financial obligations were handled in a businesslike manner. Frequently they took the form of bonds, and interest was usually charged.

It goes without saying that these large debts indicate a significant involvement in the commercial marketplace. One does not incur book debts amounting to more than a year's cash income by informally swapping goods and services with a neighbor. More research will be needed before we can understand exactly how these debts arose, but thanks to the valuable research of Mary McKinney Schweitzer we do know that in the period 1723–55 2,033 farmers took out loans from the provincial land bank. These loans had an average value of £64.78 and were evidently used to improve farms already owned by the borrower.[70] More significantly for the present discussion, some of the farmers' debts arose from credit purchases of dry goods from merchants and shopkeepers.

Inevitably, marketplace activity had its effect on the mentality of the farmers. Evidence on this subject is very difficult to come by, but records from two major wars suggest that they skillfully pursued their interest in the give-and-take of the marketplace. When dealing with a rich and open-handed government such as the British during the Seven Years' War, backcountry farmers could be most obliging. It took Benjamin Franklin just two weeks to gather 150 wagons and 259 packhorses by offering 15 shillings a day for wagons and 2

<hr />

[70] Mary McKinney Schweitzer, "Government, Capital Formation, and Colonial Economic Development: The General Loan Office of Pennsylvania, 1723–1755" (unpublished paper, 1983), pp. 11 and 16.

shillings a day for horses.[71] These were generous terms: wagoners stood to earn nearly £70 in specie for just three months' work.[72] Farmers were far less accommodating two decades later, however, when dealing with the Continental army: Washington's rebels made payment in dubious IOUs instead of hard cash. Officers were unanimous in the opinion that farmers were very tough bargainers; with characteristic hyperbole, Timothy Pickering called them "the most abominable extortioners."[73] One officer stationed in western Pennsylvania stated that "the farmers would not hire their teams for less than the wages Allowed them by the Assembly of this state, which I was under the Necessity of granting them."[74] Another official reported in 1779 that the high price of grain was inducing many farmers to leave off wagoning and return to farming because it was more profitable—a clear indication that these people were calculating the market value of their labor rather precisely.[75] And when it came to selling their grain, farmers insisted upon the highest price possible. An official in Morristown, N.J., concluded, "Unless some Law to enable us to procure grain takes place, I am pretty certain we must go without—The Farmer has the Ball at his own Foot and kicks it when he pleases."[76] Two days later

[71] Leonard W. Labaree and William B. Willcox, eds., *The Papers of Benjamin Franklin*, 24 vols. to date (New Haven, 1959–), 6:14.

[72] A farmer would earn £68.25 by serving as a wagoner for 13 weeks. Lewis Burd Walker, ed., *The Burd Papers: The Settlement of the Waggoners' Accounts Relating to General Braddock's Expedition* (N.p., 1899), contains the accounts of individual farmers, many of whom were compensated for the loss of horses and wagons. Wagoners who sustained no losses generally earned over £70. This amount may have been shared by two or more farmers, who jointly contributed 4 horses, a wagon, and teamster services.

[73] Timothy Pickering to John Pickering, Sept. 25, 1777, Timothy Pickering Papers, microfilm, Massachusetts Historical Society, Boston.

[74] John Davis to Joseph Brady, Mar. 18, 1779, John Davis Papers, vol. 4, Library of Congress.

[75] Henry Hollingsworth to Nathanael Greene, Feb. 4, 1779, Nathanael Greene Papers, American Philosophical Society, Philadelphia.

[76] James Burnside to Moore Furman, Nov. 13, 1778, James Burnside Letterbook, HSPA.

this official reported, "The Farmers are determined to keep a Head of us, let us do as we will; for Example, when 15/ was *our* price for corn they demanded 18/9, when we offered *that,* they asked 20/; now we offer 20/, and their price is between three and four Dollars."[77] Evidently these farmers (like surplus-producing farmers in Europe) considered the "just price" to be the highest price they could get. As a weathered and weary Nathanael Greene concluded after extensive dealings with Middle Atlantic yeomen, "Interest is the Governing principle with the farmers as well as almost that of every other order of men. If you propose any terms to the farmers short of those advantagious which they can make in any other Employ they will leave your service."[78] This pragmatic conclusion was borne out during the winter of 1777–78 when General Washington threw a blockade of troops around the city of Philadelphia to prevent farmers from selling food to the British troops occupying the city. Despite the threat of capital punishment, many farmers persisted in dealing with the British who, unlike Washington's army, were offering gold and silver for wheat and pork.[79]

If ever there was a time for "subsistence farmers" to stand clear of the market, it was during the political, military, and monetary chaos of the Revolutionary War. The fact that so many farmers braved a host of dangers and difficulties in order to sell their agricultural surplus to the highest bidder is compelling evidence of their significant involvement in the market. One major reason for this behavior—there were others that were just as important[80]—is that the farmers had

[77] Burnside to Charles Stewart, Nov. 15, 1778, ibid.

[78] Greene to Hollingsworth, Feb. 14, 1779, Papers of the Continental Congress, reel 193, National Archives.

[79] George Washington to John Jameson, Dec. 24, 1777, to John Armstrong, Dec. 28, 1777, to Walter Stewart, Jan. 22, 1778, to John Lacey, Jan. 23, 1778, in John C. Fitzpatrick, ed., *The Writings of George Washington from the Original Manuscript Sources, 1745–1799,* 39 vols. (Washington, D.C., 1931–44), 10:199, 215, 336, 340.

[80] In the context of an increasing shortage of land that was, by the 1760s, forcing eastern farmers to migrate to North Carolina and the Ohio

developed a taste for the goods that money could buy. A quickening flow of European and tropical imports had accustomed farmers to consuming a gigantic array of products that made life more interesting, comfortable, and stylish.[81] In this respect, it is highly misleading to consider the farmers preindustrial. There may have been very few factories in the America of 1775, but there were plenty of factory-made goods. The Industrial Revolution had not yet spread to the New World, but its twin brother, the Consumer Revolution, had. This fact was of the utmost importance to the economic development of the United States, for it meant that America's earliest industrialists, unlike such English pioneers as Wedgwood and Boulton, did not have to stimulate consumer demand for their wares. Instead, American manufacturers merely needed to meet a demand that already existed by displacing English producers. This process of "import substitution" first occurred on a large scale during the Embargo of 1807 and the War of 1812, and it continued with the effective aid of tariff barriers until the Civil War.

---

valley, farmers needed money simply to maintain the living standards of themselves and their families. The farmer who failed to take prudent risks in order to benefit from market opportunities stood the chance of pauperizing his family. A large and prosperous farm, like a thriving family business, was an excellent vehicle for promoting the material welfare of future generations.

[81] There is good reason to suspect that a similar pattern characterized New England. The volume of New England's British imports in the period 1750–75 exceeded those of Pennsylvania by a third, and Alice Hanson Jones's study of wealth patterns in 1774 reveals that the value of consumer goods in New England inventories amounted to £4.4 sterling, as compared to £4.0 sterling in the middle colonies. Contemporary newspapers and standard works of business history likewise suggest no great differences in the dry goods trade of the two areas. See McCusker, "Current Value," pp. 624–25; Alice Hanson Jones, *Wealth of a Nation to Be: The American Colonies on the Eve of the Revolution* (New York, 1980), p. 96; *Boston Evening Post;* John W. Tyler, "The First Revolution: Boston Merchants and the Acts of Trade, 1760–1774," Ph.D. diss., Princeton University, 1980, pp. 182–88, 195.

JOSEPH A. ERNST

The Political Economy of the Chesapeake Colonies, 1760–1775: A Study in Comparative History

THIS ESSAY HAS ITS ORIGINS in an awareness of the failure of the various economic interpretations of the American Revolution in the Chesapeake to explain the striking fact that the course and nature of revolution in Virginia differed radically from that in neighboring Maryland. Economic interpretations have focused on two broad and overlapping considerations of life in the Chesapeake. The first is that the Chesapeake country was above all tobacco country, the Bay shore a "Tobacco Coast." The second is that following the end of the Seven Years' War the area suffered from a series of economic crises that were greatly aggravated by Britain's postwar revenue and currency policies. Yet despite common regional features and experiences, it is still the case that Virginia and Maryland were out of step with each other during a Revolutionary movement bracketed by the depressions of 1760–68 and 1772–75. Further, Virginia's lead in 1774 in an independence movement aimed at achieving economic sovereignty won no support at all from Maryland.[1]

[1] See the discussion and extensive bibliography in Marc Egnal and Joseph A. Ernst, "An Economic Interpretation of the American Revolution," *William and Mary Quarterly*, 3d ser. 29 (1972):3–32; see also Arthur P. Middleton, *Tobacco Coast: A Maritime History of Chesapeake Bay in the Colonial Era* (Newport News, Va., 1953).

The present paper is an argument for the central importance of "political economy" to an understanding of these fundamental differences between Virginia and Maryland in the period 1760–75 and the complex character of the Revolutionary and independence movements in the Chesapeake. A view of political economy that informs the following discussion draws on a remark of John Stuart Mill in his *Principles of Political Economy*—a work that looked back to the writings of the Scottish Enlightenment and forward to the analysis of Karl Marx. Political economy, according to Mill, should not be considered as "a thing of itself, but as a fragment of a greater whole; a branch of Social Philosophy." Social Philosophy, or "Moral Philosophy" as it was called in the eighteenth century, traditionally included economics, politics, *and* social ideas and ethics. Not until the later nineteenth century did political economy come to be equated with the abstracted, "dismal science" of economics alone.[2]

At mid-century British imports of tobacco from the Chesapeake reached 70 million pounds by weight. They rose to 85 million in 1760. That same year British exports to the region were around £175,000 sterling, or 30 percent better than the previous record set twelve months earlier. The surge in trade reflected the recent growth in European demand for tobacco, but more significant was a heavy influx of British funds into Virginia and Maryland as a consequence of renewed business activity in the mother country after 1745 and important

[2] In his study *The Elusive Republic: Political Economy in Jeffersonian America* (Chapel Hill, N.C., 1980), chaps. 1–3, Drew R. McCoy discusses the eighteenth-century view of "political economy." Sections of the work concerning the Chesapeake are almost entirely concerned with the period following Independence and with the impact of the Scottish Enlightenment on American political-economic thought.

It should be noted that as used in this paper the various elements in political economy are not mutually exclusive but complementary. In the abstract it would be all too easy to elevate any one of the elements over the others. In fact it is always the concrete historical situation that determines the hierarchy of importance among economics, politics, and ideas.

The quotation is from John Stuart Mill, *Autobiography* (London, 1971), pp. 140–41.

structural changes in the marketing of tobacco in the Chesapeake.[3]

Glasgow firms began rapidly expanding their share in the tobacco industry in the late 1740s. They extended their operations throughout the Virginia backcountry, the Northern Neck, and adjacent areas of Maryland by setting up a network of "stores" where agents bought tobacco, sold goods, and gave credit. It would be another twenty years before they caught up with their English rivals; meanwhile the Scots financed the rise of a new generation of smaller planters who opened up fresh lands in the west and southwest, producing higher yields and superior crops, and adding greatly to the increasing tobacco shipments from the Chesapeake. A similar infusion of credit in the consignment trade likewise benefited the "great party" of tidewater planters, especially in Virginia. Yet their situation became increasingly precarious. Often burdened with heavy, fixed investments in land and slaves, depleted soils, declining yields, and an inferior quality of leaf, and with the gentry's propensity "for luxury and expensive living," these planters suffered severely from the glut of tobacco, the accompanying collapse of prices, and the tightening of credit that affected all interests in the Chesapeake trade beginning in 1760.[4]

"Any person with half an eye," William Allason reported from his store at Falmouth on the Rappahannock in the sum-

[3] See Jacob M. Price, *France and the Chesapeake: A History of the French Tobacco Monopoly, 1674–1791,* 2 vols. (Ann Arbor, 1973), 1:604–17, 671–73, and Marc Egnal, "The Economic Development of the Thirteen Continental Colonies, 1720 to 1775," *William and Mary Quarterly,* 3d ser. 32 (1975):191–222.

[4] Jacob M. Price, "The Rise of Glasgow in the Chesapeake Tobacco Trade, 1707–1775," *William and Mary Quarterly,* 3d ser. 11 (1954): 179–99. See also James H. Soltow, "Scottish Traders in Virginia, 1750–1775," *Economic History Review,* 2d ser. 12 (1959):83–98, and idem, *The Economic Role of Williamsburg* (Charlottesville, 1965), chap. 2. Older but still useful is Calvin B. Coulter, Jr., "The Virginia Merchant," Ph.D. diss., Princeton University, 1944.

The study of the pre-Revolutionary Chesapeake economy is a vast industry. A good introduction to the literature is to be found in John J. McCusker and Russell R. Menard, *The Economy of British America, 1607–1789* (Chapel Hill, N.C., 1985).

mer of 1760, could "see that there is more tobacco in the country than could be sold." As a new, independent merchant in the area, Allason had just entered into an agreement with the district Scots to hold tobacco at 16s. 8d. per hundred-weight, but "some timorous people who had some ships arrived" bid up the price to 20 shillings. Even so prices everywhere fell by half or more from their 1759 peak to near prewar levels. They were still too high for the great Glasgow houses, however, which even before any of the new crop had arrived were already complaining of poor markets and a slackening demand. The consignment trade proved no better. With many planters overestimating the value of current and future crops and drawing bills of exchange against inadequate remittances, London firms began protesting great numbers of sterling bills at the end of 1760.[5]

The turn of the year brought no relief. Glasgow merchants despaired of vast quantities of tobacco on hand and declining prices. When peace rumors in the spring prompted the French Farmers General—the major buyers in the Scottish market—to try undercutting existing low prices, the Scots temporarily halted all sales, impressing upon their Chesapeake correspondents the need to buy less tobacco and pay less for it. Prices did tumble a shilling or two in some places but averaged 17 shillings for the year, or just under the level for 1760. The buoyancy of prices reportedly reflected the obstinancy and competition among storekeepers who pushed business in expectation of great profits when there was "none but considerable loss, and this not known 'til too late." The resulting price gap between Glasgow and America was, of course, anything but a loss to the "rising generation" of planters.[6]

[5]See Robert W. Spoede, "William Allason: Merchant in an Emerging Nation," Ph.D. diss., College of William and Mary, 1973, pp. 127–29, from which the quotations are taken. See also James O'Mara, "Urbanization in Tidewater Virginia during the Eighteenth Century: A Study in Historical Geography," Ph.D. diss., York University, 1979, fig. 2.6, p. 123, and Price, *France and the Chesapeake*, 1:673–74.

[6]Spoede, "Allason," p. 129, and Edward C. Papenfuse, Jr., "Planter Behavior and Economic Opportunity in a Staple Economy," *Agricultural History* 46 (1972):297–311.

More important for Chesapeake interests was the spreading economic collapse in Britain in 1761. By late summer, reports told of financial distress, falling stocks, tightening credit, and weakening markets for colonial products. Harassed at home, tobacco firms cut back the flow of funds to Maryland and Virginia, calling upon their agents "to collect their debts and walk softly 'till better times" and above all to curtail "credits all of us have too foolishly given to people of little capital." As the pressure on debtors increased, so did the protesting of sterling bills. Conditions in 1762 were no better. The news from Glasgow in January was that "tobacco is dull," the "French price a low 2d. a pound" and "very slow demand; great quantities upon hand, so the prospect is very bad" with nothing ahead to "mend matters." With tobacco declining and markets relatively tight, Scottish and English merchants were understandably cautious; the volume of goods bound for the Chesapeake slid to the lowest figure for six years. The reduction did little to relieve the excess inventories and poor sales of the storekeepers, although it clearly affected the price of tobacco "in the country" which fell nearly 2 shillings per hundredweight.[7]

In Virginia the deepening economic distress in 1760 and 1761 catalyzed political antagonisms and regional divisions that preceded the coming of the Revolution. During the score of years after 1725 the oligarchy of great planters that controlled the House of Burgesses split into rival factions over the acquisition of western lands. One group, the "Robinson party," represented tidewater tobacco interests between the Potomac and the James Rivers; the other, the "Lee-Ohio Company" party, those of the Northern Neck. The Robinson party remained intact through the Revolution. The Lee faction fell apart as an organized political force around mid-century. During the 1750s questions of wartime expenditures and slavery also produced divisions within the oligarchy and

[7] See the entries for 1761 in the Richard Corbin Letterbook, 1758–68, Colonial Williamsburg Foundation Research Library, and the discussion in Joseph A. Ernst, *Money and Politics in America, 1755–1775: A Study of the Currency Act of 1764 and the Political Economy of Revolution* (Chapel Hill, N.C., 1973), pp. 66–67. The quotation is from Mar. 10, 1761, in William Allason Loose Papers, Virginia State Library (VSL), Richmond.

among the regional interests but generated no lasting alignments. More consequential was the management of the Treasury.[8]

A wartime emission of £180,000 currency early in 1757 as lawful tender for debts payable in Virginia, including sterling obligations, raised an outcry among merchants on both sides of the Atlantic for protecting the value of paper money and of British loans and credits. One suggestion was the burning of all paper notes coming into the Treasury for redemption in order to prevent their recirculation; the planter-dominated assembly rejected the scheme as an infringement upon its control of the purse. But persistent rumors of laxity and corruption in the management of the Treasury divided the burgesses, and as early as 1760 gave rise to legislative proposals for destroying at first some and later all retired paper money. The Robinson faction steadfastly opposed these actions as an assault upon the party leader and treasurer, John Robinson.[9]

Earlier crises had been surmounted. In the last months of the war, however, the charges against Robinson came to a head. One effect of the tightening credit conditions and fall-

[8] Pre-Revolutionary Virginia factionalism involving the Lee and Robinson "parties" is considered in David A.Williams, "Political Alignments in Colonial Virginia Politics," Ph.D. diss., Northwestern University, 1959. Compare Marc Egnal, "The Origins of the Revolution in Virginia: A Reinterpretation," *William and Mary Quarterly*, 3d ser. 37 (1980):405–16, which offers some evidence for the persistence of a Northern Neck, or Lee, faction into the 1750s and beyond. Egnal's focus on western expansion and factionalism in Virginia causes him to overlook other issues, especially the management of the Treasury. See pp. 403–4 for definitions of "party" and "faction."

For somewhat different interpretations of the Treasury question and the role of the Robinson party, compare David J. Mays, *Edmund Pendleton, 1721–1804: A Biography*, 2 vols. (Cambridge, Mass., 1952), 1:chap. 2, and Ernst, *Money and Politics*, chap. 3. An indication of the link between slavery and regional politics is to be found in George Reese, ed., *The Official Papers of Francis Fauquier, Lieutenant Governor of Virginia 1758–1768* (Charlottesville, Va., 1981), pp. 372–73. A recent analysis of economic regionalism in Virginia is James O'Mara, *An Historical Geography of Urban System Development: Tidewater Virginia in the 18th Century*, Atkinson College Geographical Monograph no. 13 (York University, Downsview, Can., 1983).

[9] Ernst, *Money and Politics*, pp. 49–62.

ing tobacco prices that took place in 1760–61 and continued through 1762 was to boost sterling exchange rates. The consequent drop in the cost of tobacco relative to sterling gave little solace to local merchants, who were paid in currency and had enormous sterling obligations to meet in England and Scotland. Facing considerable losses on their sterling remittances, they blamed an excess of paper money for their predicament.[10]

Late in 1762 major tobacco merchants in Britain, who were reportedly "acted upon" by traders in Virginia, besieged the Board of Trade with demands for the creation of adequate redemption funds for all the dominion's outstanding currency and the elimination of currency as lawful tender for sterling debts payable in America. The Board was sympathetic to the complainants and adopted resolutions in February 1763 threatening that if the Virginia legislators refused to do justice, the commissioners would seek parliamentary support for a ban on all currency and for anything else necessary to restore the public credit and relieve the injured merchants. The resolutions arrived in Virginia at a time of spreading economic disorder. Anticipation of peace had led British firms to ship their largest cargoes to the Chesapeake since 1760. Yet even reduced wholesale prices on some goods and efforts to lower markups on all items failed to generate much demand. In sum, all economic classes were feeling the pinch of a deepening depression and financial crisis.[11]

The House of Burgesses took up the Board's resolutions in May. On the twenty-third a member of a committee to audit the Treasury books, Richard Henry Lee, interrupted proceedings to raise a question of fraud he had been hinting at since at least 1760, when he began a campaign for destroy-

[10] For the movement of exchange rates in Virginia, see John J. McCusker, *Money and Exchange in Europe and America, 1600–1775: A Handbook* (Chapel Hill, N.C., 1978), pp. 205–14.

[11] Jacob M. Price, *Capital and Credit in British Overseas Trade: The View from the Chesapeake, 1700–1776* (Cambridge, Mass., 1980), appendix D, pp. 160–62, gives British tobacco imports and British exports to the Chesapeake for the years 1740–76. The quotation is from Lt. Gov. Francis Fauquier to the Board of Trade, Nov. 3, 1762, in Reese, ed., *Official Papers of Fauquier*, 2:818–19. See also Ernst, *Money and Politics*, pp. 65–73.

ing retired paper money. Almost £35,000 was "only reported to be in the treasury." Lee demanded a "strict" investigation to determine whether the money—an amount "sufficient to alarm not the merchants of Britain only, but every thinking person"—was really there. The action would dog his political career as long as he lived and profoundly affect the course of Revolution in Virginia.[12]

John Robinson, treasurer of the colony and Speaker of the House, had indeed been dipping into the public till for years, appropriating vast sums for his own use and for the purpose of making loans to party supporters and friends who had fallen hopelessly into debt from the "unhappy circumstances of the colony." Admittedly, Robinson had pledged his sizable estate as security for his ventures, but by 1763 British creditors had determined that the great man was no longer creditworthy and were protesting his bills of exchange. When challenged by Lee, Robinson, like many of his debtors and the Treasury, was virtually bankrupt.

Having betrayed the public trust and endangered the public credit, Robinson was desperate to keep Lee's charges within doors. He shrewdly placed his accuser on the very committees responsible for probing the Treasury accounts and replying to the British petitioners and the Board of Trade. Caught between "foreign" interests and those of his countrymen at a time when a prolonged slump threatened the entire planting class, Lee chose not to make his charges public and personally drafted Virginia's response to the British merchants. The address exonerated the colony's currency system and duly reported existing taxes sufficient to redeem every note in circulation; the merchant-creditors were depicted as avaricious harpies preying upon the hapless planters.[13]

[12] "Speech of Richard Henry Lee in Committee of Whole House," May [23], 1763, in "Selections and Excerpts from the Lee Papers," *Southern Literary Messenger* 30 (1860):133–35.

[13] Draft of house reply in Lee's hand, Revolutionary Lee Papers, 1750–1809, University of Virginia Library, Charlottesville; Lidderdale Exors. vs. Pendleton and Lyons, Adms., May 1797, Circuit Court Book 120, U.S. Circuit Court, Virginia District, VSL.

For all his equivocating, Lee had dared to say in the privacy of the House what some burgesses already knew and other doubtless more than half suspected. Yet a number willingly engaged in their own conspiracy of silence in order to protect the currency system, their own fortunes, the public credit, and above all the power of their class against the intervention of the English and Scottish merchants and the Board of Trade. Conscience made no further calls for a "strict" accounting of the Treasury, not that year, not any year—until Robinson's untimely death in 1766 made it unavoidable. Meanwhile, James Abercromby, one of Virginia's two colonial agents, had made it clear that if the assembly failed to satisfy the merchant-petitioners, the Board of Trade "will go to parliament against the legislature," a Parliament, Abercromby noted, with no great regard for America when put in competition with English interests. Within a year the Currency Act of 1764 was law, and as predicted the new law responded to metropolitan, not colonial, needs.[14]

News of the Currency Act reached the Chesapeake during perilous times. "Never was so many suits depending in this country," Allason wrote in June 1764. Before setting off from Falmouth to press for payment of "old balances" from small planters in the countryside, Allason took care to order a brace of pistols; intimidating the merchants and law officers, wrecking debtors' prisons, or just skedaddling were becoming all-too-common occurrences. Collecting from the great planters was safer, not easier. Many simply refused to pay and had to be sued; they then connived, often with success, at obstructing the law courts. The situation reflected the continuing decline of the economy. Credit grew tighter than ever, and tobacco exports actually fell in 1763 and 1764, while markets in Glasgow and London remained depressed. In the Chesapeake tobacco prices fluctuated more than usual in 1764 but were marginally better than at home. Some merchants, including Allason, began selling the weed locally for cash and buying whatever goods they needed. This seemed the "safest way these hard times to conduct business," and

---

[14] Robert Carter Nicholas to the printer, *Virginia Gazette* (Purdie and Dixon), June 27, 1766; Reese, ed., *Official Papers of Fauquier*, 2:905–6.

Allason meant to pursue "the same method 'til an absolute alteration in the trade," which he correctly guessed to be "very far off."

Despite the hard times the initial reaction to the Currency Act among Virginia's political leaders was a collective sigh of relief. Robinson, his debtors, his political followers, and the silent defenders of the provincial currency and credit had feared that Parliament would legislate all paper money "null and void." Then not only the Treasury books but the coffers would come under scrutiny. Now, until the sinking of the last wartime issue in 1769, considerable sums would circulate as lawful currency, time enough to scheme a way to replace embezzled funds, settle the accounts, and restore public credit.[15]

At the beginning of 1765 the depression in the tobacco economy deepened, with both Glasgow and London firms reporting rock-bottom prices. The only hope for tobacco was said to be a "scarcity of it in America." In fact a severe dry spell, especially in Virginia, led to predictions that the coming harvest would be the smallest in years. It was, and that fall British prices briefly edged forward, particularly for the better grades of leaf. The country price of tobacco in Virginia likewise advanced as sterling exchange rates rose to their highest levels yet, making tobacco a relatively more attractive remittance than bills of exchange.[16]

Fluctuating but generally depressed markets for tobacco in 1765 were accompanied by a second set of problems: a sharp curtailment of credit, continuing pressure for debt payment, and a shortage of coin. A proposed solution to the various

[15] William Allason to Alexander Walker, June 24, 1764, to Messrs. Bogle and Scott, July 29, 1764, in William Allason Letterbook, 1757–70, VSL; see also John Baylor to John Norton, Sept. 18, 1764, in Frances Norton Mason, ed., *John Norton and Sons, Merchants of London and Virginia . . . 1750–1795* (1937; reprint ed., New York, 1968), p. 11. Economic conditions are discussed in Price, *France and the Chesapeake*, 1:674, and Spoede, "Allason," pp. 131–32. See also Ernst, *Money and Politics*, pp. 86–87.

[16] Economic conditions are discussed in Ronald Hoffman, *A Spirit of Dissension: Economics, Politics, and the Revolution in Maryland* (Baltimore, 1973), pp. 32–33, and William S. Sachs, "The Business Outlook in the Northern Colonies, 1750–1775," Ph.D. diss., Columbia University, 1957, pp. 144–56, 193–203.

economic problems of Virginians was a public loan. Late in May 1765 a number of prominent burgesses learned privately that the legislative session would be extended a few days in order to vote on an omnibus bill for a loan office. Discussion on the plan's appeal to indebted planters and men of property had appeared in the *Virginia Gazette* a week earlier. A consideration not discussed was the recent default of the Treasury of some £50,000 currency.

As Richard Henry Lee had suggested two years earlier, and as everyone now knew was true, money reported to be in the Treasury was not there. Merchants privately condemned the treasurer as either too lax with the tax collectors, some of whom were thought to be using their receipts as a personal loan fund, or too loose in his own practices. Both suspicions were justified. A provision of the proposed loan arranged for the borrowing of sufficient money from British merchants to create not only a public loan office but also to redeem the existing currency supply, or money enough to bail out the tax collectors, Robinson, his debtors, and even the provincial credit. Taxes were to provide the needed security for the loan.[17]

On May 24, when the House of Burgesses met to consider the omnibus measure, protest against the Stamp Act seemed out of the question. The loan scheme required utmost cooperation with the crown. Like everyone else, Lee understood, and he stayed away. The perfect blend of idealist and opportunist, Lee had been conspicuous in 1764 in attacking the rumored stamp tax but secretive in efforts at becoming provincial Stamp Act collector. Whether or not Robinson knew the whole story at the time, Lee kept away from the House, if only to avoid the same dilemma he had fallen into two years before. As for the other burgesses, despite the Treasury default and growing evidence of a financial scandal, they main-

[17] Joseph A. Ernst, "The Robinson Scandal Redivivus: Money, Debts, and Politics in Revolutionary Virginia," *Virginia Magazine of History and Biography* 87 (1969):146–73. For a contrasting interpretation see Jack P. Greene, "'Virtus et Libertas': Political Culture, Social Change, and the Origins of the American Revolution in Virginia, 1763–1766," in Jeffrey J. Crow and Larry E. Tise, eds., *The Southern Experience in the American Revolution* (Chapel Hill, N.C., 1978), pp. 55–108.

tained their conspiracy of silence, and Robinson had no difficulty in lining up votes for his plan. The only opposition came from a newly elected member from Hanover County, Patrick Henry.

As Thomas Jefferson recollected these events many years later, in the House discussion of the loan a spokesman for the measure made the point that "from certain unhappy circumstances of the colony, men of substantial property had contracted debts which, if exacted suddenly, must ruin them and their families but with a little indulgence of time might be paid with ease." Henry rose to object. "What, Sir! . . . Is it proposed then to reclaim the spendthrift from his dissipation and extravagance by filling his pocket with money?" Henry's rhetoric did not carry the day; it did not impede the progress of the loan bill through the burgesses, nor, it should be noted, raise the matter of fraud. Yet in his remarks the junior burgess did convey a challenge; he challenged both Robinson's leadership and his party's claim to represent the true interests of Virginia.

The Council killed the bill, and for the reasons Henry had hinted at. "To tax people that are not in debt to lend to those that are is highly unjust," councilor Richard Corbin observed; "it is in fact to tax the idle, the profligate, the extravagant, and the gamester." After losing the fight, advocates of the loan departed Williamsburg, leaving behind a half-empty House of Burgesses. It was there that Henry found support to overcome Robinson's determined resistance and pass five of seven "treasonous" resolutions against the Stamp Act.

When the burgesses reassembled in November 1766, elections had replaced forty-one members. The many new faces reflected popular dissatisfaction with the mother country and the precarious times. Meanwhile, Robinson had died. Although the news of his peculations was spread across the pages of the local gazettes, his party was intent on keeping power, with Attorney General Peyton Randolph replacing the dead leader as Speaker and treasurer. Events deemed otherwise. A faction headed by Henry and Lee, who had redeemed himself by his forceful direction of the Sons of Liberty in Virginia's Northern Neck, received the backing of three prominent burgesses—Richard Bland, Robert Carter

Nicholas, and George Wythe; cast in the role of honest brokers, the three had political ambitions of their own. The faction attracted sufficient votes to divide the offices and elect Nicholas treasurer. Randolph gained the Speaker's chair, yet he could take little pleasure in a victory that marked the end of the Robinson party's supremacy.

Henry and Lee had stood up to the power structure, to the tidewater "aristocracy" associated with the Robinson faction, and emerged as major Revolutionary figures. They also had laid the foundation for the creation of a Revolutionary coalition of "rising" politicians—of Henry, Lee, Jefferson, and George Washington—representing the agrarian interests and outlook of the backcountry and Northern Neck. As the Revolutionary movement gathered momentum, the coalition was to draw more and more power into its hands—both in the assembly and, more important, in the extralegal associations "out of doors." Thus did regional and intraclass struggles for power, domestic and imperial reform, and economic relief give a determinate shape to the Revolutionary movement in Virginia.[18]

[18] For a different interpretation see J. A. Leo LeMay, "John Mercer and the Stamp Act in Virginia, 1764–1765," *Virginia Magazine of History and Biography* 91 (1983):3–38. See also John C. Matthews, "Two Men on a Tax: Richard Henry Lee, Archibald Ritchie and the Stamp Act," in Darrett Rutman, ed., *The Old Dominion: Essays for Thomas Perkins Abernethy* (Charlottesville, Va., 1964), pp. 96–108. For quotations see: Thomas Jefferson to William Wirt, Aug. 14, 1814, in Paul L. Ford, ed., *The Writings of Thomas Jefferson*, 10 vols. (New York, 1892–99), 9:466, and Richard Corbin to Capel and Osgood Hanbury, May 31, 1765, in Corbin Letterbook. For confirmation of the fact that the members of the Revolutionary coalition were "rising politicians," see Jack P. Greene, "Foundations of Political Power in the Virginia House of Burgesses, 1720–1775," *William and Mary Quarterly*, 3d ser. 10 (1959): 493–502.

The term *backcountry* as used in this paper includes the piedmont as well as the southside. Critical elements in the definition of the term are population density and the fact that the backcountry embraced new areas of tobacco and wheat production that had access to the expanding Scottish store system. After 1763 the spread of the "wheat belt" into the Northern Neck and piedmont would introduce a common interest to these two regions. By contrast, tidewater Virginia outside the Northern Neck was tied to the London consignment trade and contained the older and less productive lands in the province.

But this was in the future. For the moment, despite Virginia's leadership of the Revolution during the summer of 1765, the province fell out of step with radical efforts emanating from the northern colonies later that year to defy the Stamp Act by opening the courts and boycotting British goods. Few Virginia courts opened for business before repeal of the stamp tax, and even then some justices conspired not to hear the debt cases. Lee defended such behavior by explaining that it proceeded "from no regard for the Stamp Act, but the very different situation of our affairs," an allusion to the fact that the planters had long since come into control of most county courts. And it was common practice whenever the planters found themselves in straitened circumstances for these courts to delay suits for debt. Indeed, certain courts and sheriffs were already employing such tactics as early as 1760 when tobacco prices first collapsed and the merchants began pressing for payment of overdue accounts. The Stamp Act may well have forced local courts to shut their doors, yet keeping them shut provided a moratorium on debts. Hard-pressed planters welcomed the decision; the mercantile community did not.[19]

For the same reason the boycott of British goods never took hold in Virginia. Nonimportation was a commercial affair giving merchants in the great port cities an opportunity to retrench and dispose of unsold British stock, especially dry goods; it also levered British suppliers into lobbying for repeal of the stamp tax. Originating in New York just before the tax took effect, the boycott spread to Philadelphia within days and shortly after to Baltimore. The movement bypassed Virginia. The planters had no interest in it; moreover, the dominion lacked a major urban hub and an independent trading community. An urban grid spread throughout the countryside, while the province's many and competitive merchants acted as factors and agents for tobacco houses in Glas-

---

[19]Concerning the courts see William Allason to his brother, Robert Allason, Sept. 8, Nov. 8, 1765, Allason Letterbook, and David J. Mays, ed., *Letters and Papers of Edmund Pendleton, 1734–1803*, 2 vols. (Charlottesville, Va., 1967), 1:22. The quotation is from the letter of Richard Henry Lee to Landon Carter, Feb. 24, 1766, in James C. Ballagh, ed., *The Letters of Richard Henry Lee*, 2 vols. (New York, 1911–14), 1:15.

gow, or as buyers for the London market. The one significant port town, Norfolk, served as an entrepôt for Virginia's grain trade to the West Indies and a regional center for the tobacco trade. Only a handful of Norfolk merchants took an active part in the Sons of Liberty, and they made no move to adopt nonimportation. Nor did Norfolk's Liberty Boys link up with compatriots in the Northern Neck. Sons of Liberty or no, merchants—and especially the Scots—would find no allies among the Potomac planters.[20]

In Maryland the great planters also formed a hegemonic class. But the oligarchy had long before split into "proprietary" and "antiproprietary" factions, or "Court" and "Country" parties, to use the language of the time. Between 1756 and 1761 an angry and prolonged struggle over the wartime need for taxing the Calvert lands had polarized the factions; the intensity of the antiproprietary feelings aroused finally led to efforts in 1762 to eliminate the proprietorship in favor of making Maryland a crown colony. The coming of peace removed the major source of friction. Thereafter assembly politics degenerated into party wrangling over control of the lower house and the counties—a matter ruefully dismissed by some observers as the old greedy game of the "Ins" versus the "Outs"—as well as payment of the clerk of the council from proprietary rather than public funds. The arrival of hard times after 1760 had little effect on party alignments. But then no Robinson scandal roiled the political waters, and the political elite was not riven by the Currency and Stamp Acts as in next-door Virginia.[21]

[20] Egnal and Ernst, "An Economic Interpretation," pp. 17–23, and William J. Van Schreeven, Robert L. Scribner, and Brent Tarter, eds., *Revolutionary Virginia: The Road to Independence*, 7 vols. (Charlottesville, Va., 1973–83), 1:46–48. The urban question is discussed in Jacob M. Price, "Economic Function and the Growth of American Port Towns in the Eighteenth Century," *Perspectives in American History* 8 (1974):164–73. See also Joseph A. Ernst and H. Roy Merrens, "'Camden's Turrets Pierce the Skies!': The Urban Process in the Southern Colonies during the Eighteenth Century," *William and Mary Quarterly*, 3d ser. 30 (1973):549–74, and Carville V. Earle and Ronald Hoffman, "Staple Crops and Urban Development in the Eighteenth-Century South," *Perspectives in American History* 10 (1976):19–50.

[21] Pre-Revolutionary party politics in Maryland is the subject of part one

The vital difference in the Revolutionary movements in the two Chesapeake colonies turned on the role of the merchants. In Maryland, in contrast to Virginia, the merchants—excluding the Scottish factors, who seem never to have achieved even the commercial importance they did in the Old Dominion—played a significant part in Revolutionary politics; not in the House of Delegates, but in the extralegal associations of the time that shattered tradition by giving out-groups like the merchants entrée to political power. Thus did the successive pushes of economic depression and the oppressive stamp tax produce a radical coalition of Baltimore merchants and antiproprietary Annapolis politicos. It was this coalition that formed the vanguard in Maryland's Revolutionary movement during 1765 and 1766. And if the coalition did not outlive repeal of the Stamp Act and the first signs of an economic upswing, nonetheless as a class the merchants would continue to act as a major political force in the growing struggle against the mother country.[22]

Reaction to the Currency Act in Maryland was entirely different from the response in Virginia. There had been little or no fraud in handling the currency, public accounts were in reasonable order, and the question of paper money united, not divided, the interests of the dominant planting class. Wartime emissions had long since been retired by 1764, while the few remaining bills from a public loan struck before the war were reported to be locked safely away "in the chests of the wealthy" awaiting their redemption in sterling at a highly favorable exchange rate. In addition, hundreds of thousands of silver dollars had reportedly drained away to England during the last two years leaving the channels of trade to be supplied by a trickle of coins, the paper money of neighboring Pennsylvania, and "notes issued by private persons."

---

of Charles A. Barker's classic study of the *The Background of the Revolution in Maryland* (New Haven, 1940). David C. Skaggs, *Roots of Maryland Democracy, 1753–1773* (Westport, Conn., 1973), is also relevant, especially chaps. 2, 5, and 6.

A reference to the "Ins" and "Outs" may be found in Jonathan Boucher, *Reminiscences of an American Loyalist* (Boston and New York, 1925), p. 68.

[22] My debt to Hoffman's *A Spirit of Dissension* for an understanding of the role of the merchant class in Revolutionary Maryland should be clear to the reader.

True, critics in faraway London lamented the fact that Maryland's paper currency had fallen into the hands of rich speculators, "merciless wretches that grind the very poor." But the provincial view best expressed by Daniel Dulany, chief spokesman for the bastion of wealth that was the Maryland Council, was more understanding. Rich people had invested "a good deal of their property" in paper, and the risks incurred entitled them to whatever profits came their way.[23]

Yet for Dulany, as for both factions in government and for political leaders generally, a more significant consideration was the conflict between the Currency Act and the public interest. Popular opinion held paper money to be indispensable. With British coin banned by statute "and much more effectively" by an imbalanced trade, provincial bills had become a necessary medium of "internal intercourse." "We can no more do without circulation of paper in America than you can in England," Dulany lectured Secretary of the Province Cecil Calvert, who had testified before the Board of Trade against the currency. Whatever offense Virginia had given by flooding the dominion with depreciated paper—paper that found no welcome in Maryland—Parliament had sacrificed the interests of Marylanders to the demands of British creditors. Certainly it had sacrificed the interests of Dulany, who was heavily involved in real estate sales in and around Frederick Town; the depressing effect of the monetary stringency on property values elicited considerable comment at the time. If Parliament "may prevent our emitting bills of credit under one denomination," Dulany warned, "we shall have a paper circulation under another"; still a "new channel will be made."[24]

A new channel was made, but it took a while. Confronted by a deepening depression in trade and agriculture and a

[23] Cecil Calvert to Lord Baltimore, Jan. 10, 1764, in "The Calvert Papers, Number Two," Maryland Historical Society *Fund Publications* 10 (Baltimore, 1894):218–19; see also Calvert to Lt. Gov. Horatio Sharpe, Feb. 29, 1764, in William H. Browne, ed., *Correspondence of Governor Horatio Sharpe, 1761–1771*, Archives of Maryland, vol. 14 (Baltimore, 1895), pp. 141–42; Daniel Dulany to Calvert, Sept. 10, 1764, "Calvert Papers," pp. 245–46.

[24] Dulany to Calvert, Sept. 10, 1764, "Calvert Papers," pp. 245–46.

growing shortage of credit and coin, Maryland officials railed against the Currency Act yet waited two years until the meaning and scope of the new law became clearer before doing anything.

Likewise, opposition to the Stamp Act came from all sections of the Maryland economy. Tobacco's importance to Britain, however, led to its being singled out for attention. In protesting against the stamp tax, for instance, the House of Delegates cited the low price of the weed as a principal reason for the widespread opposition and confusion. More pointed was the analysis in Daniel Dulany's celebrated pamphlet *Considerations on the Propriety of Imposing Taxes.* Dulany took a hard look at the place of the tobacco trade in the British commercial system. The Chesapeake, he noted, exported some 90,000 hogsheads to Britain; 60,000 were reexported. Yet Virginia and Maryland "not being permitted to send their tobacco immediately to foreign markets *distributively,* in proportion to their demands, the re-exported tobacco pays double freight, double insurance, commission and other shipping charges." "The whole quantity," he went on, was "of course much depreciated; for going all to Great Britain, the *home market* is overdone by which circumstances the quantity required for home consumption is without doubt purchased cheaper than it would be if no more than *that* were imported into Great Britain, and of this glut foreigners and purchasers on speculation also avail themselves." In addition the two colonies paid more, "even by 50 percent," in the case of certain "foreign commodities" that could not be ordered directly from abroad. These impediments in the tobacco economy only revealed to Dulany a larger flaw in Britain's trading empire: an indifference to the colonial interest. "Every shilling gained by America," he asserted, "hath entered in Britain and fallen into the pockets of the British merchants, traders, manufacturers and land holders, and it may therefore be justly called the British commerce."[25]

Far more effective than petitions and pamphlets in defeat-

[25] Bernard Bailyn, ed., *Pamphlets of the American Revolution, 1750–1776* (Cambridge, Mass., 1965), pp. 653–54, and Dulany to Calvert, Sept. 10, 1764, "Calvert Papers," p. 244.

ing the Stamp Act in Maryland was the boycott of British goods, the opening of the court, and the cooperation of the various groups of Sons of Liberty from throughout the province. These actions were in striking contradiction to developments in Virginia at the time. At the core of the difference between the two colonies was the rapid emergence of Baltimore as the "Grand Emporium" of the Maryland trade in wheat and flour and of the Baltimore merchants as a political force in the Revolutionary movement.

By the 1760s Maryland showed unmistakable signs of economic and regional diversification. The colony straddled the Chesapeake and may be said to have "resembled a horseshoe, with a plantation district raising tobacco for export to Europe in the center and a farming area yielding foodstuffs, forest products, hemp, and flax for a variety of markets around the periphery." Baltimore's central position on the western side of this configuration gave it distinct advantages as a marketplace. Crucial to the town's growth was the construction of connecting roadways with the expanding frontier lands of Maryland and Pennsylvania; from here farmers from the Shenandoah and Susquehanna valleys sent down cereal grains in increasing amounts. By the mid-1760s Baltimore grain merchant William Lux could legitimately boast that "the situation of our town to an extensive back country, which is well cultivated and from which we draw quantities of wheat, flour, and flaxseed, renders it fair for a place of considerable trade."[26]

Such developments did not pass unnoticed. Philadelphia merchants, rivals with Baltimore's for western markets, petitioned the Pennsylvania assembly for competitive roads. But others from that city saw the wisdom of investing in Baltimore's future, in her trading establishments, or in the flour mills, distilleries, ropewalks, and other industries springing up in and around the port town. These structural ties bound

[26] The rise of Baltimore is discussed in Hoffman, *A Spirit of Dissension,* pp. 74–80. For quotations see McCusker and Menard, *Economy of British America,* p. 129, and Pamela Satek, ed., "William Lux of Baltimore: 18th Century Merchant," M.A. thesis, University of Maryland, 1974, p. 704.

mercantile and manufacturing interests in Philadelphia and Baltimore more and more tightly. So did business conditions.[27]

During the 1760s merchants in Philadelphia and Baltimore had to contend with the same fluctuating grain markets in the West Indies and southern Europe. In January 1765 grain shortages led Parliament to ban cereal exports and open domestic markets to the Americans. As major suppliers to southern Europe, English wheat dealers also turned to colonial sources. That year Baltimore alone shipped nearly 120,000 bushels to the Mediterranean, the middle colonies another 350,000. But the heavy cargoes from America and the European continent soon overturned trade; the last half of the year William Lux recorded "a very poor price for our wheat" and "uncertain" demand in Iberia and the Madeiras. West Indian conditions proved no better. In addition there was a persistence in the stringency of coin and credit and in the depressed sales of British imports.[28]

While the trading class in Philadelphia early in 1765 was complaining of overstocked inventories and "too large importation" from the mother country "for some time past," Lux was writing from Baltimore of his determination "to quit the drygoods trade at least for some time." When the Philadelphians heeded a call from the neighboring port of New York and adopted nonimportation in a joint effort to extri-

[27] Satek, ed., "William Lux," p. 704; Geoffrey N. Gilbert, "Baltimore's Flour Trade to the Caribbean, 1750–1815," Ph.D. diss., The Johns Hopkins University, 1975, and G. Terry Sharrer, "Flour Milling in the Growth of Baltimore, 1750–1830," *Maryland Historical Magazine* 81 (1976):322–33.

[28] The Chesapeake grain trade is the subject of a number of recent studies. See especially Gaspare J. Saladino, "The Maryland and Virginia Wheat Trade from Its Beginnings to the American Revolution," M.A. thesis, University of Wisconsin, 1960, O'Mara, "Urbanization in Tidewater Virginia," pp. 89–92, David C. Klingaman, *Colonial Virginia's Coastwise and Atlantic Grain Trade* (New York, 1967), Malcolm C. Clark, "The Coastwise and Caribbean Trade of the Chesapeake Bay, 1696–1776," Ph.D. diss., Georgetown University, 1970, and Earle and Hoffman, "Staple Crops and Urban Development," pp. 19–50. The quotation is from Satek, ed., "William Lux," p. 484.

cate themselves from shared difficulties, it was logical that Baltimore's trading community would follow suit. Likewise it was the logic of the situation that pushed Lux into organizing Baltimore's branch of the Sons of Liberty early in 1766 and supporting another northern initiative, defying the Stamp Act and normalizing business operations by forcing the opening of the courts and other public offices in the spring of that year.[29]

These developments quickly led to the forging of a "Baltimore-Annapolis axis" and a political alliance among the Sons of Liberty. Following the organization of their own town's Liberty Boys in February 1766, the Baltimore leaders invited groups of Sons of Liberty, which in contrast to Virginia had formed throughout the colony, to converge upon Annapolis in a move to compel the provincial court and other public offices to open without stamps. The action was orchestrated by Baltimore's William Lux and Annapolis's Samuel Chase, an antiproprietary politician, lawyer, and militant leader of the local Sons. Chase used the incident to consolidate his hold on Annapolis politics and the city's seat in the House of Delegates by attacking and driving from the local Common Council those officials who wore the proprietor's colors. A similar attempt at bringing the power of the Sons of Liberty to bear on party disputes occurred in connection with a stalled bill for paying the public debt and providing a much-needed currency issue. When a deadlock developed between the upper and lower chambers at the end of 1765 over an appropriation in the bill for the clerk of the Council, mobs began gathering to pull down the clerk's house, while rumors from western Maryland warned of a march upon the capital by vast numbers of Sons of Liberty to force a settlement.[30]

[29] John Chew to Samuel Galloway, Nov. 7, 1765, in Samuel Galloway Papers, Library of Congress, and William Lux to James Russell, Apr. 12, 1765, in Satek, ed., "William Lux," pp. 443–44.

[30] Hoffman, *A Spirit of Dissension*, pp. 50–58. It should be noted that opposition to the Stamp Act and the appearance of groups of Liberty Boys was more widespread in Maryland than in Virginia where, for self-serving reasons, the Robinson party and its planter allies moderated their response.

The Baltimore-Annapolis axis fell apart following the repeal of the Stamp Act and the first signs of recovery of the Chesapeake economy. Sharp cutbacks in imports associated with the postwar depression, the credit crisis, and the Stamp Act had given the merchants time to retrench, reduce inventories, and liquidate a portion of their British debts. Equally important markets for primary products had revived. During the early months of 1766 there was a rush to ship tobacco and wheat that continued throughout the year. Prices reflected increased demand, although having made gains during the first half of 1766, the country price for tobacco at least in Virginia dropped just below 17 shillings per hundredweight in September. More heartening for Chesapeake tobacco planters and sterling debtors, exchange rates fell dramatically; the closing of the courts and the moratorium on debts had their effects. So had reduced imports and revived exports.[31]

In Maryland a shortage of cash was hampering economic recovery. The provincial currency had disappeared from circulation years before. The availability of coin was not much better, and this at a time when the increased activity in grain and flour markets meant a rapid growth in money transactions. As Lux explained to English correspondents, cash could no longer be "got" on bills of exchange in Maryland and was exceedingly scarce at Philadelphia. Yet Lux and the other merchants could not purchase "either wheat or flour for bills, for the millers want cash to pay the farmers and the farmers having no connections with London" had no use for bills. The problem was alleviated later in 1766 when, as Dulany had predicted, the Treasury issued 175,000 paper dollars rated at 4*s*. 6*d*. under a "new denomination." While not lawful tender, the money was backed by Bank of England stock and easily passed in ready payment. Lux now exulted that "as our town increases in its trade daily and the importation of European goods much enlarged, and as we have lately had a currency emitted, we are of opinion that in future

---

[31] Ibid., pp. 42–43, and Price, *France and the Chesapeake*, 1:675. For fluctuating exchange rates see McCusker, *Money and Exchange*, pp. 197–214.

near as good an exchange can be got for bills here at Philadelphia."[32]

Even pessimists within the Chesapeake merchant community anticipated an upturn in the economy during 1767. Certainly the grain trade offered more encouraging prospects than ever. For the second year in a row crop failures occurred in Portugal, Spain, and the Levant, and so severe were the shortages that in many parts of Europe there was famine in the land, and in France there were bread riots. "Such large orders from Europe for wheat and flour, and the prices have run so high," Lux enthusiastically reported early in 1767, "that there was no chance of sending any to the West Indies." It was left to Virginia to provision the islands.[33]

Demand for wheat and flour rose even higher in 1768. That spring reports of a scarcity in southern Europe and Britain reached America, followed by large orders for what was left of the old crop. Chesapeake grain handlers began complaining of depleted supplies by early summer, a condition reflected in the swift advance of wheat prices from just under 6 shillings in Maryland during February and March, to 6s. 6d. in May, to over 7 shillings at the close of the shipping season; by July growing demand had made wheat strictly a cash item. Prices during the fall and winter, however, slipping just below the average level for the previous year as a heavy supply of new wheat came to market. Maryland alone sent 135,000 bushels to Europe in 1768, virtually all of it to Mediterranean countries. Virginia in contrast shipped some 65,000 bushels to Iberia and almost as much to England; another 45,000 went to the West Indies, in all nearly double the total exported in 1767.[34]

[32] The quotations are from Lux to William Molleson, Nov. 9, 1766, and to William Alexander and Sons, Jan. 29, 1767, Satek, ed., "William Lux," pp. 638, 702. See also Lux to Reese Meredith, Nov. 10, 1766, ibid., p. 641.

[33] Economic conditions in this period are discussed in Hoffman, *A Spirit of Dissension*, pp. 80–81. The quotation is from Satek, ed., "William Lux," p. 727.

[34] O'Mara, "Urbanization in Tidewater Virginia," fig. 2.16, has wheat export figures by naval district from 1725 to 1775; see also the regional

Conditions in the tobacco economy at the time were more unsettled. Reduced crops in 1766 and 1767 meant that exports over the next two years fluctuated around 68 million pounds by weight, the low point for the decade. On the other hand prices advanced both in the British market and the Chesapeake, where they were marginally better as the Scots, "determined to have what they choose," sought to improve their trading position at the expense of the consignment merchants. Such short swings in volume and price accelerated broader developments already taking place within Virginia's increasingly regionalized economy. In addition, these changes strengthened a sense of crisis among the great planters from the "lower and long inhabited parts of the country" and suggested the need for restructuring the economy.[35]

Several recent studies have shown that dramatic shifts in Virginia's markets, marketing arrangements, population, and land settlement after mid-century combined to ensure that the area of the piedmont served by the Naval Office District, Port Upper James, became the dominion's major producer of tobacco—and of foodstuffs and lumber products as well. For the same reasons and in the same period, Port York, the center of the tidewater consignment trade, fell from the preeminent position it held during the first half of the century, becoming a relatively minor tobacco-growing area. Indeed, according to one scholar, by the 1760s the records of tidewater planters indicate "a steady decline in prosperity, and a steady increment in indebtedness." Many growers had already begun to diversify in an effort to extricate themselves. Some, responding to the parliamentary

---

and provincial figures in Merrill Jensen, ed., *American Colonial Documents to 1776*, English Historical Documents, vol. 9 (London, 1955), pp. 391–441. For wheat prices consult Harold B. Gill, Jr., "Cereal Grains in Colonial Virginia," unpublished paper, Colonial Williamsburg Foundation, Inc., 1974, and O'Mara, *Tidewater Virginia*, fig. 6, p. 92. See also "Calvert Papers."

[35] Export figures are given in Price, *Capital and Credit*, appendix D, pp. 161–62, Edward C. Papenfuse, *In Pursuit of Profit: The Annapolis Merchants in the Era of the American Revolution, 1763–1805* (Baltimore, 1975), p. 177, and in the appendix to Ronald Hoffman, "Economics, Politics, and Revolution in Maryland," Ph.D. diss., University of Wisconsin, 1969.

bounty, turned to hemp; others, attracted by the high prices, to grain and commodities shipped outside the British commercial system, "a thing," as the planter Landon Carter observed in 1767, Virginians were "in great measure strangers to." Still others simply extended their holdings beyond the tidewater into the upland areas of the colony. A number of plans supporting these developments appeared in the newspapers at the time and advocated public support.[36]

That despite everything many tidewater planters stuck with tobacco was only witness to the fact that their way of life was closely identified with the weed's cultivation. Efforts to enlarge their crops in the 1750s, when markets were favorable and credit easy, had left them deeply indebted to and hence dependent on the consignment merchants who were dunning for debts more than a decade later and only reluctantly making new loans. It came as no surprise, therefore, that the Robinson party resurrected a scheme for a public bank, which in the spring of 1768 fell to the ground for the same reasons as three years earlier.[37]

Closely related to these considerations of political factionalism and economic dislocation and distress in the Chesapeake is the third element in political economy as an explanation of the Revolutionary movement, namely, an intense ideological concern with virtue and interest. In the

[36] See O'Mara, *Tidewater Virginia*, chap. 2, and Peter V. Bergstrom, "Markets and Merchants: Economic Diversification in Colonial Virginia, 1700–1775," Ph.D. diss., University of New Hampshire, 1980. See also George M. Herndon, "The Story of Hemp in Colonial Virginia," Ph.D. diss., University of Virginia, 1959, and Sinclair Snow, "Naval Stores in Colonial Virginia," *Agricultural History* 37 (1963):86–93. Further references and a brief discussion of the subject may be found in Ernst, *Money and Politics*, pp. 193–94, 236–38.

The quotations are from Robert P. Thompson, "The Merchant in Virginia, 1700–1774," Ph.D. diss., University of Wisconsin, 1955, p. 285, and Stephen Patterson, "Economic Dislocation and the Coming of the Revolution in Virginia, 1756–1776," unpublished paper, p. 22.

[37] A recent study that takes a different approach to the question of diversification is Raymond C. Bailey, *Popular Influence upon Public Policy: Petitioning in Eighteenth-Century Virginia* (Westport, Conn., 1979), p. 37. See Timothy H. Breen, "The Culture of Agriculture: From Tobacco to Wheat in Tidewater Virginia, 1760–1790," unpublished paper, and Ernst, *Money and Politics*, pp. 235–36.

"Libertarian" lexicon, virtue was tied to interest in two principal ways. First, the ideology of virtue was rooted in a vision of the good society. At its heart was a traditional bias stressing the inseparability of virtue from agrarianism, the independence of landed property, the subordination of the commercial, manufacturing, and "monied" interests, and the greater need for freedom in trade. Second, virtue was a moral and rational quality that allowed man to rise above narrow, selfish interest—to allow him to discover among the many claims competing for attention in the political realm the legitimate interest, or good, of the public. Selfish interest on the other hand was deemed to be natural, and its satisfaction, according to the theory and practice of the age, was associated with the demands of functional economic classes, namely, merchants, farmers, artisans, and the like. Selfish interest played a critical and legitimate role in politics; however, narrow and partial considerations of self-interest were expected to take second place to the larger public interest. Accordingly, Libertarians had no difficulty with a union of self-interest and civic morality in support of the public good.[38]

This perception of an alliance between virtue and interest is central to the dynamic of Revolution in Virginia after 1769, and to the differences in the Revolutionary movements in the two great Chesapeake colonies and to the leading role of Virginia from that time on. Thus in the eyes of Virginia's Revolutionaries, merchants—and especially the Scots—constituted a selfish minority that lacked the virtue to rise above

[38] John A. W. Gunn, *Politics and the Public Interest in the Seventeenth Century* (London, 1969), remains the best introduction to the question of interest and the public good. Explorations of other aspects of the question include: Rodger Parker, "The Gospel of Opposition: A Study in Eighteenth-Century Anglo-American Ideology," Ph.D. diss., Wayne State University, 1975; John G. A. Pocock, *The Machiavellian Moment: Florentine Political Thought and the Atlantic Republican Tradition* (Princeton, 1975); idem, "Virtue and Commerce in the Eighteenth Century," *Journal of Interdisciplinary History* 3 (1972):119–34; Joyce Appleby, "The Social Origins of American Revolutionary Ideology," *Journal of American History* 65 (1978):935–58; Michael G. Kammen, *Empire and Interest: The American Colonies and the Politics of Mercantilism* (Philadelphia, 1970); J. E. Crowley, *This Sheba, Self: The Conceptualization of Economic Life in Eighteenth-Century America* (Baltimore, 1974); and Albert O. Hirschman, *The Passions and Interests: Political Arguments for Capitalism before Its Triumph* (Princeton, 1977).

the petty concern of profit, and the Revolutionary leadership sought to exclude them from any major role, or indeed any role at all, in the Revolutionary movement. But in Maryland, as we have seen, merchants—whether or not they were deemed to be virtuous men—were recognized leaders in the struggle against economic stringency and British oppression during the Stamp Act crisis, and they were not to be denied an active part in the agitation against the Townshend Acts.

In Virginia the ideology of interest was not merely linked to notions of the public good; it also affected views of empire. At one level, as noted above, the Revolutionary outlook was revealed in complex, long-range schemes aimed at expanding the areas of colonial control and advantage within the Atlantic trading world by diversifying agriculture and producing foodstuffs for Mediterranean and Caribbean markets as well as raw materials for British industry. At the higher level or worldview, however, the ideology of interest looked beyond economic change to reform of the navigation system. Basic to this perception was a notion deriving from principles embodied in Harringtonian thought, early eighteenth-century efforts to revise England's trade relations with France, and the Freeport Act of 1766. As summarized by Thomas Paine in *Rights of Man*, published in 1791, the tradition held that "whether with respect to the intercourse of individuals or of nations," the laws of trade and commerce were "laws of mutual and reciprocal interest. They are followed and obeyed, because it is in the interest of the parties to do so, and not on account of any formal laws their governments may impose or interpose." George Mason said as much to George Washington in 1769. The economic bands that fastened the colonies to the mother country, Mason remarked, "if not broken by oppressions, must long hold us together by maintaining a constant reciprocation of interest." A fundamental objective of the Revolutionary movement in Virginia, therefore, was to make metropolitan regulation of the local economy—of agriculture, commerce, money, manufacturing, and land—more evenhanded and responsive to colonial and not simply British interests.[39]

[39] Thomas Paine, *Rights of Man* (New York, 1982), p. 187, and Robert A.

These aspects of the ideology of interest went to the core of the difference in the nonimportation movements in Virginia and Maryland directed against the Townshend duties. Nonimportation originated in Boston early in 1768 and within a year spread to New York, Philadelphia, and Baltimore. Economic hardship in the three older and larger ports pushed merchants and tradesmen into a political alliance aimed at two broad objectives: halting the inflow of British goods so that dry goods merchants could reduce inventories and foreign indebtedness, and undertaking a program of local manufacturing in order to ease unemployment among artisans and mechanics.[40]

Baltimore's merchants in contrast adopted nonimportation at the behest of their Philadelphia correspondents out of a sense of loyalty and dependency. The form of nonimportation agreed to in Baltimore and the provincewide Association adopted in late June by both merchants and planters were, however, in the words of one scholar, "lax," "partial," and "studded with exceptions." Promising tobacco markets and, more important, a flourishing wheat and flour trade made the Baltimore trading community—which led the Revolutionary movement in 1766—and the merchants in general reluctant to stop British imports. Even so Maryland's merchants made a good thing out of the boycott. By allowing "a too general importation," as one Philadelphia rival put it, they "carry'd the frontier trade" of Pennsylvania back to Bal-

---

Rutland, ed., *The Papers of George Mason, 1725–1792*, 3 vols. (Chapel Hill, N.C., 1970), 1:96–98.

The notion of reciprocity within the empire is, of course, related to the interpretation of Revolutionary ideology by Edmund S. and Helen M. Morgan; see the recent study by Thomas P. Slaughter, "The Tax Man Cometh: Ideological Opposition to Internal Taxes, 1760–1790," *William and Mary Quarterly*, 3d ser. 41 (1984): esp. pp. 568–70. Slaughter's own position ignores entirely the discussion by Mason and Revolutionary events in Virginia between 1769 and 1774.

[40] The standard account of nonimportation remains Arthur M. Schlesinger, Sr., *The Colonial Merchants and the American Revolution, 1763–1776* (New York, 1917). Merrill Jensen, *The Founding of a Nation* (New York, 1968), chap. 5, updates Schlesinger in a number of places. See also Charles M. Andrews, *The Boston Merchants and the Non-Importation Movement* (1918; reprint ed., New York, 1968).

timore and Annapolis. There was consequently nothing contradictory about the political response of Maryland's merchant-revolutionaries to the stamp tax and Townshend duties. In both cases they "acted on the fundamental principle of self-interest."[41]

In Virginia no less than in Maryland selfish interest was a recognized principle of human behavior. But the failure of any of the Virginia merchants to initiate nonimportation meant that the task belatedly fell to George Washington and George Mason. A revealing exchange of letters between the two men gives credence to the observation by Friedrich Engels that "everything which sets men in motion must go through their minds; but what form it will take in the mind depends very much upon the circumstances."[42]

Early in 1769 Washington and Mason received copies of the Philadelphia nonimportation agreement of March of that year, together with some letters that had recently passed between Philadelphia and Annapolis. Washington put his thoughts down on paper and sent them to his neighbor and friend in April. He began by affirming the need for an association but warned that "clashing interests" and "selfish designing men (ever attentive to their own gain, and watchful of every turn that can assist their lucrative views, in preference to every other consideration)" would hamper the execution of any boycott. Nowhere was this more of a problem than in "the tobacco colonies where the trade is so diffused and in a manner wholly conducted by factors for their principals at home." Tobacco merchants in short constituted an interest group that threatened the struggle against tyranny precisely because they could not be counted on to subordinate selfish concerns to the public weal. It was the tobacco planters who had to agree not to buy British goods "either

[41] Hoffman, *A Spirit of Dissension*, pp. 80–91. A discussion of tobacco markets in the period is to be found in Price, *France and the Chesapeake*, 1:675–76. The quotations are from Hoffman, pp. 88 and 90.

[42] Friedrich Engels, "Ludwig Feuerbach and the End of Classical German Philosophy," in Karl Marx and Friedrich Engels, *On Religion* (London, 1957), p. 255.

out of any of the stores . . . nor import nor purchase any themselves."

As a member of the landed gentry and a suffering servant of the dominion in the past war, Washington was reckoned to be a virtuous man and consequently a wise judge of the public good. His reliance upon the planters had much to do with the happy confluence of class interest and virtue. Planter indebtedness to some degree affected all producers in the tobacco economy and was to be the impetus to right conduct. It was "universally acknowledged," Washington asserted, that many families because of their British debts were "reduced almost, if not quite, to penury and want," their "estates daily selling for the discharge of debts"; for these distressed planters nonimportation offered the "best plea." The "extravagant and expensive planters" faced a different problem. "How can I, *says he,* who have lived in such a manner change my method? I am ashamed to do it; and besides such an alteration in the system of my living will create suspicions of a decay in my fortune, and such a thought the world must not harbor." Nonimportation gave this man "a pretext to live within bounds." Only one set of people would not "wish well to the scheme," thinking it "hard to be curtailed in their living enjoyments": those living "genteely and hospitably on clear estates." Could not these few, Washington pondered, be depended on to heed the call of virtue and consider "the valuable object in view and the good of others?"

Self-interest and virtue in tandem, these were clearly to be the mainsprings in the operation of any Virginia Association. And where an individual could not be brought into line by the one or the other, Washington believed that those responsible for the public interest could make such a man an object of "public reproach." Indeed, the more he reflected upon it, the "more ardently" Washington wished success to nonimportation, a plan which "more effectually than any other" could relieve the country of its distress.

Another issue related to interest agitating Washington was that of economic sovereignty. An imperium that assumed a right to tax, might it not also "attempt at least to restrain our manufactories; especially those of a public nature?" Should not the "same equity and justice prevail in the one instance as in the other, it being no greater hardship to prevent any manufacturing, than it is to order me to buy goods of them loaded with duties for the express purpose of raising a revenue?" This "additional exertion of arbitrary power" should be put to the test. Clearly this was pushing matters further than the "Letters from a Pennsylvania Farmer," but Washington's concern touched on one of his grand schemes for the future of Virginia: the creation of a great entrepôt on the Potomac that would surpass even Baltimore and Philadelphia in the competition for the burgeoning wheat trade of the west. And, like Philadelphia, this new metropolis was to be a center of manufacturing.[43]

[43] George Mason to George Washington, Apr. 5, 1769, in Rutland, ed., *Papers of Mason*, 1:96–98. The gentry ethic is the subject of numerous books and articles, but see especially Parker, "Gospel of Opposition," pp. 427–32. See also Jack P. Greene, "Society, Ideology, and Politics: An Analysis of the Political Cultures of Mid-Eighteenth Century Virginia," in Richard M. Jellison, ed., *Society, Freedom, and Conscience: The American Revolution in Virginia, Massachusetts, and New York* (New York, 1976), pp. 54–57. The Potomac issue is discussed in Peter J. Albert, "George Washington and the Improvement of the Potomac, 1754–1785," M.A. thesis, University of Wisconsin, 1969.

Arthur Lee and John Dickinson were the first public protesters against the Townshend Acts. The *Virginia Gazette* printed Lee's letters alongside those of the Pennsylvania "Farmer" from February to April 1768. Lee effectively coordinated his efforts with those of Dickinson. The Virginian focused upon questions of polity and the constitution, drawing heavily on classical sources and Whig opposition thought, to bring his countrymen to a "just hatred of tyranny and a zeal for freedom." For a discussion of economic matters Lee directed his readers to Dickinson. In addition Lee seconded Dickinson's two-part strategy for defeating the Townshend Acts: the assemblies were to inaugurate a petition campaign against the law, backed by a continent-wide association for the nonimportation of British goods and the promotion of American manufactures. While Lee and Dickinson warned Americans of the latest British threat to their prosperity and "public liberty," events conspired to give the House of Burgesses the lead in adopting the first of Dickinson's proposals. Early in 1768 the Virginia assembly drafted a petition to king, Lords, and Commons for repeal of the offending acts, dispatching copies of their resolutions to their London agent and the other colonies. Lee was not involved in the move to create an association, however; by 1769 he had abandoned America for London to join the cause of English Radicalism, and the task of forming an "Asso-

Mason for the most part agreed with Washington. With an eye to tailoring nonimportation to local circumstances, Mason suggested two possible courses of action. One, a variation on Washington's plan, rested on the premise that Virginia could not, like Philadelphia, New York, and Boston, circumscribe "importations within such narrow bounds"; accordingly the planters were to "retrench all manner of superfluitys" and "finery of all denominations," confining themselves to "linens, woolens, etc. not exceeding a certain price." Even a limited restriction, Mason insisted, harkening back to the Stamp Act repeal, would awaken British merchants and manufacturers to American rights. The second plan differed radically in scope and purpose. It declared for nonexportation and aimed not only at distressing tobacco houses but also the British Treasury which stood to lose in revenue "fifty times more than all their oppressions here could raise."

Mason, however, dissented from Washington's views concerning manufacturing. Washington had argued for the colonists' right to manufacture for themselves, thereby raising this question from the level of tactics to that of ideology. Mason believed it was "not the interest" of the colonies to refuse British manufactures except as a means of defeating parliamentary taxation in America. "Our supplying our mother country with gross materials and taking her manufactures in return is the true chain of connection between us," Mason averred; "these are the bands which, if not broken by oppressions, must long hold us together by maintaining a constant reciprocation of interest."[44]

---

ciation for Non-Importation" fell to Washington and Mason. See Glenn C. Smith, "An Era of Non-Importation Associations, 1768–1773," *William and Mary Quarterly*, 2d ser. 2 (1939):87–89; Paul C. Bowers, "Richard Henry Lee and the Continental Congress," Ph.D. diss., Duke University, 1964, pp. 41–46; John P. Kennedy, ed., *Journals of the House of Burgesses of Virginia, 1766–69* (Richmond, 1906), pp. 139–48, 165, 174, and William J. Van Schreeven, ed., *The Farmer's and Monitor's Letters to the Inhabitants of the British Colonies* (Richmond, 1969).

[44] Mason to Washington, Apr. 5, 1769, in Rutland, ed., *Papers of Mason*, 1:99–100. The question of colonial manufacturing is an old and much-disputed issue; see McCoy, *Elusive Republic*, chaps. 1 and 2.

It should be noted that Washington and Mason analyzed the prospects for nonimportation as if the province's "second staple," wheat, was an irrelevancy. And it was, politically speaking. Wheat was of growing significance, especially in the Northern Neck; yet tobacco remained Virginia's primary export, accounting for better than 70 percent of the value of total exports at the time. More than that, nonimportation aimed at pressuring British firms into lobbying as effectively against the Townshend Acts as they had earlier against the stamp tax. And it was the great tobacco houses, not wheat traders, that had played and continued to play a leadership role in the Committee of North American Merchants.

Events now awaited the convening of the burgesses. At that time Washington and Mason would join in the Revolutionary coalition representing the agrarian concerns of the back-country and Northern Neck and introduce their "uniform plan" of nonimportation to be concerted and sent to the different counties.[45] Meanwhile a new governor, the baron de Botetourt, had arrived in Virginia, necessitating the holding of elections. These had taken place late in 1768 against the background of rising anxiety over the Townshend duties and a vigorous newspaper debate concerning the nonimportation movement developing in the northern colonies. It was only in May 1769, however, when Botetourt consented to call the assembly into session and announced the king's rejection of the burgesses' petition for repeal of the Townshend Acts passed back in the spring of 1768 that matters came to a head.[46]

Botetourt lectured the house about the crown's determination to abide by the provision of the Declaratory Act affirming Parliament's right to pass laws binding in "all and every part" of the empire. Despite his tough stand, Botetourt had ignored the text of an even stronger speech written expressly for him by the ministry. Moreover the governor had done what he could in private to ensure that the members of

[45] Mason did not, of course, sit in the House; his brother Thomson did and was a sometime member of the coalition. For the other members see above.

[46] See Smith, "Era of Non-Importation Associations," p. 90.

the assembly would "come together in a good humor" and moderate their stance on parliamentary taxation. But, led by the Revolutionary coalition, the House reaffirmed the position taken the year before, and once again distributed the resolutions throughout the colonies. In addition it adopted a memorial to the king attacking the constitutionality of recent legislation requiring Americans suspected of treason to be tried in England. Botetourt had no choice but to call for a dissolution, whereupon, headed by Richard Henry Lee and Patrick Henry, the body of representatives withdrew only to reassemble in the Apollo Room of the Raleigh Tavern. Their business was opposition to Britain. Meanwhile Botetourt secretly informed the ministry that he had lost control of events in Virginia and counseled immediate and vigorous action.[47]

On May 11 George Mason—or someone with access to his correspondence with Washington—adopting the pen name "Atticus," outlined in the *Virginia Gazette* a plan of nonimportation and nonexportation. Britain's foreign trade, Atticus informed his readers, was in decline: the Spanish trade "almost reduced to nothing," and trade with Portugal "lessening every year." As for France the balance had long been against the mother country, and "but for the article of tobacco would be immensely so." The fact was that British merchants were being "undersold," and all because of the "luxury diffused through all ranks of Britons whereby the price of labor and manufactures is raised above the value in other countries." British luxury and extravagance was a Libertarian commonplace. Casting it in mercantilist balance-of-trade terms "proved" the colonies' economic importance and the effectiveness of nonintercourse. "That upon the whole the wealth, the trade, the shipping, and the maritime power of Great Britain have increased beyond the idea of former times," Atticus concluded, could only be owing to the colonies, which offered the one market where Britain "cannot be rivalled." Yet Parliament taxed British manufactures without American

[47] Dianne J. McGann, "The Official Letters of Norbonne Berkeley, Baron de Botetourt, Governor of Virginia, 1768–1770," M.A. thesis, College of William and Mary, 1971, pp. 12–24. See also ibid., pp. 135–39, and Bowers, "Lee," pp. 45–46.

consent. Was it now time to show "the inhabitants of *Great Britain* that our enemies are equally theirs; and by refusing to take their manufactures, and withholding from them our commodities, until our grievances are redressed demonstrate to them that we cannot be wounded but through their sides?"

Atticus conceded that there was a practical difficulty with an economic boycott in Virginia: too many merchants were Scottish factors, and the Scots could not "destrain their imports without the consent of their principals." The only solution was to bypass the trading community and rely upon the planting interest. Planters would be expected to purchase nothing but necessary items, from the cheapest dry goods to linens and woolens "not exceeding a certain price." They would, moreover, neither make nor export tobacco, and slaves would be put to manufacturing. In short a "general spirit of frugality and industry" could be expected to prevail as individual interests were subordinated to public ones, and the work ethic incorporated into a larger, nobler, transcendent purpose. Finally, the "principal gentlemen," as men of Virtue, could be expected to set the example for the "bulk of the people." "What will not the love of liberty inspire!" Atticus apostrophized.[48]

Whatever the inspiration for Virginia's nonimportation association, the agreement, signed May 18, 1769, by eighty-nine former burgesses, has been variously credited to George Mason and Richard Henry Lee. More certain is that the committee responsible for drafting the resolves drew heavily on the Philadelphia document of the previous March and on corrections to that document made by Mason in late April. With tobacco prices on the rise Mason presumably had dropped the question of an embargo. Instead association members were to bind themselves not to import or buy locally: goods taxable under the Townshend Acts, slaves, alcoholic beverages, luxuries from furniture through carriages to silks, and dry goods, other than the cheapest grades used for clothing slaves; not to import anything made by Virginia artisans—from leather goods, wool, tallow, and candles to hoes

---

[48] Rutland, ed., *Papers of Mason*, 1:106–9, and Kennedy, ed., *Journals, 1766–69*, pp. xl–xliii.

and axes; and finally not to purchase from outside the dominion commodities produced domestically such as beef and pork. The general intent of the several provisions was clear. For those Virginians, however, who were anxious to hasten the development of plantation autarky, the artisans being protected would be slaves; for those like Washington who dreamed of a new system of farming based upon grain, entrepôt towns, and western expansion, they would be white.[49]

The association agreement appeared in the *Virginia Gazette* on May 25 together with a request—strictly pro forma—that British factors prepare a general representation setting out for their suppliers the need for nonimportation. Instead when the merchants met in Williamsburg, as they regularly did in June, they confined themselves to their usual business of settling the exchange rate and clearing their obligations. Individual merchants may have adhered to the association, but the class conspicuously failed to join in the nonimportation throughout 1769.[50]

Meanwhile the newspapers carried report after report of the planters' enthusiastic support. Typical was the response of John Page, Jr. He informed his London correspondent that as an association member he would not "send to England for anything this year. I like the Association," Page declared, "because I think it will repeal the disagreeable acts of Parliament, open the eyes of the people with you, and must certainly clear us of our debts." Page was right about two things. The association did reduce great-planter indebtedness by stifling luxury purchases: between 1769 and 1771 custom records show no listings of carriages, chairs, English china, furniture, silverplate, wine, or lace. And nonimportation did open British eyes to the truth about Virginia's reputation as a staunch opponent of the Townshend Acts. The assembly resolutions of 1768 and the patriotic hoopla surrounding the association, in the words of one English writer, had given

[49] Kennedy, ed., *Journals, 1766–69*, pp. 109–13, and Carville V. Earle, *The Evolution of a Tidewater Settlement System: All Hallow's Parish, Maryland, 1650–1783* (Chicago, 1975).

[50] Dale Benson, "Wealth and Power in Virginia, 1774–1776: A Study of the Organization of Revolt," Ph.D. diss., University of Virginia, 1972.

Virginia "a name in opposing Revenue Acts," a name "not merited."[51]

In the spring of 1769 Richard Henry Lee confidently wrote his brother Arthur in London that liberty's flame burned "bright and clear" in Virginia. That summer, however, as local scribblers beat the drum for nonimportation, the flame was more like a flicker. Reports in the fall from Glasgow and London confirmed the worst: British trade with Virginia was booming, and an embittered Lee changed his metaphor. "The cause of public liberty like the setting sun is going to disappear," he wrote in December. But in no time at all Virginia's patriots discovered that the collapse of the "glorious Association so late erected . . . so soon forgotten" was the fault of the "damned Scots."[52]

Scapegoating the Scots was a familiar ploy in eighteenth-century Anglo-America. Yet there was more to it than that. The Scots were rapidly expanding their chain of stores in a struggle with English consignment merchants and independent Virginia storekeepers for control of the tobacco trade. In 1769 the Scottish factors gave so high a price for tobacco that for the moment consignment merchants and others could not compete. Some tobacco was purchased for cash, but most for store goods—cottons, woolens, blankets, linens, hardware, leather, and the like. Of these items the association permitted only cheap dry goods—if the price did not exceed 1s. 6 d. per yard; the rest came under a ban, or were specified as protected products for domestic manufacture. Thus the Scots did seem willing to violate nonimportation—as long as the good people of Virginia made it worth their while.[53]

During the second half of 1769 the association came under increasing pressure for modification for two concurrent reasons: the devastating news that, first, the Virginians had

[51] John Page, Jr., to John Norton, May 27, 1769, in Mason, ed., *Norton and Sons*, pp. 93–94. Page was close to Jefferson and was a member of the Revolutionary coalition.

[52] May 19, 1769, in Ballagh, ed., *Letters of Lee*, 1:34, and Dec. 10, 1769, in Richard Henry Lee, *The Life of Arthur Lee*, 2 vols. (Boston, 1829), 1:35.

[53] Price, "Rise of Glasgow," pp. 187–90, discusses the Scottish advantages in the tobacco trade.

failed to observe nonimportation, and, second, the ministry would ask for repeal of the Townshend Acts at the upcoming session of Parliament. Botetourt confirmed the second story in November. Levies presently in effect on paints, paper, and glass were to be dropped; only the tax on tea would be retained. Virginia's patriot leaders now switched tactics, calling upon their fellow countrymen to reform their ways and stand up bravely in the fight for the association until Britain abolished *all* constitutional taxes. Virtue, not interest, was in the ascendency.[54]

Early in 1770 the associators announced plans for an April meeting to revise and strengthen the nonimportation agreement. Supporters wrote in to the local press citing the heavy volume of British imports as a sign of how "trifling the business of the Association had been attended to," and then ritualistically cursed the Scots, and the merchants generally, for their efforts to break the organization. The arrival of news that Parliament had indeed repealed all the duties save the tax on tea forced a delay in the meeting until May 22, when the original group of associators and burgesses appointed a committee of twenty to amend the agreement. This committee split into two opposing interests. One was led by Edmund Pendleton, head of the Robinson party, which had traditionally aligned itself with the court and gave whatever support it could to Botetourt, the other by the Northern Neck faction within the Revolutionary coalition that favored a new and strengthened association.[55]

This deadlock produced a call for yet another gathering set for June 1. The day before, the Revolutionary coalition rushed into print with a letter in the *Virginia Gazette* from Arthur Lee in London. Only the British merchants could bring about the repeal of every tax including tea, and only an effective boycott would make them feel American griev-

---

[54] Kennedy, ed., *Journals, 1766–69,* pp. 226–27, and *Virginia Gazette* (Rind) Nov. 30, 1769; see also Schlesinger, *Colonial Merchants,* pp. 137–38.

[55] *Virginia Gazette* (Rind), Feb. 8, 15, 1770, and *Virginia Gazette* (Purdie and Dixon), Mar. 22, 1770. See also Thompson, "Merchant in Virginia," pp. 323–24, and Jack P. Greene, ed., *The Diary of Landon Carter of Sabine Hall, 1753–1778,* 2 vols. (Charlottesville, Va., 1965), 1:418.

ances as their own. Nothing, Lee argued, could be expected of the ministry and king. This was propaganda pure and simple. In 1770 Scottish *and* English merchants were aggressively expanding the flow of credit and goods to the Chesapeake, where commodity prices continued to rise and exchange rates fall. The firm of Perkins, Buchanan, and Brown snidely commented on these matters to its factor, Thomas Adams, that spring. Virginia's association had been "esteemed the most effectual and strongest upon the continent, and, with concern we say it, was soonest and most publicly broke through. Our bills of entry have for a long time past proclaimed this, as almost every prohibited article appears to have been shipped of which Lord Hillsborough (very naturally) took great advantage when the Committee of Merchants waited on him with a copy of the petition to parliament."[56]

On June 1 the associators met and arrived at an understanding: unless the merchant community would lend its active support, nonimportation was lost. Consequently arrangements were made, and at a session held two weeks later Andrew Sprowle, the so-called chairman of the trade in Virginia and leader of the Norfolk business community, was conspicuously present. At the next meeting, on June 22, the extent of the compromises between the rival factions became clear. First, the Revolutionary coalition surrendered leadership of the revamped association to the Robinson party and the merchants, as Pendleton took over as moderator with Sprowle second in command. Second, the new agreement made no mention of the grievances set out in May 1769; but this time nonimportation was to have some teeth, which, as Mason explained to Richard Henry Lee, was exactly what was necessary. The virtue of the planters, no less the merchants, had been found wanting. The association, operating through the various county committees, would now have the authority

[56]"Monitor," *Virginia Gazette* (Rind), May 31 and Apr. 9, 1770, in Thomas Adams Papers, 1770–78, Virginia Historical Society, Richmond. Commodity markets are described in Hoffman, *A Spirit of Dissension*, pp. 81–82; British exports, in Price, *Capital and Credit*, appendix D, p. 162. Thompson, "Merchant in Virginia," pp. 335–38, breaks down and analyzes the gross figures.

to police the agreement and enforce the public good by inculcating "in the strongest manner" a "sense of shame and fear of reproach" among all those—planters, gentlemen, merchants, and commoners—who dared to violate the regulations. Names of transgressors would be published "and themselves stigmatized as enemies to their country," while the county courts were empowered to search for prohibited articles and to seize and store them until the association disbanded.[57]

Despite a flurry of newspaper publicity during the next few months, the new operation turned out to be a "sham affair." Not economic boycott but recovery was the issue, as British credit and commodity exports continued to expand along with the sale of imported goods. Tobacco and wheat prices rose higher than ever, while sterling exchange rates fell to a new low. Finally the breakup of nonimportation in Philadelphia during the summer of 1770, and in New York, Massachusetts, and Maryland that fall, made the Virginia exercise increasingly irrelevant. Even Arthur Lee conceded that the new association would have no more impact on British merchants and manufacturers than did the old. And it did not. When Washington and Mason finally called an end to the pretense in July 1771, imports had skyrocketed to their highest levels yet.[58]

The collapse of nonimportation in Virginia has been a sore point from that time to this without consensus being reached

[57] *Virginia Gazette* (Purdie and Dixon), June 7, 1770. The new agreement is reprinted in John P. Kennedy, ed., *Journals of the House of Burgesses of Virginia, 1770–1772*, pp. xxvii–xxxl. Merchant efforts to organize and protect their interests are discussed in Thompson, "Merchant in Virginia," pp. 327–28, and in Robert W. Coakley, "Virginia Commerce during the American Revolution," Ph.D. diss., Princeton University, 1944, pp. 75–84. See also Donald M. Sweig, "The Virginia Nonimportation Association Broadside of 1770 and Fairfax County: A Study in Local Participation," *Virginia Magazine of History and Biography* 87 (1979):316–25.

Mason's remarks and an analysis of the authorship of the revised agreement are in Rutland, ed., *Papers of Mason*, 1:116–19; see also Thompson, "Merchant in Virginia," pp. 327–35.

[58] The state of the Chesapeake economy is discussed in Hoffman, *A Spirit of Dissension*, pp. 81–82. See Jensen, *Founding of a Nation*, chap. 10, for a general account of the breakup of nonimportation.

about the cause of failure. Perhaps the last word belongs to Mason, who by late 1770 had come around to a position remarkably like the one enunciated by Washington in the spring of 1769. If Virginia and the other colonies, Mason reflected, had formed a plan "in the nature of a sumptuary law, restraining only articles of luxury and ostentation together with the goods at any time taxed, and at the same time giving all possible encouragement to American manufacturers and invitations to manufacturers from Europe to remove thither and settle among us, and as these increased from time to time still decreasing our European imports, [such] an Association then formed upon these principles would have gathered strength by execution, and however slow in its operation, it would have been certain in its effects." Here was a view of a new and dynamic Virginia economy—in a new and changing relationship with the mother country.[59]

The nonimportation movement in Virginia expressed a need for economic relief and repeal of threatening British revenue and commercial measures. It also revealed the desire of the Revolutionary leadership to remedy a perceived weakness in the very structure and operation of empire, the absence of any "constant reciprocation of interest" between the mother state and the colonies. Nonimportation failed, yet the boom years of 1770–71 and the repeal of the Townshend Acts had done much to allay anxieties about the future. It was the severity of the credit collapse and depression of 1772–75 together with the commercial retaliations imposed by the Intolerable Acts that renewed old fears about the place of the Chesapeake within the British Empire. This time, however, such considerations triggered a debate that went beyond any concern with reciprocity of interest and raised the penultimate issue in the Revolution—the economic sovereignty of the colonies.

The Chesapeake's trade in wheat and flour declined in 1771, while tobacco prices remained favorable and exports turned out to be the largest yet recorded, 105,000 pounds.

[59] Mason to [George Brent], Dec. 6, 1770, in Rutland, ed., *Papers of Mason*, 1:128.

As late as December, British merchants scrambled to get their ships off to the Chesapeake and back home again as soon as possible. Competitiveness and optimism were characteristic of the Virginia and Maryland economy through the first few months of 1772.[60]

In the spring of 1772 tobacco prices in London and Glasgow began to weaken. That summer they crashed and did not fully recover until just before American Independence. One difficulty was the record shipment of around 100,000 pounds of the leaf for each of the next three successive years. Another was the panic and depression of 1772–73, one of the most severe in British history. As funds in England and Scotland dried up and creditors pressed for payment, liquidity demands and exchange rates soared. Whenever possible, debtors attempted to settle their accounts by shipping commodities. Tobacco markets were quickly "overdone," and then late in 1771 grain and flour markets also slumped. Meanwhile excessive British exports beginning in 1770 created a glut in the American dry goods trade. It was 1762–63 all over again. Enormous new debts had piled up during the years of easy credit and high commodity prices—not to mention outstanding old debts—and could no longer be paid. The number of small debtors in both agriculture and the retail trade, however, appears to have been greater than previously. Throughout the Chesapeake the common cry once again became the "distressed situation of the times" and the need for relief.[61]

At the end of May 1774 in the midst of the economic disorder, a circular letter arrived in the Chesapeake from Massachusetts condemning Parliament's closing the port of Boston and asking for nonimportation and nonexportation

[60] Hoffman, *A Spirit of Dissension*, pp. 98–101, describes trends in the economy in 1771 and 1772.

[61] Richard B. Sheridan, "The British Credit Crisis of 1772 and the American Colonies," *Journal of Economic History* 20 (1960):161–86; Thompson, "Merchant in Virginia," pp. 342–47; Coakley, "Virginia Commerce during the Revolution," pp. 820–92; Hoffman, *A Spirit of Dissension*, pp. 125–39; and Price, ed., *Joshua Johnson's Letterbook, 1771–1774: Letters from a Merchant in London to His Partners in Maryland* (London, 1979), pp. xvi–xxxi.

agreements to defeat the measure. In addition the colonies were called upon to send delegates to a Continental Congress for the consideration of the rights of America. According to one contemporary account the letter precipitated a "violent debate" among Virginia's politicians. Leaders of the Revolutionary coalition—Patrick Henry, Richard Henry Lee, George Mason, and their ally, treasurer Robert Carter Nicholas—came out strongly in favor of "paying no debts to Britain, no exportation or importation, and no courts here." In opposition was the Robinson faction represented by Speaker Peyton Randolph, Edmund Pendleton, Carter Braxton, and a supporter within the merchant community, Thomas Nelson, Jr. The conflict ended in a stalemate and an agreement to await the outcome of a convening of county delegates at a general assembly to be held in August.[62]

In the meantime, during the late spring and early summer, the Northern Neck counties took the lead in demanding the closing of the courts. By July merchants reported that many of the county courts were "as good as put up," while "the warm patriots" were "bustling hard for a general Association against imports and exports." Two months later most courts had shut down, but in or out of court no monies could be collected, even if the creditor's "salvation was to rest on it." This campaign to advance the Revolutionary cause by attacking the merchant interest, providing debtor relief to planters and farmers, and imposing sanctions against British trade was merely the opening blow in a larger struggle—the demand for repudiation of Parliament's right to regulate the colonial economy and for the economic sovereignty of America. Whatever other effect it may have had on Virginia's Revolutionary leadership, the Boston Port Act precipitated an ideological move away from an expressed desire for a reciprocity of interests within the North American trading empire to an insistence upon the colonies' need, and constitutional right, to control their own economic destiny.[63]

[62] James Parker to Charles Steuart, June 17, 1774, in Charles Steuart Papers, National Library of Scotland, Edinburgh.

[63] These events are carefully and fully analyzed in Benson, "Wealth and Power in Virginia," chap. 2. See also George M. Curtis III, "Virginia

Economic sovereignty was the core issue in the Fairfax Resolves adopted July 18 in preparation for the August convention. The third resolution drew on arguments concerning
virtual representation made at the time of the Stamp Act
crisis: the colonies were not and "from their situation" could
not be represented in Parliament. Thus "the legislative power
here can of right be exercised only by our own provincial
assemblies or parliaments" subject to a royal veto within a
"proper and limited time." The radical conclusion was that
parliamentary regulation of trade appeared "repugnant" to
constitutional principles, however necessary to the "general
good" of the empire. Such were the sentiments of Mason,
Washington, and "at least the ruling elite" of the county—
except for Bryan Fairfax. He informed his friend Washington that the claim about Parliament having "no right to make
any laws for us," especially laws concerning trade, was unacceptable. Washington ignored him.[64]

Fairfax may have been put off at home, but his notions
found support in many parts of the province. A Caroline
County resolution, for instance, espoused a view proclaimed
by Mason only five years before, namely, that "a firm and
mutual intercourse and reciprocation of interests and affec-
tions between Great Britain and her colonies" was both "de-
sirable and beneficial." In any event the provincial convention
that met during the first week in August sidestepped any
controversy over parliamentary rights in matters of trade and

Courts during the Revolution," Ph.D. diss., University of Wisconsin, 1970,
chaps. 4–6. Compare Emory G. Evans, "Planter Indebtedness and the
Coming of the Revolution in Virginia," *William and Mary Quarterly*, 3d ser.
27 (1971):511–33.

The quotes are from Charles Yates to Samuel Martin, July 5, 1774, in
Charles Yates Letter Book, 1773–83, University of Virginia Library, Charlottesville, and William Reynolds to George Norton, Aug. 18, Sept. 6,
1774, in William Reynolds Letterbooks, 1771–79 and 1772–85, Library of
Congress.

[64] Nan Netherton et al., *Fairfax County Virginia: A History* (Fairfax, 1978),
pp. 95–103; Donald M. Sweig and Elizabeth S. David, eds., *A Fairfax
Friendship: The Complete Correspondence between George Washington and Bryan
Fairfax* (Fairfax, 1982), p. 68. Van Schreeven, Scribner, and Tarter, eds.,
Revolutionary Virginia, has conveniently reprinted all the existing county
resolutions from the period (1:111–68).

commerce in favor of a simple affirmation of the fact that "wanting the protection of Britain" Virginia had "long acquiesced" in the Acts of Navigation. It then went on to approve an economic boycott of the mother country and the call for a Continental Congress. Elected delegates to the Philadelphia convention came from both the Robinson party and the Revolutionary coalition. Delegates, however, were enjoined from taking any formal position in Congress on the Navigation Laws. This did not in the end stop two of Virginia's seven delegates, Patrick Henry and Richard Henry Lee, from airing their personal opinions on the subject.[65]

Economic sovereignty was not a question in Maryland politics during the period. A "popular party" had emerged in 1773 in connection with a notorious newspaper debate between Daniel Dulany and Charles Carroll of Carrollton over the "fee controversy" and the hard times. This new faction embraced elements of the old country party and the former Baltimore-Annapolis alliance of merchants and radical politicians, but it remained on shaky grounds and was just beginning to consolidate its position in the House of Delegates. The arrival of the Massachusetts circular and the calling of county conventions to address the issue of a British boycott confronted the popular party with more difficulties. These conventions quickly became the locus of Revolutionary power and authority in the province, and the party found itself having to vie for leadership with a small, albeit politically dangerous, republican faction. Popular party leaders in sum feared political and social turmoil if the Revolutionary cause were pushed too hard and tried to reach some possible accommodation with the mother state.[66]

In contrast to Virginia, the very question of parliamentary regulation of trade split the Revolutionary vanguard in Maryland. Samuel Chase, for one, conceded Parliament's right in

[65] Van Schreeven, Scribner, and Tarter, eds., *Revolutionary Virginia*, 1:114–16, 228, 236–39.

[66] The popular party's development and actions during these years are analyzed in Hoffman, *A Spirit of Dissension*, chaps. 5–6. Compare William A. O'Brien, "'Challenge to Consensus': Social, Political and Economic Implications of Maryland Sectionalism, 1776–1789," Ph.D. diss., University of Wisconsin, 1979, chaps. 1–2.

the area, while Baltimore's merchants and Charles Carroll appear to have been of another mind. Yet in the interests of party unity such differences were set aside throughout 1774 and 1775. Not until 1776, when events made it seem that a complete break with Britain was inevitable—and not with Parliament alone but with the crown as well—did Maryland's Revolutionaries reluctantly join the representatives of the other colonies to vote for independence.[67]

The First Continental Congress had to decide a number of difficult issues during the months of September and October 1774. Foremost among them was the nature and content of the *Declaration of Rights* of the American colonies. Central to this problem was the validity of the Navigation Acts. The Virginians were supposed to remain silent on the question, the provincial convention having restricted them to considerations that "would not retrospect farther back than 1763." Yet Richard Henry Lee entertained no doubt about the acts; they were a "capital" violation of the colonies' rights, and he made his views known. Delegate Patrick Henry was no less forthcoming in his remarks to Congress. Before the colonists were "obliged to pay taxes as the subjects of Britain did," Henry declared, "let us be as free as they: let us have our trade open with all the world." Nevertheless, as Lee explained to John Adams, who supported his position, the great danger was that striking at the navigation system "would unite every man in Britain against us," as it did so many of the delegates in Congress.[68]

[67] See James Duane to Samuel Chase, Dec. 29, 1775, in Edmund Cody Burnett, ed., *Letters of Members of the Continental Congress,* 8 vols. (Washington, D.C., 1921–36), 1:87–89. The views of Charles Carroll of Carrollton on this question are not so clear as one would like. The editor of a new and complete edition of Carroll letters, Ronald Hoffman, has generously made the correspondence of the Revolutionary period available to me, and even more generously has shared with me his knowledge of and insights into the Revolutionary and independence movements in Maryland. In any event, Carroll's moods, if not his ideology, may be judged from a letter to the British firm Wallace and Co., written as early as Jan. 8, 1775.

The position of the Baltimore merchants is touched on by Hoffman, *A Spirit of Dissension,* pp. 164–65.

[68] The quotations are from Paul H. Smith, ed., *Letters of Delegates to Congress, 1774–1789,* 9 vols. to date (Washington, D.C., 1976–), 1:8, 46, 68–69, 111, 292–93.

In the end Congress deferred "to a future time" the need to take any constitutional stand on the navigation laws. For the moment the *Declaration of Rights* merely asserted that the colonies would "from the necessity of the case, and a regard to the mutual interest of both countries . . . cheerfully consent to the operation of such acts of the British parliament as are *bona fide* restrained to the regulation of our external commerce." Compromise and reciprocity of interests, not economic sovereignty, were to form the bases of any accommodation with Britain.[69]

Thomas Jefferson had just missed out on being elected to the first Congress and illness had kept him from attending Virginia's August convention. He nevertheless prepared a statement of rights he hoped the provincial convention would adopt. Jefferson had sent a copy of the document to his political ally Patrick Henry, expecting him to present it to the county deputies. But Henry failed to act—possibly out of indolence, or out of fear that the statement was too radical for the occasion. Fortunately, Jefferson had taken the precaution of placing a second copy in the hands of Peyton Randolph, who at least tabled it for the delegates' perusal. The "young" reportedly applauded its sentiments; the "old" did not. In any event, after the convention and upon the advice of friends, Jefferson went ahead and published his sentiments in the celebrated pamphlet *A Summary View of the Rights of British America*. A central claim was that the "exercise of a free trade with all parts of the world" was "possessed by the American colonies as of natural rights." Jefferson went on to explain, not in any detail but with much passion, how parliamentary regulations of trade, manufacturing, and agriculture had injured American interests.[70]

As Richard Henry Lee had feared, American insistence on the right to control their own economic lives united the British political nation against the colonies. *A Summary View* arrived in England at about the same time as Congress's

[69] Worthington C. Ford, ed., *Journals of the Continental Congress*, 34 vols. (Washington, D.C., 1904–37), 1:63–74.

[70] Van Schreeven, Scribner, and Tarter, ed., *Revolutionary Virginia*, 1:234–56; see also Ford, ed., *Writings of Jefferson*, 1:9–13, 183–84, 211–16.

Declaration of Rights. The ministry and Parliament focused on Jefferson's pamphlet. In arguing against a conciliatory measure introduced by William Pitt in 1775, the earl of Sandwich observed that "it was clear the Americans were not disputing about words, but realities"; what they wanted was "to free themselves from the restrictions laid on their commerce."[71]

Sandwich was close to the mark. The Revolutionary movement in the Chesapeake reflected, indeed, embodied, the need for a mutual "reciprocation of interest" between the mother state and her colonies. And the First Continental Congress settled upon that very formula in its *Declaration of Rights.* But an independence movement that had originated in Virginia in the summer of 1774 aimed at achieving economic sovereignty. The Declaration of Independence in 1776 was a logical extension, but not a forgone conclusion, of Virginia's position.

[71] The quotation is from Staughton Lynd, "An Economic Interpretation of the Declaration of Independence," unpublished paper. Lynd makes the question of Parliament's right to regulate trade and commerce central to the problem of independence; this is also the thesis of James L. Cooper, "Interests, Ideas, and Empire: The Roots of American Foreign Policy, 1763–1779," Ph.D. diss., University of Wisconsin, 1964, chaps. 1–6. I have followed Lynd and Cooper on this matter.

RUSSELL R. MENARD

Slavery, Economic Growth, and Revolutionary Ideology in the South Carolina Lowcountry

THERE ARE TWO MAJOR PROBLEMS in the historiography of the American Revolution in the South. One concerns the relationship between economic and political developments. In an older historiographical tradition the connection was clear. Mercantilist restrictions, customs racketeering, and grasping English merchants forced planters to put up with unacceptable constraints, corrupt officials, and, especially, a burdensome debt. The combination made life within the old empire intolerable and drove colonists into resistance and independence. That view now finds few defenders. Indeed, most historians are now persuaded that the colonial economy was strong and flexible and that it delivered an impressive prosperity, especially to those privileged men who led the Revolution.[1]

This essay, a preliminary report on a study of the lowcountry political economy during the eighteenth and early nineteenth centuries, has benefited from comments by Paul G. E. Clemens, Marc Egnal, Joseph A. Ernst, Jacob M. Price, and the members of the Minnesota Social History Workshop. Research support was provided by the Graduate School, University of Minnesota.

[1]The literature on these issues is reviewed by John J. McCusker and Russell R. Menard, *The Economy of British America, 1607–1789* (Chapel Hill, N.C., 1985), pp. 351–58.

The collapse of this paradigm has led some scholars to separate the Revolutionary process from social and economic developments. Thus, Bernard Bailyn argues, "the outbreak of the Revolution was not the result of social discontent, or of economic disturbances, or of rising misery, or of those mysterious social strains that seem to beguile the imaginations of historians straining to find peculiar dispositions to upheaval." Instead, political and constitutional issues were primary. "American resistance," Bailyn continues, "was a response to acts of power deemed arbitrary, degrading, and uncontrollable—a response in itself objectively reasonable, that was inflamed to the point of explosion by ideological currents generating fears everywhere in America that irresponsible and self-serving adventurers . . . had gained the power of the English government and were turning first . . . to that Rhineland of their aggressions, the colonies."[2]

Slavery is the second historiographical problem. No one has improved on the way Samuel Johnson put the question: "How is it that we hear the loudest yelps for liberty among the drivers of negroes?"[3] Responses to that query fall into three categories. One response, still all too common, has been to ignore the fact of slavery, to write as if the South were not a slave society, to pretend that the Revolutionary leaders in the South were not men whose intimate daily involvement with black bondsmen and bondswomen shaped their behavior and their view of the world.

A second response has been to point out how slavery made southern planters particularly sensitive to any challenge to their own freedom. It did so, Jack P. Greene suggests, in two ways, both of which operated with special force in South Carolina. "Slavery," Christopher Gadsden announced in 1766, "begets slavery." South Carolina's black majority and the ever-present fear of "domestic insurrections" made for "a very weak Province" with a limited capacity to resist metropolitan

[2]Bernard Bailyn, "The Central Themes of the American Revolution: An Interpretation," in Stephen G. Kurtz and James H. Hutson, eds., *Essays on the American Revolution* (Chapel Hill, N.C., 1973), pp. 12–13.

[3]"Taxation No Tyranny," in Donald J. Greene, ed., *Samuel Johnson: Political Writings* (New Haven, 1977), p. 454.

aggression. To Gadsden, at least, the moral was clear. Surrounded by "very dangerous Domestics," South Carolinians had "to take a militant stand against any threat to their liberty before the threat had become so formidable that they, like their slaves, lost all 'power of resistance.'"[4]

Moreover, immediate knowledge of slavery gave Revolutionary rhetoric a special meaning and intensity in the South. When planters spoke of slavery, tyranny, and oppression, they did not deal in abstract political categories but instead described a real and degrading human condition. The "language of slavery," common to patriots throughout the colonies, had a special force in the South, where it evoked apocalyptic fears of a world turned upside down. "In the southern colonies," David Ramsay explained, "slavery nurtured a spirit of liberty. . . . Nothing could more effectively animate the opposition of a planter to the claims of Great-Britain, than a conviction that those claims . . . degraded him to a degree of dependence on his fellow subjects, equally humiliating with that which existed between his slaves and himself."[5]

A third answer is Edmund S. Morgan's exploration of the paradoxical relationship between slavery and freedom in American politics. Simply put, black slavery made the South safe for white liberty. Slavery isolated blacks and removed them from the political process; racism united whites by concealing class differences behind a republican rhetoric that asserted the equality of free men. "In the republican way of thinking," Morgan argues, "slavery occupied a critical, if am-

[4]Jack P. Greene, "'Slavery or Independence': Some Reflections on the Relationship among Liberty, Black Bondage, and Equality in Revolutionary South Carolina," *South Carolina Historical Magazine* 80 (1979):193–214, quotation on p. 203; Christopher Gadsden to William Samuel Johnson, Apr. 16, 1766, and to Samuel Adams, May 23, 1774, in Richard Walsh, ed., *The Writings of Christopher Gadsden, 1746–1805* (Columbia, S.C., 1966), pp. 72, 93; George Milligen-Johnston, *A Short Description of the Province of South-Carolina* (London, 1770), pp. 25–26.

[5]Philodemos [Thomas Tudor Tucker], *Conciliatory Hints . . . Submitted to the Considerations of the Citizens of the Commonwealth of South Carolina* (Charleston, 1784), p. 10; David Ramsay, *The History of the American Revolution*, 2 vols. (Trenton, N.J., 1811), p. 46.

biguous position: it was the primary evil that men sought to avoid by curbing monarchs and establishing republics. But it was also the solution to one of society's most serious problems, the problem of the poor." Elsewhere the poor were disorderly and dependent, a constant threat to property, and easily manipulated by tyrants. In the South, however, most of the poor were black slaves effectively disciplined by their masters. "Virginians"—and South Carolinians also—"could outdo English republicans as well as New England ones, partly because they had solved the problem." Southerners, Augustus John Foster observed early in the nineteenth century, "can profess an unbounded love of liberty and of democracy in consequence of the mass of people, who in other countries might become mobs, being there nearly altogether composed of their own negro slaves."[6]

Despite their contradictions—slavery both threatened order and made America safe for Revolution—Morgan and Greene have gone a good distance toward answering Dr. Johnson's question. This essay extends their analysis by exploring the connections between economic growth, slavery, and Revolutionary politics in the South Carolina lowcountry. In that region of British America the issues had a special clarity. The great planters and merchants of South Carolina prospered within the old empire, more so than any other group in the mainland colonies. And their prosperity rested on the backs of slaves. Prosperity, slavery, and Revolutionary politics were thoroughly entwined.

"Few Countries," David Ramsay observed in 1808, "have at any time exhibited so striking an instance of public and private prosperity as appeared in South Carolina between the years 1725 and 1775." Ramsay could be accused of special pleading. He was, after all, an advocate for a particular interpretation of the Revolution in which South Carolinians, satisfied, prosperous, and loyal citizens of the empire, were

[6]Edmund S. Morgan, *American Slavery, American Freedom: The Ordeal of Colonial Virginia* (New York, 1975), p. 381; Richard B. Davis, ed., *Jeffersonian America: Notes on the United States of America Collected in the Years 1805–6–7 and 11–12 by Sir Augustus John Foster, Bart.* (San Marino, Calif., 1954), p. 307.

pushed into independence by the villainous, unprincipled actions of British officials. Carolinians, Ramsay argued, "did not covet independence." Rather, it was their "only means of extrication from the grasp of tyranny, exerted to enforce novel claims of the mother country, subversive of liberty and happiness."[7] Assertions of prosperity strengthened his case that colonists were disinterested patriots, reluctant Revolutionaries forced to defend their liberties. Still, Ramsay did not exaggerate, or at least not much. There is abundant evidence in the growth of population and the spread of settlement, in the rise of the export sector and the balance of payments, in the accumulation of wealth and its distribution that the great planters and leading merchants prospered by the empire. That evidence merits a careful review, for it suggests the dimensions of the risks assumed by Revolutionary South Carolinians and where they found the nerve to take the chance.

Population figures provide striking evidence of South Carolina's remarkable progress. Despite high mortality, especially in the lowcountry where malaria and yellow fever took a heavy toll, the colony's population grew rapidly, even by the demanding standards of British America. The data describe a pattern often encountered in the colonies in which an initial period of high but decelerating growth gave way to a fairly steady expansion. In South Carolina the turning point occurred in the 1740s, an especially troubling decade when restrictions on slave imports stunted the growth of the black population. Thereafter, the annual rate of population increase hovered about 3.3 percent, nearly sufficient to double the number of inhabitants every twenty years. On the eve of the Revolution, South Carolinians numbered about 150,000. Some 90,000 of them were enslaved.[8]

The growth of population was paralleled by an equally re-

[7] David Ramsay, *The History of South Carolina, from Its First Settlement in 1670, to the Year 1808*, 2 vols. (Charleston, S.C., 1809), 1:123, 220.

[8] For South Carolina population estimates see U.S. Bureau of the Census, *Historical Statistics of the United States: Colonial Times to 1970*, 2 vols. (Washington, D.C., 1975), 2:1168 (ser. Z16–17). For the pattern of growth see McCusker and Menard, *Economy of British America*, pp. 217–21.

markable increase in exports. Success was not immediate, however, at least by the standards of the early colonists, many of whom measured their performance against the great fortunes earned by sugar planters. The first several decades were years of experimentation during which Carolinians discovered their possibilities, explored the local resource base, and tested overseas demand. In the process they built a diverse economy by colonial standards. Self-sufficient agriculture and farm building were the major activities, but settlers also produced exports that could be exchanged for manufactures, servants, and slaves. The early export trade centered on the supply of provisions and wood products to Barbados supplemented by a trade in furs and naval stores to England. The economy did not generate great fortunes, but it provided local merchants and planters a variety of opportunities for small-scale production and exchange.[9]

The period of experimentation ended with the emergence of rice as the major commercial product early in the eighteenth century, the crop that "soon became the chief support of the colony, and its great source of opulence," as much the "staple Commodity" of the region "as Sugar is to Barbados and Jamaica, or Tobacco to Virginia and Maryland." Rice propelled South Carolina from a Barbadian appendage to a major producer for the metropolitan market, it undermined the early diversity of the export sector as a growing share of the

[9]The economic history of colonial South Carolina is surveyed in McCusker and Menard, *Economy of British America*, pp. 169–88. See also Peter A. Coclanis, "Economy and Society in the Early Modern South: Charleston and the Evolution of the South Carolina Low Country," Ph.D. diss., Columbia University, 1984, and, for the early years, Converse D. Clowse, *Economic Beginnings in Colonial South Carolina, 1670–1730* (Columbia, S.C., 1971). For rice exports see U.S. Bureau of the Census, *Historical Statistics*, 2:1192 (ser. Z481–485). For prices see Arthur Harrison Cole, *Wholesale Commodity Prices in the United States, 1700–1861: Statistical Supplement* (Cambridge, Mass., 1938); George Rogers Taylor, "Wholesale Commodity Prices at Charleston, South Carolina, 1732–1791," *Journal of Economic and Business History* 4 (1932):356–77; and Peter A. Coclanis, "Rice Prices in the 1720s and the Evolution of the South Carolina Economy," *Journal of Southern History* 48 (1982):531–44. These can be reduced to sterling using the exchange rates in John J. McCusker, *Money and Exchange in Europe and America, 1600–1775: A Handbook* (Chapel Hill, N.C., 1978), pp. 222–24.

colony's resources were devoted to its cultivation, and it left a distinctive imprint on lowcountry society.[10]

Data on prices and exports suggest a three-stage periodization in the growth of the rice industry during the eighteenth century. The first, lasting to about 1740, was characterized by a rapid but steadily decelerating expansion of exports achieved in the face of generally falling prices. Output grew more rapidly than prices fell, however, and the value of the crop grew impressively, from perhaps £20,000 sterling in 1720 to about £100,000 by 1740. Rice had quickly become the dominant export of the lower South and one of the major staples of British America. The second period, a transitional decade extending from the early 1740s to the early 1750s, was marked by low prices and a stagnant output. These were, as we shall see, difficult times for lowcountry planters and Charleston merchants. The third period, beginning in the 1750s and lasting to the Revolution, was again one of expansion, although output grew more slowly than in the years before 1740 and prices drifted up rather than down. By 1770 the South Carolina rice crop was worth more than £300,000 sterling, placing it third among exports from the British continental colonies, behind tobacco and wheat products, and accounting for 10 percent of the value of all commodities shipped from the mainland.[11]

In addition to its rapid rise, a second point about the rice industry is important to an understanding of the Revolutionary movement in South Carolina. "The culture of rice in Carolina," David Ramsay observed, "has been in a state of constant improvement." The major changes included the

[10] Alexander Hewatt, *An Historical Account of the Rise and Progress of the Colonies of South Carolina and Georgia*, 2 vols. (London, 1779), 1:119; [James Glen], *A Description of South Carolina . . .* (London, 1761), p. 87.

[11] James F. Shepherd and Gary M. Walton, *Shipping, Maritime Trade, and the Economic Development of Colonial North America* (Cambridge, 1972), p. 98. Lewis C. Gray, *History of Agriculture in the Southern United States to 1860*, 2 vols. (Washington, D.C., 1933), 2:277–90, remains the best introduction to the colonial rice industry. See also the recent essays by James M. Clifton, "The Rice Industry in Colonial America," *Agricultural History* 55 (1981):266–83, and Henry C. Dethloff, "The Colonial Rice Trade," *Agricultural History* 56 (1982):231–43.

shift of production first from moist uplands to inland swamps and later to the tidewater, the spread of irrigation, the discovery of varieties better suited to local resources, and improvements in the cleaning process. Gains in productivity combined with improvements in packaging, shipping, and marketing to permit planters and merchants first to lower the price of rice and later to hold it down in the face of rising costs for land and labor. The rapid changes in techniques testify to the flexibility of the South Carolina plantation system and the inventiveness of the men who ran it.[12]

The rapid development that began with the discovery of rice was interrupted in the 1740s. The slave rebellion at Stono brought the first shock. Although small and quickly crushed, the Stono slave rebellion of 1739 frightened lowcountry planters, led them to worry about the direction their region had taken, to question the wisdom of making South Carolina "more like a negro country than like a country settled by white people." The rebellion persuaded them to place a prohibitive duty on slave imports and to step up efforts to recruit European settlers. The result was dramatic. Fewer than 1,000 slaves arrived at Charleston between 1741 and 1749, and the black population failed to grow during the decade while the number of whites increased by 10,000. South Carolina still had a black majority, but it was no longer so overwhelming.[13]

Planters were able to indulge their unease over blacks and restrict slave imports throughout the 1740s because they had neither the need nor the ability to pay for new workers. King George's War (1739–48) proved a disaster for the lowcountry,

[12] Ramsay, *History of South Carolina*, 2:206. Useful materials on rice cultivation appear in Samuel B. Hillard, "Antebellum Tidewater Rice Culture in South Carolina and Georgia," in James R. Gibson, ed., *European Settlement and Development in North America* (Toronto, 1978), pp. 91–115; David Leroy Coon, "The Development of Market Agriculture in South Carolina, 1680–1775," Ph.D. diss., University of Illinois, 1972; and David Doar, *Rice and Rice Planting in the Carolina Low Country* (Charleston, 1936), pp. 7–41.

[13] On Stono see Peter H. Wood, *Black Majority: Negroes in Colonial South Carolina from 1670 through the Stono Rebellion* (New York, 1974), quotation on p. 132. The slave trade and the growth of South Carolina's black population are discussed below.

particularly in its later stages. War disrupted trade, diverted ships and sailors to other tasks, and drove freight and insurance charges sharply upward, to more than two or three times their peacetime norm. Rice, among the most bulky of American staples, was particularly hard hit, "for it is an article that will not bear the advanced price of an extraordinary fr[eigh]t. insurance etc. which are incident in war time." Prices, which had reached 9 shillings per hundredweight in the late 1730s, fell to just over 2 shillings in the mid-1740s. Exports too declined, although less dramatically than prices, and the value of the crop plummeted, from a peak of £145,000 sterling in 1741 to a low of £29,000 in 1746 at the bottom of the depression. Since rice was clearly "king" in the lowcountry, the troubles of the 1740s reverberated through the entire economy. The land boom of the 1730s came to an abrupt end, imported goods became scarce and expensive, and planters who had borrowed heavily during more prosperous times were forced into bankruptcy. Other export trades were less severely affected than rice—indeed, the declining naval stores industry received a needed boost from war-induced demand—but these were simply too small to carry planters through the long depression. "This Province," Gov. James Glen complained, "was brought to the Brink of Ruin." [14]

Planter confidence in the potential of South Carolina's economy was quickly restored in the aftermath of the war. For one thing, the slaves now seemed firmly under control as planters acted resolutely to discipline their workers. Fear of the black majority—"an intestine enemy the most dreadful of enemies"—could still send an occasional shiver down a planter's spine, but Stono proved the last major scare of the colonial period. There is evidence that both the composition

[14] William Pollard to B. and J. Bower, Feb. 1, 1774, in H. Roy Merrens, ed., *The Colonial South Carolina Scene: Contemporary Views, 1697–1774* (Columbia, S.C., 1977), p. 277; James Glen to Robert Dinwiddie, Mar. 13, 1754, in William L. McDowell, Jr., ed., *Colonial Records of South Carolina: Documents Relating to Indian Affairs, May 21, 1750–August 7, 1754* (Columbia, S.C., 1958), p. 478. Stuart O. Stumpf, "Implications of King George's War for the Charleston Mercantile Community," *South Carolina Historical Magazine* 77 (1976):161–88, provides a detailed account of the depression.

of the slave population and the attitudes of planters toward blacks changed during the 1740s. Many slaves, James Glen explained in 1751, "are natives of Carolina, who have no notion of liberty, nor no longing after any other country." Country-born slaves "have been brought up with white people, and by white people have been made, at least many of them, useful mechanicks, as coopers, carpenters, masons, smiths, wheelrights, and other trades." Even the Africans in the colony "can all speak our language, for we imported none during the war." Such slaves, Glen concluded, "are pleased with their masters, contented with their condition, reconciled to servitude, seasoned to the country, and expert at the different kinds of labor in which they are employed." One need not accept Glen's account of slave *mentalité* to recognize that he isolated an important truth: the growth of creole majority among blacks, a process given a considerable boost by the stoppage of African imports in the 1740s, transformed the slave population in ways that made them less terrifying to their owners.[15]

Second, planters responded to the hard times of the 1740s with an effort to diversify their plantations and to reduce costs by producing more of the things they needed internally. Training slaves in various plantation crafts was part of that effort. In addition, they reorganized workers to produce their own food instead of purchasing it from abroad or from small planters on the edge of the plantation district. And they began to make at least some of the shoes and clothing for slaves rather than relying entirely on imported British manufactures. While there was a tendency to return to the highly specialized organization of the initial boom years with the postwar recovery, lowcountry plantations emerged from the depression with more flexibility and diversity and with at least

[15] Wood, *Black Majority*, p. 321; Glen to the Lords Commissioners for Trade and Plantations, March 1751, in Merrens, ed., *Colonial South Carolina Scene*, p. 183. On the ways in which the rise of a creole majority tended, paradoxically, to both increase the autonomy of blacks and lower white anxiety see Philip D. Morgan, "Black Society in the Lowcountry, 1760–1810," in Ira Berlin and Ronald Hoffman, eds., *Slavery and Freedom in the Age of the American Revolution* (Charlottesville, Va., 1983), pp. 83–141.

some cushion against the uncertainties of producing staple commodities for an international market.[16]

The emergence of indigo as a major staple in the quarter century before Independence also boosted planter confidence, persuaded Carolinians that their creativity played a major role in delivering the colony from depression, that they could deal with adversity, and that they were competent to shape the future. South Carolina planters had responded to the depression by experimenting with new crops in hope of diversifying their operations, of finding "a means of dividing the labour of our hands so that we may not glut the Market with any one Article." With indigo they had a spectacular success, since the British were unable to obtain the dye from their usual source in the French Caribbean during King George's War. The 1749 crop was worth more than £17,000 sterling, roughly 20 percent of the value of rice exports. The industry nearly collapsed in the early 1750s as English textile manufacturers again found an adequate supply from the French West Indies and as planters concentrated on rice. But there was a rapid recovery when the Seven Years' War again cut off supplies from the French islands, and indigo established itself as a central product of South Carolina's economy.[17]

Indigo served the lowcountry economy well. In addition to helping insulate South Carolina against war-induced depression, it provided employment for slaves during slack times in rice cultivation, uses for land unsuitable for the major staple,

[16] George D. Terry, "'Champaign Country': A Social History of an Eighteenth-Century Lowcountry Parish in South Carolina, St. Johns Berkeley County," Ph.D. diss., University of South Carolina, 1981, pp. 255–59; Philip D. Morgan, "The Development of Slave Culture in Eighteenth-Century Plantation America," Ph.D. diss., University College, London, 1977, pp. 20–47.

[17] Henry Laurens to John Knight, July 24, 1755, Philip M. Hamer, George C. Rogers, Jr., and David R. Chesnutt, eds., The Papers of Henry Laurens 10 vols. to date (Columbia, S.C., 1968–), 1:299. Gray, History of Agriculture, 1:290–97, remains the best introduction to the South Carolina indigo industry. See also David Leroy Coon, "Eliza Lucas Pinckney and the Reintroduction of Indigo Culture in South Carolina," Journal of Southern History 42 (1976):61–76.

and a marketable export for those who could not grow rice. The success of indigo led some to view the prospect of another war with optimism. "We hope," Henry Laurens wrote on the eve of the Seven Years' War, that "a new War will learn us how to propogate other useful Articles which would not be attempted with any Spirit whilst the Planter can find his Account in continuing in the old Track."[18]

South Carolina's export sector expanded rapidly during the quarter century from the end of King George's War to the Revolution. Rice exports worth on average £128,000 sterling in the early 1750s, fluctuated around £330,000 by the early 1770s. The value of the indigo crop grew at a spectacular rate, from an annual average of less than £10,000 in the early 1750s to nearly £150,000 between 1770 and 1774. According to a contemporary estimate, South Carolina's exports were worth about £160,000 sterling in 1748; between 1768 and 1772 exports were worth an average of more than £450,000 annually, a nearly threefold increase in just over two decades. The author of *American Husbandry* described an even faster growth: he reported exports worth £243,000 in 1754, £396,000 in the early 1760s, and £756,000 in 1771. Perhaps the best evidence of the success of South Carolinians as producers of exports is provided by the per capita estimates generated by James F. Shepherd and Gary M. Walton. Over the years 1768 to 1772, exports per inhabitant from South Carolina averaged £3.7 sterling, more than three times the figure for the remaining mainland colonies.[19]

[18] Coon, "Eliza Lucas Pinckney," p. 64; Laurens to Sarah Nickelson, Aug. 1, 1755, Hamer, Rogers, and Chesnutt, eds., *Papers of Laurens*, 1:309.

[19] Glen, *Description of South Carolina*, pp. 50–55; Harry J. Carman, ed., *American Husbandry* (New York, 1939), pp. 311–13; James F. Shepherd, "Commodity Exports from the British North American Colonies to Overseas Areas, 1768–1772: Magnitudes and Patterns of Trade," *Explorations in Economic History* 8 (1970):13–50; idem and Samuel H. Williamson, "The Coastal Trade of the British North American Colonies, 1768–1772," *Journal of Economic History* 32 (1972):809; Shepherd and Gary M. Walton, "Economic Change after the American Revolution: Pre- and Post-War Comparisons of Maritime Shipping and Trade," *Explorations in Economic History* 13 (1976):397–422. For rice and indigo exports see above, n. 9, and U.S. Bureau of the Census, *Historical Statistics*, 2:1189 (ser. Z432–435).

There were, of course, breaks in the general prosperity. War, metropolitan recession, and crop failures led to occasional downturns in the value of exports, although rice and indigo tended to offset each other and the export sector did not again approach the depths reached in the 1740s.[20] And there were certain structural difficulties stemming from South Carolina's colonial position as a producer of plantation crops for external markets. There were recurring currency shortages, planters—whose "desires . . . increase faster than their riches"—sometimes overextended themselves to purchase slaves, manufactures, and luxury goods, and the colony's trade was thoroughly dominated by British merchants.[21] Nevertheless, the colony prospered. "The planters here all get rich," Robert Wells, publisher of the *South Carolina and American General Gazette,* reported in 1765. And the Charleston merchants, too, he might have added, who, "almost to a Man . . .[had] risen from humble and moderate Fortunes to great affluence." On the eve of Independence, South Carolina, if not "the most thriving Country perhaps on this Globe," was at least "the most oppulent and flourishing colony on the British Continent of America."[22]

That wealth reflected the ability of South Carolina to exploit opportunities available within the old empire. Table 1

[20] The best guide to short-term fluctuations in South Carolina's export sector is the letters of Henry Laurens in Hamer, Rogers, and Chesnutt, eds., *Papers of Laurens.* See also Leila Sellers, *Charleston Business on the Eve of the Revolution* (Chapel Hill, N.C., 1934).

[21] Thomas Smith to Isaac Smith, Jr., Apr. 11, 1772, as quoted in George C. Rogers, Jr., *Evolution of a Federalist: William Loughton Smith of Charleston (1758–1812)* (Columbia, S.C., 1962), p. 56. On currency shortages and structural difficulties see Joseph A. Ernst, *Money and Politics in America, 1755–1775: A Study in the Currency Act of 1764 and the Political Economy of Revolution* (Chapel Hill, N.C., 1973), and Jacob M. Price, "Economic Function and the Growth of American Port Towns in the Eighteenth Century," *Perspectives in American History* 8 (1974):161–63.

[22] Robert Wells to [?], Aug. 13, 1765, as quoted in Carl Bridenbaugh, *Myths and Realities: Societies of the Colonial South* (Baton Rouge, 1952), p. 57; Robert M. Weir, *Colonial South Carolina: A History* (Milwood, N.Y., 1983), pp. 218, 263; "Dr. Milligen-Johnston's 'Additions' to His Pamphlet," in Chapman J. Milling, ed., *Colonial South Carolina: Two Contemporary Descriptions* (Columbia, S.C., 1951), p. 109.

Table 1. Average annual value of commodity exports from South Carolina, 1768–72, by destination (in thousands of pounds sterling)

Commodity	Great Britain	Southern Europe*	West Indies	Mainland colonies	Total
Rice	164.8	50.2	50.8	15.0	280.8
Indigo	108.5				108.5
Deerskins	16.4				16.4
Naval stores	4.8			.7	5.5
Wood products	.3	.1	2.4	.1	2.9
Grains, grain products	.2	.3	4.2	4.2	8.9
Livestock, beef, pork	.1	.1	2.8		3.0
Other	3.2	.4	1.9	4.9	10.4
Total	298.3	51.1	62.1	24.9	436.4

SOURCES: James F. Shepherd, "Commodity Exports from the British North American Colonies to Overseas Areas, 1768–1772: Magnitudes and Patterns of Trade," *Explorations in Economic History* 8 (1970):13–50; idem and Samuel H. Williamson, "The Coastal Trade of the British North American Colonies, 1768–1772," *Journal of Economic History* 32 (1972):809.

*Includes Africa

provides a summary of South Carolina's export trade at the end of the colonial period. Two features stand out. First, this was a highly specialized export economy, heavily dependent on its two major plantation crops, rice and indigo. Together, they accounted for nearly 90 percent of the total value of exports. Contemporaries were much impressed with the rapidly growing volume of backcountry products that poured into Charleston, but these had not yet had much impact on the structure of exports.[23] Second, trade was largely confined to Great Britain's Atlantic world. The mother country took all of Carolina's indigo (on which the British government paid a substantial bounty) and, together with its West Indian colonies, it took the bulk of the rice crop. True, there was a sizable direct trade in rice to southern Europe, shipments to foreign sugar islands were growing, and much of the rice sent to Britain was reexported to Holland and Germany. But low-country prosperity was tied closely to the British Empire.[24]

It could be argued that this was a false prosperity, however, that Carolina planters lived well by mortgaging the future to British merchants. At first glance, the size of their debt would seem to support such a view. On the eve of the Revolution, South Carolinians owed some £350,000 sterling to British merchants. That works out to £2.3 per head, roughly the equivalent of the debt owed by Chesapeake planters. While most historians now agree that the debt was not a major source of Revolutionary protest in Maryland and Virginia, it is still argued that chronic indebtedness "heightened the sense of unease" felt by many residents of the Tobacco Coast late in the colonial period.[25] That was not the case in South Carolina, for reasons that become clear when the debt is

[23] See, for examples, William Bull to Lord Hillsborough, Nov. 30, 1770, Public Record Office Transcripts, vol. 32, pp. 393–96, South Carolina Department of Archives and History, Columbia; *South Carolina Gazette*, Dec. 5, 1771; and Rachel N. Klein, "Ordering the Backcountry: The South Carolina Regulation," *William and Mary Quarterly*, 3d ser. 38 (1981):663–65.

[24] Gray, *History of Agriculture*, 2:284–87.

[25] Jacob M. Price, *Capital and Credit in British Overseas Trade: The View from the Chesapeake, 1700–1776* (Cambridge, Mass., 1980), p. 137; Weir, *Colonial South Carolina*, p. 155.

placed in perspective. For one thing, the average yearly value of exports from South Carolina to Britain alone during the early 1770s was substantially larger than the debt, while the value of exports to all places was perhaps twice as large. South Carolina planters were good risks, and the debt they carried was in fact modest given their incomes. Nor were South Carolinians overdependent upon Britain for investment capital. Indeed, by the 1770s the internal debt—loans by some South Carolinians to other residents of the province—was much larger than the external one, indicating that the colony possessed the resources to finance continued growth.[26] This is not to deny the importance of British credit. It financed the purchase of manufactures and slaves and it was a much-valued convenience, as events of the 1780s would demonstrate.[27] But Carolina's prosperity did not rest on a chronic indebtedness that permitted planters to live beyond their means. It rested instead on the productive capacity of their plantations and their ability to produce crops much valued in other parts of the Atlantic world.

Rice and indigo shaped the Carolina lowcountry, made it into a plantation society more similar in structure to the British Caribbean than to the other North American colonies. The most striking similarity is in the size of the slave population. The growth of rice production led to a sharp rise in demand for labor. That demand was met largely by African slaves. On average, Charleston imported 275 blacks a year during the 1710s, nearly 900 in the 1720s, and over 2,000 in the 1730s. Slaves were a majority in South Carolina as early as 1708, when a substantial number of them were Indians. By 1740 slaves—then largely black—comprised more than 70 percent of the total population, a proportion more like that found in the sugar islands than elsewhere on the mainland. Few blacks arrived at Charleston in Stono's immediate aftermath or dur-

[26] See the reports of "Monies at interest" in the South Carolina tax returns for the 1760s in General Tax Receipts and Payments, 1761–69 (1771), S.C. Dept. Arch. and Hist.

[27] See Jerome J. Nadelhaft, *The Disorders of War: The Revolution in South Carolina* (Orono, Maine, 1981), pp. 143–54.

ing the depression of the late 1740s, and, in consequence, the black share of the population fell to about 62 percent of the total at mid-century, still very high by mainland standards.[28]

With the recovery after 1750, the combined demand of rice and indigo planters drove slave imports sharply upward. They remained high for the rest of the colonial period, excepting the years 1766–68, when a prohibitive duty stopped the trade. Slave imports averaged nearly 1,600 annually in the 1750s, 2,000 in the 1760s, and more than 4,000 between 1770 and 1774. In 1770 there were more than 80,000 slaves in South Carolina, just over 60 percent of the total population. Blacks were a much larger proportion in the plantation districts along the coast, however, where their share exceeded 80 percent. Rice and indigo made the lowcountry a slave society.

The growth of slavery is not the only demographic parallel between South Carolina and the West Indies. The white population in the lowcountry plantation district declined with the growth of slavery, just as it had earlier in the sugar islands. Much of the decline was a consequence of white emigration, but it also reflected higher death rates that accompanied the introduction of African diseases.[29] Rapid growth also transformed the slave population. African imports swelled the sex ratio, turning a population that had been growing by repro-

[28] On the growth of slavery and the slave trade see Peter H. Wood, "'More like a Negro Country': Demographic Patterns in Colonial South Carolina, 1700–1740," in Stanley L. Engerman and Eugene D. Genovese, eds., *Race and Slavery in the Western Hemisphere: Quantitative Studies* (Princeton, 1975), pp. 131–72; Elizabeth Donnan, "The Slave Trade in South Carolina before the Revolution," *American Historical Review* 33 (1928):804–28; John Donald Duncan, "Servitude and Slavery in Colonial South Carolina, 1670–1776," Ph.D. diss., Emory University, 1972; W. Robert Higgins, "Charles Town Merchants and Factors Dealing in the External Negro Trade, 1735–1775," *South Carolina Historical Magazine* 65 (1964):205–17; idem, "The Geographical Origins of Negro Slaves in Colonial South Carolina," *South Atlantic Quarterly* 70 (1971):34–47; and Daniel C. Littlefield, *Rice and Slaves: Ethnicity and the Slave Trade in Colonial South Carolina* (Baton Rouge, 1981).

[29] The best introduction to the demography of South Carolina whites is Wood, *Black Majority*. Terry, "'Champaign Country,'" pp. 90–142, contains rough but useful estimates of several demographic parameters.

duction into one that registered a net natural decline. Rice in particular consumed workers. "No work can be imagined more pernicious to health," Alexander Hewatt argued, "than for men to stand in water mid-leg high, and often above it, planting and weeding rice." It was a "horrible employment," the author of *American Husbandry* added, "not far short of digging in Potosi." As late as the 1830s, when blacks elsewhere in the United States were growing at near Malthusian rates, Samuel Patterson noted that rice planters "never expected that the number of their people should increase—if they could keep up the force—which in many cases they could not do—it was all they hoped." Twenty years later, Robert Russell confirmed Patterson's observation, reporting mortality so high that rice planters often were forced to rely on purchases to maintain the size of their work force. Plantation agriculture brought the demographic regime of the sugar islands to lowcountry South Carolina.[30]

Demographic changes were not the only ones that accompanied the spread of rice and indigo nor the only ways in which the lowcountry repeated earlier developments in the West Indies. For one thing, there was a sharp increase in scale as large plantations "swallowed up" small farms. Further, the growth of plantation agriculture brought increased wealth and greater inequality, declining opportunities for poor men, and a high rate of out-migration as rice and indigo pushed small, diversified farmers to the periphery of the plantation district. There is evidence as well of growing absenteeism, as some successful planters chose not to live in the society they helped create. Rice and indigo, in short, turned the lowcountry into a plantation society and produced, in the process, a

---

[30] Hewatt, *Historical Account*, 1:159; Carman, ed., *American Husbandry*, p. 277; Samuel Patterson, June 6, 1832, as quoted in William H. Freehling, *Prelude to Civil War: The Nullification Controversy in South Carolina, 1816–1836* (New York, 1968), p. 33; Robert Russell, *North America: Its Agriculture and Climate* (Edinburgh, 1857), p. 179. On slave demography in South Carolina see, in addition to Wood, *Black Majority*, Terry, "Champaign Country," and Morgan, "Black Society" and "The Development of Slave Culture," Cheryll Ann Cody, "Slave Demography and Family Formation: A Community Study of the Ball Family Plantations, 1720–1896," Ph.D. diss., University of Minnesota, 1982.

region more similar in social structure, population composition, and economic organization to the sugar islands than to the mainland colonies to the north.[31]

That transformation was not complete, however. South Carolina avoided the extremes of plantation society that appeared in the West Indies. Perhaps the most important difference concerns scale. Rice and indigo plantations, although large by comparison with agricultural enterprises to the north, were much smaller than sugar plantations, and lowcountry planters were less wealthy than sugar magnates. In consequence, owner absenteeism was more limited in South Carolina than in the West Indies. While sugar planters often moved to London, merged with the English gentry, and left their estates in the hands of resident overseers, lowcountry planters managed their plantations, leaving only for the Charleston social season or to escape the heat and diseases of late summer. Like the sugar magnates, lowcountry planters spent much of their income on imported luxuries, but a large share of their profits were spent at home. The limited, temporary nature of planter absenteeism in the lowcountry also had important political consequences, for—and again in contrast to the West Indies—it permitted the growth of an indigenous ruling class, a powerful, self-conscious group capable of shaping the region's future.[32]

Recent work with tax lists, probate documents, and land records provides helpful detail on the rise of the great lowcountry rice and indigo planters and the structure of lowcountry society. We can begin with the distribution of slaves in three especially well-documented parishes, all near Charleston in the heart of the plantation district: St. Georges to the southwest on the Ashley River, St. James Goose Creek to the west on the Cooper, and St. Johns Berkeley, also on the Cooper, northwest of Charleston.

[31] Wood, *Black Majority*, describes the impact of rice culture on South Carolina. For the West Indian comparison see Richard S. Dunn, *Sugar and Slaves: The Rise of the Planter Class in the English West Indies, 1624–1713* (Chapel Hill, N.C., 1972).

[32] The South Carolina–West Indian comparison is explored in McCusker and Menard, *Economy of British America*, pp. 181–86.

In St. Georges, where rice was introduced during the mid-1710s, there were nearly eight slaves per household as early as 1720, twelve by 1726, and twenty-four by 1741. A census for 1726 describes the distribution of slaves a mere decade after the beginning of commercial rice production. It suggests how rapidly those planters who took advantage of the early rice boom could rise to wealth. Of the 108 households in the parish, only 21 contained no slaves, a remarkably small proportion (although in fact high by later lowcountry standards) that speaks eloquently of the importance of slavery to the region. Doubtless it was this group that James Glen had in mind when he reported that roughly 20 percent of the whites in South Carolina "have a bare subsistence." Another 40 planters, perhaps the two-fifths "who have the necessarys of life" in Glen's standard, were small planters with one to five slaves. The 29 households reporting six to twenty-four slaves might be classified as middling planters "who have some of the conveniencys of life." Finally, there are the great planters of St. Georges, that fifth of the population with "plenty of the good things of life," 18 households with more than twenty-five slaves.[33]

If the St. Georges Parish census testifies to the rapid rise of the great planters, it also suggests the limits of the process during the first quarter of the eighteenth century. None of the planters there in 1726 owned more than 100 slaves and only two owned more than 90. Evidence from St. James Goose Creek demonstrates that the great planters would become even greater as the rice boom continued. St. James, one of the first regions opened to rice cultivation, contained 19 slaves per household as early as 1720, and blacks outnumbered whites by roughly four to one. By 1745 a partial tax list reports an average of 43 slaves per household and suggests a black/white ratio of more than seven to one. Only two of the fifty-nine households on the list reported no slaves, while sixteen reported more than 50 and five over 100. Three of the planters, Henry Izard, James Kinloch, and Sara Mid-

[33]Glen to the Lords Commissioners for Trade and Plantations, March 1751, in Merrens, ed., *Colonial South Carolina Scene*, p. 184; Wood, *Black Majority*, pp. 146–65.

dleton owned 218, 230, and 215 slaves respectively. These three also paid taxes on an average of 11,000 acres of land and nearly £3,500 sterling in money at interest. Clearly, the great planters of St. James Goose Creek could afford "plenty of the good things of life" by mid-century.[34]

A similar pattern appears in St. Johns Berkeley, although the planters there were not so wealthy as their neighbors in St. James. There were more than 2 slaves per household in St. Johns in 1705, a figure that reached to 15 by 1720, about 24 in 1740, and nearly 30 in 1762. Over time the ownership of slaves became both more widespread and more concentrated in the hands of the large planters. During the 1720s and 1730s, 18 percent of the inventoried decedents owned no slaves, a proportion that fell to 13 percent in the two decades centered on mid-century and to only 5 percent for the 1760s and 1770s. There was also a marked increase in concentration and in the number of large planters. Between 1720 and 1739, only 13 percent of the decedents owned more than 25 slaves and none owned more than 50. In the 1740s and 1750s, 35 percent of the inventories reported more than 25 slaves, 18 percent more than 50, and 7 percent more than 100. Between 1760 and 1779, 14 percent of the inventoried decedents owned over 100 slaves.[35]

The distribution of land in the lowcountry, although less well documented, resembled the distribution of slaves: it was both widely held and concentrated in the hands of the great planters. Only 13 of the 59 households on the tax list for St. James Goose Creek in 1745 reported no land, while 27 paid taxes on more than 1,000 acres and 7 on more than 5,000 acres. In St. Johns Berkeley land was equally concentrated and even more widely held. During two four-year periods centered on 1763 and 1773, George Terry identified, respectively, 115 and 98 landowners in the parish. Given roughly 110 households there at that time, there is little possibility of a sizable landless population. While there were many small

[34] Philip D. Morgan, "A Profile of a Mid-Eighteenth Century South Carolina Parish: The Tax Return of St. James, Goose Creek," *South Carolina Historical Magazine* 81 (1980):51–65.

[35] Ibid.; Terry, "'Champaign Country,'" p. 249.

holdings, large landowners predominated: 44 of the 115 landowners of 1763 had more than 1,000 acres, as did 55 of the 98 in 1773. While the data are inadequate to permit a precise description of trends, they do suggest that, as was the case with slaves, the share of lowcountry households owning land increased from the 1720s to the end of the colonial period while the estates of the great planters grew.[36]

Studies of probate records by William G. Bentley and Alice Hanson Jones provide a regionwide perspective on the wealth of the lowcountry (table 2). While much additional work is needed before it will be possible to describe with precision the wealth of the living or even of decedent property owners, certain patterns are evident. These data clearly confirm the importance of slavery in South Carolina's economy. In most years more than three-quarters of the decedents owned slaves, while among those who earned their income from agriculture that proportion was greater than 95 percent. There were, on average, 9 to 12 slaves per estate in the 1720s and 1730s, 15 to 18 in the 1740s and 1750s, and 28 by 1774. Slaves accounted for 40 to 50 percent of the movable wealth of South Carolinians from the 1720s to the 1760s and for an extraordinary 68 percent in 1774. The data also reflect the prosperity of the lowcountry in the decades before Independence: mean movable wealth per decedent doubled between 1740 and 1760 and grew at an even faster rate in the next fifteen years. In 1774, decedents who entered probate in the Charleston district were worth £2,700 sterling on average, more than six times the figure for the thirteen colonies as a whole. Nine of the ten wealthiest men to die in the mainland colonies in 1774 had lived in the lowcountry.[37]

[36] Morgan, "Profile of a South Carolina Parish"; Terry, "'Champaign Country,'" p. 248. For additional evidence on the distribution of land and slaves see Jackson T. Main, *The Social Structure of Revolutionary America* (Princeton, 1965), pp. 57–61; Weir, *Colonial South Carolina*, pp. 213–18; and Richard Waterhouse, "South Carolina's Colonial Elite: A Study in the Social Structure and Political Culture of a Southern Colony, 1670–1760," Ph.D. diss., The Johns Hopkins University, 1973.

[37] Alice Hanson Jones, *Wealth of a Nation to Be: The American Colonies on the Eve of the Revolution* (New York, 1980), pp. 171, 177, 379. Peter Coclanis reports that "white per capita wealth grew at an annual compound rate of

Table 2. Some characteristics of South Carolina probate inventories, 1722–74

| Date | Percent decedents with slaves | | Slaves per estate | Percent of wealth in slaves | Sterling value, mean movable wealth |
	All decedents	Farmers and planters			
1722–26	78.7%	96.2%	9.5	45%	£417
1727–31	81.2	92.8	11.4	48	382
1732–36	69.5	93.4	11.2	40	430
1737–41	78.2	98.1	17.1	48	425
1742–46	76.1	96.1	15.5	48	575
1747–51	82.6	100.0	16.1	50	706
1752–56	80.9	95.1	18.1	51	769
1757–62	79.0	95.2	16.0	51	863
1774	81.0	95.1	28.0	68	1955

SOURCES: William G. Bentley, "Wealth Distribution in Colonial South Carolina," Ph.D. diss., Georgia State University, 1977, pp. 82, 84, 104; Alice Hanson Jones, *American Colonial Wealth: Documents and Methods*, 3 vols. (New York, 1977), 3:1473–1619, 2165–67. Values reduced to sterling using the exchange rates in John J. McCusker, *Money and Exchange in Europe and America, 1600–1775: A Handbook* (Chapel Hill, N.C., 1978), pp. 222–24.

Clearly, the lowcountry gentry prospered within the British Empire, accumulated slaves and land, and built impressive fortunes by eighteenth-century standards. Why, then, did they place their wealth at risk and quit the empire? At one level their answer was clear enough. They did so to preserve their liberty and to prevent their enslavement. They were pushed out by the "whole System of British Policy" designed "to put in practice every means, that arbitrary, diabolical cunning, clothed with power, could devise, to reduce us to the most miserable and abject subjection," to refuse "every right, which distinguishes you from galley slaves," and "to compel America to bow the Neck to Slavery."[38] Granted that "the language of slavery" had a special precision in the lowcountry, that answer seems abstract, confined to the realm of constitutional principle and political philosophy, separated from the realities of everyday life in a plantation society. Liberty to do what? we might ask. Revolutionary South Carolinians did not provide a clear answer to that question, but pursuing what they did say yields insight into their motivations, into the society they sought to preserve, and into their aspirations for the future.

The rapid growth of the South Carolina economy during the eighteenth century had a profound impact on the world-view of Revolutionary leaders. South Carolina offered a seemingly boundless opportunity, placed few limits on the abilities of the industrious and frugal to rise in the world. "It was," David Ramsay announced, "preeminently a good poor man's country," an "excellent refuge to the poor, the unfortunate, and oppressed."[39] The loyalist Alexander Hewatt, South Carolina's first historian, agreed: "In that growing colony, where there are vast quantities of land unoccupied, the poorest class of people have many opportunities and advantages, from which they are entirely excluded in countries

---

2.0 to 2.3 percent" from the 1720s to the 1760s ("Bitter Harvest: The South Carolina Low Country in Historical Perspective," *Journal of Economic History* 45 [1985]:255).

[38] William Henry Drayton, Christopher Gadsden, and John MacKenzie, as quoted in Greene, "'Slavery or Independence,'" p. 198.

[39] Ramsay, *History of South Carolina*, 1:115, 117.

fully peopled and highly improved." Although initially "exposed to many dangers in providing for themselves and families an habitation for a shelter against the rigours of the climate, and in clearing fields for raising the necessaries of life," those with "the good fortunes to surmount the hardships of the first years of cultivation," find that "the inconveniences gradually decrease in proportion to their improvements." Once planters had "established their characters for honesty and industry," they could obtain credit and purchase "hands to assist them in the harder tasks of clearing and cultivation. . . . Having abundance of waste land, they can extend their culture in proportion of their capital. They live almost entirely on the produce of their estates, and consequently spend but a small part of their annual income. The surplus is yearly added to the capital, and they enlarge their prospects in proportion to their wealth and strength." "They labour," Hewatt concluded, "and they receive more and more encouragement to persevere, until they advance to an easy and comfortable life."[40]

Such sentiments were echoed over and over again. South Carolina, contemporaries were persuaded, promised the "frugal and industrious" white man "a sure road to competancy and independence," a chance to "find employment and high wages for his labour; so that with economy, he has a prospect of acquiring a tolerable fortune, in the space of sixteen or twenty years." "You are now in a land," Christopher Gadsden lectured recent Irish immigrants, "that with half the industry and prudence you were obliged to use in Ireland, you may gain a landed property, all really your own, sufficient to support yourself and families decently and independently."[41]

For some the colony offered more than a simple "competance," "a comfortable life," or "a tolerable fortune." Contemporaries were amazed at the wealth accumulated by the

[40] Hewatt, *Historical Account*, 2:127–30, 182–83.

[41] Greene, "'Slavery or Independence,'" p. 212; Lionel Chalmers, *An Account of the Weather and Diseases of South-Carolina* (London, 1776), p. 30; Christopher Gadsden, *A Few Observations on Some Late Public Transactions* . . . (Charleston, 1797), p. 24.

lowcountry's leading citizens, by "the rapid ascendency of families which in less than ten years have risen from the lowest rank, have acquired upward of £100,000, and have, moreover, gained this wealth in a simple and easy manner." Josiah Quincy's account of the rise of Joseph Allston, a Winyah Bay planter of "immense income all of his own acquisition," is typical. Allston started just "a few years ago," Quincy noted, "with only five negroes," but now owned several plantations and more than 500 slaves which netted £5,000 to £6,000 sterling a year. And, Quincy added, as if his report were not yet sufficiently impressive, "he is reputed much richer."[42]

There was an occasional dissent. Some were distressed by the impact of such possibilities on behavior in the lowcountry, claiming that they induced even "the best of men . . . to take every Step of aggrandizing their Fortunes" and made life among "the polite Part of this Country . . . one continued Race; in which every one is endeavouring to distance all behind him, and to overtake, or pass by, all before him." Others complained that easy money encouraged self-indulgence, luxury, heavy gambling, hard drinking, and social irresponsibility, while some sneered at the vulgar pretensions of newly rich merchants and planters. A few even sounded a note of realism, pointing out that South Carolinians were not rich by English standards.[43]

But the dominant tones conveyed optimism, wonder, confidence, and self-congratulation. Most commentators agreed that the "Men and Women who have a Right to the Class of Gentry" were "more numerous than in any other Colony in North America," that there were "more persons possessed of between five and ten thousand pounds sterling in the province than are to be found any where among the same number of people." For the majority of observers, South Carolina's opportunities more than compensated for its shortcomings.

[42] Mark A. DeWolfe Howe, ed., "Journal of Josiah Quincy, Jr., 1773," Massachusetts Historical Society *Proceedings* 49 (1916): 453; Bridenbaugh, *Myths and Realities*, pp. 65–66.

[43] "A Back Settler," *Some Fugitive Thoughts on a Letter Signed Freeman . . .* (Charleston, 1774), p.34; *South Carolina Gazette*, Mar. 1, 1773; Bridenbaugh, *Myths and Realities*, pp. 54–118.

"The Success of a Crokatt, a Shubrick, or a Beswicke, but a few years here in a Mercantile Way," a contributor to the *Gazette* boasted, "or of a Lynch, or a Huger, or a Serre, in a Planting Way, with many other such Instances, proves more in Favor of Carolina, than all the Pamphlets that were ever wrote about it."[44]

Behind the fabled wealth of the lowcountry lay the equally fabled profits earned on its principal exports, rice and indigo. Reports of "frugal industrious planters" who "every three or four years, doubled their capital" were common, as were assertions that slaves paid for themselves—"cleared their first cost and charges"—in a short time.[45] The author of *American Husbandry* calculated that with an initial investment of £2,000 sterling a careful planter could build an estate yielding £12,000 net annually in little more than a decade. No one in South Carolina earned so much because the typical planter "frequents the taverns and concerts of Charles Town more than his plantation," but it was clear "that planting in this country may be made the way to immense fortunes." "No husbandry in Europe can equal this of Carolina," he concluded, "no agriculture in England will pay anything like this."[46]

Even efforts at realism succumbed to Carolina's near mythical possibilities. Those "Gentlemen were too sanguine who informed your Lordship that 33 Negroes ought to clear £500 a year," James Grant told the earl of Egmont, for "a Planter does a great deal if he makes at the rate of eight pounds a Year of his Negroes, clear of all expenses. To do that a plantation must be well established, and the Slaves must all be

[44] Milligen-Johnston, *Short Description*, p. 24; Hewatt, *Historical Account*, 2:180; *South Carolina Gazette*, Dec. 4, 1749.

[45] Hewatt, *Historical Account*, 2:127–28, 140, 184; Ramsay, *History of South Carolina*, 1:114, 118, 2:211; Peter Manigault to William Blake, n.d. [Dec. 1772?], in Maurice A. Crouse ed., "The Letterbook of Peter Manigault, 1763–1773," *South Carolina Historical Magazine* 70 (1969):191; Philip D. Morgan, "Work and Culture: The Task System and the World of Lowcountry Blacks, 1700 to 1880," *William and Mary Quarterly*, 3d ser. 39 (1982):576–77; John Murray to Robert Laurie, July 12, 1757, as quoted in Terry, "'Champaign Country,'" p. 263.

[46] Carman, ed., *American Husbandry*, pp. 292–301.

seasoned able working hands." While there are "Instances of Indigo planters doubling their Capital in a Year ... at an average Carolina planters do not make as much as I have mentioned, I mean of produce to go to Market, so as to remit the Money to Europe." Such income was not the whole story, however, "for many things are consumed in a plantation which are of great utility in point of Living, tho' they cannot be converted into Cash." Grant "always reckoned that an Intelligent Carolina Planter with a Capital from two to three thousand sterling (if his Negroes & Lands were to be disposed of) lives as well as any Man can do in Great Britain with an Income of £500 a year."[47]

Slaves were essential to lowcountry prosperity, most Carolinians admitted, to the high profits earned on rice and indigo, to the great fortunes accumulated by the leading planters and merchants, and to the "comfortable circumstances" of the more ordinary colonists. "There is no living here" without slaves, a colonist reported as early as 1711. Slaves "were the riches" of South Carolina, "the very means of our industry," "to this country what raw materials were to another," for "no planter could cultivate his lands without slaves."[48] "White servants would have exhausted their strength in clearing a spot of land for digging their own graves, and every rice plantation would have served no other purpose than a burying ground to its European cultivators," Alexander Hewatt explained. "The low lands of Carolina, which are unquestionably the richest grounds in the country, must have long remained a wilderness, had not Africans, whose natural constitutions were suited to the climate and work, been employed in cultivating this useful article of food and commerce."[49]

[47] James Grant to the earl of Egmont, Feb. 9, 1769, quoted in Littlefield, *Rice and Slaves*, p. 70.

[48] "A Letter Written in 1711 by Mary Stafford to Her Kinswoman in England," *South Carolina Historical Magazine* 81 (1980):4; *Charleston Evening Gazette*, Sept. 28, 1785, Oct. 18, 1785.

[49] Hewatt, *Historical Account*, 1:120. See also David Ramsay to Benjamin Rush, Jan. 23, 1780, and to John Eliot, Nov. 26, 1788, in Robert L. Brunhouse, ed., "David Ramsay, 1749–1815: Selections from His Writings,"

For South Carolinians, the ill-fated Georgia experiment provided the most powerful testimony to the necessity of blacks. "This country was not capable of being cultivated by white men," Charles Pinckney argued, "as appeared in the attempt made in Georgia, during General Oglethorp's administration, but entirely failed, and ended in the white people emigrating from that state into this, where they could have negroes to cultivate their lands." Without slaves, "the one thing needful," "as essentially necessary to the cultivation of Georgia, as axes, hoes, or any other utensil of agriculture," colonists would be reduced "to want and begary" and "the Colony deserted and brought to destruction." Once the prohibition of slaves was lifted, however, and planters "got the strength of Africa to assist them . . . they laboured with success, and the lands every year yielded greater and greater increase." "S. Carolina & Georgia," Charles Cotesworth Pinckney concluded, "cannot do without slaves."[50]

Slaves were not only the way to wealth and the basis of lowcountry prosperity. Slaveowning also represented success and defined achievement. Commentators on South Carolina identified success as "plantations and slaves in the country," described the "industrious man" as one with "lands and negroes around him" who could "manage and improve them as he thinks fit." In Revolutionary South Carolina liberty meant the chance to exploit all the available opportunities, acquire land, and drive blacks, the possibility to achieve that "Satisfaction of Mind which a free born subject of America tastes

American Philosophical Society *Transactions*, new ser. 55, pt. 4 (1965):65, 123; Ramsay, *History of the American Revolution*, 1:37, 39; and James Habersham to the earl of Hillsborough, Apr. 24, 1772, "The Letters of the Hon. James Habersham, 1756–1775," Georgia Historical Society *Collections* 6 (1904):173.

[50] *Charleston Evening Gazette*, Sept. 28, 1785; Milton L. Ready, *The Castle Builders: Georgia's Economy under the Trustees, 1732–1754* (New York, 1978), pp. 281–83; Ralph Gray and Betty Wood, "The Transition from Indentured to Involuntary Servitude in Colonial Georgia," *Explorations in Economic History* 13 (1976):353–70; Betty Wood, *Slavery in Colonial Georgia, 1730–1775* (Athens, Ga., 1984); Max Farrand, ed., *The Records of the Federal Convention of 1787*, 3 vols. (New Haven, 1911), 2:371.

in seeing a stately Slave stand on every Perch of his extensive Plantation."[51]

Of course, South Carolinians idealized the society they had built, but that idealization rested on a bedrock of accomplishment plainly evident to all who troubled to look. The economy had grown rapidly in the eighteenth century, especially so in the years leading up to Independence. South Carolinians had developed a profitable plantation agriculture characterized by technical innovation and had demonstrated that they could respond creatively to economic difficulties. And, although some were bothered by qualms of conscience, more by fears of rebellion, they had shown themselves capable of managing slaves. Many had acquired substantial fortunes, and the wealth of some was spectacular by colonial standards. Most lowcountry planters did own land and slaves, even if the spread of rice and indigo had forced many small farmers to leave. Those accomplishments made some citizens aggressive and self-confident, filled them with pride in their achievements, persuaded them that they could manage their own affairs, made them resent British interference. Robert Pringle captured the prevailing spirit in his 1769 charge to a grand jury. "Some of your progenitures arrived in this country when it was a dreary wilderness," he asserted, "inhabited only by wild beasts, and great numbers of savages." Despite "the great hazard they ran of losing their lives, and the many hardships and disadvantages they labored under . . . they bravely maintained their ground, and withstood and defended themselves against the frequent assaults and attacks of the savages, though attended with a great effusion of blood." Subsequently, "by their great industry," they "improved and cultivated the colony to so great maturity, that it became the land of plenty, as well as of liberty, and fruitful, like the land of Egypt." And "all this done," Pringle boasted, "without one farthing expense or charge to the mother country."[52]

[51] Chalmers, *Weather and Diseases of South-Carolina*, p. 30; Hewatt, *Historical Account*, 2:130; "Back Settler," *Fugitive Thoughts*, p. 34.

[52] Quoted in Weir, *Colonial South Carolina*, p. 262.

British policy, many South Carolinians claimed, threatened those accomplishments and their prosperity. Certainly British policy restricted the gentry's ability to govern the colony, to address a range of local issues, and to nurture the economy, especially after 1769, when a prolonged confrontation between the assembly and crown appointees brought provincial government to a halt. But the Revolutionary movement was more than a fearful response to real or imagined threats. Colonial achievements were projected into the future and served as a source of self-confidence. There seemed no limits on South Carolina's possibilities, and few among the gentry doubted that they could manage the future and capture the region's full potential. In New England and the middle colonies, David Ramsay noticed, "few of the very rich were active in forwarding the revolution . . . but the reverse took place in the southern extreme of the confederacy. There were in no part of America, more determined whigs, than the opulent slaveholders." In the lowcountry, at least, that ardor reflected more than an intense fear of degradation and enslavement. It was fed instead by the successes of the past and by a vision of a slaveholder's republic with a rich and bountiful future. The "opulent slaveholders" belonged to that "active and spirited part of the community, who felt themselves possessed of talents, that would raise them to eminence in a free government." They "longed for the establishment of independent constitutions," for it was their "turn to figure on the face of the earth, and in the annals of the world." "The Almighty," William Henry Drayton knew, "has made choice of the present generation to erect the American Empire. . . . An Empire that as soon as started into Existence, attracts the Attention of the Rest of the Universe; and bids fair, by the blessing of God, to be the most glorious of any upon Record."[53]

[53] Ramsay, *History of the American Revolution*, 2:399–400, 452; William Henry Drayton, *A Charge, On the Rise of the American Empire* . . . (Charleston, 1776).

JOHN J. McCUSKER

Growth, Stagnation, or Decline? The Economy of the British West Indies, 1763–1790

THE ISLANDS OF THE WEST INDIES have been compared to a necklace of jewels strung in a curving line along the outer edge of the Caribbean Sea. Anchored at the north end by

For help with this present effort I wish to thank Paul G. E. Clemens, Stanley L. Engerman, the other participants in the conference on the Economy of Early America: The Revolutionary Period, 1763–1790, and the members of the Indiana University Economic History Workshop, the University of Illinois Economic History and Comparative Systems Workshop, the seminar on the Histoire Economique sur l'Atlantique et Ses Rivages of the Université de Bordeaux III, the Quantitative Economic History Discussion Group of the London School of Economics, and the Forsker- og Hoved-fagsseminar i Økonomisk Historie of Universitetet i Bergen for helpful comments and suggestions. This paper is part of an ongoing investigation into the economic history of the production, trade, and consumption of sugar, molasses, and rum in the Atlantic world during the seventeenth and eighteenth centuries. I am pleased to acknowledge my debt of gratitude to the Institute of Early American History and Culture, Harvard University, the National Endowment for the Humanities, the American Council of Learned Societies, the American Enterprise Institute, the American Historical Association, the American Philosophical Society, the University of Maryland, the fellows of St. Catherine's College, Oxford, and the John Simon Guggenheim Memorial Foundation for support of various aspects of this project. Revisions were completed while I was a visiting research fellow at the Centrum voor Economische Studiën, Katholieke Universiteit Leuven, Belgium, to the faculty and students of which I am especially grateful.

Jamaica and at the south by Barbados, the chain of the British West Indies was interspersed with other islands variously held by France, Spain, the Netherlands, Denmark, and even Sweden. Jamaica and Barbados stood apart. The other British islands belonged to one or another of two geographical groups: to the north, the Leeward Islands; to the south, the Windward Islands. In the first group were four chief islands—Antigua, Montserrat, St. Christopher (shortened to St. Kitts), and Nevis—and a subgroup of smaller islands, the British Virgin Islands. In the Windward Islands were Dominica, St. Vincent, Tobago, and Grenada and the Grenadines. The Windward Islands were also called the Ceded Islands because they had been turned over to Great Britain by France in 1763 as part of the settlement ending the Seven Years' War. All of the British West Indies are listed, with their estimated populations, 1760–90, in table 1.

There were other changes in the ownership of the individual islands during the seventeenth and eighteenth centuries for all but the two most important British islands, Jamaica and Barbados. From the time these two had been first settled by Englishmen, they continued without interruption to be productive members of the old empire. Sugar manufacture started on Barbados in the 1630s, underwent a period of very rapid expansion in the 1640s and 1650s, and continued to grow during the next two decades, though at a much slower rate. Decline had set in by the 1680s and lasted for the next half century. The recovery that began in the 1720s persisted until the time of the Revolutionary War. The Leeward Islands followed a path similar to that of Barbados, differing only in the timing and intensity of their own "sugar revolutions." None experienced this transformation as early, as suddenly, or as completely as Barbados. Jamaica, captured from Spain in 1654, benefited from a steady growth that continued until the Revolutionary War, merely slowing somewhat between the 1680s and the 1730s.

The economies of all of the British sugar islands were similar in structure, and one can easily talk about them as one entity. The chief difference in sugar growing between Barbados and Jamaica was the restriction imposed on the former by the limited supply of land available to its planters—and

Table 1. Population estimates for the British West Indies, 1760–90 (in thousands)

Colony	Category	1760 (1)	1770 (2)	1780 (3)	1790 (4)
Jamaica	White	10.0	12.2	17.9	18.3
	Black	172.9	201.7	243.2	275.6
	Total	183	214	262	294
Barbados	White	17.8	17.2	16.9	16.2
	Black	86.6	92.0	82.4	75.4
	Total	104	109	99	92
Antigua	White	3.2	2.8	(2.3)	5.0
	Black	35.2	38.6	37.9	45.0
	Total	38	41	40	50
Montserrat	White	1.4	1.3	1.1	0.8
	Black	9.1	9.9	9.3	8.5
	Total	10	11	10	9
Nevis	White	1.2	1.6	2.0	1.5
	Black	8.5	8.8	9.0	8.4
	Total	10	10	11	10
St. Christopher	White	2.6	2.1	2.1	4.0
	Black	22.3	23.4	24.6	26.3
	Total	25	26	27	30
British Virgin Islands	White	1.2	1.2	(1.2)	(1.2)
	Black	6.8	8.5	10.2	(10.2)
	Total	8	10	11	(11)

Table 1. Population estimates for the British West Indies, 1760–90 (continued)

Colony	Category	1760 (1)	1770 (2)	1780 (3)	1790 (4)
Dominica	White	1.6	3.1	1.2	1.2
	Black	5.7	14.8	18.8	15.4
	Total	7	18	20	17
St. Vincent	White	0.8	2.0	1.5	1.4
	Black	5.4	8.3	11.9	11.8
	Total	6	10	13	13
Grenada	White	1.3	1.6	1.1	1.0
	Black	12.4	24.7	31.5	27.0
	Total	14	26	33	28
Tobago	White	—	0.2	0.7	0.5
	Black	—	3.2	11.1	15.4
	Total	—	3	12	16
Subtotals Leeward Islands	White	9.6	9.0	8.7	12.5
	Black	81.9	89.2	91.0	98.4
	Total	91	98	99	110
Windward Islands	White	3.7	5.9	4.5	4.1
	Black	23.5	51.0	73.3	69.6
	Total	27	57	78	74

Table 1. Population estimates for the British West Indies, 1760–90 (continued)

Colony	Category	1760 (1)	1770 (2)	1780 (3)	1790 (4)
Totals British West Indies	White	41.1	45.3	48.0	51.1
	Black	364.9	433.9	489.9	519.0
	Total	405	478	538	570

SOURCES: Estimates are based on materials assembled and methods discussed in John J. McCusker, "The Rum Trade and the Balance of Payments of the Thirteen Continental Colonies, 1650–1775," Ph.D. diss., University of Pittsburgh, 1970, appendix B, supplemented by additional research. Data for the period after 1790 are especially fragmentary and the estimates for 1790 are based on figures for 1785–89, thus understating somewhat the actual population levels for that year.

NOTES: "Black" includes slaves, free blacks, maroons, and Amerinds; the last three groups constituted an insignificant percentage of the total.

Not all totals agree because of rounding. Figures in parentheses are essentially guesses. The subtotals for the Leeward Islands add together the figures for Antigua, Montserrat, Nevis, St. Christopher, and the British Virgin Islands (Anguilla, Tortola, and others). The subtotals for the Ceded, or Windward, Islands add together the figures for Dominica, Grenada and the Grenadines, St. Vincent, and Tobago. The Windward Islands did not become British until 1763. It is therefore technically incorrect to add the population of this group to the total of the British West Indies for 1760 though not to have done so in this case would have distorted unacceptably any calculations of the changes between 1760 and 1770.

The figures presented in Alex[andre] Moreau de Jonnès, *Recherches statistiques sur l'esclavage colonial et sur les moyens de le supprimer* (Paris, 1842), pp. 36–45, are not strictly comparable to the above estimates since his numbers were not subjected to the same adjustments to correct for undercounting and other problems with the raw data (see the discussions in the text and notes of McCusker, "Rum Trade," appendix B).

even that difference was muted somewhat by the availability of new lands for sugar in neighboring colonies. Jamaica suffered from no such restriction, its land being effectively limitless, at least in this era. As a result of this difference the planters of Barbados (and the Leeward Islands) tended to farm more intensively, whereas Jamaican planters engaged in land-extensive agriculture. Nevertheless, all the British West Indies were prosperous places by the time of the War for American Independence.[1]

The American Revolution ended that period of prosperity not only in the British West Indies but throughout British America. All will agree that the years immediately following 1776 were not so good, economically speaking, for the colonies in rebellion as the years preceding the war. A recent study of the colonies' economic history has even suggested that the decline in the United States during the War of Independence approached the levels recorded during the Great Depression of the 1930s.[2] Nevertheless, renewal had set in by the middle of the 1780s. It is probable that, for the United States, economic historians will eventually agree to characterize the whole era of the American Revolution in terms of three subperiods: 1763–75, a time of general prosperity; 1776–83, a time of severe depression; and 1783–90, a time of slow recovery.[3]

[1] For an account of the economic history of the British sugar islands, see Richard B. Sheridan, *Sugar and Slavery: An Economic History of the British West Indies, 1623–1775* (Barbados, 1974). For a more recent, shorter synthesis see John J. McCusker and Russell R. Menard, *The Economy of British America, 1607–1789* (Chapel Hill, N.C., 1985), pp. 144–68. Older treatments are Frank Wesley Pitman, *The Development of the British West Indies, 1700–1763*, Yale Historical Publications, Study 4 (New Haven, 1917), and Lowell Joseph Ragatz, *The Fall of the Planter Class in the British Caribbean, 1763–1833: A Study in Social and Economic History* (New York, 1928). For general histories see Sir Alan Burns, *History of the British West Indies* (London, 1954), and J[ohn] H. Perry and P[hillip] M. Sherlock, *A Short History of the West Indies*, 2d ed. (London, 1963).

[2] McCusker and Menard, *Economy of British America*, pp. 373–74.

[3] This is not to say that there were no fluctuations within these subperiods. See ibid., pp. 60–65. The standard work on the latter two subperiods

However apropos that characterization may be of the economy of the United States, we cannot be sure it serves equally well for the other British colonies in the New World—Canada and the West Indies. Indeed, for the West Indies, there is reason to think that it is much too sanguine a picture. The standard works on the subject—insofar as there are any works on the subject of the economy of the British West Indies in the late eighteenth century—designate the whole period after 1763 as one of decline. Sir Alan Burns, in his *History of the British West Indies,* entitled his chapter on the two decades after 1764 the "years of disaster."[4] Lowell Joseph Ragatz also dated the decline of the British Caribbean as having begun with the Treaty of Paris that ended the Seven Years' War.[5]

(and beyond) is still Curtis P. Nettels, *The Emergence of a National Economy, 1775–1815,* The Economic History of the United States, vol. 2 (New York, 1962).

[4] Burns, *History of the British West Indies,* pp. 501–35. Compare Robert Livingston Schuyler, *The Fall of the Old Colonial System: A Study in British Free Trade, 1770–1870* (London, 1945), for whom "the fall" began in 1770 and the somber tone in Perry and Sherlock, *History of the West Indies,* pp. 127–41.

[5] Ragatz, *Fall of the Planter Class.* Compare Eric Williams, *Capitalism and Slavery* (Chapel Hill, N.C., 1944). For the broader historiographical traditions within which these works fit, especially Williams's, see Elsa V. Goveia, *A Study on the Historiography of the British West Indies to the End of the Nineteenth Century,* Instituto Panamericano de Geografía e Historia, publicacion no. 78 (Mexico, 1956), Seymour Drescher, *Econocide: British Slavery in the Era of Abolition* (Pittsburgh, 1977), pp. 3–9, William A. Green, "Caribbean Historiography, 1600–1900: The Recent Tide," *Journal of Interdisciplinary History* 7 (1977):509–30, and McCusker and Menard, *Economy of British America,* pp. 17–50 (esp. 41–45), and 144–68.

Ragatz's book began where the other standard book on the subject (Pitman, *Development of the British West Indies*) left off. In contrast, Richard Pares, the fine historian of the West Indies, called the period ending with the War of Independence a "silver age," a view concurred in by Richard B. Sheridan (Pares, *Merchants and Planters* [*Economic History Review,* supplement 4 (1960)], p. 40; Sheridan, *The Development of the Plantations to 1750* [*and*] *An Era of West Indian Prosperity, 1750–1775* [Barbados, 1970], p. 74). The "golden age" is supposed to have been the halcyon days of the 1640s. Compare Jacques Godechot, "La période revolutionnaire et impériale," *Revue Historique* 539 (1981):225, summing up Michel Devèze, *Antilles, Guy-*

Yet much of the evidence that the economic fortunes of the West Indian possessions of Great Britain peaked before that war and fell steadily thereafter is at least worthy of reexamination. Most of what Ragatz and others have relied on to demonstrate their case is simply a repetition of contemporary fears and complaints uttered in petitions and papers presented before Parliament pleading the particular purposes of the sugar lobby. The island planters had a good deal to fear and, indeed, they had been complaining mightily for years. But their jaundiced views of their expectations during the decades after 1763, and especially after 1783, have become accepted by many as historically accurate. What the economic situation of the British West Indies actually was over these years remains to be discovered.

The British West Indian sugar planters traditionally pursued two interrelated goals as they sought to maximize the returns from their enterprises. On the one hand, they tried to keep high the prices they received for things they sold; on the other hand, they tried to keep low the prices they paid for the things they purchased. They exported sugar, molasses, rum, and other, less important, tropical commodities. In order to maintain high prices for their exports, they strove both to preserve their monopoly on the supply of these goods to Great Britain and Ireland and to extend it to the entirety of the British Empire. One such attempt produced the Molasses Act of 1733, but it proved less than effective. Another of their efforts resulted in the return to France after the Seven Years' War of Martinique and Guadeloupe—but not the Windward Islands.

Just as the sugar planters tried to extend their monopoly on supply to maintain high prices for their exports, they also tried to keep their costs low. The planters needed to purchase and import almost all their supplies—food, timber products, work animals—and they tried to keep these costs down by limiting the markets to which their suppliers could sell such items. The Molasses Act was designed to do that, too, by preventing the North American colonists from trading with

anes, la mer des Caraibes de 1492 à 1789 (Paris, 1977): "Les Antilles françaises connaissent, entre 1763 et 1789, l'apogée de leur prospérité."

the West Indian colonies of the French, the Danes, the Dutch, or the Spanish. It surprised no one, then or later, that the North Americans were not comfortable with attempts to prevent them from buying or selling in the "foreign" West Indies. But the British West Indian sugar planters were not overconcerned about the plight of the North Americans. In pursuit of their own profits, in ways as mercantilistic as those of the mother country, they tried every device they could to maximize returns and minimize costs.[6]

They persisted in these efforts after the Seven Years' War. We are all more or less familiar with the events of the period 1763–90 as seen from the perspective of the British sugar planters. They continued to be unhappy that the Treaty of Paris had introduced four new sugar islands into the old select circle of British producers, thus diluting the monopoly on supply previously enjoyed by the older colonies. They were unhappy with the events of the War of Independence because it cut off their trade with the continental colonies, disrupted their trade with Europe, and introduced foreign produce into the British market as captured cargoes, the prizes of war. And they were particularly unhappy after the war when the British government, enforcing the Navigation Acts with new orders and acts, tried to close down for good most of the trade with the United States. Each of these de-

---

[6] For the details of all this see Pitman, *Development of the British West Indies*. See also Richard B. Sheridan, "The Molasses Act and the Market Strategy of the British Planters," *Journal of Economic History* 17 (1957):62–83. However aggrieved the West Indians may have felt, it is important to appreciate the preferential treatment accorded them within the old empire. Just as the passage of the Molasses Act attests to Parliament's willingness to give special help to the planters, so also did the government cater to West Indian mercantile interests. As Jacob M. Price has put it: "The original laws [of trade] too, whatever they said on paper, were never seriously intended to apply to the West Indies where 'international trade' remained the rule rather than the exception. How really serious were the British ministers after 1763 in wishing to alter the trade [between the British and the non-British colonies]? The establishment of free ports, *inter alia*, suggests a greater interest in legitimating rather than stopping it" (review of Thomas C. Barrow, *Trade and Empire: The British Customs Service in Colonial America, 1660–1775* [Cambridge, Mass., 1967], in *Journal of Economic History* 27 [1967]:400). The West Indians' complaints were intended simply to induce a continuation or expansion of such privileged treatment.

velopments threatened the position of the sugar producers of the British West Indies, either by weakening the market for their produce or by increasing the cost of their provisions and supplies. They complained before the fact that such actions would harm them. They complained over the years that these actions were harming them. And they complained later that they had suffered greatly as a result of these actions.[7] Given the obvious self-serving content of the complaints, the questions to be answered are: Were they harmed? and How much were they harmed? Ragatz and others, by relying almost exclusively on the public petitions and protests of the complainants, have answered just as the they did themselves. We might want to have another look.

Ideally, of course, we could turn to a range of data to answer these questions, but in reality we cannot. Economic data are much less abundant for the British West Indies than they are for Great Britain itself or even for the continental colonies. And economic data for the British West Indies, however difficult to find for the period before 1775, are still more difficult to find for the years afterwards. The last two phases of the Second Hundred Years' War between England and France—1776–83, 1793–1815—disrupted and destroyed the records and record keeping of the British West Indies. We are left with limited evidence to answer our questions.[8]

Despite such constraints, several considerations suggest that the effort is worthwhile. It is clear that the British West Indies were the most important colonial possessions of Great Britain's first empire. British economic growth in the eigh-

---

[7] For the details of all this, see Ragatz, *Fall of the Planter Class,* esp. pp. 81–201. Compare Alice B. Keith, "Relaxations in the British Restrictions on the American Trade with the British West Indies, 1783–1802," *Journal of Modern History* 20 (1948):1–18.

[8] Even the records kept in England are deficient from this period; a fire in the Custom House in London in 1814 destroyed many of the English Ledgers of Imports and Exports for the 1780s and later. See John J. McCusker, "Colonial Civil Servant and Counterrevolutionary: Thomas Irving (1738?–1800), in Boston, Charleston, and London," *Perspectives in American History* 12 (1979):344. For these materials see also McCusker and Menard, *Economy of British America,* pp. 73–78.

teenth century depended on all her colonies as producers and consumers, and the West Indies fulfilled both functions superbly, far better per capita than did their neighbors in the continental colonies. Over the period 1763–75, the British West Indies were the destination of 7.6 percent of all British exports and accounted for 22.1 percent of all British imports. They were the largest supplier of imports and the fourth largest overseas consumer of British produce and manufactures. A good portion of the commodities imported into Great Britain from the British West Indies were reexported for sale abroad. Much of British overseas trade depended on its Caribbean colonies. Anything that harmed Great Britain's trade with the West Indies threatened the development of the metropolitan economy.[9]

It is clear, too, that a major change in the economy of the British West Indies did occur sometime between the middle of the eighteenth century and the middle of the nineteenth century, just as Ragatz has said. Islands that had been lively, viable contributors to an imperial economy in 1750 were dead in the water by 1850. In order to discover the causes of the change and to identify the particular results of what happened, we need first to find out when things started to go bad. If the decline began about 1763, then perhaps Ragatz is

[9] These data are from Board of Trade Papers, 6/185, Public Record Office. In this volume are some contemporary extracts from the English and Scottish Ledgers of Imports and Exports mentioned in the notes to table 2. See also the notes to table 4, where this same source has been used. The base for these constant-value figures is 1700–1702 (John J. McCusker, "The Current Value of English Exports, 1697 to 1800," *William and Mary Quarterly*, 3d ser. 28 [1971]:618). The importance of the West Indies to British economic growth has long been recognized in the literature. See Phyllis Deane and W[illiam] A. Cole, *British Economic Growth, 1688–1959*, 2d ed. (Cambridge, 1969), pp. 86–88, and, especially, Jacob M. Price, "Colonial Trade and British Economic Development, 1660–1775," *Lex et Scientia: The International Journal of Law and Science* 14 (1978), 106–26. Compare Stanley L. Engerman, "Notes on Patterns of Economic Growth in the British Colonies in the Seventeenth, Eighteenth, and Nineteenth Centuries," in Paul Bairoch and Maurice Lévy-Leboyer, ed., *Disparities in Economic Development since the Industrial Revolution* (New York, 1981), pp. 46–57. This was originally given as a paper before the Seventh International Economic History Congress at Edinburgh in 1978. See also McCusker and Menard, *Economy of British America*, pp. 35–50.

right in relating it to the difficulty that the older sugar islands had in competing with the newly ceded Windward Islands. As he argued, poor farming practices and an inability or unwillingness to innovate may have been the reason for the decline of Barbados, Jamaica, and the Leeward Islands. If the decline began about 1776, then perhaps it was the disruption and devastation of the War of Independence that caused it. The war at first cut off the continental colonies as suppliers and as markets. After 1778, when the French entered the war on the side of the United States, their naval forces upset trade still further and then captured several British islands. Maybe the War of Independence, as in the words of David H. Makinson, "cost the British West Indies their economic life."[10]

But if the economy of the British West Indies came through the war years without too much damage, then maybe the causes of the decline have to be sought in the 1780s. Perhaps, as the West Indians feared, continued restrictions on their trade with the North Americans wrought irreparable harm to their economy. The Orders in Council of 1783 and the subsequent laws that prevented the postwar resumption of the old patterns of trade certainly raised the ire of both the sugar planters and the Americans. Arranging for the resumption of free trade with the British West Indies became a major goal of United States foreign policy over the next fifty years. Whether the closing of these ports to most American vessels harmed the British West Indies—and, if so, to what extent—is, however, still an unsettled issue. If it did not, if the economy of the British West Indies made it through the 1780s relatively unharmed, maybe the causes of their ultimate decline need to be sought later, perhaps in the Napoleonic Wars or, perhaps, even in the abolition of the slave

[10] David H. Makinson, *Barbados: A Study of North-American–West-Indian Relations, 1739–1789*, Studies in American History, no. 3 (The Hague, 1964), p. 132. Richard B. Sheridan would seem to agree ("The Crisis of Slave Subsistence in the British West Indies during and after the American Revolution," *William and Mary Quarterly*, 3d ser. 33 [1976], 615–41, and "The Slave Trade to Jamaica, 1702–1808," in B. W. Higman, ed., *Trade, Government and Society in Caribbean History, 1700–1920: Essays Presented to Douglas Hall* [Kingston, Jamaica, 1983], pp. 1–16).

trade and the emancipation of the slaves. Perhaps, as Seymour Drescher has suggested, Great Britain killed off the British West Indies in the nineteenth century by an act of "econocide." We need to find out when the turning point in the economic fortunes of the British West Indies happened before we can start to look for its causes.

The argument presented here is that Ragatz was wrong in his choice of 1763 as marking the beginning of the economic deterioration of the British West Indies and that any decline started only after 1790.[11] Up to that point the economy of the British Caribbean continued to grow and change in several significant ways. While the data discussed herein do not address fully the issues of development or decline, they do reflect the state of the economy well enough to support these contentions. In particular they challenge any ideas that the

[11] Engerman, "Economic Growth in the British Colonies," has already established that the decline only began with the changes attendant upon emancipation, and not before. Drescher, *Econocide*, reached a similar conclusion in an analysis of the West Indies that borrowed heavily both in method and in content from John J. McCusker, "The Rum Trade and the Balance of Payments of the Thirteen Continental Colonies, 1650–1775," Ph.D. diss., University of Pittsburgh, 1970. Compare Seymour Drescher, "Le 'déclin' du système esclavagiste britannique et l'abolition de la traite," trans. C. Carlier, *Annales: Economies, Sociétés, Civilisations* 31 (1976):414–35. Nevertheless Engerman's message—and, more importantly, its implications—have not been fully appreciated by historians. See, for example, Selwyn H. H. Carrington, "Teaching and Research of United States History in the English-Speaking West Indies," in Lewis Hanke, ed., *Guide to the Study of United States History outside the U.S., 1945–1980*, 5 vols. (White Plains, N.Y., 1985), 1: 423–32, citing "my own works *The West Indies during the American Revolution: A Study in British Colonial Economy and Politics* (book manuscript, 1979) and *Crisis in the Caribbean Economy, 1775–1787* (monograph manuscript, 1982)." Compare his "Economic and Political Development in the British West Indies during the Period of the American Revolution [1770–82]," Ph.D. diss., University of London, 1975, and "The American Revolution and the British West Indies' Economy," *Journal of Interdisciplinary History* 17 (1987): 823–50. See also Herbert C. Bell, "British Commercial Policy in the West Indies, 1783–93," *English Historical Review* 31 (1916):429–41, Charles R. Ritcheson, *Aftermath of Revolution: British Policy toward the United States, 1783–1787* (Dallas, 1969), and John Philip Wise, "British Commercial Policy, 1783–1794: The Aftermath of American Independence," Ph.D. diss., University of London, 1972.

British West Indies began a downward slide in the 1760s from which they never recovered. Rather, as we will see, the dozen years after the Treaty of Paris in 1763 witnessed a major expansion in the islands. The period of the War of Independence was one of depression for the British West Indies, as it was in the United States, but one of less severity in the islands than on the North American continent. Moreover, in the post-1783 era the West Indies recovered more quickly and more fully than did their continental cousins. By every available measure, the British West Indies were in better shape in 1790 than they had been in 1770—and that was distinctly not true of the United States. Whenever the planter class of the British West Indies began to fall, it was not before 1790.

We begin by formulating and analyzing estimates of the population of the British West Indies. While no one would argue that short-term changes in human population necessarily relate causally and directly to parallel changes in an economy, there are several reasons to examine these figures for the British Caribbean. Primarily this is indicated because over 90 percent of the West Indians were black slaves. They were the work force of the plantations, a term much too dry to convey the reality of their economic exploitation or their human suffering. "Work animals" better describes how they were treated and how we can view their role in the economy. As plantation slaves they were fed, clothed, and housed only well enough to keep them in the fields during their prime working years. They were literally worked to death and then replaced with new slaves from Africa. Thus there are some economic inferences to be drawn from short-term changes in the size of the black population of the islands.

Certainly some of the West Indian planters thought so. They argued, especially in the 1780s, that the war just over had nearly devastated them and that the changed trade regulations about to come into effect would finish the job. Numbers of slaves had died during the war from malnutrition and other causes and the expected continuation of high prices for provisions would only exacerbate the problem. In other words, they implied that the depressed state of the economy could be read in the population figures for their colonies, at least in the black population figures.[12] We are interested in population statistics for the British West Indies not only because they allow us to test these notions but also because they provide us with the necessary capability of reducing other economic data to a per capita basis, thus rendering comparisons more valid.

A critical point to be made about the decennial estimates of population in table 1 is their relatively unreliable or "fragile" character, especially those for the year 1790. They are probably all in the right order of magnitude, and those for each decade are all of roughly equal fragility so that comparisons among them are valid, but that is the best that can be said for them. Data collection in the British West Indies, which had been poor before the 1780s, seems to have broken down completely during the years after 1790. As a result these figures are at their worst when we need them most. Insofar as the figures for 1790 are wrong, however, it is most likely as underestimates.[13] Nevertheless these data do allow us to make a point or two—points that, of course, take into account the weakness of the data.

First, and most significantly, the population of the British West Indies continued to grow throughout the period. In forty years the total population of the islands increased 40 percent. Although growth was not uniform across all the colonies—and, indeed, the population declined on some of the older islands, notably Barbados—the number of both whites and blacks grew during the period. Because many of the complaints mentioned before emanated from Barbados, it is significant historiographically that Barbados lost nearly 20

---

[12] See, for example, Bryan Edwards, *The History, Civil and Commercial, of the British Colonies in the West Indies*, 2 vols. (London, 1793), 2:415. See also the "extracts of two letters from Jamaica," Sept. 21, 1786, Board of Trade Papers, 6/76, P.R.O. Compare Ragatz, *Fall of the Planter Class*, pp. 142–53, and Sheridan, "Crisis of Slave Subsistence," pp. 615–41.

[13] Any underestimation of the data on population for 1790 in table 1 would result in an overstatement of the per capita figures in column 3 of table 4. That undesirable effect is offset by using data from somewhat earlier in the decade (1784–90) to compile the estimates for 1790.

percent of its own black population between 1770 and 1790.[14] But the tendency for the older islands to weaken relative to islands with newer lands was a continuing process in the Caribbean. Involved was the shift in resources from less productive to more productive fields of endeavor, a development most often effected by the actual migration of planters, equipment, and slaves. Whatever this may have meant for one island, it can hardly be equated with the economic decline of the British West Indies.[15]

While the total population of the islands did grow, the second fact to emerge from table 1 is that the rate of growth decreased over the era. But this deceleration in the growth rates of the white and black populations is probably not very significant. To begin with, the decennial estimates for 1790 are most likely underestimates, and the growth rates for the decade of the 1780s are therefore lower than was the case in fact. Even so the white population grew at a faster rate in the

[14]See Makinson, *Barbados*, pp. 83–136. The nadir was reached in 1784; the slave population of Barbados increased slowly and unevenly after that date. See "An Account of the Number of Slaves [in Barbados] returned to the Treasurer's Office . . . from . . . 1780 to 1787," C.O. 28/61, fol. 204, P.R.O. Compare "Barbados. Report of a Committee of the General Assembly, upon the Several Heads of Enquiry, &c., related to the Slave Trade," 1790, in Great Britain, Parliament, House of Commons, *Sessional Papers to 1801*, 29 (Accounts and Papers), No. 697 (1), p. 3; and "An Account [from the] . . . British West India Islands [of] . . . the Number of Negroes Imported [and] . . . Exported [in 1787 and 1788]," 1790, ibid., 31 (Accounts and Papers), No. 705 (4). For a discussion of the slave trade during this period see Philip D. Curtin, *The Atlantic Slave Trade: A Census* (Madison, Wis., 1969), pp. 127–62.

[15]In much the same way, we need to be wary of statements that the number of sugar plantations declined when, indeed, the acreage under cultivation and/or the quantity of sugar grown and manufactured increased. Any "decline" in the number of plantations may be explained by consolidation, for example. See the report in Jamaica, Assembly, *Proceedings of the Hon[ourable] House of Assembly of Jamaica, on the Sugar and Slave-Trade* (St. Jago de la Vega, 1792), appendix 12, which contrasts the 775 plantations on the island in 1772 with the 767 there in 1791. Patented acreage in Jamaica grew from 1,671,569 acres in 1754 to 1,907,589 acres in 1789 (McCusker, "Rum Trade," p. 242, n. 21). Even the assembly's figures for the number of plantations is suspect. Edwards, *History of the British West Indies*, 1:312–14, shows 1,061 sugar plantations in Jamaica in 1786.

1780s (6.5 percent) than it had in the 1770s (6.0 percent), though not so rapidly as it had in the previous ten years (10.2 percent).[16] The rate of growth of the black population in the 1780s was much slower than in earlier decades—6.0 percent as opposed to 12.9 percent in the 1770s, 18.9 percent in the 1760s, and 23.6 percent in the 1750s. Nevertheless, just as these figures suggest, the declining rate of growth was a continuing phenomenon and not something that we can necessarily blame on anything peculiar to this time. Even more to the point of this analysis, however, is the importance of changing population size on the economy. Increases or decreases in the size of the labor force were less important than were changes in output.

The produce of the sugar islands was, of course, sugar—or, more accurately, sugar and its by-products, molasses and rum. We have no real figures on the quantity of sugar harvested and manufactured annually in the British West Indies; our best data are the amounts of sugar exported from the islands and imported elsewhere.[17] Such data are reasonable proxies for sugar production only if the product mix—the relative proportion of sugar, molasses, and rum made from a given quantity of raw cane juice—stayed the same. Assuming no real change in product mix over the short term (a fair assumption), we can attempt an assessment of changes in the

[16] Some of this growth was due to immigration. Many of those who immigrated into the British West Indies in the 1780s were loyalists fleeing from the United States (see Ragataz, *Fall of the Planter Class*, pp. 194–99).

[17] Many of these and subsequent points about the nature of the West Indies sugar industry are developed more fully in the appendixes and text of McCusker, "Rum Trade." The standard English-language treatise on the sugar industry, Noel Deerr, *The History of Sugar*, 2 vols. (London, 1949–50), 1:193–203, presents the figures for sugar imported into England as if these data showed the quantities produced in each island. Even such careful scholars as Engerman ("Economic Growth in the British Colonies," table 3) have been misled by Deerr's work. Compare Elizabeth Boody Schumpeter, *English Overseas Trade Statistics, 1697–1808* (Oxford, 1960), pp. 61–62, and McCusker, "Rum Trade," pp. 885–87, 891–929, esp. p. 991, n. 24. The most authoritative work on sugar is still Edmund O. von Lippmann, *Geschichte des Zuckers seit den ältesten Zeiten bis zum Beginn der Rübenzucker-Fabrikation: Ein Beitrage zur Kulturgeschichte*, 2d ed. (1929; reprint ed., Niederwalluf [bei Wiesbaden], 1970).

Table 2. Sugar and rum exports from the British West Indies, 1770–73 and 1784–87

Year	Imported from the British West Indies into			
	England	United States	Canada	Total
	(1)	(2)	(3)	(4)
Sugar (hundredweight)				
1770	1,818,229	65,489	653	1,884,371
1771	1,492,096	46,994	840	1,539,930
1772	1,786,045	44,456	979	1,831,480
1773	1,762,387	39,365	393	1,802,145
1784	1,815,510	47,595	14,744	1,877,849
1785	2,173,468	46,116	12,214	2,231,798
1786	1,813,098	35,801	18,836	1,867,735
1787	1,926,121	19,921	9,891	1,955,933
Rum (gallons)				
1770	2,631,210	3,250,060	38,310	5,919,580
1771	2,728,565	2,180,060	67,588	4,976,213
1772	2,284,163	3,332,750	85,715	5,702,628
1773	2,282,544	3,049,298	82,505	5,414,347
1784	1,981,308	2,742,271	888,170	5,611,749
1785	3,558,380	2,188,000	677,412	6,423,792
1786	2,229,231	1,399,040	953,743	4,582,014
1787	2,251,341	1,620,205	874,580	4,746,126

SOURCES: The data for England are from the Custom House Ledgers of Imports and Exports for these years. Not all totals agree because of rounding. For the data cited here, only the ledgers for 1770–73 survive. See Custom and Excise Records 3/70–73, Public Record Office.

Although the later ledgers are lost, the data continued to be collected and compiled and there are contemporary extracts from them, some of which were published. See, for example, Bryan Edwards, *The History, Civil and Commercial, of the British Colonies in the West Indies*, 2 vols. (London, 1793), 2:509–10. Compare "An Account of the Quantity of Sugar Imported into Britain between 1772 and 1791," Nov. 8, 1792, Long Manuscripts, Add. Ms. 12:432, fol. 18, British Library, and the data presented by Thomas Irving, the Inspector General of Imports and Exports, in April 1791 to the "Select Committee appointed to take Examination of Witnesses on the Slave Trade," among the "Minutes of the Evidence . . . respecting the African Slave Trade," 1791, in Great Britain, Parliament, House of Commons, *Sessional Papers to 1801*, 34 (Accounts and Papers), No. 748, pp. 264–75. Irving used 1772–75 and 1787–90 as the two four-year periods for his comparison because "I am of opinion, that the Islands did not recover [from] the . . . consequences of war, sooner than about the year 1787" (ibid., p. 265). For the origins and original compilation of the data see G[eorge] N. Clark, *Guide to English Commercial Statistics, 1696–1782*, Royal Historical Society Guides and Handbooks, no. 1 (London, 1938); John J. McCusker, "The Current Value of English Exports, 1697 to 1800," *William and Mary Quarterly*, 3d ser. 28 (1971):607–28; "Colonial Civil Servant and Counterrevolutionary: Thomas Irving (1738?–1800), in Boston, Charleston, and London," *Perspectives in American History* 12 (1979):315–50; and *Bills of Entry and Marine Lists: Early Commercial Publications and the Origins of the Business Press* (Cambridge, Mass., 1985). The data for the continental colonies (United States) and for Canada are from local custom house records, compiled at the time. See "Account of the Quantity of British West Indies products imported into the thirteen colonies and British North America," 1770–74, Liverpool Papers, vol. 153, fol. 51, Add. Ms. 38,342, British Library; and "Account of the Quantity of West Indian products imported into the United States and British North America," 1783–89, in the "Report of the Lords of the Committee of the Privy Council . . . for Trade and Plantations . . . on the Trade to Africa," 1789, in Great Britain, Parliament, House of Commons, *Sessional Papers to 1801*, 26 (Accounts and Papers), No. 646a, Part 4, appendixes 13 and 21. Compare the "State of the Trade with America from 1783–1789," Colonial Office Records, 325/6, P.R.O.; David Macpherson, *Annals of Commerce, Manufactures, Fisheries, and Navigation . . . to . . . 1801*, 4 vols. (London, 1805), 4:161; and the "Report on the Commercial State of the West Indian Colonies," in Great Britain, Parliament, House of Commons, *Sessional Papers*, 1807, 3 (Report), no. 65. For rum one can compare the Custom House figures with those generated by the Excise Office. See "An Account of the Amount of Excise Duties received yearly on Rum imported from the British West India Islands into England," 1734–88, Treasury Office Papers, 38/363, P.R.O. Comparable data for Scotland and Ireland have yet to be compiled, but see John J. McCusker, "The Rum Trade and the Balance of Payments of the Thirteen Continental Colonies, 1650–1775," Ph.D. diss., University of Pittsburgh, 1970, pp. 886, 894–95, 942–43. See also the discussion of all these data by Thomas Irving in several reports and letters dated the fall of 1787 and spring of 1788 in the Correspondence and Papers of George Grenville, Dropmore Papers, Add. Ms. 59:238, fols. 62–76, 91–95, 107, 122–23, British Library.

economy of the sugar islands by comparing the quantities of sugar exported from the British West Indies.

Recent studies have shown than the quantity of sugar produced and exported from the British Caribbean grew steadily from the 1730s through to the end of the first of the three periods that interest us here, 1763–75.[18] The growth was shared by all of the British islands and continued until the beginning of the War of Independence. We do not know what happened during the war—although we can expect that there was some falling off—but, as table 2 shows, the increase in production resumed in the 1780s. A comparison of 1784–87 with 1770–73 shows an increase in sugar production in the British West Indies by nearly 11 percent. The increase in rum production was slightly less (3.0 percent). Even though the war had disrupted considerably the production and marketing of sugar and its by-products, sugar output in the British islands during the decade of the 1780s nevertheless ran ahead of what it had been before the war. This is revealed all the more clearly if we value the quantities exported in each period by the London price for raw muscovado sugar (table 3). The annual average crop in the early 1770s was worth about £3,300,000 sterling (in current pounds), in the mid-1780s about £4,200,000. We can reduce this to an estimate of output per worker by dividing the value produced by the number of blacks in the colonies. On that basis, each West Indian black worker can be credited with producing £7.58 worth of sugar in the early 1770s and £8.63 worth of sugar in the mid 1780s. Productivity in sugar went up by about 14 percent.[19]

These figures of value of output per worker probably underestimate the increase in productivity in the sugar industry.

[18] McCusker, "Rum Trade," pp. 128–301, esp. p. 230.

[19] From table 3, the average price for muscovado sugar for 1770–73 was 36s. 9d. per hundredweight; for 1784–87, 42s. 7d.½. The Phelps Brown and Hopkins commodity price index records a 5.7 percent rise between 1770–73 and 1784–87 (John J. McCusker, "An Historical Price Index for Use as a Deflator of Money Values in the Economy of Early America" [forthcoming]). Thus £8.43 in mid-1780s pounds was the equivalent of £7.98 mid-1770s pounds. On a constant value basis, productivity rose 5.3 percent.

Table 3. The price of muscovado sugar at London, 1760–87 (in shillings sterling per hundredweight)

Year	Price
1760	32–47
1761	32–50
1762	28–49
1763	25–37
1764	27–40
1765	32–44
1766	29–42
1767	33–42
1768	32–41
1769	33–42
1770	31–42
1771	32–44
1772	29–43
1773	28–45
1774	27–44
1775	25–39
1776	29–47
1777	39–67
1778	45–68
1779	50–59
1780	45–59
1781	56–73
1782	40–73
1783	28–45
1784	26–46
1785	35–45
1786	40–56
1787	41–52

SOURCES: Bryan Edwards, *The History, Civil and Commercial, of the British Colonies in the West Indies,* 2 vols. (London, 1793), 2:267. These are the prices of the lowest grade of raw, muscovado sugar as taken in by the Customs on the islands in payment of the 4½% Duty, imported into London, and sold there at auction. See John J. McCusker, "The Rum Trade and the Balance of Payments of the Thirteen Continental Colonies, 1650–1775," Ph.D. diss., University of Pittsburgh, 1970, pp. 1142, 1187, n. 273. English sugar brokers believed that, because they were of lower quality, these sugars averaged 3s. the hundredweight less than the average price paid for the planters' sugars sold in the same market (*An Account of the Late Application to Parliament from the Sugar Refiners, Grocers, &c. of the Cities of London and Westminster, the Borough of Southwark and the City of Bristol* [London, 1753], p. 2n).

Any such underestimate is an artifact of the premise implicit in using the total black population as the divisor for both periods—that is, that the proportion of black workers involved in sugar production was the same in the 1770s and the 1780s.[20] But the proportion changed. Despite the suggestions by Ragatz and others that the West Indian planters were tradition-bound and unusually adverse to adopting new methods, there were many innovations introduced into West Indian agriculture during the last half of the eighteenth century.

Some of these had to do with the way sugar was produced. There was a very early (and technologically significant) attempt to adapt the steam engine to the sugar mill, one example of an ongoing interest in making milling more efficient. A new variety of sugar cane was introduced, experimented with, and eventually widely adopted; it yielded more juice of a higher sugar content. Planters appear to have varied the product mix considerably, producing more crystalline sugar or more molasses and rum as the relative prices of each shifted. The Barbadian planters turned increasing quantities of their raw muscovado sugar into white clayed sugar, as did the planters on Grenada.[21]

Other innovations had to do with the development of new crops, among them cocoa, coffee, indigo, and cotton being notable additions to the increased output of the several islands. They had traditionally occupied a role subservient to sugar and its by-products but, during the years after 1763

[20] Another potential cause of distortion might have arisen if there had been a significant change in the age structure of the black population. There is no evidence for any such change nor any reason to believe it took place.

[21] Despite his conclusions, Ragatz, *Fall of the Planter Class*, esp. pp. 37–80, 199–202, is the source himself of much of the information about the developments mentioned in this and next paragraph. For clayed sugar in Barbados and Grenada see McCusker, "Rum Trade," pp. 198–220, 221–24. Compare the argument in W[illiam] A. Green, "The Planter Class and British West Indian Sugar Production, before and after Emancipation," *Economic History Review*, 2d ser. 26 (1973):448–63. For the steam engine and sugar milling see McCusker and Menard, *Economy of British America*, p. 324.

and, especially after 1783, these commodities assumed some-what greater importance. Whereas such goods had consti-tuted perhaps 6 percent by value of the exports of the British West Indies in the 1760s, the percentage had probably doubled by the late 1780s.[22] It would go higher later.

All of these developments suggest that a smaller propor-tion of the black population was involved in making the sugar produced in the mid-1780s than in the early 1770s. If a rel-atively smaller number of black laborers worked at sugar pro-duction in the 1780s than in the 1770s, then the output per worker rose in the period by even more than the 14 percent calculated above. The diminishing rate of increase in the black population of the British West Indies might simply have reflected this increase in productivity. To the extent that ag-ricultural and technological innovations improved labor pro-ductivity, they worked as well to decrease the need for fresh supplies of slaves and, thus, to diminish demand in the slave trade.

A growing population, increasing sugar production, and greater productivity, even given a hiatus during the war years, suggest the possibility that the economy of the British West Indies was not yet in decline by the 1780s. Other data support this contention. Table 4 presents figures showing the level of imports into Great Britain from the British West In-dies (in other words, British West Indian exports) and ex-ports from Great Britain to the British West Indies (or British West Indian imports) in constant value terms on a per capita basis for the three subperiods of the era after 1763: 1763–75, 1776–83, and 1784–90.

[22] The figure for the 1760s is based on *American Husbandry* (1775), ed. Harry J. Carman (New York, 1939), pp. 429, 439, 445–46, 448–49, 462, and elsewhere; that for the 1780s is a guess founded in impressions gained from reading, among others, Edwards, *History of the British West Indies*, 2:268 *et seq.* D. J. Pope, "Shipping and Trade in the Port of Liverpool, 1783–1793," 2 vols., Ph.D. thesis, University of Liverpool, 1970, 2:153–61, developed figures for cotton imports into Liverpool from the British West Indies that show a fourfold increase between 1770 and 1791–92 al-though, as the author is careful to point out, some of that cotton had been grown in the non-British islands and imported into them for reexport to the British market.

In table 4 British exports to the West Indies and imports from the islands are reduced to a per capita basis in two ways, either by using the total population of the several islands or by using only a part of that total population. In the second series of reductions British imports/West Indian exports are reduced to a per capita basis using the figures for just the black population of the islands in 1770, 1780, and 1790; and West Indian imports/British exports are reduced using the figures for just the white population. This second series of reductions is the more revealing because production of West Indian exports is more likely to have varied significantly with the black population, the producers, than with total population, and because consumption of imports from Great Britain is more likely to have varied significantly with the white population, the consumers. The per capita level of consumption—the standard of living—of the black population, especially as it was reflected in imports from Great Britain, is unlikely to have changed much, if at all, over a short space of time, especially in constant value terms.[23]

As we might have expected, both imports into the islands and exports from them were lower in constant value terms during the war than they were before the war according to three out of four of these per capita measures (table 4, column 2). (Using constant values, the base of which is outside this period [1700–1702], discounts for any wartime induced price differences.)[24] Less expected, but in line with the general argument presented here, all three measures rose again

---

[23] The subject of changes in the standard of living of blacks in the British West Indies (and elsewhere in the Western Hemisphere) is a topic of current debate. For a summary of this debate see McCusker and Menard, *Economy of British America*, p. 58, n. 8, and pp. 295–96. This all needs to be understood within the context of the discussions engendered by Robert William Fogel and Stanley L. Engerman, *Time on the Cross: The Economics of American Negro Slavery*, 2 vols. (Boston, 1974). The point here is merely that any change is unlikely to have been reflected over the short term by variations in the value of goods imported from Great Britain if only because so very small a proportion of those things that blacks in the British West Indies consumed was imported from Great Britain.

[24] See John J. McCusker, "The Current Value of English Exports, 1697 to 1800," *William and Mary Quarterly*, 3d ser. 28 (1971):607–28

Table 4. Average annual exports and imports between Great Britain and the British West Indies and the United States, 1763–89 (in constant pounds sterling)

	1763–75	1776–83	1784–89
	(1)	(2)	(3)
Exports to the British West Indies			
From England and Wales	1,189,698	1,185,148	1,295,992
From Scotland	72,017	167,610	182,283
Total value	1,261,715	1,352,758	1,478,275
Per capita value			
white population	27.85	28.18	28.93
total population	2.64	2.51	2.59
Imports from the British West Indies			
Into England and Wales	2,763,593	2,511,998	3,515,218
Into Scotland	150,985	154,603	279,335
Total value	2,914,578	2,669,601	3,794,553
Per capita value			
black population	6.72	5.43	7.31
total population	6.10	4.94	6.66
Exports to the United States			
Total value	2,563,397	699,521	2,333,171
Per capita value			
total population	1.19	0.25	0.59
Imports from the United States			
Total value	1,702,309	160,473	928,097
Per capita value			
total population	0.79	0.06	0.24

SOURCES: These data are from Board of Trade Papers, 6/185, Public Record Office. In this volume are some contemporary extracts from the English and Scottish Ledgers of Imports and Exports that are mentioned in the notes to table 2. The base for these constant value figures is 1700–1702 (John J. McCusker, "The Current Value of English Exports, 1697 to 1800," *William and Mary Quarterly*, 3d ser. 28 [1971]:618). Compare B[rian] R. Mitchell and Phyllis Deane, *Abstract of British Historical Statistics* (Cambridge, 1962), pp. 310–11; U.S. Bureau of the Census, *Historical Statistics of the United States: Colonial Times to 1970*, 2 vols. (Washington, D.C., 1975), 2:1176–78 (ser. Z 213–44, with corrections for ser. Z 227–34). Florida is included as part of the continental colonies/United States. The population data for the British West Indies are from table 1, using 1770 for the 1763–75 calculation, 1780 for the 1776–83 calculation, and 1790 for the 1784–89 calculation (see n. 13, above). Population data for the continental colonies for the same decennial years are from U.S. Bureau of the Census, *Historical Statistics*, 1:8, 2:1168 (ser. A 1, Z 1).

after the war to levels nearly the same as or higher than they had been before. Only the level of British exports/West Indian imports measured against the number of white consumers failed to conform to the general pattern of decrease then increase. Instead it increased during *both* periods. During the war it rose by 1.1 percent. And it rose again after the war by an additional 2.7 percent. On a per capita basis, the white inhabitants of the British West Indies were steady customers of the mother country.[25]

At a constant value, West Indian exports/British imports measured per capita against the black population exhibited the same general three-part pattern but with a much wider variation than West Indian imports/British exports. The figures for West Indian exports/British imports combine the total value of all goods shipped, sugar included. The decrease during the war was sharp—exports fell 19.2 percent, and the postwar increase was even steeper—exports rose again by 34.6 percent. West Indian exports to Great Britain in the 1780s, on a per capita constant value basis, were 8.8 percent higher than they had been in the 1760s and early 1770s. To the extent that either or both imports or exports approximated the changing levels of West Indian gross national product, the economy of the islands certainly did not suffer materially during this period. Indeed, it seems by these data to have improved.

This is all the more striking for the contrast with the United States, where the struggle for independence cost the colonists dearly. According to James F. Shepherd and Gary M. Walton, exports per capita in the United States were 25 percent lower in 1791–92 than they had been in 1768–72.[26] Table 4 shows that per capita exports from the United States to Great Britain decreased by 70 percent between 1763–75

[25] Some of the British goods imported into the British West Indies were, of course, destined for reexportation to other markets. Traditionally these had been in the non-British Caribbean, especially the Spanish settlements on the Main. During and after the War of Independence some of these goods were also reexported to North America.

[26] James F. Shepherd and Gary M. Walton, "Economic Change after the American Revolution: Pre- and Post-War Comparisons of Maritime Shipping and Trade," *Explorations in Economic History* 13 (1976):397–422.

and 1784–89. Wealth estimates show wealth per capita to have been 14 percent lower in 1805 than in 1774, and that after a considerable period of recovery.[27] Estimates of gross national product show a 46 percent decline between 1774 and 1790.[28] Stanley L. Engerman and Robert E. Gallman conclude that, if these estimates are found to be accurate, then something "truly disastrous" happened to the economy of the United States between 1775 and 1790.[29]

To the extent that we can rely on the data offered here, we can say that, in comparison with the experience of the United States, the West Indies did very well indeed over this period. For the British West Indian planters the years 1763–75 were a time of prosperity, 1776–83 was a time of disruption, even depression, but 1783–90 was a time of great recovery to levels of prosperity that exceeded 1763–75. Over the whole era, imports in real, per capita terms stayed constant. Exports in real, per capita terms increased markedly. The output of sugar, the West Indies' major crop, stayed steady in terms of

[27] Alice Hanson Jones, *Wealth of a Nation to Be: The American Colonies on the Eve of the Revolution* (New York, 1980), p. 81, in comparison with data assembled in Samuel Blodget, *Economica: A Statistical Manual for the United States of America* (Washington, D.C., 1806), p. 196.

[28] McCusker and Menard, *Economy of British America,* pp. 373–76.

[29] Stanley L. Engerman and Robert E. Gallman, "U.S. Economic Growth, 1783–1860," *Research in Economic History* 8 (1983):19. Compare Nettels, *Emergence of a National Economy,* pp. 45–88, and elsewhere.

Sheridan, *Sugar and Slavery,* pp. 229–32, presents data for 1771–75 that argue a total wealth for the island of Jamaica of £18,000,000. On average each of the estimated 15,000 white inhabitants was worth £1,200 sterling, therefore. (The population estimate is from table 1, above.) Compare Engerman, "Economic Growth in the British Colonies," table 4, where he excludes the value of slaves from the total wealth and includes the slave population in the total population of wealth producers. Sheridan's calculations originally appeared in his article "The Wealth of Jamaica in the Eighteenth Century," *Economic History Review,* 2d ser. 18 (1965):292–311. Michael Craton, *Sinews of Empire: A Short History of British Slavery* (London, 1974), pp. 132–56, presents an alternative, lower set of estimates that Engerman, "Economic Growth in the British Colonies," n. 4, suggests are too low. Jamaican estate inventories in the Jamaica Archives, Island Record Office, Spanish Town, could be used to extend these wealth estimates.

volume and increased in market value both absolutely and on a per capita basis. Theirs was not an economy in decline—yet. The decline and fall of the British West Indies began sometime after 1790.

JACOB M. PRICE

Reflections on the Economy of Revolutionary America

THE ESSAYS PRESENTED IN THIS VOLUME rather remind me of going through a family's photograph album. We get fascinating details about some important aspects of the family's life—usually happy events—but little or nothing about other features of their existence about which we might be a little curious. In this article I should like to try to put the separate, valuable contributions of these papers into the broader context of what we know, have recently learned, and still need to know about the economy of the thirteen colonies before, during, and after the Revolution.

During the past fifteen or twenty years there has been a striking and most rewarding revival of scholarly interest in the precensus population history of the colonies. Research in this area has made us aware of the marked difference between the seventeenth- and eighteenth-century population structures. In most colonies in the seventeenth century, males outnumbered females by a substantial margin. As one moved south from New England, mortality rates rose and life expectancy fell. All this added up to populations that did not reproduce themselves and were heavily dependent on immigration not just for growth but even for survival. By the first half of the eighteenth century—the transition took place at different times in different colonies—almost all continental colonies had reached a stage in which there was a more even distribution of sexes, more normal family life and very significant indigenous population growth with only a marginal dependence on immigration.

This pattern of population growth held true for the black population as well as for the white. This was in marked contrast to the West Indies where, throughout the eighteenth century, slave populations failed to reproduce themselves. Russell R. Menard suggests that part of this may be ascribed to the wider geographical dispersion of slaves in North America and to the rising proportion of creoles in the total slave population: both would have tended to isolate blacks to a greater degree from African diseases. Work routines—except in rice—should have been lighter in most parts of the continent than in the islands,[1] and food was definitely cheaper, hence probably more available. The teeming rivers and forests of the thirteen colonies should have offered slaves an effective opportunity to obtain in fish and small game a diet richer in protein than that available to their counterparts in the Antilles.

The high rate of natural increase in the total population apparently cushioned most of the deleterious population effects of the Revolution. Immigration was cut off for seven or eight years. Tens of thousands of loyalists left the colonies. Thousands of slaves were evacuated or removed by the British, or otherwise escaped from the control of their masters. Recent scholarship suggests that deaths in military service were heavier than previously imagined.[2] Yet the population estimates in the *Historical Statistics of the United States* show a population increase between 1770 and 1790 (82.9 percent) almost the same as that for 1750–70 (83.5 percent).[3] Even war could not check the fecundity of the American people celebrated by Benjamin Franklin.

However, if population increased without a corresponding

[1] On the demographic implications of fieldwork, compare John Campbell, "Work, Pregnancy, and Infant Mortality among Southern Slaves," *Journal of Interdisciplinary History* 14 (1984):793–812.

[2] Howard H. Peckham, ed., *The Toll of Independence: Engagements and Battle Casualties of the American Revolution* (Chicago, 1974), pp. 131–33.

[3] U.S. Bureau of the Census, *Historical Statistics of the United States: Colonial Times to 1970*, 2 vols. (Washington, D.C., 1975), 1:8, 2:1168.

increase in total income, there may, as we shall observe later, have been a decline in income per head. This I see as the central problem in the economic history of the Revolutionary era.

The economist's affection for elegantly simple models frequently spills over into economic history, where we read much about staple economies and subsistence economies. These concepts are useful provided that one does not use them too literally in attempting to describe reality. Even the self-reliant and self-sufficient Daniel Boone needed guns and shot and salt, at the very least, and the demands of the tax collector extended deep into frontier areas. At the other extreme, although West Indian plantations purchased a good share of their food from abroad—much to their grief during the Revolutionary War[4]—continental plantations grew most of their own. Recent scholarship has emphasized that a substantial fraction of the labor on tobacco plantations in the Chesapeake had to be devoted to growing food and similar nonmarket activities.[5] Nevertheless, some geographic areas were clearly more oriented than others toward external markets.

The lines that marked the boundaries between areas of more significant, and areas of less significant, market orientation were not fixed. They varied with commodity and with temporal changes in what Harold Innes called the penetrative powers of the price system. Thomas Doerflinger has pointed out that farmers in the middle colonies commonly sold more than one commodity or service on the market and thus had some powers of adaptation when the price of any given commodity became less attractive. Whether it paid to send a wagonload of wheat to Philadelphia would vary with the distance, costs of transport, and the market price at Phil-

[4] Lowell Joseph Ragatz, *The Fall of the Planter Class in the British Caribbean, 1763–1833: A Study in Social and Economic History* (New York, 1928), chap. 5.

[5] For example, Paul G. E. Clemens, *The Atlantic Economy and Colonial Maryland's Eastern Shore: From Tobacco to Grain* (Ithaca, N.Y., 1980), pp. 172–74; David C. Klingaman, "The Significance of Grain in the Development of the Tobacco Colonies," *Journal of Economic History* 29 (1969):268–78.

adelphia. For any given price per bushel one could draw an encircling line on the map representing the limits of the zone within which it was then feasible or attractive to send wheat to market. The zone would, of course, extend farther from Philadelphia in areas where cheaper water transport was available. Similar zones could be indicated for Baltimore and for the overland shipment of tobacco to Petersburg, Va., from places to the southward. The fact that some inland localities were only marginally part of the Atlantic economy meant that they could experience exceptionally rude shocks when downward fluctuations in world prices in effect cut them off from outside markets. The traditional turbulence of such regions can be seen not simply as a manifestation of frontier culture but also as evidence of the pains of adjustment arising from originally overoptimistic expectations of market opportunities. For example, when tobacco dropped precipitously in world price in a few years (1759–63, 1769–73),[6] growers in the Regulator country of north central North Carolina, whose tobacco had to pay land carriage to Petersburg, were bound to suffer much more than Virginia planters with access to cheaper water transport.

If the reach of the market was ill defined and variable, the economic boundaries between free and slave labor were hardly more precise. Of course, the differences between the archetypes of the free yeoman family farmer of New England and the great slave plantation owners of Jamaica, Barbados, or South Carolina were distinct enough; but all reality did not fit into one or another of these models. Writers on slave economies almost always tell us that slavery was a precondition for this or that colonial economy. But does this usually mean more than that slaves were necessary for a slave plantation economy? It is by no means clear that slaves were

[6]Compare Maryland local prices in Clemens, *Atlantic Economy*, pp. 226–27, and Carville V. Earle, *The Evolution of a Tidewater Settlement System: All Hallow's Parish, Maryland, 1650–1783* (Chicago, 1975), pp. 228–29, and European prices in Jacob M. Price, *France and the Chesapeake: A History of the French Tobacco Monopoly, 1674–1791*, 2 vols. (Ann Arbor, 1973), 1:672–76, 2:852. The Amsterdam prices (because of the method of averaging used) do not reflect price fluctuations as clearly as does the "French price" in Britain.

equally needed in all commodity productions that came to use slaves. Blacks constituted almost 12 percent of New York's population in 1770,[7] but no one would argue that slaves were necessary for any particular productive activity in that colony. How much more necessary were they in Virginia and Maryland? Since Thomas J. Wertenbaker's time we have understood that tobacco cultivation in Virginia and Maryland developed first in the seventeenth century as an activity of relatively small "yeoman farmers" assisted only by a few indentured servants who, on the completion of their service, commonly became first tenant farmers and then very frequently yeoman farmers employing indentured servants of their own.[8] Slavery was not necessary for the small-scale system of cultivation then prevalent and technically adequate. The chief competition for the tobacco cultivators of Virginia and Maryland came from the small peasant cultivators of southwest France, the Low Countries (including French Flanders and Artois), and the valleys of the Rhine and Main. Even in Cuba tobacco was a crop of smallholders.[9] Slavery came to flourish in the tobacco colonies because the larger landed proprietors found that in a world in which land was plentiful they could earn more from their land as planters than as landlords collecting rents from tenants. As planters they found at a certain point that it was rational to pay more and invest in slaves rather than indentured servants. Edmund S.

[7] U.S. Bureau of the Census, *Historical Statistics*, 2:1168.

[8] High points in this vast literature include Thomas J. Wertenbaker, *Patrician and Plebian in Virginia* (Charlottesville, Va., 1910), idem, *The Planters of Colonial Virginia* (Princeton, 1922), Edmund S. Morgan, *American Slavery, American Freedom: The Ordeal of Colonial Virginia* (New York, 1975), Gloria L. Main, *Tobacco Colony: Life in Early Maryland, 1650–1720* (Princeton, 1983), Clemens, *Atlantic Economy*, Russell R. Menard, "From Servants to Slaves: The Transformation of the Chesapeake Labor System," *Southern Studies* 16 (1977):354–90, and Allan L. Kulikoff, "Tobacco and Slaves: Population, Economy and Society in Eighteenth-Century Prince George's County, Maryland," Ph.D. diss., Brandeis University, 1976.

[9] Fernando Ortiz, *Cuban Counterpoint: Tobacco and Sugar* (New York, 1947), chap. 1, esp. pp. 30–33; Price, *France and the Chesapeake*, chaps. 6, 18; idem, *The Tobacco Adventure to Russia*, American Philosophical Society *Transactions* 51 (1961), chaps. 1, 9.

Morgan sees this as primarily a social-political decision; I see it more as a rational market decision, as do Russell R. Menard, Gloria L. Main, and others of the "Maryland School."[10] The decision was, of course, made easier by the increasing relative scarcity of indentured servants after 1689. The end result is the same: the rise of slave cultivation and the large estate. What if slaves had not been available or not available on as attractive terms? In the first instance, less tobacco would have been cultivated, as in fact happened in the years immediately following the return of peace in 1713. This would inevitably have led to higher prices. At higher prices, planters could pay for both indentured and free labor. This should ultimately have drawn at least some more free labor to the Chesapeake and have established a new equilibrium with both higher labor costs and higher prices.

Such an adjustment would have been much more difficult in the Caribbean, for David W. Galenson has shown us that those considering indentured servitude were well aware of the difference in working and health conditions in different colonies and demanded much more favorable terms (that is, shorter service) to induce them to go to the Antilles rather than to the Chesapeake or Pennsylvania.[11] We can conceive, at least hypothetically, of an equivalent equilibrium involving higher labor costs and higher prices in the British sugar colonies. It would probably have been totally unrealizable, however, without significantly higher tariff protection as long as the rest of New World and African sugar was produced by slaves—as the British West Indian sugar industry found out to its discomfort in the half century after emancipation in 1833. In the extreme case of South Carolina rice cultivation, Russell Menard's essay is persuasive that no realistically imaginable system of nonslave labor could have attracted the needed free labor to that area and cultivation.

If the market can substitute one labor system for another, it can much more readily substitute manufactures of one origin for those of another. James A. Henretta's essay reminds

[10] See note 8.

[11] David W. Galenson, *White Servitude in Colonial America: An Economic Analysis* (Cambridge, 1981), chaps. 6 and 7.

us that in the seventeenth and eighteenth centuries most manufactures of standardized nonluxury products took place in the countryside. We may follow the advice of D. C. Coleman and put aside for the present the elusive concept "protoindustrialization" and speak simply of rural manufactures.[12] This rubric in fact embraced three separate manufacturing systems. In the first, the household manufacturing system, the family fabricates needed goods for itself without recourse to the market: spinning its own yarn, weaving its own cloth, tanning its own leather, making its own shoes. In the second, which I shall call the independent rural artisan system, the rural craftsman owns his tools and raw materials but works for an initially local market that does not involve him directly in complex merchandizing or credit operations, though the ultimate market for his goods may be at some distance. (A well known example of this last was the woolen manufacturing industry of the West Riding of Yorkshire, whose weavers sold their cloth at local markets as they manufactured it—one piece at a time. The system developed to the extent it did only because there were in the Halifax and other cloth markets merchants able to buy the cloth as it came to market and handle its finishing and marketing.)[13] Finally, there was a third organizational mode, the full putting-out or merchant-manufacturer system. The clothier or other merchant-manufacturer put out raw and semifabricated materials to cottage workers of diverse skills who processed them on piecework. The cottage workers generally, but not necessarily, owned their own spinning wheels, looms, and the like, but the merchant-manufacturer owned the material being processed. To work well, the putting-out system required the concentration of a good number of spinners, weavers, and related workers in a fairly compact area so that the traveling agents of the clothier, for example, could reach an economical number of them in a single day's travel. In the English case, the clothier or other merchant-manufacturer was gen-

[12] D. C. Coleman, "Proto-Industrialization: A Concept Too Many," *Economic History Review*, 2d ser. 36 (1983):435–48.

[13] Compare Herbert Heaton, *The Yorkshire Woollen and Worsted Industry* (1920; reprint ed., Oxford, 1965), pp. 203–5, 293–301.

erally tied to a factor (commission merchant) in a port town who supplied him with raw materials on credit and sent him the most detailed instructions about the qualities and varieties most in demand.[14] In this way, the humblest cottage weaver who never strayed more than a dozen miles from his native parish was tied to the imperatives of national and international markets.

To what extent was each of these three forms of rural industry present in colonial America? Tradition and some historiography has it that there was much household manufacture, particularly in the northern colonies and frontier areas, but this is difficult to document quantitatively. Only 1 percent of the Virginia inventories prepared between 1660 and 1676 contained reference to spinning wheels. There was, however, an enhanced incentive to attempt domestic manufactures during the wars of 1689–1713, when supplies from Europe became more irregular and much more expensive. Gloria Main reports that during the depression of tobacco prices in the 1690s, sheep-rearing increased in several parts of Maryland and with it the number of spinning wheels in postmortem inventories. She found no looms in her Maryland inventories before 1705, however, and in only 8 percent thereafter. The situation in New England was more advanced but not as different as one might expect. There are frequent references to spinning wheels in seventeenth-century inventories, but looms are less in evidence. Inventories prepared in Essex County, Mass., in New Hampshire, and in Maine between 1670 and 1730 show 40 percent of households with spinning wheels but only 7 percent with looms. In a group of 91 printed inventories for Providence, Rhode Island, dating from 1716 to 1726, spinning wheels are mentioned in 55 percent but looms in only 10 percent! Despite all the agitation encouraging local manufactures between 1765 and 1775, the situation was not too different on the eve of the Revolution. Carole Shammas has analyzed the 284 Massachusetts inventories of 1774 printed by Alice Hanson Jones. These show

[14] Jacob M. Price, *Capital and Credit in British Overseas Trade: The View from the Chesapeake, 1700–1776* (Cambridge, Mass., 1980), pp. 102–8.

that 48.9 percent of the households there contained spinning wheels but only 5.7 percent were equipped with the wheels, looms, and other equipment needed to make both linen and woolen cloth. (There was, however, a significant regional variation in this, ranging from the mere 2.1 percent in urban Suffolk County to 14.8 percent in remote frontier Hampshire County.) Slaveowners had a particular incentive to find useful occupations for different kinds of slaves at different seasons; spinning must have been perceived as an efficient indoor occupation for female slaves in winter and other free times, for Shammas reports that analysis of Jones's group of Virginia and Maryland inventories for 1774 shows 71 percent mentioning spinning wheels. The relative ubiquity of spinning wheels and the rarity of looms confirm what common sense suggests would follow from the greater technical difficulty of weaving as compared with spinning. Rural housewives could use only some of their yarn for knitting, and Shammas reports that in New England they sold the surplus to local storekeepers who arranged for its weaving locally on the putting-out system. Henretta similarly cites evidence in his paper for Virginia planters also arranging for weaving locally on the putting-out system. Although there were so-called cloth "factories" in New York and Massachusetts employing a number of weavers, most colonial weavers in both town and country appear to have been independent craftsmen who probably worked both on the putting-out system and on their own as opportunity offered.[15] In shoemaking,

[15] Main, *Tobacco Colony*, p. 73; Carole Shammas, "How Self-Sufficient Was Early America?" *Journal of Interdisciplinary History* 13 (1982):254–59; Laurel Thatcher Ulrich, "A Friendly Neighbor: Social Dimensions of Daily Work in Northern Colonial New England," *Feminist Studies* 6 (1980):395; Rolla Milton Tryon, *Household Manufactures in the United States, 1640–1860: A Study in Industrial History* (Chicago, 1917), pp. 81–85, 91–92 (Tryon reports that in the description of runaway servants and slaves in New Jersey, 1704–79, about 30 percent are indicated as wearing homespun clothing); Rita S. Gottesman, comp., *The Arts and Crafts in New York, 1726–1776*, New-York Historical Society *Collections* 69 (1938 for 1936): 258, 261. Arthur Harrison Cole was skeptical about the existence of any putting-out in the colonial period; the subject obviously needs further work (*The American Wool Manufacture*, 2 vols. [Cambridge, Mass., 1926], 1:19–20).

too, we find the beginnings of a partially articulated putting-out system emerging in the Lynn shoe trade before the Revolution.[16]

Independent craftsmen in the countryside need not have been totally cut off from agricultural activities. Pierre Goubert observes that in the late seventeenth century in the rural Beauvaisis—where morcellement, or subdivision of holdings, had gone very far—agricultural smallholders very frequently acquired part-time second occupations by which they described themselves in the records. Peter H. Lindert similarly observes that in contemporary late seventeenth-century England a significant proportion of the rural population had some sort of craft designation but suggests that here too most could not have been occupied full time in their crafts. In the areas of New England where subdivision had gone relatively far by the mid-eighteenth century there would have been a comparable pressure to acquire supplementary part-time occupations.[17] However, insofar as manufacturing crafts were part-time occupations of smallholders, the labor market would have been markedly imperfect and slow to respond to changes in demand.

We have very little hard data on manufacturing output in the colonies except for such items as the imports of cotton wool given by James Henretta. There are, of course, all kinds of hints that manufacturing activity was increasing in the late colonial period. One clue for the textile industry which no one—as far as I know—has pursued systematically is the appearance of fulling mills. In a celebrated article, the late Eleanora Carus Wilson described their first appearance in England as an "industrial revolution of the thirteenth century." Fulling mills were waterpower-driven washing machines for cleaning the great "pieces" of woolen cloth (usually

[16] Paul G. Faler, *Mechanics and Manufacturers in the Early Industrial Revolution: Lynn, Massachusetts, 1780–1860* (Albany, 1981), pp. 20–24.

[17] Pierre Goubert, "The French Peasantry of the Seventeenth Century," *Past and Present* 10 (1956):60; Peter H. Lindert, "English Occupations, 1670–1811," *Journal of Economic History* 40 (1980):701–6; Jackson Turner Main, *Society and Economy in Colonial Connecticut* (Princeton, 1985), pp. 241–56.

about seventy-five yards long) after they came from the loom. With them were associated the tenteryards in which the cloth was dried after washing. Fulling mills were of necessity rural, and in Carus Wilson's view they greatly facilitated the movement of the woolen industry from town to country.[18]

The appearance of fulling mills in New England in the mid-seventeenth century suggests the existence of weaving on a commercial scale. It would be extremely useful to have periodic censuses of eighteenth-century fulling mills comparable to what we have for 1810 (when 1,682 were reported in sixteen states).[19] They were then much more common in the North but were also to be found in the South: they were first advertised in the *Virginia Gazette* in the years between 1763 and 1775 but were more frequently mentioned during the war. The phraseology of the advertisements suggests that the fullers expected patronage from the kind of planter already mentioned who put out his wool to be woven by a local craftsman.

The *Atlas of Early American History* contains excellent maps indicating the location of sugar refineries, rum distilleries, potteries, paper mills, silversmiths, glassworks, and ironworks in both pre-Revolutionary and Revolutionary America. Unfortunately the editors omitted fulling mills and shipbuilding yards, although shipbuilding was the most important colonial export industry. Some of the activities covered—particularly sugar refineries, distilleries, glassworks, and probably paper mills—required substantial capital and are not to be confounded with the activities of independent rural craftsmen.[20] In the case of iron, we must distinguish between the earlier stages of production—furnaces, forges, rolling and slitting mills—that required substantial capitali-

[18] Eleanora Carus Wilson, "An Industrial Revolution of the Thirteenth Century," *Economic History Review,* 1st ser. 11 (1941):1–20. On fulling mills in New England from the 1660s, compare William B. Weeden, *Economic and Social History of New England, 1620–1789,* 2 vols. (1890; reprint ed., Williamstown, Mass., 1978), 1:271, 306, 394, 2:679.

[19] Tryon, *Household Manufactures,* pp. 249–50.

[20] Lester J. Cappon, *Atlas of Early American History: The Revolutionary Era* (Princeton, 1976), pp. 26–31.

zations and the later stages of fabricating (nail and hardware making) that could be carried on by small independent smiths and cottage artisans. It would be extremely useful to have a census distinguishing the number and location of iron furnaces and forges at ten-year intervals from approximately 1740 to 1790.

In different colonies the iron trade had different characteristics. Much of the pig iron made in Virginia and Maryland was shipped at low freight rates to Britain as ballast on tobacco ships. There it was converted at foundries into cast iron or at forges into purified bar iron from which hardware and other forms of wrought iron were later fashioned. Britain in turn sent substantial amounts of bar iron as ballast on ships to New England and New York.[21] This would suggest that in those northern colonies the iron-fabricating trades outstripped local pig iron production, in contrast to Pennsylvania and New Jersey where there appears to have been a better balance between ironmaking and iron fabricating. Furthermore, the importation of bar iron into the more northerly colonies suggests that there may have been rather more iron-working there than the map of furnaces and forges would suggest, for the map would not pick up the processing of imported bar iron by petty smiths and cottage nailmakers.

The evidence on American industry in the decades leading up to the Revolution is therefore mixed. On one hand there is much evidence, particularly in textiles, of a predominance of independent rural craftsmen working largely for a local market with a relatively limited systematic putting-out system. On the other hand, in shipbuilding, ironworks, glassworks, distilleries, and paper works we find distinct evidence of more heavily capitalized forms of industrial organization becoming more conspicuous in the decades immediately preceding the Revolution. Nevertheless, the increase in internal manufacture, however large, did not diminish the significance of the import trades, either absolutely or per capita, as the contributions of Thomas Doerflinger, James F. Shepherd, and James Henretta all make clear. A great part of the economic life of Boston, New York, Philadelphia, Annapolis, and

---

[21] U.S. Bureau of the Census, *Historical Statistics*, 2:1185.

Charleston, in particular, centered on their role as distribution centers for imported European and Asian products. These imports competed effectively with domestic manufactures in both price and quality. Some imports were luxury goods not readily procurable in America; others, such as inexpensive linens, shoes, and "slops" (work clothes), were cheaper than anything produced locally.

We know much more about the organization of these import trades and related exchanges than we did thirty years ago, though some matters still remain in the dark. What proportion of the port merchant community was native, what proportion immigrant? Did these proportions change over time after the passing of the first generation? Equally important, how many port merchants were really trading on their own capital and at their own initiative, and how many were acting primarily as factors or commission merchants for, or as partners in, British firms? Such factors and junior partners can be found all through the South from Maryland to Georgia. Were they unknown in the North?

Some historians get terribly upset, indeed bristle, at any trace of debt. But debt, as Rabelais and Winifred B. Rothenberg remind us, is only the side of the ledger opposite credit. Increasing credit, indeed increasing debt, per capita, are most likely signs of increasing wealth per capita and increasing confidence in trading relations. Your local Campus Toggery doesn't pay cash for its gear nor did eighteenth-century merchants and shopkeepers. In an agricultural society, credit is more complex because of the payment schedules necessitated by the crop year and the risks implicit in vagaries of weather, crops, and prices. Most dealings between American and British merchants were based on the one-year credit allowed by the big British wholesalers who supplied the export trades.[22] However, when American merchants or shopkeepers or Scottish stores in the Chesapeake or North Carolina sold to planters or farmers, they had to take their chances on repayment, and long delays were not unanticipated. In general, good prices for agricultural produce meant speedier repayments while poor prices slowed everything down.

[22] Compare Price, *Capital and Credit*, chap. 6.

The burden of debt was then really a variable dependent on the movement of prices—the ultimate unpredictable variable. When one looks at the postwar debt claims, one is struck by how much heavier the burden of unsettled debt was for the Chesapeake than for the colonies to the north and south of it.[23] This difference cannot all be ascribed to the superior moral character of Quakers and Yankees (whose reputation was not that good) but reflects the different price histories of different commodities. Tobacco prices were falling in Europe between 1770 and 1774 when they reached desperately low levels.[24] By contrast, world wheat prices were high in 1772–74[25] and only fell in 1775 when tobacco recovered. The rise of tobacco prices in 1775 liquidated most of the debt of consigning planters who were normally kept on relatively short credit by the London and Bristol consignment merchants—but not the debts of the more numerous smaller planters who dealt at the Scottish and other stores where they were allowed longer credits.

When we observe price depression in tobacco but not in wheat in the early 1770s, Joseph A. Ernst's paper suggests that we may be dealing with possible causes of the greater radicalization of tobacco growing as opposed to wheat growing areas at that time. To say this does not mean that one must treat price movements as a *cause* of the Revolution in a philosophically rigorous sense; it may be enough to say that they were attendant circumstances facilitating revolutionary mobilization in some areas. Professor Ernst has dealt extensively with the ideology of revolutionary elites-to-be. But provincial ideologues usually become revolutionary elites only

[23] Ibid., pp. 6–14.

[24] The low tobacco prices of the early 1770s were an inevitable result of the overproduction of a heavily taxed commodity facing relative inelasticity of demand in the short run. In a country where land is plentiful, overproduction followed inevitably from an increasing labor force (particularly an unfree labor force) with few attractive and immediately available alternative uses. Slaves tended to be imported most heavily when tobacco prices were high, but their reproduction could ensure a rising labor force even when prices were falling.

[25] For example, B[rian] R. Mitchell and Phyllis Deane, *Abstract of British Historical Statistics* (Cambridge, 1962), p. 487.

when external conditions facilitate the activation or mobilization of some hitherto politically inert elements in society. Even a Lenin had to wait in Zurich until circumstances over which he had no control gave him the historically momentous opportunity to proceed to the Finland Station. Price movements in the 1770s, as pointed out by Ernst, are important as just such an independent circumstance facilitating if not causing Revolutionary mobilization.

More generally, when we approach political economy as a subject of historical research, we may be talking about two rather different sets of questions. Some historians of political economy—and this would include Ernst in part of his paper—investigate the publications, speeches, correspondence, and other expressions of political actors and publicists to establish as clearly as possible their analytic mode, goals, and programmatic or tactical recommendations. In this sense, historical political economy is a combination of the history of ideas and political propaganda techniques. There is, however, another variety of historical political economy that is concerned rather with the relationship of economic institutions and conditions to political life, and seeks in particular to investigate the ways in which changes in economic conditions or relationships may have had socially destabilizing results and thus helped create the conditions in which sharp political change become more possible. In this latter type of historical political economy, changes in prices or debt levels are important whether or not they are prominent in the publicistic work of political agitators and actors.

The Revolution distorted almost every aspect of the colonial economy. Few really prospered except blockade-runners, privateers, and government contractors. The fact that Chesapeake tobacco prices rose tenfold in Europe during the war gives us a classic example of inelasticity of demand but suggests that very little of that product was reaching Europe.[26]

[26] Prices in London rose from around 2*d.* per pound in 1774 to 23*d.*–24*d.* per pound in early 1782; prices in the free port of Dunkirk (where supplies would have been slightly easier) rose from under 20 *livres tournois* per quintal in 1774 to 125–150 *l.t.* around 1777 (Price, *France and the Ches-*

Tobacco production during the war could not have exceeded one-third of prewar and may have been much less. Much of what was grown was destroyed by enemy raids in the war or lost at sea. Food producers probably did better because of demand from the victualing officers of three nations. More intractable was the cutting off of supplies of imported goods. Some, of course, trickled in at fantastically inflated prices but this could have been little consolation to the average consumer.

As James Henretta graphically points out, the war was the golden hour of homespun, the moment of opportunity for every domestic industry. Some could profit from this hour more than others. Those manufacturers who depended on imported components or raw materials were severely embarrassed. Shipbuilding was seriously restricted by the shortage of imported sails, cables, and cordage. New England trades based on imported raw materials, whether molasses or cotton, must have been similarly circumscribed. It was even difficult to make and sell snuff in Virginia during the war because of the shortage of bottles.[27] The woolen and iron trades should have prospered much more. The frequency of advertisements for fulling mills in the *Virginia Gazette* increased markedly with the war. And one finds it hard to imagine that ironworks did not prosper. (In Britain, even Quaker-owned ironworks prospered in wartime without taking any defense contracts.) If the war was a moment of extraordinary opportunity for many manufacturing entrepreneurs, how many of them lasted into the peace? Or, like Jonah's gourd, did they flourish and wither in a day?

With its opportunities the war also brought suffering, death, and destruction. As already mentioned, recent research suggests that battle losses may have been larger than

---

apeake, 2:721, 744, 852, though the averaging employed makes the Amsterdam series less useful; compare 2:721, 723–25, 727, for Chesapeake leaf reaching Europe in wartime).

[27]Jacob M. Price, "The Beginnings of Tobacco Manufacture in Virginia," *Virginia Magazine of History and Biography* 64 (1956):15; Harrold E. Gillingham, "Pottery, China and Glass Making in Philadelphia," *Pennsylvania Magazine of History and Biography* 54 (1930):128.

previously supposed.[28] Lost too were the thousands of loyalists and thousands of slaves who left with the departing British forces, and the tens of thousands of immigrants who did not reach America in these years because of the war. Yet we have already seen that the fecundity of the American population more than made up for the population losses ascribable to the war. Only in Virginia did the loss of slaves appear to have left evidence of reduced productive capacity after the war. We know that some Virginia loyalists resettled in British occupied Georgia during the war, however, and were followed to that state by other Virginians after the war. Their presence helps explain the postwar spurt in tobacco exports from South Carolina and Georgia.[29] We may be dealing here with a problem of relocation rather than diminished capacity.

But the war more seriously disturbed the old trading patterns, and these could not always be so easily restored. British ports were open to American (i.e., United States) ships and goods after the war, and American demand for British goods remained strong. If Americans gained greater familiarity with French luxury goods, they usually found the British competition more attractively priced and more familiar. But Britain was no longer a market for American-built shipping, nor could American-built and owned ships be used in the British West Indian or intraimperial trades. These were significant losses, for before the war one-third of the British merchant navy had been built in the thirteen colonies and earnings on shipping services did much to right the unfavorable trade balances of many colonies. The British West Indies were now closed to United States ships—the cause of decades of friction between Britain and the new United States government.[30]

[28] Peckham, *Toll of Independence.*

[29] Price, *France and the Chesapeake,* 2:729–31.

[30] Robert Livingston Schuyler, *The Fall of the Old Colonial System: A Study in British Free Trade, 1770–1870* (1945; reprint ed., Hamden, Conn., 1966), pp. 85–97. Compare also Joseph A. Goldenberg, *Shipbuilding in Colonial America* (Charlottesville, Va., 1976), and Jacob M. Price, "A Note on the Value of Colonial Exports of Shipping," *Journal of Economic History* 36 (1976):704–24; James F. Shepherd and Gary M. Walton, "Estimates of 'In-

James Shepherd has ably sketched for us the varying success of United States merchants and shipowners in adjusting to the changed circumstances of the difficult postwar decade, 1783–92. "Overall," he points out, "there was an increase in the real value of exports from the late colonial period to the early 1790s. But since the population increased by 80 percent over this period, the rise of exports did not keep pace with population growth. The relative importance of foreign markets to the American economy declined somewhat." If there was not a compensating rise in production for the home market, there *may* have been a decline in per capita income in the United States between 1775 and 1790.[31] The real commercial rewards of freedom, Shepherd explains, came to the new country only after the start of the long European wars in 1792–93, wars that, for a time at least, gave the United States some of the windfall profits of neutrality.

The British West Indian islands also experienced serious wrenching effects from the breakdown in the pre-Revolutionary trading patterns. The war years were particularly difficult for the islands because of the interruption in food and other supplies from North America, which led to serious suffering among the slave population. Yet the British West Indies taken as a whole—if not every part—recovered in the end, for they still had their greatest asset, the British market, and in peace were able once more to get supplies from what was left of British North America and even from the United States in one way or another. John J. McCusker defers the decline of the islands' agricultural economy until after 1790; some would put it in the nineteenth century.[32]

---

visible' Earnings in the Balance of Payments of the British North American Colonies, 1768–1772," *Journal of Economic History* 29 (1969):230–63.

[31] The literature on the problem (particularly the contributions of Gary Walton and James Shepherd) is discussed in Stanley L. Engerman and Robert E. Gallman, "U.S. Economic Growth, 1783–1860," *Research in Economic History* 8 (1983):8, 18–19. They also discuss the work of Alice Hanson Jones, suggesting a possible decline in per capita wealth between 1774 and 1805.

[32] For example, Seymour Drescher, *Econocide: British Slavery in the Era of Abolition* (Pittsburgh, 1977), pp. 16–25.

The restoration of trade after the war reactivated some if not all of the old credit relations. American merchants once more found long credits available on purchases in Britain a strong magnet drawing their custom thither. But transatlantic credit was only one small part of the American credit picture. Aubrey C. Land's work on Maryland indicates that even before the Revolution internal credit flows were more important than external.[33] That is, Marylanders owed each other much more than they owed to persons in Britain. These internal credit flows, as Professor Rothenberg indicates, became much deeper and more intricate in the postwar years, encouraged as they were by the founding of banks, the growing density and complexity of trade, the establishment of public debt, and ever higher land values supporting the mortgage market.

Viewing the eighteenth century as a whole, we can readily see that down to 1775 the main features of the economic history of the thirteen colonies were aggregate growths in population, output, and foreign trade and a growing complexity of institutions (including monetary and credit) within the economy. Compared with the increases in the aggregates, the increases in per capita income were most likely quite moderate and probably significant only over long periods of time. The war years saw a marked decline in every aspect of foreign trade and in the production of the principal export staples. Part of the income lost in these sectors was made up by the import-substituting increase in domestic manufactures though, on final reckoning, there had to be a decline in per capita income during the war. In the first postwar decade, 1783–92, there was a gradual restoration of prewar levels of external commerce, though the increase in population made these prewar levels of production and trade less of a contribution to per capita income. The great increases in foreign trade came only after the start of the Anglo-French war in 1793. We do not know how much of the wartime gains in internal manufactures proved lasting nor how much in-

[33] Aubrey C. Land, "Economic Behavior in a Planting Society: The Eighteenth-Century Chesapeake," *Journal of Southern History* 33 (1967):478–80.

creases in the domestic economy could have contributed to per capita income after 1775. Nor can we as yet measure exactly when per capita income recovered its prewar levels; it may have been only after 1793.

In recent years a new quantitative rigor has added greatly to our understanding of colonial population growth, servile institutions, and the history of the family, as well as to more obvious topics such as foreign trade. There is clearly a need and very likely an opportunity for the application of such more rigorous quantitative methods to still other, chronologically later and quite important topics, including manufactures and the macroeconomy during the war and immediate postwar years.

Contributors
Index

Contributors

THOMAS M. DOERFLINGER is a securities analyst in the Research Department of PaineWebber Incorporated, where he specializes in investment strategy. The holder of a B.A. from Princeton and a Ph.D. from Harvard, he has written seven scholarly articles and *A Vigorous Spirit of Enterprise: Merchants and Economic Development in Revolutionary Philadelphia* (1986), which was completed while he was Fellow and Visiting Editor of Publications at the Institute of Early American History and Culture at Williamsburg, Virginia. Mr. Doerflinger's second book, coauthored with Jack L. Rivkin, is *Risk and Reward: Venture Capital and the Making of America's Great Industries* (1987).

JOSEPH A. ERNST is a professor of history at York University, Ontario, Canada, and author of *Money and Politics in America, 1755–1775: A Study in the Currency Act of 1764 and the Political Economy of Revolution* (1973). He is currently extending his political-economic analysis of the currency question to New England.

LEWIS R. FISCHER is associate professor in the department of history and a member of the Maritime Studies Research Unit at Memorial University of Newfoundland. His publications include *The Enterprising Canadians: Entrepreneurs and Economic Development in Eastern Canada, 1820–1914* (1979), *Merchant Shipping and Economic Development in Atlantic Canada* (1982), *Change and Adaptation in Maritime History: The North Atlantic Fleets in the Nineteenth Century* (1985), and *Shipping and Shipbuilding in Atlantic Canada, 1820–1914* (1986). He has concentrated primarily on the maritime and economic history of the eighteenth and nineteenth centuries, and is currently working on monographs on the Canadian and Norwegian merchant marines before World War I.

JAMES A. HENRETTA is Priscilla Alden Burke Professor of American History at the University of Maryland, College Park. He is the author of *"Salutary Neglect": Colonial Administration under the Duke of Newcastle* (1972), *The Evolution of American Society, 1700–1815: An Interdisciplinary Analysis* (1973), "Social History as Lived and Written," *American Historical Review* (1979), and various articles on early American history. Professor Henretta is the coauthor of *Evolution and Revolution: American Society, 1600–1820* (1987) and *America's History* (1987). His present research project is entitled "Law and the Creation of the Liberal State, 1770–1860."

JOHN J. MCCUSKER is a professor of history at the University of Maryland, College Park, where he teaches economic history and the history of colonial America. His research and writing center on various aspects of the economy of the Atlantic world in the seventeenth and eighteenth centuries. His most recent book, written with Russell R. Menard, is *The Economy of British America, 1607–1789* (1985).

RUSSELL R. MENARD, professor of history at the University of Minnesota, is the author of *The Economy of British America, 1607–1789* (with John J. McCusker), *Economy and Society in Early Colonial Maryland,* and numerous articles on early American economic and social history. His current research focuses on long-distance trade in the early modern era, transitions to slavery in the Americas, and the political economy of the Carolina lowcountry.

JACOB M. PRICE is professor of history at the University of Michigan, where he has taught since 1956. His publications include *The Tobacco Adventure to Russia* (1961), *France and the Chesapeake* (1973), *Capital and Credit in British Overseas Trade* (1980), and many articles. He is past president of the Midwest Conference of British Historical Studies and president-elect of the Economic History Association.

Contributors

WINIFRED B. ROTHENBERG is visiting assistant professor of economics at Tufts University. She received her Ph.D. in history from Brandeis University. Her essay in this volume is from her forthcoming book *Markets and Massachusetts Farmers, 1750–1855: A Paradigm of Economic Growth in Rural New England,* a study of the emergence of markets for farm produce, capital, and hired labor in Massachusetts.

JAMES F. SHEPHERD is professor of economics at Whitman College, Walla Walla, Washington. His research on American trade and economic development during the late colonial period has led to a number of articles and collaboration with Gary M. Walton on two books: *Shipping, Maritime Trade, and the Economic Development of Colonial North America* (1972) and *The Economic Rise of Early America* (1979). He is currently examining the transition of the American economy in the 1780s.

Index